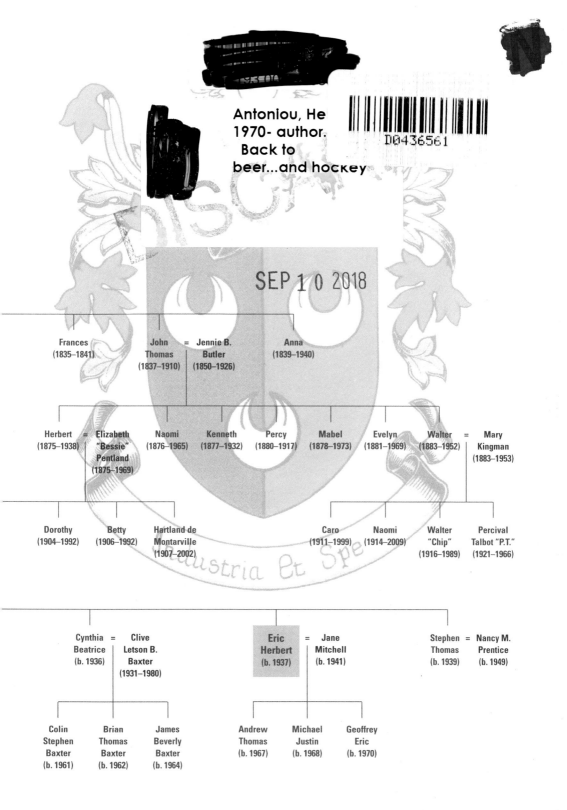

Frances
(1835–1841)

John = Jennie B.
Thomas   Butler
(1837–1910) (1850–1926)

Anna
(1839–1940)

Herbert = Elizabeth
(1875–1938) "Bessie"
Pentland
(1875–1969)

Naomi
(1876–1965)

Kenneth
(1877–1932)

Percy
(1880–1917)

Mabel
(1878–1973)

Evelyn
(1881–1969)

Walter = Mary
(1883–1952) Kingman
(1883–1953)

Dorothy
(1904–1992)

Betty
(1906–1992)

Hartland de
Montarville
(1907–2002)

Caro
(1911–1999)

Naomi
(1914–2009)

Walter
"Chip"
(1916–1989)

Percival
Talbot "P.T."
(1921–1966)

Cynthia = Clive
Beatrice   Letson B.
(b. 1936)   Baxter
(1931–1980)

Eric = Jane
Herbert   Mitchell
(b. 1937) (b. 1941)

Stephen = Nancy M.
Thomas   Prentice
(b. 1939) (b. 1949)

Colin
Stephen
Baxter
(b. 1961)

Brian
Thomas
Baxter
(b. 1962)

James
Beverly
Baxter
(b. 1964)

Andrew
Thomas
(b. 1967)

Michael
Justin
(b. 1968)

Geoffrey
Eric
(b. 1970)

BACK TO BEER ... AND HOCKEY

Eric Molson at the Notre Dame brewery soon after he was named president of
Molson Breweries Canada in October 1980. Molson Coors Brewing Company
collection.

BACK TO
BEER
... AND
HOCKEY

The Story of Eric Molson

HELEN ANTONIOU

McGill-Queen's University Press
Montreal & Kingston | London | Chicago

To the eighth generation, with love and hope

ISBN 978-0-7735-5287-6 (cloth)
ISBN 978-0-7735-5310-1 (ePDF)
ISBN 978-0-7735-5311-8 (ePUB)

Legal deposit first quarter 2018
Bibliothèque nationale du Québec

Printed in Canada on acid-free paper that is 100% ancient forest free
(100% post-consumer recycled), processed chlorine free

Funded by the Government of Canada Financé par le gouvernement du Canada | Canadä Canada Council for the Arts Conseil des arts du Canada

We acknowledge the support of the Canada Council for the Arts, which
last year invested $153 million to bring the arts to Canadians throughout
the country. Nous remercions le Conseil des arts du Canada de son
soutien. L'an dernier, le Conseil a investi 153 millions de dollars pour mettre
de l'art dans la vie des Canadiennes et des Canadiens de tout le pays.

LIBRARY AND ARCHIVES CANADA CATALOGUING IN PUBLICATION

Antoniou, Helen, 1970–, author
Back to beer ... and hockey : the story of Eric Molson / Helen Antoniou.

Includes index.
Issued in print and electronic formats.
ISBN 978-0-7735-5287-6 (cloth). – ISBN 978-0-7735-5310-1 (ePDF). –
ISBN 978-0-7735-5311-8 (ePUB)

1. Molson, Eric, 1937–. 2. Molson family. 3. Molson Canada (Firm) –
Biography. 4. Businesspeople – Canada – Biography. 5. Brewers –
Canada – Biography. 6. Beer industry – Canada. 7. Brewing
industry – Canada. 8. Biographies. I. Title.

TP573.5.M64A58 2018   663'.42092   C2017-906840-7
                                         C2017-906841-5

Set in 11/15 Minion Pro with Univers LT
Book design & typesetting by Garet Markvoort, zijn digital

CONTENTS

PART III THE RETURN

PROLOGUE
The Age-Old Recipe

There are only four ingredients in beer – well, three really: grain, water, and hops. Yeast is not an ingredient, although it needs to be there. It is an activator. It goes in, does its thing, and goes out. It doesn't stay in the beer. It *makes* the beer.
ERIC H. MOLSON, brewmaster

The recipe for beer is thousands of years old. Combining only four ingredients, it creates one of the world's most complex beverages, certainly one of the most popular and preferred.

Beer has been the drink of kings as well as the drink of the people. According to the *Oxford Companion to Beer*, ancient Egyptians were buried with it, Noah brought it aboard the ark, and Queen Elizabeth I took it with breakfast. It has graced the tables of every president of the United States. Canadian Prime Minister Stephen Harper and US President Barack Obama chose beer as the payout for their friendly Olympic hockey wagers. When Team Canada won the men's gold in overtime at the 2010 Vancouver Games, Obama delivered a case of Molson Canadian to Harper. Four years later Obama repeated the gesture following the Canadian hockey victory in Sochi.

Yet beer is also the great democratizer. In our modern world, it has come to symbolize hard-working, honest folks.

The process of beer-making is one of purity, precision, and chemistry. Its chemical reaction is not explosive; rather, it is slow and measured, quietly working its age-old magic. Beer's natural ingredients – grain, water, hops, and yeast – offer a profound metaphor of integrity, longevity, and unsuspected depths. Yeast especially is a model of modest

Theo Moudakis cartoon of Barack Obama delivering a case of Molson Canadian to 24 Sussex Drive, official residence of the prime minister of Canada, after losing a bet on the winner of the 2010 Olympic gold medal game in hockey. Team Canada beat Team USA 5–3 on 21 February 2010. *Toronto Star*, 3 March 2010. Reprinted by permission.

alchemy. This common fungus is the soul of beer. It creates the beer, and yet there is no yeast in beer.

Scientists have long studied yeast, but its workings remain somewhat mysterious. We do know that through fermentation, yeast converts sugars into carbon dioxide and alcohol. During this process, the yeast reproduces and creates another generation of healthy new yeast, which can be reused *ad infinitum*. As a living organism, yeast has particular requirements to survive and thrive. It needs to be kept clean and robust, neither malnourished (with insufficient oxygen, for example) nor rushed (breweries have attempted to accelerate the yeast, only to go broke trying). Under such conditions, yeast will work faithfully, and a brewery can use the same yeast throughout its enterprise, even over hundreds of years.

Molson is one of Canada's oldest companies. Launched in 1786, its beginnings were as humble as those of a strand of yeast. And, like yeast, it has enjoyed remarkable longevity, the company brewing under the stewardship of Molson family members for seven generations.

The founder, John Molson, was only twenty-two years old and a recent immigrant when he established his brewery in Montreal. He had drive, entrepreneurial spirit, and a little money from his parents, who had died before he left Lincolnshire, England. In Canada, John Molson's brewery became his family, and this family – its bricks and mortar, barley and malt – was passed on to his children and the generations that followed. He had a grand vision: his beer must be "honest," his company a "steady, patient industry," and his family "prudent" and "vigilant." For more than 230 years, Molson and his descendants have

Brewery on Notre Dame Street, Montreal, ca. 1886, the oldest brewery in North America. Molson Coors Brewing Company collection.

assumed this responsibility. Like the brewer's yeast, each generation grows; many move off to different pursuits, but at least one strand stays on to watch over the brewing and the preparation of the next batch.

As the great-great-great-great grandson of John Molson, Eric Molson quietly worked behind the scenes, maintaining and stewarding an empire. Tossed into the world of big business, this unassuming man, against his own nature, persevered, adapted, and took up his ancestor's torch. This story is the evolution of Eric Molson, from behind-the-scenes brewer to the head of North America's oldest brewery, from reluctant heir to the steward of an international public corporation in its third century of operation, and from a young man in the shadow of his uncle and father to the leader of the family, taking care of his siblings and raising his children in accordance with his values of humility, perseverance, and long-term mindedness.

Beer is made through a series of tumultuous processes – whirlpool, boiling, centrifuge – but it is in the silence and calm of the cooling that the yeast works its magic: making the beer, regenerating itself, providing for all, and then slipping aside. The journey of yeast, of beer, is Eric Molson's journey.

Author's Note: I have tried to use gender-neutral pronouns throughout the book where appropriate, but at times masculine pronouns predominate, particularly in quoted speech. In part this is because Molson, like many breweries, has traditionally been a male environment. In our interviews, Eric frequently used "him or her" when he talked about leaders and businesspeople, but I found it cumbersome to use "him/her" or "he/she" throughout the text. Wherever possible, I used the plural pronouns "they" or "them," but at times I opted for the masculine; for this reason I am adding this explanatory note.

PART ONE

THE CALL TO
ADVENTURE

1 Growing Up in Eric's World

Knowing how contented, free, and joyful is life in the world of science, one fervently wishes that many would enter its portals.
DMITRI MENDELEEV (1834–1907)

Sitting across the table from Eric watching him write, I can't help but notice his meticulous penmanship. The letters are small, evenly spaced, upright, and rounded. My father-in-law's script is almost a reflection of his nature, I think – introverted, logical, practical, and yet creative.

We're on the back porch of his home in Kennebunkport, Maine, overlooking the Atlantic. It's a beautiful spot. Bright reflections of sunlight dance on the waves to the horizon. The seawater breaks rhythmically on rocks below. And occasionally, the cries of seagulls pierce the ocean's pulse. Very soothing.

I wait for Eric to complete his to-do list. After a few minutes, he puts down his pen, tucks his notepad in his breast pocket, and raises his light-brown eyes to me. "Okay," he says, "where do you want to start?"

And so begins my journey with Eric. I'm not really sure what I'm getting myself into, but I am curious and eager to discover what this seventy-five-year-old man has to share. Initially, I was surprised he agreed to the project. His shyness is legendary, and so is his aversion to the public spotlight. But thanks to the gentle persistence of my husband, Andrew, he eventually got on board. "Dad, your story can help others," Andrew reasoned. "They can learn something from all you've been through." Eric accepted, but not before setting out two

Eric Molson on the back porch of his home in Kennebunkport, Maine, 1998. Molson family collection.

conditions: first, that we tell the story as it happened, "warts and all," and second, that the book be published simultaneously in English and French – "We are Canadian, after all."

Secretly, Andrew and I had another reason for encouraging Eric to work on this book. We wanted to re-engage him in something. After he retired from Molson Coors in 2010, he underwent a serious back operation, and his recovery was slow, painful, and isolating. It was as if he withdrew from everything and everyone. This book was our way to help him. We figured that by having him revisit the past through interviews and discussions, we would reignite the fire that once motivated him.

Besides, I wasn't going to lose another opportunity to capture the thoughts and experiences of a man I loved and admired. I missed that chance with my own father. From the time he was diagnosed with Alzheimer's until his death ten years later, I was too overcome with grief to record his words. All I could do was watch in dread as the disease chipped away at the doting father, caring friend, and accomplished orthopaedic surgeon he once was, leaving behind a mute, glassy-eyed figure slumped in a wheelchair. To this day I can't listen to Neil Young's "Prairie Wind" without my heart tightening and my eyes welling. Young sings, "Trying to remember what my daddy said before too much time took away his head …" I lost my father, Dr Antonio Antoniou, in 2010, and I wish I had more of him than just memories.

With Eric, I have had the chance to try to capture his essence, not only for my own sake but for that of my children. One day they may want to know more about their grandfather's challenges and accomplishments than they can glean from bits of family conversation.

There are many facets of "Grandpa Eric" that intrigue me. Did he want to go into the beer business, or did he do it out of a sense of duty and familial obligation? How did he shoulder the responsibility of continuing the Molson enterprise? Was he fearful of messing up or, even worse, being the Molson who lost it all? It is well documented that only 30 per cent of family businesses last to the second generation, 12 per cent to the third, and 3 per cent to the fourth or beyond. Eric's challenge was to pass the torch to the seventh generation. Did he succeed? Did he manage to fulfill his vision for the company and for what Molson represents? If so, what principles guided him? How did he handle the inevitable greed around him? What about those who tried to push him aside, have him resign as chairman of Molson, and take control? How did he cope when he discovered that one such person bore the Molson name?

I was eager to address these issues with him, yet there were two other reasons that motivated me to undertake this book.

The first had to do with Eric's style. In my twenty-five plus years in the corporate world, I've encountered a wide variety of managers. And it seems to me that those who prevail usually have great charisma, excellent communication skills, and an ease in murky political waters. Those are all useful qualities, but if that's all there is or if they're accompanied by a big ego (which is often the case), things can go terribly

According to the *Harvard Business Review*, only 3 per cent of
family companies operate into the fourth generation and beyond.
Yet family-owned or family-controlled companies make up 80 per
cent of the world's businesses and are in most countries the major
source of long-term employment. "Imagine the benefit, then, if
these companies mastered key people management, leadership
development, and succession practices. How? By learning from
the best in their class: large, family-owned or family-controlled
organizations that have prospered for decades, if not centuries"
("Leadership Lessons from Great Family Businesses," Claudio
Fernández-Aráoz, Sonny Iqbal, and Jörg Ritter, *Harvard Business
Review*, April 2015).

wrong. This is especially true today when form consistently trumps
content. The emphasis on appearances and soundbites, fuelled by In-
stagram and Twitter, is quashing the value of real substance. So I often
wonder: what about the quiet ones? What about people like Eric, more
introvert than extrovert, yet strongly principled and insightful? Can
they too be compelling leaders? Can they succeed? In the fifth century BC, Lao-Tzu wrote, "The highest type of ruler is one of whose
existence the people are barely aware … The Sage is self-effacing and
scanty of words. When his task is accomplished and things have been
completed, all the people say, 'We ourselves have achieved it!'" Can
that still be true today?

A further impetus for this book is that I am inspired by Eric's values.
Today, money seems to be the ultimate goal and the measure by which
we judge ourselves and others. Not that money is unimportant, but
we seem to have gone overboard in our adulation of it, Kardashian
style. It's all about the bling and how much stuff one can buy, even as
the chasm between the haves and have-nots grows wider. But for Eric,
money has always been linked with responsibility and stewardship.
How many people would say no to $50 million for the sake of a higher

principle, to ensure that something of value – Molson – survived in the long term?

Turning to Eric in the morning light of Maine, I put these thoughts aside and say, "Why don't you tell me about your childhood and what it was like growing up in Tom's household?"

And Eric starts.

"My father, Tom Molson, was a hard worker," he says. "He was an engineer and an excellent builder of breweries. He always stuck to the basics, top-quality ingredients, modern equipment, accurate temperature controls, efficient processes, and good bricks for the buildings. He studied things well and just cranked it out. Tom set the example for hard work.

"But he wasn't necessarily the warmest guy. And he didn't talk much … I don't remember having long conversations with him. He was tough, you know. Tom was tough and abrupt … smart as hell, but tough."

🍁

"Eric! Stephen! Get in the car. Not another word. Red will drive you to school!"

The two boys scurried to the Hillman, out of range of their father's wrath. Eight-year-old Eric winked at his younger brother. Stephen's face relaxed, and once in the car, they collapsed in giggles.

The boys were driven to school each morning, even though they found it supremely embarrassing to be delivered to the gates of Selwyn House School by a uniformed chauffeur. Eric hated "all that crap." More than anything, he just wanted to "be one of the guys." He eventually managed to convince Red, the driver, to drop him and Stephen a few blocks from school so that they could walk the rest of the way.

Coming from one of Canada's most prestigious families, growing up in Westmount, the wealthy Anglo area of Montreal, and attending a private boys school staffed with highly qualified British educators, these boys might have been expected to have a different attitude, one of privilege and superiority. That idea is laughable to anyone who knows them. Eric and Stephen, like their older sisters, Deirdre and Cynthia,

Brothers Eric and Stephen Molson in their Selwyn House uniforms, 1945. Molson family collection.

were the same as countless other kids. They wanted to have fun, play sports, and mess about. There was no arrogance or superciliousness in any of them. And, except for the odd reference to "the Molson name" from a relative or neighbour, they had little sense of their family's long, eminent place in Canadian society.

The boys' school-ride dilemma was eventually resolved by Frank Carlin, a neighbour who offered to carpool them with his own children, Nan and her brother Taylor. Each morning they wound through the streets of Westmount, letting Nan off at Sacred Heart School for girls, and the three boys at Selwyn House.

Frank Carlin was a hockey guy, head coach of the amateur Montreal Royals. "That's how we all became rink rats," says Eric. "Frank was in charge of the Royals, which was the farm team for the Montreal Canadiens. He'd give us tickets to some of the games. Stephen and I would sit in those rink-side seats at the Forum right around the ice, and at the time there was no glass to separate us from the players. Sometimes we'd get to see two games in a row – Sunday afternoon doubleheaders – amazing! Frank's team was so good it could easily have been in the NHL. One year, Dick Irwin Sr, the coach of the Canadiens, was behind 2–3 in the playoffs. He brought up five of Frank's players to the big team, and they won the Stanley Cup!"

Young Eric looked up to the players. He admired their speed, strong skating skills, and deft handling of the puck. A self-described "little runt" or "shrimp," he was far from an imposing ice-hockey player, but he loved the game. He was out on the rink every chance he got – either as a centre or left wing but never in defence. (Quoting former Canadiens goalie Ken Dryden, Eric says, "The puck hurts! Every shot hurts!") But above all, Eric and his siblings delighted in watching the professionals play. They were passionate about the Montreal Canadiens. Their family's close affiliation with the NHL team (their father, Tom, and their uncle Hartland would later own it) was not a factor. They were true fans.

Sports were an important part of the Molson household. Tom encouraged all four of his children, sons and daughters alike, to enjoy a variety of activities: hockey, cross-country skiing, tennis, sailing, canoeing. They all participated. And while Stephen excelled on the ice and court, Eric played mostly for pleasure and to fit in. Deirdre, the eldest, remembers the contrast between her two brothers: "Stephen was a beautiful athlete. But my father would push Eric, saying stuff like, 'You've got to be manly! You have to be on the hockey team and on the football team. You have to compete!'"

Above: Celia Molson canoeing in 1943 with her children: *left to right*, Deirdre, Cynthia, Eric, and Stephen, on Lac Violon in the family property at Ivry in the Laurentians. Molson family collection. *Below*: Eric, Cynthia, and Deirdre Molson, March 1944, about to go cross-country skiing in Ivry. Molson family collection.

Cynthia, second born after Deirdre, has similar memories. "I have a few visual recollections of Eric as a shivery little boy, because he was very skinny and a bit retiring. Stephen was the imp. He was the one who always got into trouble and made us laugh with his pranks. He was the athletic one." Nonetheless, Eric kept up. Tom sometimes took the boys skiing on Mount Royal. Skis balanced on their shoulders, they climbed the steep hill – a lot of work for a kid like Eric who wasn't as sturdy as some of his contemporaries.

One thing Eric and his father agreed wholeheartedly on, however, was the brewery on Notre Dame Street – an imposing and iconic edifice along the St Lawrence River in Montreal's east end. Every few weeks Tom Molson took his children down after dinner for the night shift. Eric still remembers his amazement: "We walked in and *wow*, our eyes would be popping out. There were these big refrigeration machines painted red with gold trim. They looked like giant fire trucks!" Who could resist the shiny compressors, the clanging bottles, the sweet smell of fermentation? Heaven for little boys.

During his rounds, Tom spoke to the workers and checked things like temperatures, timing, and cleanliness. Cynthia recalls, "When we'd go down to the brewery, I saw everyone tip their caps to Tom. That's when I realized he was a fairly important figure there."

🍁

Thomas Henry Pentland Molson was not the typical Anglo boss. His French was good, and he addressed employees in their mother tongue. As well as the vocabulary of the operations, Tom transmitted to his children the importance of respecting rules. Eric remembers the night his father caught a worker smoking beside the highly flammable power room of the brewery. "We didn't hear much, but we knew what was going on because we could see the guy's face as he was backing up slowly while Mr Tom gave him shit." (At the brewery, Molson family members were generally referred to by their first name preceded by "Mr".)

Tom introduced his children to the business in this hands-on way, but he rarely talked to them about Molson Brewery Ltd when they were growing up. He never held family meetings, didn't discuss the

Tom and Celia Molson, Mount Royal Hotel, 30 August 1940. Molson family collection.

responsibility that came with the Molson name or what it meant to own one of Canada's oldest corporations. In fact, Deirdre says, "I was well into my teens before I realized that 'Molson' was something different. It slowly dawned on me. Tom never spoke much about that. He may have talked about the history of Molson and how they were entrepreneurial and hard-working people, but never about money, how much they had, or what we stood to inherit."

To young Eric, all these questions relating to his well-known surname were immaterial. "Whether I was a Smith or a Jones, I wanted to please my father. I wanted to get good marks, come in first in my class, and make my parents happy."

But his parents' happiness was beyond Eric's control. Neither Tom nor his wife, Celia, were particularly warm towards their children, and their relationship with each other often seemed strained, albeit polite.

It hadn't always been that way. When thirty-year-old Tom Molson first noticed Celia Cantlie in 1931 aboard a ship crossing the Atlantic, he was struck by her beauty. This was no longer the little girl he had seen at the house years before. She was now an elegant, eighteen-year-old debutante, travelling to London with her aunt, Lady Mount Stephen. Tom was determined to get to know her. He discovered she was smart, witty, and musical, a captivating piano player. He was besotted. The relationship flourished, and within a year they were married.

Meanwhile, the Great Depression was taking its toll across Canada. Companies closed and unemployment rose to an all-time high. By 1933, 30 per cent of the labour force was out of work. Molson's beer business, however, remained largely unaffected. And while Celia was grateful to be spared the hardship, she felt uncomfortable enjoying herself when others were suffering. Tom was the same. Some say that the experience of seeing close friends lose all they had changed him forever.

His sense of duty, however, remained steadfast. In 1939, when Canada declared war against Germany, Tom readily enlisted even though he was thirty-eight. Too old to be sent overseas, he went to Garrison Petawawa, Canada's largest military base, in Ontario, where he served his country for six years.

Major Thomas Henry Pentland Molson, Petawawa military base, 1941. Molson family collection.

Above: Celia and Tom Molson's children, 20 March 1940, when Tom left to serve in Petawawa (*left to right*): Stephen (six months), Deirdre (five years), Eric (two), and Cynthia (three). Molson family collection. *Below*: Eric Molson's childhood home, 10 Ramezay Road, Westmount, QC, 1941. Molson family collection.

Celia was left behind to manage four children all under the age of six. The red-brick house at 10 Ramezay Road was a complicated residence to run. Tom the engineer had designed and overseen its construction, and with his usual meticulousness outfitted it with the latest equipment, built-in amenities like heating units and central air conditioning, and a basement full of carefully labelled machinery.

"Celia was busy during the war," Deirdre recalls. We are having tea in her homey yet elegantly decorated condominium next to the Montreal Museum of Fine Arts. "She worked at the Red Cross, the VON [Victoria Order of Nurses], at the maternity hospital, the symphony ... And she ran Ramezay Road, because my father was away. She also ran Ivry" – the family's country residence. Deirdre continues, admiration in her voice, "She did it all. She learnt from her father, as the youngest of five ... and her mother dying when she was only nine. Her father taught her how to run a household early on. Besides, Celia was smart, and she was also a lot of fun."

Eric remembers two things of his childhood home: his father's detailed instructions on how it should be operated, and his mother's music. "Celia played a lot at Ramezay Road, beautiful music. She had a grand piano downstairs that we weren't allowed to touch. We messed around with the upright on the top floor ... Sometimes we played, but mostly we used it as a goal for floor-hockey games."

The differences between Tom and Celia – he being strict and fastidious, she more carefree and adventuresome – started to abrade their relationship even before Tom left for Petawawa. Back then, however, Eric was too young to notice. His early memories were of music and fun.

After the war, the distance between the two grew. Celia became more involved with volunteer work and Tom threw himself into his duties at the brewery. Even so, Tom was strongly invested in his sons' futures, encouraging them both into eventual roles in the company. "Eric, you'll be the engineer – study science," Tom would say. And to Stephen, who longed to be a teacher, "You'll be the accountant." Tom was replicating a familiar sharing of responsibilities: he was the engineer and builder of some of Molson's brewhouses, while his brother Hartland was the finance guy and dealmaker. Tom did not envision corporate roles for his daughters, even though Cynthia and Deirdre were quick and bright, always top of their classes.

Deirdre sits a little straighter as she describes Tom's attitude. Although close to eighty, she has an athletic frame and still plays tennis two to three times a week. "My father gave us the idea that family and responsibility are very important. He had a great sense of duty with all the jobs that he took on. Of course, he always cut out the girls, in the sense that he didn't feel we should take on any business roles. It was a very English – not American – thing to do, not to involve the girls. With the boys, however, he was quite tough. He felt that they had a position in Montreal, and that they had a responsibility not only to the company but also to the community. Tom instilled this sense of duty in them – in all of us, really."

"Tom was different from his predecessors, though." She raises her hand absentmindedly to the locket around her neck. "In the past, none of the women who inherited shares in the company got voting shares. My aunts, Tom's sisters Dorothy and Betty, for example, only got non-voting shares. So Tom was more modern that way. Both Cynthia and I got Class B voting shares. Regardless, neither Cynthia nor I showed any interest in the business world. We were not that way inclined. In fact, I don't know if Eric was that way inclined either. Even Tom – I'm not sure Tom would have gone into business if he didn't have the brewery to go into. Tom loved boats, sailing, engines. He could have been a naval architect or something ... He was a scientist, like Eric."

❦

The time came to send the kids to boarding school. "It was fairly typical for English Canadians who had grown up in a system that was a copy of the British system of education to go to boarding school quite young," Eric says. At eleven, he went at the same time as Deirdre, and two years later, Stephen and Cynthia followed. The boys were sent to Bishop's College School (BCS) in Lennoxville, and the girls to King's Hall, Compton. The two institutions, both in the picturesque Eastern Townships, were about a two-hour train ride from Montreal.

Brothers Stephen and Eric Molson head off to Camp Nominingue, June 1947. Molson family collection.

Eric never liked leaving home. Even going to summer camp at Petit Lac Nominingue in northern Quebec, he went with tears in his eyes. Boarding school was much worse. Instead of Camp Nomininge's canoeing, campfires, and sing-alongs, BCS was a school with a strong military tradition. Rules were often enforced with corporal punishment.

"I hated leaving home to go there," Eric says. "It was awful. I'd be crying like crazy, and Tom would say, 'Put him on the train.' That's the way it was in those days. You didn't tell your dad you didn't want to go … at least I didn't. I wouldn't dream of it. I couldn't say, 'I can't stand

Eric Molson in the marching band of Bishop's College, spring 1953. Molson family collection.

this place. I want to leave.' Besides, where would I go? Those schools were all the same."

One teacher at BCS, however, helped smooth the transition to boarding-school life for Eric: Walter McMann, also known as Mickey, after the famous mouse. (His wife, a piano teacher, was nicknamed Minnie.) Aside from being an exceptional educator who taught math "very, very well," McMann showed Eric great kindness on his first train ride from Montreal to BCS. "I guess he saw me crying at Windsor

Station, thought I was a cute little guy, and really looked after me," says Eric. "He tried to reassure me … I had serious doubts about the place."

Bishop's College was considered a top boarding school. Its compulsory cadet program, affiliated with the prestigious Black Watch Regiment of Montreal, was viewed as one of the best for making leaders out of young boys. Students drilled daily in full uniform, heavy rifles on their shoulders, to the beat of a sergeant's orders. For Eric, this was far too intense: "That's why I joined the band. I played a snare drum in the marching band, and that way I didn't have to carry a rifle." Besides, he secretly enjoyed practising. Music gave him a sense of escape.

When it came to avoiding activities he disliked, Eric was resourceful. He managed to be president of the BCS Debating Society without once getting up to argue a viewpoint. He refined this technique years later in the boardroom. He would hear out all the opinions around the table first, waiting to see if his idea was expressed by someone else, and only then, if it wasn't, would he speak up.

"What usually happens is that the people who like to talk start speaking first, using their clichés and latest business jargon – stuff like 'bolt-on,' or 'headwinds,' or 'reading the deck' – it drives me nuts. And then you listen for those who have real insight." He was delighted when someone made his point ahead of him; that way, he didn't have to intercede. It made him a great listener and a keen observer. It also allowed him to deliberate different points of view before coming to a decision. And while some people may have considered his reticence a sign of weakness, as Lao-Tzu, the ancient Chinese philosopher, once wrote, "Those who know do not speak. Those who speak do not know."

Eric excelled academically at BCS, always finishing first or second in his class. Outside the classroom, though, disadvantaged by his small size, he learned to "stay out of trouble and keep my head down." A few of the larger, older boys had fun at his expense. Some would say it was bullying. He remembers once being picked up by his feet and dumped into a barrel head first.

Stephen, although two years younger than Eric, fared a little better: he was stronger and more athletic. "I was a skinny little runt," Eric says. He depended instead on his sense of humour to build friendships and alliances, becoming one of ten head boys in his last year at BCS. Overall, the social lessons Eric learned in boarding school powerfully informed his style and his attitude of disdain towards *les péteux de bretelles* or "blowhards."

But Eric's biggest discovery at BCS was in the school's labs. Arthur Campbell – known by boys who feared his temper as Beaky, for his long nose – was one of those legendary teachers. For Eric, he opened the doors to the world of chemistry: "All of a sudden, something clicks, and you get it. Beaky did that for me, and I grew to love science."

Chemistry became a lifelong passion and Dmitri Mendeleev, the father of the Periodic Table, Eric's hero. It was the precision, clarity, and elegant simplicity of the Russian's work that impressed him – all that order lurking behind the chaos of everyday life.

♦

Eric would soon discover that life could get messy.

A few weeks into the start of his third year at BCS and Stephen's first, Celia came from Montreal to see her sons. A light breeze rustled the maple leaves on the circular driveway in front of the school's main entrance. Celia paused, gripping the brass handle of the heavy wooden door before pushing it open. She had come to tell the boys that she would be going away and spending the coming months in England with her father. She and Tom were going to divorce.

Eric was surprised. He hadn't noticed any flare-ups between his parents when he was at home and assumed the distance between them was normal. Yet he wasn't particularly unsettled by the news. Divorce was becoming more common among the parents of his peers. Stephen, on the other hand, was devastated. When Eric visited him in his dorm room that night, he found him on the edge of his bed, staring dolefully at the floor. Eric sat down and put his arm around his brother's shoulders. "You'll see, we'll be okay," he told him. "It will be all right ... Don't worry. We're together, right?"

In Cynthia's view, the divorce affected Stephen the most of the four children, "probably because he was the youngest. We learned of it soon after the two of us were sent to boarding school – Deirdre and Eric were already gone. My parents must have thought it best for all the

Eric Molson sitting on top of Stephen, at Ivry, July 1943. Molson family collection.

Tom Molson at Ivry, summer 1943, with his children (*left to right*) Deirdre, Stephen, Eric, and Cynthia. Molson family collection.

children to leave for boarding school at that point, because we were all going to remain with our father and not live with our mother. I was thirteen years old, but Stephen was only nine. Eric would have tried to reassure Stephen. One thing that was always very evident was that Eric and Stephen were so closely bonded as children. They tolerated us girls, but they were just devoted to each other."

At the time it was unusual for a father to get custody of the children. For Tom, however, the point was non-negotiable. If Celia wanted to divorce, the children would remain with him.

Deirdre, as the eldest, was probably the first to have been told. "My mother came to speak to me alone," she recalls. "She said, 'Your father and I can't live together happily anymore, so we are going to get divorced. You are going to stay at Ramezay Road with your father, and I will find a place to live nearby' … She felt it was fair. She was the one who wanted to leave; he had the purse strings. He had built the house, it was a family house, and I guess she felt that she could have the divorce, but the kids were going to stay with him … It was tough."

Tom did his best to be a good father. Says Cynthia, "I'm sure we weren't easy to handle, but he stuck it out. From the time he and

Mummy divorced, we would have dinner with him in the main dining room every night when we were home. He would tell us stories of El Alamein, or some other World War II conflict, but we would hardly listen. We were busy making jokes and being rather naughty. Daddy was a little deaf, you know – he was in the artillery in the war, after all – so we could easily carry on a separate conversation under our breath at the table, which he couldn't really hear. He was very patient about all that, but he was kind of boring and pretty strict. He didn't have a great sense of humour, and he was always interested in teaching us a little bit, you know. Basically, Tom's outlook on life was pretty serious."

Echoing his sister, Eric says, "My father was quite a boring and serious man. Celia was a much more exciting person, and she was younger. I saw that she needed to get away." Eric's main regret about the divorce was that he didn't get to see as much of his mother.

"Progressive" is how Eric describes Celia. She wasn't the kind of mother who said no to much, and she always encouraged Eric to follow his own path. "She would slip me books to read when I was fourteen or fifteen which were a little more advanced and quite spicy for the times. She wanted me to do things that were different. She exposed me to art and music, so that I could get something else under my belt than the usual crap."

Eric was even okay with Celia's decision to remarry. He liked Henry "Laffey" Lafleur, the man she had fallen in love with. It didn't matter that she had probably started seeing him while still living with Tom. Eric thought Laffey was "smart as hell" – a Rhodes scholar with a sense of humour, "a tolerant and a liberal thinker," and "an absolutely brilliant lawyer, tops in Montreal." Eric and Stephen also got along with the Lafleur boys. In the summers they all went together to Smith's Cove, Nova Scotia, for a few weeks. The kids spent carefree days by the ocean, digging for clams, fishing from log rafts, and picnicking – simple, undemanding activities that Eric always enjoyed.

The Nova Scotia holidays contrasted the more structured summertime routine with Tom at Métis-sur-Mer, where Eric's grandparents, Herbert and Bessie Molson, owned a big house overlooking the St Lawrence River. On the porch, there was a beautiful telescope, which Eric was allowed to use. Always the observer, he loved scanning the

Eric (*standing*) and Stephen Molson on a raft, Smith's Cove, Nova Scotia, summer 1949. Molson family collection.

horizon, watching ships go by. But the time at Métis felt less like a vacation than the days at the ocean with Celia. In some ways Métis was much like Montreal: the same Westmount families (including other Molson relatives) transplanting themselves by the water for July and August, having the same parties, with the same conversations at different houses every night. Then and as he grew older, Eric avoided such social scenes. "I inherited from Celia the ability to say no to all those cocktail parties. I never liked that kind of stuff. Nor did Celia. She thought there was too much socializing at Métis."

Tom played golf and encouraged Eric to practise with him, thinking it would serve him well later on. Eric resisted. "I never thought I would be any good at it, so why try? Why start? It's inefficient for exercise. I would much rather go off with Stephen on our bikes."

Still, Tom persisted in giving his children access to whatever he thought would benefit their development and education. He took each of them on a trip to Europe soon after their eighteenth birthdays to immerse them in culture and history.

Deirdre remembers that experience fondly. "The year I got out of Smith College, my father came over to take myself and Eric on this tour of Italy over the Easter holidays. Celia was much more interested in culture than Tom, but my father thought he *should* be, so he took us to Rome, Florence, Venice, and Naples over a period of two weeks. It was a wonderful trip, with guides and everything. Cynthia and Stephen got it two or three years later. Everybody got a turn to a European tour. Tom showed us all this art, not because he was really interested in it himself – except maybe for the architecture – but because he thought we should have that as part of our education."

In Italy, Tom took Deirdre and Eric to Cassino, a town that had been all but destroyed ten years earlier. "Cassino was wiped out by the Allies during the war and there were still some unexploded bombs left," Eric says. "I remember my father was nervous as hell." Eric's favourite part of the trip, however, was their visit to Pompeii. The volcanic eruption piqued his scientist's curiosity, and "that little dog smothered in ash" captured his imagination.

In the same vein of broadening his children's horizons, Tom sent Eric for his final year of high school to L'Institut Le Rosey in Switzerland. Le Rosey, one of the world's most prestigious schools, has been favoured for generations by royalty, celebrities, and the very wealthy, the Aga Khan, the Borgheses, and the Rothschilds among them. There was no messing around when it came to Tom selecting the best for his son's education, although he never missed a chance to remind Eric of the exorbitant cost – three times that of Bishop's back home!

"Le Rosey was a neat experience, completely different," Eric recalls. "All in French. And it was fun: we played, we skied, and we studied." By seventeen, Eric was filling out and getting stronger. He could now outperform his classmates on the ice. "I knew hockey much more than those guys because I was Canadian and had been skating all my life. I taught them a lot of the dirty tricks from back home, and they loved it!"

Seventeen-year-old Eric Molson skiing in Switzerland as a student at Le Rosey, 1954. Molson family collection.

Enjoying his new physical expertise, Eric would even sneak out at night and play on the local village team. He recalls cheerfully, "The boards were only waist high, so if you ever got checked against them, you'd fly out. One of the rinks had a river right over the bank of snow, so we would get checked right into the river." Playing in a relaxed, non-competitive environment was a great pleasure for Eric, who simply loved the game.

As at BCS, Eric did well academically at Le Rosey, particularly in chemistry. Private lessons from the principal's wife, Mme Joannot, advanced his understanding of the subject. By the end of the year, he turned his attention to college applications. Tom was pushing for the Royal Military College of Canada, where he'd studied engineering nearly twenty-five years earlier. For Eric, this was a non-starter. No way was he going back to marching and military drills. He much preferred the looks of Dartmouth, which "had a ski scene on the cover of the school brochure. It seemed like my kind of place."

Tom didn't agree but, fortunately for Eric, his father had heard good things about Princeton. Two things would have sold Tom: it was far away from a big city, so offered fewer temptations, and it had an excellent reputation. "Whoever sold my father on Princeton was a great salesman," Eric says. "It was the best break of my life. I had fun there, but I also really learned how to work in an organized fashion, how to eliminate the unimportant and concentrate on key concepts – values I later instilled in my family and in the company."

🍁

Tom continued to try to direct his son's path by insisting on Princeton's engineering program. Eric dutifully acquiesced but didn't really enjoy it. "I didn't like the overly assertive, macho guys around me in engineering, and I didn't like doing things like surveying and drawing and all that kind of stuff." Mostly, however, he disliked being "shoved around" by his father.

At the end of his freshman year, as he was planning to look for a summer job, Eric fell gravely ill. He could barely breathe, suffered intense chest pains, and rapidly lost weight. Diagnosed with severe pneumonia, he was transferred from his college to Columbia's Presbyterian Hospital in New York City. The pneumonia evolved into empyema, a life-threatening infection caused by pus accumulating in the cavity between the lungs and the inside of the chest wall. Doctors decided to operate to drain the pus.

"We thought he was going to die," Cynthia says. She reaches out to stroke the head of her Bernese mountain dog. "He was terribly ill. He had to have the fluid drained from his lungs. Daddy was there and I joined Mummy going down to the hospital. I was at Wellesley and she was coming down from Montreal. The three of us were at his bedside. The only thing that saved him was an unproven new antibiotic that he was really a guinea pig for. We were all so worried." Her eyes tear up. As if on cue, the Bernese lets out a long sigh and lowers himself to the floor.

Eric's perspective on his ailment is more clinical. "I got really interested in the medical side of my illness. I was one of the first patients in the world to use bacitracin, a new antibiotic developed in the mid-1950s. I was operated on and then I spent that whole summer walking around with a tube hanging out of my back. But what I remember most was how I pummelled the doctors with questions about what they were doing to me. They were all sure I was going to go into medicine."

Cynthia sees the experience as a defining moment in Eric's journey. "I've always wondered if that period when he was hospitalized in New York for his terrible sickness, whether that was a turning point in his life. He came so close to dying. It may have been just my interpretation, but it seems that from then on he got more serious. It was as if the possibility of advancing his own interests became less important to him and he felt he should do what was expected of him."

The three months in New York Presbyterian gave Eric time to reflect on his future career path, but he says he didn't feel constrained in his choices. His sense of duty towards Molson grew as he thought of what he wanted to do, and by the end of the summer he knew he would join the family business. But not via engineering, as Tom had dictated. Instead, he would follow his passion: pure chemistry. Since this was still a pathway to the beer business, Tom did not object.

❦

In the fall of 1956, Eric started in Princeton's chemistry program under Professor John Turkevich, known as "The Turk" (although he was "Russian as hell," Eric says). A world-famous physical chemist, Turkevich was an expert in small particles and colloids and a popular lecturer. Eric was impressed. "I was so happy when I got him as my thesis advisor. I liked chemistry, I liked his lectures, so I asked for him. And I guess he liked me, because he accepted."

Eric recalls walking up Princeton's Washington Road towards the Frick chemistry building, worrying about his first interview with The Turk. It turned out that his professor was interested in Eric's plans after college: "When he asked me, he was expecting me to say something like 'go to medical school' or 'do a PhD in chemistry.' Instead, I blurted out, 'Make beer!'"

"Become a brewer?" The Turk pushed back his thick, unruly hair. "It's the first time I've heard that!" He added, "Then we must study yeast." The big, bulky man got up from his chair. "Come. I have an electron microscope in my lab."

What pleased Eric was that The Turk said "we," not "you." Here was an authority figure who not only supported his chosen path but was willing to travel it with him. Yeast became a shared passion between them over the next three years, and the topic of Eric's thesis.

Viewing yeast up close was for Eric in many ways like seeing himself clearly for the first time. Even today, when describing yeast and its role in the production of beer, Eric could be talking about himself: the quiet but essential factor in a long brewing tradition that steps in to work its beer-making magic, and steps away again, having prepared a new generation to continue the work. Eric explains: "Midway through the brewing process, yeast is added to wort that's been cooled to a precise temperature. Yeast is very specific about what it wants, and without the right environment and ingredients, it won't make the beer you want. Once you add the yeast, you wait. You can't rush it. It's a natural mechanism, and you can't accelerate it.

"In the brewing process, each yeast cell multiplies, and this yeast is used again in future brews. It never loses its characteristics. With good yeast practices, a brewery can have the same yeast for all its history. And we do."

Eric's thesis focused on the yeast cell wall and the structure within. Under The Turk's tutelage, he used a special atomic oxygen burner to thin the cell wall and then experiment with different stains to best see the interior of the cellular structure. Eric was fascinated. "The skin is

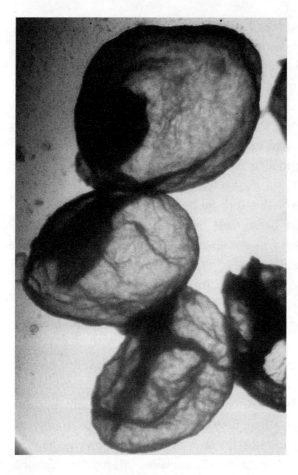

Electron micrograph image of partly burnt, freeze-dried yeast cells (24,000 times magnified), taken by Eric Molson as part of his senior thesis, "Microincineration by Atomic Oxygen and the Three Dimensional Study of the Structure of Biological Species," submitted to Professor John Turkevich, Department of Chemistry, Princeton University, 1 May 1959.

tough and thicker than many other cell walls. That way you could do a lot of genetic engineering inside it. So, if you want to study a new drug or pharmaceutical, and you want to do it under controlled conditions, you're better off doing it inside the yeast cell." Eric's enthusiasm persisted for years, and later he motivated people at Molson to get involved in research using yeast cells as the vehicle for studying the potential of various cancer drugs.

Eric worked hard at Princeton and he liked it. The Turk understood and encouraged his love of chemistry. "He gave me a ridiculous grade," says Eric with pride. "An A plus!" For a brief period, Eric considered going all the way to become a professional chemist working in a lab. But his earlier desire of "I want to make beer" persisted.

The Turk, a mentor as well as a teacher, encouraged him to stay with his first passion. "You know, Eric," he said, "in life you've got to get on a high wave and stay on it. And for you, that's beer." It was an aphorism that Eric would remember and use – especially years later when the time came to steer the company back to the beer business, after many years as a diversified conglomerate.

It would have been a quieter and perhaps simpler life for Eric to have stayed in a lab as a scientist. It would certainly have better suited his introverted nature. But he trusted his instinct and followed The Turk's advice. "I stayed on that wave and continued on the path of getting in the beer business. It was in my first interview with The Turk that I finally resolved to be a brewer, and I studied yeast with his electron microscope. Then I spent the rest of my life at Molson, with yeasts – protecting, manipulating, and encouraging them to make huge batches of first-class ales and lagers. I've never regretted it. It was a lot of fun and a good operation to be part of … it gave me a purpose in life." For Eric, it would be a way to bring value to the larger world around him.

🍁

Despite Turkevich's profound influence, Eric did not see him socially outside the lab. He sometimes regrets this. "One day The Turk had ballet dancers over for brunch at Princeton. I definitely should have gone to that one. I would have met some interesting people!" The societal side of things would always be a challenge for Eric, and the Princeton milieu was no exception. Besides the usual cliques of jocks and snobs, there was also another layer of segregation to contend with: "eating clubs." These were private institutions along Prospect Avenue where undergraduates ate their meals and socialized. A student had to go through a series of interviews – a process known as "bickering" – to be admitted (or rejected) by the members of the club. Unless you were a Rockefeller or a Ford, disappointment was almost guaranteed.

Eric shakes his head, remembering. "It's a horrible thing, awfully pretentious. They judge you by the clothes you wear and the people you know, things like that. People wearing tweed jackets, smoking pipes … these were twenty-year-old kids! The Ivy Club would even have a harpist entertaining them, can you believe it?"

Princeton University's Charter Club, as depicted in Princeton's 1959 *Bric a Brac* yearbook. Reprinted by permission.

In *This Side of Paradise*, F. Scott Fitzgerald refers to the Ivy Club as "breathlessly aristocratic." Eric describes it more vernacularly as "where all the big shots were at." He didn't attempt to get into that one. He tried to join the Cap and Gown Club where most of his buddies went, but didn't get in. Eventually he ended up even further down the hill of prestige at the Charter Club, where members were primarily of "degenerate Eastern wealth," or so they described themselves in soused hilarity. Eric and his Charter chums, including his cousin and childhood friend, Michael "The Rat" Huband (who couldn't get into Cap and Gown either), had the quintessential college experience of "drinking beer and having fun."

Football games were particularly lively. Eric often attended wearing a huge raccoon coat that he had found in a second-hand shop. It was old and moth-eaten but had the advantage of a thick lining that could hold up to two cases of beer. The coat became legendary, and even upstanding Uncle Hartland would slip Eric a few bucks each Christmas, whispering, "This is for your Coon Coat."

With his coat stocked to its limit, Eric could hardly stand. At games, his friends all congregated around him, surreptitiously drinking beer kept nicely cool by the insulating fur. Eric revelled in the camaraderie. In the right setting, he became more social and outgoing.

Music also played an important part of his Princeton years. Eric inherited Celia's good ear for it. He had grown up listening to his mother "playing beautifully" on her grand piano at 10 Ramezay Road and often found himself "goofing around" on the upright upstairs. Cynthia recalls, "He would be belting out songs and playing the piano while we were all being silly about singing, because none of us had much of a voice. He really seemed to relax and have fun there." And now, at Charter, he did the same. "I played every day at my club for an hour after dinner. I just sat there, and we were all in the living room and I played, every night. Not because I was any good or I wanted to get better, but just because I liked it."

He took some theoretical music courses at Princeton to deepen his understanding, but never considered it seriously. "To go into music, I

Eric Molson playing piano, Kennebunkport, Maine, summer 1999. Molson family collection.

would have had to give up my long-term career goal of being a brewer, and that came first."

During summer breaks, Eric worked – one year as a messenger boy at the Bank of Montreal, and another cutting dead trees and preparing for forest fires in the woods of New Brunswick. He chuckles as he recalls bringing his books with him to the woods to study.

Despite the family wealth, he didn't receive pocket money from his father, and so he looked forward to working, both in the summers and after graduation. "We all wanted to work. Once you make some money, you're freer. I couldn't wait to just take the streetcar to work and have that kind of autonomy."

Stephen was also in Montreal working in the summertime, and the boys went out in the evenings to listen to music. When Tom grilled them at dinner about their jaunts, Eric would start telling him details of their outings. Stephen would kick him under the table, muttering, "Don't say anything, Creep. Are you trying to suck up or something?"

Eric laughs as he remembers. "Stephen always thought I was telling our father way too much."

The brothers have affectionately referred to each other as "the Creep" ever since. "He called me 'the Creep' and I would call him 'the Creep,'" says Eric. "If I ever said anything nice to my father, he would make sure I shut up. He's funny, Stephen. I miss him when I'm not around him."

🍁

Eric's school years were also years of development and progress for the Molson Brewing Company. In 1945, when he was still at Selwyn House, Molson went through a significant transformation. After 159 years as a privately held corporation, making and distributing beer solely in Quebec, it made its company shares available to the public for the first time. The goal of this initial public offering was to gather enough capital to expand the existing brewery and to grow the business beyond the borders of the province.

John Molson started the company in 1786 from nothing and built it up into one of the larger ones in Lower Canada. It provided a solid base from which the family could invest in multiple initiatives to strengthen the community and the country, including shipbuilding,

Molsons working at the brewery. *Left to right,* F. Stuart Molson (1893–1983), Tom H.P. Molson (1901–1978), Herbert "Bert" W. Molson (1882–1955), John H. Molson (1896–1977), and Hartland de Montarville Molson (1907–2002). Molson Coors Brewing Company collection.

railways, banking, hospitals, universities, and of course hockey. The brewery, however, always remained strong, front and centre, upholding its founding father's principles of hard work, integrity, consistent quality, and community.

In each of the generations that followed, there seemed to always be one "beer man" born, and it was he who took the company forward on John's faithful path. Following World War II, Tom and Hartland joined the other Molsons at the helm of the brewery. The two were polar opposites yet complementary, the older brother behind the scenes, reserved and diligent, and the younger one up front as the charismatic face of the company.

Four years after taking the company public, Tom, Hartland, and their older second cousin Bert Molson, then president of the brewery, worried about diluting the family's control position. They didn't want to lose their grasp on the company's direction, yet they wanted to keep encouraging public shareholders. In 1949, they introduced a dual-class share structure to address this concern.

"Dual-class" means that the company issues two different categories of shares – in this case, non-voting and voting. Molson's existing shares were split into Class As (non-voting) for public purchase, and Class Bs (voting) for the founders of the brewery. This kind of structure is still used today by companies like Google, Facebook, and Rogers that want to raise capital from investors eager to share in future growth but also want to keep control with the creators of the enterprise.

Of course, there are pluses and minuses to this kind of setup. A pivotal factor is trust – trust that those who own voting shares will act in the best interest of the corporation and *all* its shareholders. If they don't, or if there's even a suspicion that they are using their privileged position for their own benefit, non-voting shareholders could rise up and revolt. When properly administered, however, the dual-class mechanism allows for a longer-range planning horizon. This is especially the case when the voting shares are held by owners who are have strong values and ethics, who thoroughly understand the business, and who are committed to the long-term growth and survival of the company (as opposed to transient share-flippers who just want a quick return).

It is both a privilege and responsibility to own a controlling block of a public corporation. Bert, Tom, and Hartland understood this. Would their successors? Time would tell.

2 Meeting the Heroine

The meeting of two personalities is like the contact of two chemical substances; if there is any reaction, both are transformed.

CARL G. JUNG (1875–1961)

"Tell me about hockey," I prompt Eric.

We are in Maine, sitting down for another one of our sessions, as Eric calls them. A light salty breeze drifts through the screens of the sunroom.

Eric takes a sip of coffee, glances out at the blue Atlantic and answers with usual brevity. "What's there to say? I'm a big fan."

I bite my tongue. I'm uncomfortable with silence. It's something I've learned about myself over the years, so I try to stay quiet to give Eric time to elaborate. Out on the horizon, a small lobster boat weaves through the waters, stopping at the buoys that mark the traps.

"Do you know what Andrew calls hockey?" Eric asks me. "The 'Great Northern Ballet.' And you know what? He's right. It's like they're dancing out there … well, at least when they're not fighting or getting dumb penalties. They're hockey players, after all." He shakes his head, smiling.

"Hockey is part of our culture," he continues. "It's very Canadian and it's part of the Molson name. Just like a good glass of beer."

I think back to the overwhelmingly positive reaction on 27 May 2009 when it became public that the Molson Brothers – Eric's sons Andrew, Justin, and Geoff – were thinking of putting in a bid for the

Front-page headline of Montreal's *La Presse*, 27 May 2009: "Vente du Canadien: Les Molson sautent dans la melée" (Sale of Canadiens, Molsons jump into the fray). Lower, a reference to a page 3 article by sportswriter Réjean Tremblay: "Vers un retour à la normalité?" (Towards a return to normality?).

Montreal Canadiens. I was taking a 6:00 a.m. flight to Toronto, and before boarding, I bought copies of all the papers – the *Montreal Gazette*, the *Globe and Mail*, *La Presse*, *Le Journal de Montréal*, *Le Devoir*, and the *National Post*. The story was everywhere. Reading the articles on the plane, I sensed unmistakable excitement that the Molson family could once again own the team. It was like a homecoming.

"You must have been happy when the boys came to you with the idea to buy back the team in 2009," I say.

"No way," Eric shoots back. "I was very negative. I tried to tell Geoff and Andrew to forget it. I said, 'It's a bad investment.' But they can be very persuasive. It's turned out all right, I think, and Geoff is doing a good job building it into a bigger entertainment business. But there are a lot of factors you don't control when you own a hockey team. Think about it – a bunch of millionaires running around on a sheet of ice! I wouldn't have done it. Besides, we'd already been through it twice before."

✦

"Molsons Buy Control of Forum, Canadiens" was the headline in the *Globe and Mail* on 25 September 1957. Tom and Hartland Molson had bought the Canadian Arena Company – the Montreal Canadiens' hockey club and the Forum where they played – from Senator Donat Raymond. It was an exciting time to own the team. The "famous Flying Frenchmen of the National Hockey League" had just won the 1957 Stanley Cup and would go on to win it another four times in a row, a streak never since duplicated.

Hockey was more than just a game, and the Habs – the team's popular nickname, referring to *les habitants*, the original settlers of New France – were more than just a team. Over the course of the twentieth century, the team became a kind of "third pillar" of Quebec society; the Catholic Church and the French language were the other two. The weekly Saturday-night broadcasts of *Hockey Night in Canada* were as imperative as Sunday-morning mass. In fact, the Canadiens' jersey is often referred to as *La sainte flanelle*, revered and sacred like the holy relic it is named after, *La sainte robe* Jesus wore to his crucifixion.

In the mid-1950s, the team unwittingly assumed an even larger societal role. Its players came to represent the rising revolt by the French-speaking Québécois against the powerful Anglos – "*les boss*" – who controlled the province's industries and natural resources. Maurice "Rocket" Richard, the team's star and top scorer, became an icon for Quebec's Quiet Revolution, a time of intense social change just starting to build momentum. It began on 13 March 1955, when Clarence Campbell, the (Anglo) NHL president, suspended Richard for the rest of the 1954–55 season (including playoffs) after he hit a linesman in a game.

The fans thought the punishment too severe. Many said it was because of Richard's French-Canadian background. The "scumbag

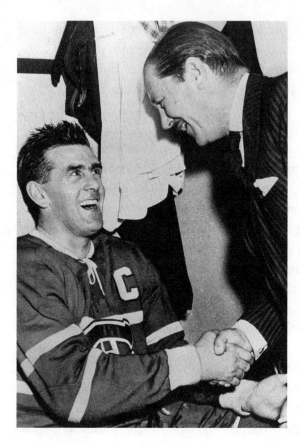

Hon. Senator Hartland de Montarville Molson congratulating Maurice "Rocket" Richard after the 1960 Stanley Cup victory. LAC/Molson fonds PA-127084. The Stanley Cup has been won on eleven occasions by the Montreal Canadiens under Molson family and/ or Molson Brewery ownership.

Anglos" running the NHL were trying to make an example out of the Franco working-class hero dominating their league. When Campbell showed up at the Forum a few days later for a game on St Patrick's Day, he sparked a riot in the streets of Montreal that released years of pent-up Québécois frustration.

Tom and Hartland were sensitive to the responsibility that came with owning the Habs. Hartland put it well: "We don't own the Canadiens, really. The public of Montreal, in fact the entire Province of Quebec owns the Canadiens. This club … is an institution – a way of life." Years later, Eric echoed this sentiment to his own sons.

❧

Being responsible, working hard, respecting others, keeping your word: Eric learned these values from his father and uncle. They were the values the fifth-generation Molson brothers relied on in 1945 when they turned to outside investors to raise money for the first time. Molson's initial public offering was done to expand the brewery outside the Province of Quebec.

The brothers first scoped out potential sites in Ontario. It was a covert operation to confound industry rivals; they travelled separately under assumed names. And rivals they had. The Labatt brothers, growing the business started by their grandfather in 1847, had just launched Labatt 50, the first light ale in Canada. And business tycoon E.P. Taylor was on a buying spree. He had amassed over twenty small breweries, including O'Keefe, to create the world's largest brewing company, Canadian Breweries Ltd. It may well have been Taylor's acquisition rampage that convinced the Molson brothers to opt for a dual-class share structure for their brewery in 1947, four years after going public.

"Control was important in those days, because you didn't want someone like E.P. Taylor raiding your stock and getting control, which is what he did to all those other breweries," Eric says. "You want to control where you're going."

Tom and Hartland settled on an Ontario site: a ten-acre prime waterfront lot on Fleet Street, with access to the railway and highway. The only problem was that it was partly owned by E.P. Taylor. The industrialist parked a couple of enormous O'Keefe beer trucks there; with thousands of motorists travelling the freeway daily, it was a good advertising location. Proceeding with caution, the brothers hired an intermediary to negotiate the purchase. They knew if Taylor found out who was interested in his property, he would never let it go. In the end, they snapped it up without his finding out it was for Molson. "It was just a piece of land available in a good location for us to have a brewery," Eric says. "You had the water, you had the trains, you had the roads ... Once it was done, our guy called E.P. Taylor and told him, 'Get your trucks off our property.' It came as a total surprise to him."

Tom threw himself into the new plant's design and construction. In August 1955, Molson's Toronto brewery was inaugurated. The six-storey structure was one of the largest and most modern breweries at the time, and Tom was justifiably proud of his creation, *his* brewery. To run it, Hartland found David Chenoweth, a precocious young man in

Sod-turning ceremony, 1954, for Molson's Toronto brewery, the most modern in Canada when completed. Standing in front of the Molson truck are (*left to right*) George H. Craig, Campbell L. Smart, Thomas H.P. Molson, and David M. Chenoweth. Chenoweth became the first non-Molson president and CEO of Molson Breweries Ltd in 1966. Molson Coors Brewing Company collection.

his twenties, then president of Pepsi-Cola Canada. Always the artful negotiator, Hartland managed to seduce Chenoweth away from Pepsi-Cola to oversee operations at Molson's Toronto plant. It would eventually service most of Ontario and some of Western Canada.

The following years were exciting ones of growth and expansion. The company reached another milestone in 1958. Again Tom went undercover, using the name Wilson, and secretly scoped out potential acquisition targets in Western Canada. That was his expertise: looking over a brewery to see if Molson should buy it, or picking a site to build a new one. The brothers settled on the unfortunately named Sick's Brewery Ltd, based in Calgary. Tom liked the nuts and bolts of the business, and Hartland approved of the finances. Sick's had five breweries in British Columbia, Alberta, and Saskatchewan as well as two in the United States.

To enable the acquisition, the Molson board modified the company's share capital. On 3 October 1958, they created an additional 500,000 Class A and Class B shares and did a two-for-one split of already issued stock. The price of Molson shares had skyrocketed in recent years. By increasing the number of shares through a split, they became more affordable, and the company could attract new investors. The measures worked. On 29 November 1958, Molson announced it had acquired control of Sick's Brewery on a share exchange basis.

The Sick's deal brought more than anyone bargained for. "When we bought those breweries out West, we went in and found that every drawer was full of money," says Eric. "That's an expression to say that what we bought was worth a lot more than we'd paid for. We went in there, and when we started looking around – opening the drawers, as it were – we realized they were full of cash. The brewing operations, the equipment, the products ... they were all worth a lot more than what we expected."

With the Sick's transaction, at the end of the 1950s Molson had grown into a pan-Canadian corporation. From a private Quebec brewery in 1945, it became a publicly held brewer with facilities across the country in a thirteen-year time span.

Sick's Brewery Ltd, Prince Albert, Saskatchewan, bought by Molson in 1958. With the Sick's acquisition, Molson expanded in the West. Molson Coors Brewing Company collection.

With so much good fortune, the Molson brothers looked for a way to give back. It was a tradition started long ago by John Molson, who once said, "We are all members of a larger community, which depends on everyone playing a part."

On 28 November 1958, the day before the Sick's acquisition, Tom and Hartland followed John's footsteps by creating the Molson Foundation. They funded it with over half of their Class B voting shares, and dedicated it to "the betterment of Canadian society." The foundation was set up to make gifts and donations to hospitals, medical research, and educational institutions across the country. The Molson Foundation has now been in existence for close to sixty years. Formed and maintained mainly from Molson stock, it relies almost exclusively on the beer company to give back to Canada, illustrating the importance of the business to the overall Molson philosophy. Over the years, it has supported a myriad of institutions across the country with multimillion dollar donations. Some of the beneficiaries closer to home include the Montreal Neurological Institute, Université de Montréal, Concordia University, Centre hospitalier Sainte-Justine, and the Montreal General Hospital.

The Molson family's affiliation with some of these establishments goes back more than a century. In the case of the Montreal General Hospital (MGH), for example, it was John Molson who lobbied the 1819 Legislative Assembly to support its construction as the city's first non-denominational public hospital. In his petition, the fifty-six-year-old Molson argued, "The strong tide of emigration that has extended itself to Canada, and the increased number of sick naturally attendant on such causes, imperiously call for some asylum where they may receive that aid and relief their impoverished and unsheltered condition urgently demand." The immigrant population's situation was made worse by limited access to the religion-based Hôtel Dieu de Montréal, the only hospital in town. While the legislature deliberated over the request, Molson and his allies took immediate action by raising private funds to open the first twenty-four beds in a temporary building. Four years later, the MGH received its Royal Charter and a permanent

Logo of the Molson Foundation, established by Tom and Hartland Molson in 1958. From the time of its inception to 2016, the foundation has supported 570 institutions, donating a total of $155,521,867.

hospital was built. John Molson and his three sons were all named to the hospital's founding board of governors. A Molson has served on the board of the MGH in every succeeding generation, down to Tom, then Eric, and now Andrew.

Eric chuckles as he describes the imprint Tom left on the Montreal General Hospital. "At the same time that Tom was expanding the Montreal brewery and building the one in Toronto, he was vice-president of the MGH, which was also being enlarged. So Tom ended up using the same stuff for the hospital that he used for the breweries – same tiles, same railings, same colours, same designing engineers, McDougall Freidman. So the hospital looks a bit like the brewery! And of course a brewery has to be a bit like an operating room in some ways. It has to be kept sterile, it has to be cold all the time, and it has to be easy to clean. So if you look at the old part of the MGH, you'll see it's very close – same colours (pale green and fawn), same bricks (bricks galore – my father liked bricks because they're solid and easy to lay) as the Notre Dame brewery."

In 1958, as Molson grew across the country in both business and philanthropy, Eric watched from the sidelines at Princeton. That spring, there had been the added thrill of the Montreal Canadiens, now owned by Tom and Hartland, defeating the Boston Bruins to win the Stanley Cup. As Eric thought about post-graduation life, he wondered how he too would eventually contribute to the Molson name, if at all.

Tom had ideas on the matter. When Eric graduated from Princeton with honours in 1959, Tom decided it was time to immerse his son in the beer business. Judging it was best for Eric to gain experience outside the family company, he made an arrangement with Phil Oland, owner of Moosehead Breweries in St John, New Brunswick.

"They swapped children so we didn't have to work for our own fathers," says Eric. "I went to Moosehead, and Derek Oland came to work at Molson." It was a principle Eric applied years later with his own son Geoff, who was eager to work at Molson. Eric insisted that Geoff get pertinent experience at another firm before joining the family brewery.

Eric's first venture in the beer business, however, was less than positive. After several months of "tasting" all day at Moosehead and crashing at the local YMCA, he was bored. "It was very much a drill. I was doing the same thing every day. I'd take samples from the tanks, bring them to the lab for testing … very routine. I didn't find it challenging." He started doubting whether he wanted to be in the beer business after all.

He called his father and told him, "I think I'd like to go back to school and do a master's in chemistry."

"Don't be ridiculous," snapped Tom. "You don't want to become one of those eggheads working in a lab for the rest of your life, do you?"

Luckily for Eric, John Turkevich came through with a solution. "I'm looking for someone," Eric's former professor said. "Why don't you come back to Princeton and work for me?"

Without hesitation, Eric agreed. He was delighted at the thought of being back in the lab, working with an electron microscope, living in Charter Club. He might even go to some of the Philadelphia debutante balls.

"They had great bands at those deb parties," he recalls. "I would take the train to Philly, listen to the band play all night, and be back in the lab the next morning."

Molson's Capilano brewery, 1966, at the southern foot of the Burrard Bridge in the Kitsilano neighbourhood of Vancouver, BC. Molson Coors Brewing Company collection.

Tom was mollified because, in addition to his lab work at Princeton, Eric enrolled at the United States Brewers' Academy in Mount Vernon, New York. There he gained an in-depth understanding of brewing science (malting, mashing, boiling, fermentation, and finishing) and brewery engineering (fluid flow, heat and mass transfer, solid-liquid separation, etc.). He graduated in March 1960 as a certified brewmaster.

Now twenty-two, he felt ready to start in the family business. But once again, Tom had his ideas of how this would work. "You're not going to work in the Montreal head office," he told Eric. "You should get some hands-on experience." He sent him out West to start as an apprentice brewer in Molson's smaller Vancouver facility.

Arriving in Vancouver in April 1960, Eric checked into the Sylvia Hotel across the Burrard Bridge from Molson's Capilano Brewery. "I have nothing but the fondest memories of those Vancouver days," he says. "I did all the things a young man dreams of doing when he finds his first real independence. I took the train across Canada, found the first apartment I ever rented, got my first pay cheque from Molson as an assistant quality-control chemist, bought my first car – a VW Beetle – made a lot of friends, played hockey and baseball with Molson employees, drank beer, and learned a lot about beer making and beer marketing."

Unlike the time at Moosehead, he was stimulated by both his peers and bosses, and felt he was part of a team. He checked temperatures and conformity of samples, recorded notes for quality assurance, and worked with the other lab employees to further improve Molson products. In this milieu, he was neither inhibited nor shy. "The people at Molson were teaching me brewing and management techniques. They helped develop me. They had good senses of humour, and I started liking it. I could never have learned all that had I worked directly for Tom in Montreal."

Tom was making sure that Eric was exposed to different facets of the business. He wanted him to be well-rounded. Not only did Eric assist in the beer-making process, he did creative work with the marketing people, he visited taverns and other client establishments with the sales guys, and he completed rotations at the other western Molson facilities in Calgary and Prince Albert. There, he took on an assortment of projects. "For instance, I had to supervise the installation of new tanks. I even designed some of the piping and stuff. The smaller the brewery, the more you can do things. I liked the additional responsibility."

✤

A year later, in 1961, Eric was moved back to Montreal to take on the position of assistant brewmaster at the Notre Dame brewery. It was a very different environment from what he had experienced in the West. Montreal was where John Molson began operations in 1786, and with his portrait hanging prominently in the main reception room, it felt to Eric as if his ancestor was still keeping a close eye on things.

A lot of other Molsons also worked at the Montreal brewery, including a number of cousins. Not all of them shared Eric's values and work ethic. "Some of them were goof-offs," Eric says bluntly. "They would sit there lining up dates and reading girlie magazines … I didn't think that was the way you earned respect." To Eric, it was important that

Eric Molson standing in front of the portrait of the Hon. John Molson (1763–1836) that still hangs today in the brewery's main reception room on Notre Dame Street.

Molson's original Montreal brewery, Notre Dame Street, 1967. The tower at the centre with the Molson sign on it was added after Hartland Molson learned that Expo 67 was to be held on Ste Helen Island across the St Lawrence River from the brewery. He estimated that that the brewery's existing sign was too low to be seen by the millions of visitors expected to attend the world fair. Since Montreal's municipal zoning laws prohibited adding a rooftop sign, he decided to rebuild the brewery's storage tower high enough that a sign on its river side could be seen from the fair. Today the storage tower is emblazoned on all four sides with a truck-sized neon sign that flashes Molson alternately in red and blue and can be seen from miles away. Molson Coors Brewing Company collection.

the same standards apply to family members as to other employees – no special favours. "The guys at the brewhouse knew me as a straight shooter, a guy who was a hard worker and consistent. I was there first thing every morning, ready to roll up my sleeves, just like them."

Moreover, it was at the brewery on Notre Dame Street that the presence of "Mr Tom" and "Mr Hartland" – chairman of the board and president, respectively – was most felt. Their watchful eyes could be intimidating. Never hesitating to intervene, they would zoom in on a detail they wanted addressed, be relentless in their reminders on how to correct it, and not let it go until it was resolved to their satisfaction. They were especially that way with family members being groomed to run the business one day, bringing up important issues of quality control or process compliance but also focusing on the most insignificant points. Says Eric, "The problem was that they were just as adamant on the larger issues as on the smaller ones – like whether a light was not working properly in the elevator or whether the clock at the top of the building was off by a few minutes. And if you didn't have the backbone to withstand the pressure, it could destroy you … It's probably what happened to P.T. Molson." Eric's voice trails off as he remembers the untimely death of forty-five-year-old P.T.

Tom and Hartland's micro-management aside, the general climate at the Notre Dame brewery was one of camaraderie. Employees and family members alike enjoyed close relationships and mutual admiration. The Molsons hired a team of doctors, nurses, and dentists for the benefit of all their employees, including players of the Montreal Canadiens. They routinely brought the staff together to share in social activities and organized pick-up hockey games at the Forum to build *esprit de corps*. A moving example of the family's commitment to the people of the brewery was when Dave Chenoweth passed away at fifty-one, leaving behind his widow, Clare, and five boys. Tom and Hartland, beholden to Chenoweth for his commitment and loyalty to Molson, arranged to pay for all his children's university studies – collectively, eleven degrees.

This kind of attention to employee welfare generated a strong sense of allegiance. In fact, it wasn't uncommon to find multiple generations of a family – fathers, uncles, and sons – working for the firm. John Patrick Rogers, who started in the payroll department at twenty-two and eventually became Molson's CEO and president, says: "It was an extraordinary company, and it was made that way by the family. They really cared about us. I still have my twenty-five-year pin with the inscription 'Member of the Molson Family' engraved on it. It meant something."

The Molsons also took great care to keep the brewery as politically neutral as possible. The early 1960s was a time of unrest in the province. The Front de libération du Québec (FLQ), an extremist group supporting separation, was gaining momentum and would eventually resort to violence in their fight against "Anglo-Saxon imperialism." In the brewery, Eric explains, "we stayed away from politics. We didn't explain why we loved Canada. We supported Pearson and Trudeau and Laurier. We said it, but we didn't preach it. And we didn't speak against separation. We had our employees to think of … there was the same percentage of separatists in our company as there were federalists."

After moving back to Montreal, Eric was eager to find his own place rather than go back home. Tom did not object; by this time, he was remarried, to Beatrice Passmore, later known as "Auntie Bea," a former neighbour along Ramezay Road. Eric rented an apartment downtown on Stanley Street with his old BCS pal Arnold Sharp, a.k.a. "Arnie," and Auntie Bea's son Godfrey. The roommates and a few others regularly met for some laughs, hockey games, and a couple of beers. Often they were joined by Stephen, now a student at McGill and a budding bridge player. Although smart and capable, Stephen was less into academics than his siblings and didn't worry as much about pleasing Tom.

The brothers' casual fun was only possible because they were living on their own, out of the public eye. When your last name was Molson, Montreal could feel like a city full of busybodies. "Back then, my mother's friends went shopping with white gloves on. They were fuss-pots ladies … always looking for something to tsk-tsk at." Eric knew his father and the fuss-pots kept a close watch on him, though his modern mother was happy for him to sow his oats. But Eric knew better than to get up to any antics around town. "I let loose in Princeton or when I was away ... not in Montreal with my aunts watching!"

The brewery was also a place where Eric could let loose a little. The company had a "Men's Bar" in Montreal where both union and staff employees could gather for free beer after their shift. (Later, as president of Molson's Ontario brewery, Eric would open a similar bar at the Reception Room of the Fleet Street facility.) Eric enjoyed going to the company bar at the end of each day. "These brewery guys spoke my language. We exchanged lots of notes, talked beer and hockey, and drank a couple of *grosses molles*" – a colloquialism used to describe a pint of Molson Export.

John Rogers remembers, "Eric was very comfortable with the people in the plant, because they were his kind of people. Of course they were comfortable with him as well, because they knew he'd been there right from the bottom up. He knew the business inside out."

While Eric loved the brewhouse, he knew that remaining a brewer was not to be his lot and accepted that without complaint. Tom's lessons of responsibility had registered. What mattered most was the company, not a young man's whims and fancies. Dutifully, Eric completed his education by taking the requisite accounting and economics courses at night school while working at the brewery. In 1963, he left the factory floor to become assistant to the president, learning about the dealings and strategies of the business world under Uncle Hartland.

❦

Hartland de Montarville Molson, a decorated war hero, Canadian senator, and president of Molson, was an almost royal presence at the brewery. Always impeccably dressed, with his shoes shone daily, he had elevated tastes and a stately bearing. Tea was served to him each afternoon from polished silver by Armand, the butler. To be invited to the boardroom for tea with Mr Hartland was to be in a position of prestige in the company.

While Eric respected Hartland's business sense, his good work in the senate, and his dedication to his responsibilities, he didn't value aspects of Hartland's style. The grand demonstrations of wealth, the flunkies

Senator Hartland de Montarville Molson, 1968, posing with the Stanley Cup won by the Montreal Canadiens in a four-game sweep against the St Louis Blues. Courtesy estate of David Bier.

who surrounded him, the airs he put on at times, and the fact that he could be a bit of a bully reflected everything that Eric had regarded with distaste at school. "He liked all the trappings around the presidency – big car, chauffeur, all that stuff. But the brewery people didn't want some guy coming to work in a Rolls-Royce … In our business, it's better to be a sidewalk man. When you're on the sidewalk, you know what people are thinking."

Regardless, Eric agreed to become Hartland's assistant ("bag man," he calls it), recognizing a great learning opportunity. For three years he travelled with Hartland across the country, doing everything from tipping waiters to writing memos for senior management meetings. In his role of assistant to the president, he was exposed to a whole new side of the business. (He's still amazed at all that he saw so early on: "I had lunch with Joey Smallwood when I still had pimples!") But Hartland often made Eric feel inadequate. He regularly lost patience with his nephew, snapping, "No, that's not the way to do it, Eric. Let me."

Tom mocked Hartland's need to have everything "tickety-boo." On weekends at Ivry (the large lake-side property north of Montreal which Tom's father and uncle had purchased so the Molson clan could build country houses for weekend getaways), Hartland's idiosyncrasies were often out of place. He donned gloves to go boating, ordered the motor-boat's gas tank polished, and had servants bring down food to the lake on a tray. "As if you can't bring your own picnic down to the wharf!" Eric laughs. "He lived like that, Hartland. Tom did not."

The two brothers running Molson couldn't have been more different. Hartland, debonair in an ascot and jacket, was the front man. He had a vision for the business and got involved in marketing and promotions. Tom was the conservative engineer. Every day he wore his "working man's blue suit," complete with a reserved necktie, and stuck to the basics. He focused on manufacturing, process efficiencies, and quality, intent on procuring the best ingredients, the best equipment, and the best supplies.

"Tom was 'Mr Inside' and Hartland was 'Mr Outside,'" says John Rogers. "Tom knew every pipe and valve in the brewery. Brewing was in his veins. But he was a shy man, as is Eric, and he was quite happy to see Hartland out in front, being Hartland. You know, shaking hands, handing out gold watches … they were a good pair."

The "good pair" worked well together. Eric would later reflect, "We've survived over the generations because we've had brothers who don't fight." There was Tom and Hartland in the fifth generation, Eric and Stephen in the sixth and now, Andrew, Justin, and Geoff.

🍁

Whereas Hartland taught Eric the importance of vision and strategy, from Tom he learned about execution through consistent high quality, rigorous discipline, and innovation. To keep up with the latest developments, Tom built relationships with brewers from around the world. They discussed technical aspects of the business, everything from new recipes to more efficient processes and better packaging. Eric would later follow Tom's example in a more structured way, joining an international brewing consortium that annually brought together brewers from North America, Europe, and Japan to exchange technical information.

Over the years, Tom also shared industrial know-how with William Coors – known as "Uncle Bill" to both relatives and employees of the Coors Brewing Company in the United States. The two brewers knew and respected one another, although they were different in many ways. In terms of their backgrounds, Tom's forefather had emigrated to Canada from England and launched his enterprise in 1786, while Adolph Coors came from Germany and founded his Golden Colorado brewery eighty-six years later. Molson also had thirty more years of experience than Coors as a publicly listed company. And while the Molson family stayed out of politics, Coors family members played prominent roles in the American political arena through their support of conservative ideals.

There was one thing that joined Molson and Coors, however: superior beer-making. Tom and Bill both strove to deliver high-calibre beer, unfailing customer satisfaction, and transformative innovation to ensure that their breweries continue to thrive for generations to come. The two men held each other in high esteem. When Tom wanted to expand from ales to get into lagers, for example, it was "Uncle Bill" he called.

Tom's relationships with his colleagues were strong, and he always adhered to the highest standards. Says Eric, "Everything he bought for the company or sold to the consumer – all ingredients, temperatures, labels – everything had to be perfect. You know the John Molson quote, 'An honest brew makes its own friends'? Well, Tom exemplified it." But Tom expected perfection not only as it pertained to the brewery but also of his son. It was a difficult, if not impossible, standard to live up to. Eric recalls, "He'd give me shit for not working on Saturday morning. I had to talk back to him: 'Dad, nowadays not many people go to work on Saturday morning. If I'm needed at the brewery, I'm on call.' I was on call every weekend, all year round."

The brewery was certainly central to Eric's life, but he also knew that he needed and wanted more.

❦

Jane Mitchell first came into Eric's life as "Tonia's little sister." The Mitchell girls were both pretty and fine-featured, but Tonia was taller with sandy hair and Jane was a petite brunette. Both were students at King's Hall, a boarding school for girls in the Eastern Townships about sixteen kilometres away from BCS. Occasionally the two schools organized coed events, and, at the age of twelve, Eric invited Tonia to one of the tea dances. These parties were a highlight of the school year. Everyone wanted to go, except perhaps for Jane who, at eight, was the school's youngest boarder. She was stuck dancing awkwardly with Miss Gillard, the headmistress. Tonia, noticing her younger sister's glum face, asked Eric, "Why don't you take her for a spin?"

It was their first dance.

Twelve years passed before Eric and Jane saw each other again. While he completed his studies and started working, Jane went to Bishop's University. By the time she finished her BA, she was eager to break out of the pastoral Eastern Townships. She found her exit with "Katie Gibbs," the venerable Katharine Gibbs School of executive secretarial programs in New York City.

"It was a wonderful experience," she tells me. We are in her kitchen in Montreal as she prepares vegetables for dinner. "I absolutely adored New York." I have no trouble believing her. In all the years I've known Jane, her curiosity and appetite for discovery have been constants.

After graduating from Katie Gibbs, Jane moved back to Montreal and got a job with the engineering firm McDougall Friedman. By then, Eric had settled back in the city after his stint out West and was working at the Notre Dame brewery. Their paths were destined to cross. Jane's new apartment was down the street from Eric's. And as she was friends with Eric's roommates, Arnie and Godfrey, she occasionally went over to visit.

Seeing Eric again after all that time, Jane was struck by how much he had changed. Gone was the skinny, pimply teen of years before. He had filled out, grown tall, and become quite handsome. He was still shy, but this only added to his mystery. "He was harder to get to know than the others," Jane says. "I was intrigued." She found herself drawn to his humour, his intelligence, his unpretentious manner and unshowy ways. The attraction was mutual.

Jane Mitchell and Eric Molson, 1964. Molson family collection.

"Jane was the prettiest of the bunch," says Eric. "I didn't take a shine to too many girls before that. I just used to hang out with the guys, drink beer, and talk hockey. I mean, I had dates, but they were more like balls of fluff … Jane was different." She was someone he could talk and laugh with, someone who listened and understood him – someone he felt he could trust.

He started giving Jane signs that he thought she was special. Whereas others might have chosen flowers or chocolates, Eric was more pragmatic. He worried about Jane's safety in her basement apartment and presented her with a baseball bat as a means of self-defence. "Can you believe it? A baseball bat?" Wiping her hands on a dishtowel, Jane laughs. "It wasn't conventional, but I don't know, I found it endearing." Eventually, the two started spending time alone, going on picnics, seeing movies or, in typical Eric fashion, doing laundry together. They delighted in each other's company and fell in love.

It was a match wholly approved of by Montreal society and by both families. Jane recalls attending a hockey game at the Forum with Eric in those early days: "To get to our places, we had to pass in front of the family seats, and when we walked through, I heard Uncle Tommy whispering to Aunt Dosh, 'Oh, wouldn't that be nice?' – referring to Eric and me."

But Eric was not ready to get married. "It took me a while to figure out what a wife ought to be," he says. "A mother, a partner, a confidante? … I don't remember when it clicked." As weeks turned to months and eventually years, one thing became clear to Jane: it was taking too long. Even her mother, Margaret Mitchell, was losing patience. "Oh, just go and find someone else," she urged. "He's not worth it!"

After a while ("of being vetted," Jane says jokingly), she got fed up. "I thought, 'Oh, come on, Eric, do something!' I was twenty-three or twenty-four years old, and in those days if you weren't attached or married by then, you were an old maid. So I decided to take off. My friend Vicki was working in Spain at the time and was urging me to go over, so I decided to go visit her for a few weeks." Jane saved enough money for a one-way ticket to Madrid. Her parents, knowing her wanderlust, paid for a return flight three weeks later.

She admits she wanted to trigger a reaction. "I was sort of hoping Eric would say, 'Don't go to Spain! And if you go, come back … I can't live without you!' Well, he didn't do that at all." Instead, he encouraged her. "Go sow your wild oats and have a great time." He believed in giving people space to make their own decisions (while keeping watch in the background) – an attitude he maintained with his children and later, as chairman of Molson, with his CEOs.

Jane's three-week trip to Spain turned to nearly two years. She moved in with Vicki, got a job at Imperio Americano del Embalaje, and perfected her Spanish. The two girls had a busy social life. Among their friends were Los Brincos, a popular Spanish rock band of the

1960s, known as the "Spanish Beatles." Jane got to know the foursome and donated the money from the sale of her parent's return-to-Canada ticket to help them buy Vox instruments in London.

But she continued to keep in touch with Eric. In their letters back and forth, she shared her adventures in Spain, and he described his experiences in the business world. Sometimes he hinted at his longer-term intentions, asking questions like "How would you handle the responsibility of running a household?" Still, he didn't propose.

As always, Eric was methodical and thorough. Using his science-based inquiry approach, he tested his hypothesis that Jane was "The One." He was clearly in love with her, but he wanted to make sure she could cope with the duties that came with the family name. In that time and place, "Molson" was an undeniably big deal.

"I can't believe the scrutiny he put me through," Jane says. "Very scientific! I think he may have been a little frightened at first. It was probably because, in his mind, he had to marry someone who could carry the flame … who could cope with the ins and outs of Molson. I think he realized the responsibility that was going to eventually fall on his shoulders, and he took that very seriously."

"I wanted to make sure it was *true* love," says Eric. "You know, the kind that lasts. If you follow Hollywood's definition of love, it's easy, but if you want the real McCoy – you know, the real thing that's going to last forever – it's harder to figure out."

As the Canadian-stamped letters continued to come, Vicki would ask, "So? Did he propose?"

Jane would shake her head. "What do you think?"

One day, a particularly tantalizing missive arrived. Eric, who had been immersed in a Molson business deal to buy the Hamm breweries in the United States, had begun detailing the specifics of the transaction in a letter to Jane. He suddenly realized he had gone too far and thought, "Jeez, this is too confidential!" Left with the choice of either rewriting the whole thing or blacking out the sensitive parts of the existing letter, he opted for the latter (more efficient, he figured), and with a marker, "made a hash of it." Jane and Vicki were convinced the blanked-out text was a marriage proposal. Jane says, "So there we were, holding up this letter to the light, trying different angles and I was hoping to read, 'Come home Jane and marry me!' … It was very funny."

After being apart from Jane for nearly eighteen months, Eric realized his initial hunch was right: she was the love of his life. He had to see her. He wrote to her and asked her to meet him in Austria. He was going skiing in St Anton am Arlberg with friends. Would she join them?

Jane agreed. In early December 1965, she took a short leave from her job, flew from Madrid to Zurich, and took a train to St Anton. Eric met her at the station. Their reconnection was immediate; it was as if they had never been apart. They spent a carefree and joyous two weeks together skiing the Tyrolean Alps. And before it was over, they decided they were going to get married.

Jane remembers the scene at the airport at the end of their holiday. They had to go through different security checkpoints as she was heading back to Madrid and he to Montreal. "So there we were, on opposite sides of this long barrier, walking along, kissing and not letting go," she says, imitating her younger, smitten self. "By the time we left Austria, we knew we were meant for each other."

There was no formal proposal. Eric didn't get down on bended knee. He didn't produce an extravagant engagement ring. Instead, they opted for simple gold bands. When they told their parents of their decision, everyone was pleased. "Finally!" said Jane's mother and offered to help with the wedding.

Jane went back to Montreal after Christmas to start getting organized. "Eric came to get me at the airport. I had told my mother I was coming in the next day so I could spend some time with him. But when I called her the following day from his apartment and she asked, 'When did you get here?' I made a complete boo-boo and said, 'I got here last night.' She was livid. She said, 'You get on that bus and come to Massawippi right away!' I told her I would take Eric's car, and she answered, 'You are not taking Eric's car. You are not going anywhere in his car. You get on that bus and I'll meet you at the station.' I was in trouble."

Fifty years later, Jane laughs. "She eventually got over it. And actually, when it was time to organize our wedding that spring, she was the one who made most of the arrangements. I had to go back to Spain to finish my job, pack my bags, and say my goodbyes, so I was very lucky she helped me with all that."

The celebration took place on Saturday, 16 April 1966. Eric was twenty-eight and Jane twenty-five. They were married in the Massawippi Union Church, close to where Jane's parents lived. Margaret Mitchell had taken great care decorating the quaint white country church. Bringing in cedar boughs as a background, she interspersed them with spring flowers, willow shoots, and birds. It was enchanting.

Eric and Jane were not interested in the pomp and circumstance of an elaborate ceremony, with hundreds of guests and a fancy reception. They would have preferred to elope or go off and get married in a small church with a few friends somewhere in Spain. But that was not possible. A Massawippi country wedding was the closest alternative. "Everybody in the family was probably quite disappointed with our little folksy wedding, but we loved it," says Jane.

When it was over, the newlyweds drove south of the border to Vermont for a late ski weekend honeymoon at Jay Peak. They ended up seeing half their wedding guests on the hill. But summer was coming, and at Molson that was the busiest time of the year. Always conscientious and responsible, Eric felt he had too much work at the brewery to take any more time off just then.

They left for their "real" honeymoon a few months later. Tom had generously gifted them a trip to Europe, and they started in Spain. "I introduced Eric to all my friends," Jane recalls. "Everybody was chatting with me in Spanish, and Eric soon realized that the word '*claro*' was a good one to know. It can mean different things, but you say it after someone makes a point, it means 'clearly' or 'obviously.' So, every once in a while during a conversation, Eric would throw in, '*claro*,' and my friends would say, 'Oh, your husband speaks such good Spanish!' But that was the only word he knew!"

Their next stop was Paris. Tom had organized for them to stay at the Ritz on Place Vendôme. It was beautiful and elegant but they much preferred the more bohemian Left Bank. Cashing in the rest of Tom's first-class bookings (saving enough money for a few more trips later on), they moved into a small *pension* in the Quartier Latin that was more their style.

Newlyweds Jane and Eric Molson leaving the Massawippi Union Church on 16 April 1966. Molson family collection.

Tom must have been pleased with their union, but, besides his largesse with their trip, he rarely expressed it. When they returned from Europe, Eric tried to tell him about their journey. "Tom just cut him off, looked at him and said something careless, something about his shoes," Jane remembers. "I could tell Eric was hurt; he just stopped talking."

Jane's father, on the other hand, would ask Eric to sit down and he would listen to him. Judge William Mitchell, or "Papa," was "like

Eric Molson and his father-in-law, "Papa," the Hon. Mr Justice William Mitchell, at the reception following the installation of Eric as fifth chancellor of Concordia University, 9 November 1993. Molson family collection.

a real father," according to Eric. "He was terrific. He believed in hard work and doing things right." What Eric appreciated most, however, was Papa's ability to tune in and pay attention to others. Unlike Tom who snapped "do this" or "do that," Papa took time to work things out with Eric.

"I didn't really have a guy I could talk to in my father. It was different with Papa." Eric clears his throat as he struggles against his emotions, eyes moistening. "Papa *listened* … and we could talk about anything. He was wonderful."

Jane recognizes the bond between the two men: "Eric loved my father. He never had a close relationship with Tom, but he could talk with my father. Eric talked with him all the time."

As she and Eric began their life together, Jane came to realize the depth of Eric's sense of responsibility. She observed his burgeoning devotion not only to the Molson enterprise but to what the Molson family name stood for. "It wasn't about pleasing Tom. Eric was committed to the Molson industry, to the tradition of the Molson family, to giving back to the community and to Canada. That's what gave him drive. Back then, he was already devoted to growing this great Canadian institution and promulgating what Molson stood for beyond the borders of our country."

A little over a year before the wedding, while Jane was still in Spain, Eric had been deeply involved in a transaction with the Hamm Brewing Company of St Paul, Minnesota. By then, Molson had grown to become Canada's second-largest brewer with operations across the country and was looking for a way to break into the US market. Molson already had a minor stake in two small breweries in Washington, but according to Eric, "That was peanuts." The acquisition of the Theodore Hamm Brewing Company – the eighth largest in the United States – was a substantial move. Dave Chenoweth, then executive vice-president of operations, spearheaded the initiative and proudly announced that it would be a reversal of the growing trend of Canadian companies getting taken over by large US corporations.

The team worked for months on the deal. Molson was about to straddle the border and Eric was excited to be part of the company's next phase of growth. His role was far from strategic, but he was engaged and learning. Chenoweth made sure of that. "He spent a lot of time talking to me and training me and coaching me," Eric recalls. When the moment came to deliver the finalized offer, Eric brought it to the Hamm people himself.

It was supposed to go through without a hitch. Even John J. McCloy, the big-shot US lawyer, banker, and presidential advisor retained by Molson, said so. He was wrong. US antitrust authorities objected to the deal and threatened to sue. Chenoweth and his team were stunned. "We had a measly 2 per cent market share with some small brewery in

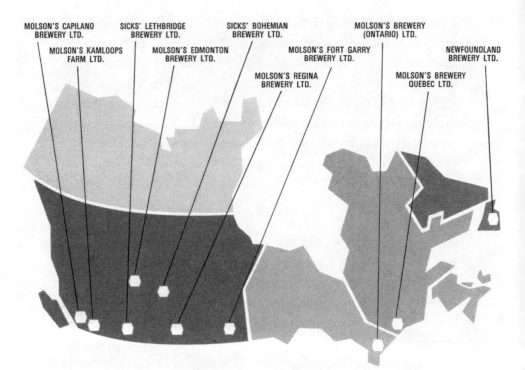

MOLSON'S CAPILANO BREWERY LTD.
SICKS' LETHBRIDGE BREWERY LTD.
SICKS' BOHEMIAN BREWERY LTD.
MOLSON'S BREWERY (ONTARIO) LTD.
MOLSON'S KAMLOOPS FARM LTD.
MOLSON'S EDMONTON BREWERY LTD.
MOLSON'S FORT GARRY BREWERY LTD.
NEWFOUNDLAND BREWERY LTD.
MOLSON'S REGINA BREWERY LTD.
MOLSON'S BREWERY QUEBEC LTD.

Molson's breweries across Canada, as depicted in the company's 1968 Annual Report. Molson Coors Brewing Company collection.

the West, and they used that against us," Eric remembers. "It was a bad decision."

The team reconvened and considered its options. They all knew what had happened a few years earlier to Labatt, Molson's Canadian rival, when it tried to buy Milwaukee's Schlitz Brewery. It got embroiled with the US Justice Department in a pricey legal battle that was still ongoing. Unwilling to go down that path, the Molson board decided to abandon the proposed merger with Hamm. The statement issued on 20 March 1965 read: "The Molson Board of directors viewed with extreme concern the prospect of engaging in time-consuming and costly litigation, particularly when the final outcome would be uncertain and might take years to resolve."

Eric was very disappointed. "That deal could have changed the course of our history and made us a completely different company," he says. "We spent a fortune trying to buy Hamm's. We got opinions from top experts, put in a 'win-win' proposal. And then we got to the antitrust level and they told us to get lost."

Once he got past his letdown, the failed deal made him realize an important difference between business and his beloved chemistry. As a chemist, he could predict the reaction of a specific combination of ingredients. In business, however, there was no such certainty; even if one took all the right steps to close a deal, the outcome was never guaranteed. There were multiple variables to grapple with, the most complex being people and their motivations.

Long discussions ensued on what to do next. In 1966, the company was flush with capital. Now that penetrating the American beer market through a US acquisition was no longer viable, Tom and Hartland, with Molson's board of directors and senior executives, had to find another way to grow their business.

They chose to diversify. Conglomerates were all the rage in the mid 1960s, partly because of low interest rates and swings in the market that facilitated leveraged buyouts. Molson's leaders decided to jump on the diversification bandwagon.

After 180 years of operating as a brewery, the company founded by John Molson was going to grow beyond beer.

3 Brewing Beer at Molson

Never be bullied into silence. Never allow yourself to be made a
victim. Accept no one's definition of your life; define yourself.
ROBERT L. FROST (1874–1963)

Eric loves beer. Most of us enjoy a cold one (or two or three) on a hot
summer day or while watching our favourite sports team on TV, but
Eric *really* loves beer. He loves the taste of it, the look of it, the smell
of it, the making of it, the ingredients that go into it … he loves its
every facet.

When he's about to try a new discovery, for instance, he tastes it as
one would a fine wine. First he makes sure the glass is clean. He recalls,
"I once told Freddy Heineken when I was in his office having a beer,
'Freddy, do you know your glasses are dirty? I can tell by the way the
foam is collapsing.' A dirty glass with oils or other residue can stop the
creation of foam and ruin the beer's flavour."

He then tips the glass to a 45-degree angle (again, for the foam),
pours, and holds it up to study the beer's colour, head, and consistency.
The visual exam complete, he gently swirls the liquid to test how the
head holds up, to stimulate carbonation and release aromas. He raises
the drink to his nose and breathes in deeply. Only then does he taste
the beer, one small mouthful at a time. It's the best way to fully appreciate the fragrances, flavours, and feel of this beverage.

When it's good, Eric's smile says it all. Pure bliss.

Eric Molson having a "rivet" with his sons Andrew (*left*) and Geoff (*middle*) at the main reception room of the Notre Dame Street brewery, December 2009, shortly after the purchase of the Canadiens. Molson Coors Brewing Company collection.

Although he doesn't consume copious amounts (usually one before dinner), he doesn't tire talking about it. "Beer recipes are all different," he explains. "Molson Export, for instance, has less malt in it, but it has more grain, more corn, and more rice, which lightens up the beer." He can detail every step of the beer-making process, from milling to lautering to fermenting, right down to packaging. "The most important and longest part of the process is fermentation. The yeast needs time to do its work and make beer out of cool wort. You can't skimp on that." Sometimes he gets into technicalities I don't understand, but I can still listen to him for hours. I relish the passion it evokes in him.

Yet it's not only the science and production of beer that enliven Eric. He cares just as much about the human bonds it helps create. I can hear it in his choice of words. For instance, he often refers to a beer as "a rivet" and explains the moniker through its joining quality: "I first heard the word 'rivet' used for beer from my friend's father. He was a steel man and in his business rivets are used to hold together things like steel beams and columns. I liked the term, so I adopted it.

And later my boys liked it too, so it stuck … I guess we felt that having another 'rivet' held us together."

Beer brings Eric to life and that's how I know he loves it. So it baffles me that back in the 1960s he went along with the plan to diversify Molson and turn it into a conglomerate. I ask him why he let it happen.

He takes a deep breath before answering. "It's not much of an excuse, but I was a kid at the time. I didn't know much about business. I didn't know much about diversification. And there were all these experts and senior guys saying it made sense and it was the right thing to do."

Eric was twenty-nine when the decision was taken to venture outside of beer. Besides his youth and limited business experience, it may have been his unwillingness to confront authority figures like his father and uncle that kept him from speaking up. They were the ones calling the shots, and as a "good" member of the younger generation, he followed suit.

I can relate to that. Like Eric, I took years to find my own path and summon the courage to pursue it. When choosing my university program, for example, I was too preoccupied with what I should do and accomplish, rather than with following my passion and using my intuition as a guide. My parents, both physicians, expected me to get a professional degree – which I did. At seventeen, I chose law and never even considered my penchant for the humanities. It was only much later in life that I tapped into what was truly compelling to me and delved into the study of human behaviour. Perhaps Eric was similar in that regard. He had all the "shoulds" of his father, his uncle, his forefathers, the Molson name, the long family history in business. So maybe it's not surprising that when they said Molson should diversify to survive for the next hundred years, he "went along with the gag" (his words) and muffled his own misgivings.

On the porch in Maine, Eric shakes his head as he recalls, "One of the lines we heard back then was, 'Why don't you get into the snow-mobile business? That way you can have a big business in the winter, and when summer comes along, you'd have another big business because they would all be drinking beer!' It's called seasonally adjusting your business. It didn't seem to matter that we didn't have the first idea on how to make snowmobiles or how to run that kind of enterprise.

We shouldn't have diversified. We didn't run any business well that was not beer. It took us a while to figure that one out."

✤

Molson's 1966 annual shareholders' meeting was held on 28 June at the Queen Elizabeth Hotel in downtown Montreal. It was a well-attended, elaborate affair, complete with a formal luncheon served by white-gloved waiters.

Senator Hartland Molson, then president and CEO of the brewery, stood at the podium and summarized the company's journey through its phases of expansion. It had gone from a private family business to a public company in 1945 and then expanded from a local brewery to a pan-Canadian one in 1955 with the opening of the Toronto brewery and the purchase of Sick's out West.

"We have reached the point where we have firmly consolidated our position in the brewing industry in Canada from coast to coast," Hartland said. "We are thus now able to turn our attention first to the determination and then to the execution of the next stage of our development." Molson, he declared, was now to get into new forms of industry and business enterprises.

A number of organizational changes were announced at the meeting. Tom Molson, then sixty-five years old, was retiring as chairman of Molson's board and being replaced by Hartland. In turn, Hartland, who had been president of the company for thirteen years, was to be succeeded by Percival Talbot ("P.T." or "Pete") Molson.

"P.T. was our type of Molson," says Eric. "He was honest, had a great reputation, and was smart as hell." He was the son of Walter Molson, the youngest brother of Herbert, Tom and Hartland's father. Born in 1921, he was twenty years younger than his cousin Tom and, like him, had gone to Bishop's College School, where he was awarded the Governor General's Medal and finished top of his class. He went on to McGill University, graduated with first-class honours in economics and political science, and won the coveted Rhodes scholarship to Oxford.

Twenty-one-year-old P.T., however, declined the prestigious award and chose instead to serve his country. In 1941, with war raging in

Percival Talbot "P.T." Molson (1921–1966). Molson Coors Brewing Company collection.

Europe, he enlisted with the Royal Canadian Navy and spent four years on transatlantic freighters bringing ammunition and other supplies from Canada to England. He rose to the rank of lieutenant-commander of the frigate HMCS *Lewis*, one of the youngest officers in that position. After the war, he could have reclaimed his scholarship to Oxford (he was offered an extension) but chose instead to join Canada's foreign service, where his genial style and unfaltering diplomacy served him well. He got an overseas posting to the Canadian High Commission in London and then to Berlin. In 1950, he returned to Canada and eventually became executive assistant to Lester B. Pearson, then secretary of state for external affairs. Pearson commented on the high quality of P.T.'s work.

While P.T. was still in Ottawa, Hartland and Tom were starting to grapple with the issue of succession. Although it would be many years before either of them retired, they regularly discussed who would next assume Molson's leadership. Tom's boys were too young and Hartland's only daughter wasn't even contemplated. There was potentially David Molson. He was part of the family (albeit more remote, a second cousin once removed) and he worked at the brewery. But Tom and Hartland thought the age gap too big. Besides, David was far more interested in the hockey team than in making beer.

The Molson brothers then considered P.T. Why not? they thought. He's smart, judicious, accomplished – just what Molson needs. Let's bring him in. We have to keep our options open. However, the thirty-two-year-old foreign service professional was not that interested in joining the brewery. He didn't even want to be a businessman.

Despite his apprehensions, after twelve years of service, P.T. joined Molson Breweries Ltd in 1953. The decision in the end was his, but he did it more out of a sense of duty and familial obligation than anything else. Hartland contacted Pearson to negotiate P.T.'s release from Canada's Department of External Affairs.

🍁

Sitting beneath portraits of founder John Molson Sr (*left*) and John Molson Jr are the five Molsons active in the brewery in 1965 (*left to right*): Hartland, Billy, Tom, P.T., and Eric Molson. National Archives Canada.

P.T. performed well at Molson and rapidly progressed through its ranks. On 1 July 1966, thirteen years after being hired, he was named president and CEO of the corporation. Moving from Toronto to Montreal, he took over Hartland's responsibilities. It was a big move, made more difficult by the fact that his wife, Lucille, refused to go with him.

The headlines on 14 September 1966, eleven weeks after P.T.'s promotion, shocked everyone connected to Molson. "Molson president dead from gunshot," was the one in the *Globe and Mail*. The rumour mill whirled at full throttle: "What happened?" people wondered. "Did you hear? I think it was because …"

The word "suicide" was not used in the papers. Instead, there were euphemisms like "accident" and "unfortunate incident." But as details leaked, it became clear: on the second weekend of September, as the leaves were just starting to change colour in the Laurentians, P.T. drove up north alone to his country house in Ivry and shot himself in the head. Three days later, on Monday, 12 September, his body was found with a 20-gauge shotgun at its side.

He was forty-five years old. Father of four children. President of the second-largest brewery in Canada. He was well liked and respected in his community. Yet unbeknownst to most, P.T. suffered from depression. It was serious enough for him to have sought treatment at the Allan Memorial Institute, a psychiatric hospital in Montreal. And although it looked like P.T. had found a way to live with his mental illness, he had a breakdown.

The exact cause of his collapse is unknown. Perhaps it was learning that Lucille had fallen in love with another man. Maybe it was the pressure of running a family-controlled business like Molson. Eric places some of the blame on his father and uncle. "Tom and Hartland used to bug him. They would harass him for petty little things. P.T. couldn't work on what *he* thought was important. Instead, he would be running around trying to please everyone else." All these aspects may have been contributing factors, but when someone suffers from depression, it is difficult to pinpoint a single reason.

"It was awful when P.T. killed himself," remembers Eric. "A real shock. It was all over the papers. He had only been president for a few months … We were all crying, it was just flooding us." Tears well in his eyes as he thinks back. "P.T. was a great guy. He just wasn't in the right place. He should have stayed a diplomat."

It was a lesson for Eric about the importance of following one's passion and true calling. P.T. had been pushed into Molson. He felt he couldn't say no. Eric vowed to himself that he would never exert that kind of pressure. Not on his sons, not on anyone. People had to choose what was right for them, especially when it came to the direction of their lives.

Eric remained faithful to this ideal and respected others' choices. Where he was tested, however, was standing up for his own vision, particularly if it involved a clash or confrontation. It would take years and multiple trials before he finally found his own voice and was able to take a resolute stance against the bullies who confronted him. One of those bullies was a member of the Molson family.

🍁

With the tragic loss of P.T., Tom and Hartland looked for a new CEO. As their options of family members were limited (Eric, for example, was still too young and inexperienced), they decided to ask David Chenoweth.

It was the first time in the company's 180-year history that a non-Molson would take the position of president and CEO. Chenoweth resisted, arguing that there must be someone in the family more qualified; it was more appropriate that a Molson be in charge. Tom and Hartland wouldn't budge. A month after P.T.'s death, on 14 October 1966, Chenoweth was elected president of Molson Breweries Ltd. His first order of business as CEO was to execute the strategy announced by Hartland at the previous annual general meeting: diversify the company's business.

🍁

Molson's foray into diversification lasted almost thirty years. From its 1966 launch, it would take the incumbency of five different CEOs – David Chenoweth, Bud Willmot, Jim Black, John Rogers, and Mickey Cohen – for the strategy to be deemed a failure. During those decades, the company's name changed to reflect its broadened scope of

David M. Chenoweth, 1967, president of Molson Breweries, 1966–68. Molson Coors Brewing Company collection.

activities. It went from Molson Breweries Ltd to Molson Industries Ltd and ultimately to The Molson Companies Ltd (TMCL).

The Molson name, once synonymous with beer and hockey, became diluted. In fact, people close to the corporation referred to it only by its acronym, TMCL. Even Eric, who was chairman of the board for the last eight years of diversification, spoke about it as TMCL. The "Molson" part of the name was silenced. Listening to Eric, it's clear to me that as much as he loves brewing and Molson's place in that industry, he was equally detached and cerebral about TMCL and its non-beer activities.

When diversification was originally proposed in the mid-1960s, Eric was not against the plan. The company had to find a way to grow, and after it was blocked from expanding into the United States when the Hamm deal fell apart, getting into other businesses seemed a logical alternative. Besides, diversification was a lauded business trend. Increasingly, management teams were turning their companies into conglomerates. In Canada, they included Argus Corporation, Brascan, Domtar, and Canadian Pacific. Molson's direct competitors were taking that route: Labatt would own Laura Secord Candy Shop, Ogilvie Flour Mills, Mannings Inc., and others. A *Globe and Mail* editorial reflected on the concept's allure: "However the pedagogues might define a conglomerate, the term seems to have stock market magic when it is applied to those aggressively managed companies that grow strong on a diet of small companies. They have been among the most glamorous of industrial issues during the past year both in Canada and in the United States."

Eric assumed that the company's new strategic direction wouldn't change much for him personally. Industry experts would manage the new, added-on businesses while he would stay with beer. And he did. Six years after starting "in the rubbers" (referring to the rubber boots used by workers on the factory floor) at the Vancouver plant, he was promoted to brewmaster of Molson's Quebec operation in November 1966. It was an exciting time for him. He was twenty-eight years old,

Eric Molson carries out his duties as brewmaster at the Notre Dame brewery, 1966. He was especially satisfied with the cleanliness of the premises: "We are very proud of our plant, which is probably number one in the world in terms of hygiene. From our copper equipment to our floors, our pipes, our tanks, our yeast culture rooms, our fermentation and storage chambers, everything is kept as clean as in a hospital" (interview, November 1966). Molson Coors Brewing Company collection.

married for seven months to his beautiful Jane (now pregnant), and entrusted with his first management position.

Eric tried not to let his family's stake in Molson influence his management skills. "It shouldn't be any different if you're a manager with just a few shares or one with a larger, controlling stake in the company. Perhaps the only thing it does is help the others at the brewery realize that I'm really being serious and that I'm in it for them because I care about the long-term future of the place."

Having experienced different types of leaders in his first six years as an employee, Eric set his own management style. First, he had an open-door policy. "I let them know they could always talk to me: 'Come on in!' I would say. 'You want to talk about your job? Your future? The company? Come on in.'" Eric connected with employees regardless of their rank. He also worked on perfecting his French, the predominant language of the Notre Dame plant.

Secondly, he embraced a "frayed collar" approach to business. He explains: "You keep your shirt going for a few more years. You don't go in with a perfectly pressed suit if you're trying to get the guys in the bottle shop on your side." Always wary of the trappings of wealth, it suited him to remain authentic and "one of the guys," even in a position of authority. He adds, "Always go to the same bathroom. Whether you're a big shot or a small shot, everyone goes to the bathroom in the same place."

Moreover, he believed in objective-based performance reviews for all, including family. "Everyone should go through the process. Set goals. Get measured. Find out if you're a winner or a loser."

Eric was good with his team, and the respect was mutual. John Rogers, who worked closely with him in those years, remembers, "People recognized Eric's authority not because of his name but because he was a highly qualified production man, trained right from the bottom up. There were no pretenses about Eric."

But even in those early management days, Eric wrestled with his strong dislike of conflict. He had a propensity to let things slide and adopt a "wait and see" approach, even when he was in disagreement. This trait, however, also served him. By taking a step back to observe, he could discern whether the enterprise's checks and balances worked.

If, for example, someone in marketing made a product label change he did not like (which happened regularly, personal tastes being what they are), he would let the approval process run its natural course rather than voice his opinion. The fact that his surname was on the label made no difference. He preferred to wait for the results of market research than to impose his will. He also thought it wasn't his place to say anything – he was in production, after all, not promotion. He didn't want (or need) the confrontation.

"I don't mind seeing somebody make a mistake. I sometimes let something happen and I don't say anything, even if I think it's a stupid thing to do, because I want to see what will happen to the person making the move. Will he be corrected? Reprimanded? Fired? How fast will his boss act? If he's kept on, is there something in place for him to learn from his mistake? Those are all important things to know about how a business is being managed." So even though some would later criticize Eric for being too permissive, his non-interventionist style allowed him to observe, pinpoint the source of the problem, and take measured action.

※

In 1968, Eric raised the issue of good management practices with Bud Willmot, who had replaced Chenoweth as Molson's CEO.

"Shouldn't we be putting in place a more formal performance review process for all the different businesses we're in?" he asked. "I mean, beer's a cinch; you look at things like market share and margin per bottle and you pretty well know how you're doing. But all these other companies … how do we know whether or not we're performing well with them?"

Willmot stared at Eric from across his desk in his office near Toronto's Pearson International Airport. "It seems to me you're getting a bit petulant, Eric." He appeared irritated by the challenge. "I know," he continued, "we'll create a committee. You can study the issue and come up with some recommendations." Eric knew he was being dismissed. Willmot was a powerful guy. Twenty-one years Eric's senior, the newly named president of Molson Industries Ltd was a renowned business executive.

Hartland Molson in discussion with Donald G. "Bud" Willmot, president and chief executive officer of Molson Industries, 1968–1973, pictured here in 1968. Molson Coors Brewing Company collection.

The changes that had taken place at Molson since Hartland announced the plan to diversify two years before were staggering. CEO David Chenoweth had started out timidly by purchasing a two-thirds interest in Vilas Industries Ltd, a small, Quebec-based furniture-maker, in June 1967. He saw similarities between the brewery and Vilas: both handled consumer products, had repetitive sales, and were engaged in extensive marketing.

Hartland, however, was impatient. They would never make Molson a conglomerate with small, piecemeal acquisitions. Molson had money to invest and a strategy to realize. They needed to make a bold move. It was in this context that Hartland thought of Bud Willmot.

Donald Gilpin "Bud" Willmot was known in Canada's business milieu as the torchbearer for diversification. As CEO of Anthes Imperial Ltd, he had grown his company from a smattering of small businesses to a powerful conglomerate with revenues matching those of Molson. Anthes had a range of operations, making cast-iron pipes and fittings, office and heating equipment, specialized industrial products, and construction equipment, to name a few. As Eric says, "Anthes was a high-flying public company, going up fast."

Willmot was also well established in the social circles Hartland frequented. He was into horses and had just founded Kinghaven Farms, a thoroughbred racing stable that became one of the most decorated in Canadian history. (He would later be known as the "race-horse king" of Canada.)

So Hartland approached Willmot. And after a promising first meeting, he instructed Chenoweth to do a deal with Anthes.

🍁

A year later, on 11 September 1968, Molson merged with Anthes, and sweeping transformations ensued. The company's name changed from Molson Breweries Ltd to Molson Industries Ltd to reflect its new structure as a holding company with multiple subsidiaries. Bud Willmot became a significant shareholder of the new entity, with a voting block second only to that of the Molson family. He replaced Chenoweth (who became vice-chairman of the board) as CEO, and the company's head office moved to the outskirts of Toronto, where Anthes was located.

Willmot told reporters in October 1968 that Molson had made the first overtures. "Molson is a long established, very successful, sound company with extensive financial resources. It is in a very stable industry, its performance is quite predictable, it has substantial cash flow, a very capable group of people, an announced desire to diversify. Combine that with a company [Anthes] that has been dealing with the question of growth and diversification. When you then meld the unusual strengths of these two companies, it is our belief this brings about an excellent result, and a large company capable of perhaps doing things collectively that individually might not have been accomplished."

John Rogers, a forty-two-year beer veteran with Molson, has a different perspective. "The merger with Anthes was the biggest turning point of the company in my time." He views the merger as "unfortunate ... It happened because we were blocked from improving our position in the American beer market [with the failure of the Hamm deal]."

Yet the idea that Anthes would be Molson's future growth vector was a good one. It made sense. The challenge, however, was in its execution.

First, there was the question of culture. Molson had always been a very tight-knit, almost family-like company. That changed with Anthes. "There was a definite Molson way when we were just a brewery," Rogers says, "We all felt close and part of the family. We lost that with the merger. All these small organizations which added up to Anthes didn't have the same spirit, and, in the end, it was not a happy time for the Molson people when the merger took place."

Then there were operational issues. Eric remembers an attempt to combine distribution efforts. "Anthes had a whole bunch of trucks in their fleet, because they were in construction. So, it was decided that they were going to pick up our beer for delivery as part of the synergy efforts between the two companies." The reaction when the Anthes trucks first came around to the brewery was immediate. "We blew our stack!" Eric remembers. "We couldn't transport our beer in those *dirty* trucks! They were going to ruin our reputation. I had to explain, 'Our trucks will be thoroughly washed every day and our logo 'Molson' will be beautifully placed on them' ... it's a culture thing." Eric concludes, "Bud may have been a good businessman – and he certainly impressed Hartland – but one thing he did not know much about was the beer business."

For Eric, however, the most important loss from the deal with Anthes – the one with the longest-term impact – was that the family lost ownership of "Molson" as a brand name. "The deal with Willmot was when we lost control of the specs of the beer. The brand names and everything else would have been part of that deal ... We should never have let that go." Eric shakes his head. "We should have always kept control of the specs for our labels, our liquids, our malts, our hops ... all the important things. We should have kept them close."

He concedes that one of the things he admires most of his competitor and partner in Canada, Freddy Heineken, is that "Freddy never lost control of his name. He ruled over the specs of his products. If someone wanted to change the graphics or anything else related to Heineken, they would have to go to Freddy for permission. We should have done the same thing."

But at the time, he didn't feel he had a voice in the matter. "I was young. I couldn't interfere. Besides, the decision was made, and Chenoweth was doing everything he could to close the deal."

Finalizing the Anthes negotiations put a terrible stress on Chenoweth. It may even have led to his death three months later. It was widely known that Chenoweth's health was fragile; he suffered his first heart attack at the age of forty-one and was outfitted with an early-model (experimental) pacemaker. Whenever he travelled for work purposes, he was accompanied by a business associate trained to give him heart compressions if he collapsed.

In early December 1968, all the resuscitation efforts failed. Dave Chenoweth died of a heart attack at fifty-one. Eric's eyes well up. "What a tragedy. Huge loss. He was a great. And his boys ... Clare and Dave had five boys and they were all still in their teens. He was too young ... We had just lost P.T., and now Dave. It was awful."

Eric conjectures, "Dave may very well have woken up one morning and realized what a huge mistake Anthes was. He was instrumental in getting that deal done, but that's what Hartland and the board wanted. Unfortunately, we jumped on the Anthes bandwagon at the worst time, when it was at its peak value. It's like buying a house that was falling down and paying a huge premium for it. Perhaps Dave realized that and the stress was too much for him. I don't know ... all I know is that Anthes was a pile of junk that collapsed, and Dave died shortly thereafter."

★

During this period of tumult at the company, Jane and Eric were settling into married life. They had rented a small, downtown apartment on Lambert-Closse street, walking distance from the Forum, where they went most Saturday nights to cheer for the Habs. And while Eric went to the brewery every morning, Jane assumed what she thought of as her wifely duties.

She smiles. "You should have seen me. I put so much pressure on myself. There I was, trying to have everything running like Betty Crocker. I decorated the house, kept it spotless, put out fresh flowers every week, prepared home-cooked meals. I tried to have it all perfect for when Eric got home from work."

It wasn't long before they were reminded that things don't always go as planned. Four months into her first pregnancy, Jane suffered a miscarriage.

Eric goes quiet recalling the loss. "It's a terrible thing to go through. Imagine: you get married, your baby is coming, and then it goes. But I always rely on modern-day medicine, and the doctors told us that Jane was going to be all right and that she would be able to have another baby in the future. Still, it was tough … terrible for Jane."

She went through a roller-coaster of emotions from shock, to anger, then guilt and sadness. Knowing how badly she wanted children, Eric did his best to comfort and reassure her. Happily, she was soon pregnant again. Within four years, the couple had three healthy boys: Andrew, born in 1967, Justin in 1968, and Geoff in 1970.

"Jane and I didn't talk much about how we would raise our kids," recalls Eric. "We didn't read many books about it either. We had the one by Dr Spock, but mainly we used common sense. Jane knew more about it than me and did most of the work. I was backup."

The two, however, shared strong values. Like all parents, they wanted their sons to be happy, curious, and confident, but they also instilled in them through example the importance of hard work, lifelong learning, respect for others, and appreciation of diversity. They resolved to give their children as normal a childhood as possible. Conscious of the presumptions associated with the Molson name (especially in Quebec), they made sure their boys did not grow up feeling entitled or superior.

For their first home, they chose to stay on "the flats" rather than go up on the hill, an area dense with Westmount's mansions. They bought an attached row house at 484 Wood Avenue. According to Eric, "The best part of 484 was the lane life it offered." Along the back ran an alley

Molson brothers Geoff (four), Justin (five), and Andrew (six), on a beach in Maine, August 1974. Molson family collection.

where neighbourhood kids congregated, organized pick-up hockey games, and rode their bikes. "We wanted the kids to mix with people from different backgrounds, and the lane was good for that," Jane says.

This notion of integrating their children into a mixed milieu guided Jane and Eric when they looked for a place to spend weekends and holidays. Historically, the Molson retreat was Ivry, the family property in the Laurentians a couple of hundred of kilometres north of Montreal. The vast plot had been bought by Eric's grandfather Herbert Molson and his brother in 1910 at the suggestion of their father, who urged them to spend time together. The spot near the village of Ivry-sur-le-Lac met all their requirements. It was easily accessible from Montreal (there was a train). It enclosed two lakes around which family members could build vacation homes, and it was good for outdoor activities year round – swimming, boating, hiking, skiing, skating. When Jane and Eric were first married, they spent time there. Eric says, "I like Ivry. It's beautiful – a lovely lake and great scenery. But I also had hassles there."

Eric and Jane Molson with (*left to right*) Geoff, Justin, and Andrew, Massawippi, summer 1977. Molson family collection.

Eric was responsible for the maintenance of the main house at Ivry, and with pressure from Tom it became a burden: "My father was nagging me about the place. He would call me late at night to remind me to 'do this', 'do that', 'take this down', or 'don't forget to talk to Henri [the property manager]', and on and on."

It was too much, Jane agrees. "Eric was so busy with work; he was travelling a lot; and then Tom relied on him to take care of Ivry."

Shortly after Justin's birth, Eric and Jane decided to start looking for a getaway place of their own. They looked within two hundred kilometres of Montreal and in April 1970 settled on the old Harris property near Massawippi where Jane's parents lived in the Eastern Townships. Eric was pleased with their purchase: "We bought this cheap farm and it was great. Once you start investing in your own place, gradually fixing it up like you want, you get hooked."

Although they all occasionally went to Ivry for weekend visits or New Year's festivities, Wippi (short for Massawippi) became the place where Eric spent time with his sons. Work often kept him late at the brewery or took him out of town, but weekends were for family. In winters, with the help of a local man, they pumped water out of the

Geoff, Andrew, and Justin Molson, Massawippi, 1977. Molson family collection.

Tomifobia River and create an ice rink next to the house. Andrew remembers fondly, "My dad played hockey with us on weekends. On a good day with an icy road, we would put on our skates at the house, skate down to the rink, and spend the whole day there. The kids in the village would come over, and all of us, including Dad, played together."

The boys enjoyed the outdoors, experienced farm life, and had a whole different set of friends in Massawippi than in the city. Jane says, "We wanted the kids to learn how to grow vegetables, tend a garden, take care of animals – we had some chickens, ducks and a couple of donkeys. We were in our sort of "beatnik" stage and did a lot of the work ourselves."

The only drawback was it fostered a certain distance from the other Molsons, as Eric's siblings and their respective families continued to congregate at Ivry. But for Eric, the simplicity of Massawippi was liberating.

At the Quebec brewery, Eric continued to develop his management skills. He noticed, for example, that a bureaucratic silo mentality had settled into the place with different departments growing apart and failing to collaborate. It affected morale and efficiency.

He raised the issue with his boss John Rogers, then president of the Quebec brewing division. (Eric was *chef d'exploitation* – "a terrible title!" he says. "Imagine, *exploitation* manager. I know it's the proper way to say it in French but it didn't translate well for me.") The two men took action. "John Rogers and I worked on a new way of doing things. Everyone was to roll up their sleeves, get down to work, call a spade a spade … no more time-consuming, internal politics. Our theme was 'back to basics.' And it worked! We turned around the Quebec division." They simplified company processes, developed the communication channels between the various departments – production, packaging, shipping, sales, marketing – and created larger, more coherent units. He and Rogers toured the province, spoke about the new approach at the brewery, and got different groups to band together. It worked.

In addition to encouraging employees to collaborate across departments, Eric urged them to surpass themselves. His aim was excellence through innovation. "How many of us can say of what we do today that it is the best way to do it?" he regularly challenged his crew. "In these rapidly changing times, it is safe to say that if we are doing something today like we did it five years ago, chances are there *is* a better way … We as employees are more familiar with the company's existing operations, methods, and equipment than anyone else. Let's work together to develop better ways of doing our work."

While the rest of the company focused on diversifying, Rogers and Eric concentrated on making beer and doing it well. They saw the market shifting, getting more competitive, and knew the teams had to stay nimble. They streamlined operations, fostered innovation, and got the groups to collaborate.

By the early 1970s, some of the more stringent beer-sale laws were being slightly relaxed in parts of Canada. Sunday drinking started to be allowed, and the drinking age was lowered to eighteen. The beer industry was growing more sophisticated, dabbling in market segmentation to match products to the tastes of specific customer groups.

Eric thought, "Why not make a premium brew – a new beer, with a higher alcohol content, for the more sophisticated drinker?"

As always, he started with research. He designed a recipe and, except for a small team that worked on the first batch, kept it confidential. It was a strong ale concoction with double the hops, double the grains, double the strength. Eric used Export Ale yeast and "put in an abnormally high number of yeast cells." When it was done, he hung a big sign on the tank: "DO NOT TOUCH. To be opened at Christmastime."

That December, Molson employees got a taste of the prototype. It had a strong Export Ale flavour and appealed to the beer drinkers of the company: "This is the best we've ever made!" Eric remembers them saying. "And they were right. It was delicious – the kind of beer that makes you want to drink the whole tank!"

The average consumer, however, didn't agree. When Eric and his team tested the new product on the street, he remembers some of their reviewers gagging and complaining, "Do I have to take another sip? This stuff is terrible!" It was too strong.

Range of Molson products available in the 1970s, including Brador at the far right. Molson Coors Brewing Company collection.

The recipe was modified accordingly.

Then there was the question of branding. The prototype was named Réveillon – French for Christmas Eve, to commemorate the occasion of its introduction at the brewery. But for the public launch of this new brew, Eric wanted something to reflect the high-prestige status of the beer. The marketing department was working on names like Triple X, Grand Prix ... not original enough, in Eric's judgment.

He spent nights in bed with a dictionary, thinking, "I need two syllables, and I want it to start with *bra*." "*Bra*" was soft in tonality and was also short for *brassin*, *brassé*, *brasserie* (French for brew, brewed, brewery). He brainstormed with Jane, and one night in Massawippi came up with "*d'or*" (golden, in French) for quality. The combination became *Bras d'or* ("golden arm") and then simply Brador. Perfect, thought Eric.

Still, he didn't obtrude his opinion on the team. He wanted to win on merit, not on the capital of his surname. Anonymously he added "Brador" to the list of names being tested by the market research group.

It came out on top. The marketing team took the name and worked on the look: a gold oval, outlined with a thick royal-blue line and "Brador" prominently in the centre; it was set against a black hexagonal label, topped with a crown cap enveloped in gold foil. A regal label for a premium-brewed, extra-strength malt liquor.

"Launching Brador was a high like you wouldn't believe," says Eric. "I didn't do it for Tom. No, it wasn't to impress my father. I did it for the brewery. We all worked on it together. The brewers loved it. The sales team, the marketing team, the production team, they all loved it."

More importantly, the public did too. After only a few days on the market, the brewery ran out. "We had to hire rows and rows of kids to crank more out," says Eric. "We were lucky because it was summertime and there were lots of students available. They were all lined up, putting those gold caps on … Brador sold like hotcakes. We even started exporting it to the United States."

It was one of Eric's happiest experiences at the brewery.

In the world of the Molson clan, hockey was almost as central as beer. All members of the family, girls and boys alike, grew up playing it, watching it, analyzing it, developing a passion for it. For them, as for most Québécois, the Montreal Canadiens were the apotheosis of hockey, a quasi-religion at whose altar they worshipped every Saturday night.

When Tom and Hartland acquired the team back in 1957, the change of ownership had been seamless. The family earned the fans' respect for their faithful management. Under their watch, the Canadiens finished first in the league's regular season eight times and won six Stanley Cups. With all its success, the team was a thrilling organization. Everyone wanted to be a part of it – including family members like David Molson.

A distant cousin of Tom and Hartland's, thirty-five-year-old David was working his way up at the brewery. He showed promise, but his interest was not in beer: it was in hockey. In 1964, he approached Hartland directly. Could he become the new president of the Montreal Canadiens? After some discussion, they agreed. The only condition

Above: Stephen and Eric Molson, 1953, dressed to play for the Abenakis, the hockey team of Bishop's College School. Molson family collection. *Below*: Playoff game at the Montreal Forum, 1968. *Left to right*, David Molson, Prime Minister-Elect Pierre Elliott Trudeau, Senator Hartland Molson, and Prime Minister Lester B. Pearson. Courtesy estate of David Bier.

Brothers David, Billy, and Peter Molson (*left to right*), shaking hands with Hartland Molson to commemorate the sale of the Montreal Canadiens by Hartland and Tom Molson to the three cousins in September 1968. Courtesy estate of David Bier.

was that David surround himself with real hockey people, experts like Sam Pollock and Hector "Toe" Blake.

Being CEO of the Canadiens, however, was not enough for David. Four years later, as Molson was heading into its merger with Anthes, David made a new offer. What if he and his brothers, Peter and Billy, were to buy the team? They had inherited Molson brewery shares from their uncle Bert Molson in 1955 and were offering them in exchange for control of the Canadiens.

The shares, however, did not come close to the team's market value. Given the extensive renovations done at the Montreal Forum only a year prior and the league's expansion from six to twelve teams, the worth of the Canadiens had increased drastically since Hartland and Tom bought the team. Nonetheless, they agreed to the sale and accepted the proffered shares. It was essentially a gift on their part. By transferring the team to the next generation, they would keep this prized possession in Molson hands. Hartland and Tom believed David and his siblings when they promised to preserve the team in the family for life.

✦

The headline of the *Globe and Mail* on 16 August 1968 read, "Relatives buy Forum, Canadiens: Control of the Montreal Canadiens and the Forum has been sold by one branch of the Molson family to another."

Thirty-year-old Eric was shocked. It was the first he had heard of it. "I found out that Tom and Hartland had sold the Canadiens to those guys by reading about it in the papers. They never talked to Stephen and me about it. They never said, 'Oh, the time will come when we'll have to get out of hockey.' I just saw it in the paper one day. I was upset. So was Stephen."

More than the actual sale of the team to the cousins, what bothered Eric was his father's lack of communication. Why hadn't he said anything? Didn't Tom trust him? Maybe he and Stephen would have been interested in running the team. They could have done it. Granted, they were younger and less experienced than their cousins, and David knew hockey, but still, Tom could have spoken to them first.

Three years later, the sting burned even deeper. In June 1971, rumours of a new deal were already circulating: David, Peter, and Billy Molson were said to be looking for someone to buy the team. The brothers, however, were emphatic: "The club is not for sale." Yet the talk persisted, enough for the stock price of the Canadian Arena Co., listed on the Montreal Stock Exchange, to climb from $9.50 to $14.50 in just a few weeks. At the time, Billy told reporters, "The stock should be worth $25!" Like his son Ian years later, Billy Molson followed the company's valuation and share price closely.

Hartland reached out to David in late November 1971. "What's this I hear about the team being for sale?" David reassured him that the sale rumours were "unfounded gossip." Then, on 31 December 1971, three years after getting the team from Tom and Hartland and promising to keep it forever in the family, David and his brothers sold it to Edward and Peter Bronfman. The price, an estimated $15 million, was more than three times what they paid for it. A great deal for them – and a huge betrayal of one branch of the family by another.

On 5 January 1972, Hartland made his disappointment public through a press release:

It was with great surprise, and it was not until twenty-four hours after the official announcement, that Senator Hartland Molson learned of the sale of the Montreal Canadiens to a group of financiers. Senator Molson did not attempt to hide his disappointment at the news of the sale, surprised by the news while he was traveling outside the country. Senator Molson could not understand the reason for the sale and was bitterly disappointed by this move on the part of David Molson and his brothers.

Hartland then sent a brief note to David: "This is to inform you that your name will not be resubmitted for the election to the board at Molson's next annual meeting." He closed the chapter by removing from his office the framed photo of the three cousins taken at the time when they bought the team from him and Tom.

Eric says, "That side of the family – David, Peter, and Billy – they let us down. They got the team for chicken feed, promised in writing to keep it in the family for life, and then turned around and sold it ... There was no loyalty there. They weren't right." The mentality of "everything has a price" was a way of thinking Eric did not ascribe to.

He understood, however, that part of his cousins' motivation to sell the team was the charged political climate in Quebec. The FLQ separatist movement had gained momentum in the late 1960s and had increasingly used violence as a way to send its "anti-Anglo" message. "It was really bad for a while," remembers Eric. "We didn't dare even *speak* English, in case they'd target us. That whole time of the FLQ was pretty tense."

It all came to a head on 5 October 1970 with the kidnapping of British Trade Commissioner James Richard Cross. Five days later, four armed men abducted Pierre Laporte, the Quebec labour minister. At 4 a.m. on 16 October, Prime Minister Pierre Elliott Trudeau called the Canadian army into Montreal and invoked the War Measures Act – a first in peacetime. The law gave police the power to round up and detain anyone suspected of involvement in the violence without bringing formal charges. A few days later, Laporte's body was found in the trunk of a car. He had been strangled. The FLQ claimed responsibility for the murder.

At that time, David Molson – like other prominent Montrealers, such as Hartland, associated with English privilege – was on the FLQ's targeted list of *maudit anglais*. With his blond hair, front-row seats at the Forum, and high-profile role as owner and president of the Canadiens, he was very visible and an easy target. Stephen remembers, "It wasn't a pleasant time to own the hockey team. David and his brothers wanted out, and I can understand that. They were getting threats and all that … What I don't understand is why they didn't come to Uncle Hartland and say, 'Look, we can't handle it. We'll sell it back to you.'" It would have been the honourable thing to do."

Eric, however, took an important lesson from these events. He would later say, "In any transaction, always have a plan B – a right of first refusal or some other mechanism – to keep your options open." But in 1971, the understanding between the two Molson branches had been based on a handshake, and the team was lost.

Looking back now, Eric sees another side to the sale by the cousins. When dealing with a large family, he says, you need to tend it like a gardener pruning sapling trees. "You pick a branch and stick with it. Sometimes that means you have to make sacrifices … But it's worth it if you get to prune off branches that are weaker and invigorate your winner." By selling the team in exchange for Bert Molson's shares, Tom and Hartland chose to reinforce their roots in beer. The branch of the family made up of David, Peter, and Billy chose hockey and were essentially cut off.

Sometimes, however, this kind of thinning encourages new growth – a bloom in the next generation, who may one day yearn to get back into the principal line of business and take over.

4 Becoming the Boss

You're nothing special because you're a Molson. Never expect
anybody to give you anything because of your name.

ERIC H. MOLSON, interview with Andy Holloway, 21 May 2007

I sit in my usual spot in the back porch of the Kennebunkport house,
waiting for Eric to join me. Outside, ominous grey clouds camouflage
the morning sun, giving the landscape a steely appearance. The ocean
is still, eerie almost. It's the calm before the storm, I think.

"Here we go." Eric comes in with a thermos full of freshly brewed
coffee and pours us each a cup. "So, tell me, what's on your mind today?
I'm ready for anything."

If he only knew. Earlier that morning, going through my research
material, I came across a 2004 *Wall Street Journal* article. Its headline
caught my eye: "A Brewing Family Feud Poses Risks for Molson Beer
Empire – Two Cousins Vie for Control as Industry Consolidates. Who
is a Real Molson?" It was all about the "family schism" between Eric
and his distant cousin Ian Molson.

So the question I want to blurt out to Eric as we sit with our coffee
on this grey morning is, "What made you do it? How could you let
someone like Ian come in? Why did you trust him?"

But I don't. I know I'll eventually get there, and it's best not to jump
ahead. Otherwise, we could spend the whole time talking about this
breakdown with Ian. But that's not Eric's whole story. The "Ian saga" is
just one stumbling block in his journey.

I rein in my curiosity and start with a general question. "I was wondering, Eric – what does it take to be a good owner?"

He looks thoughtful. "Well, it depends. Are you in a start-up phase? Are you in a crisis? Or is it business as usual? Also, it depends whether or not you're dealing with a public company. I mean, if you control a public company with super-voting shares, it's not the same as if you're the founder and sole shareholder of a private company. It all depends."

"I guess I'm wondering about you. In your context, what does it take to be a good owner?"

"There are a number of basics you need to stick to." He holds up his hand and raises each finger in turn as he lists his points: "One, you understand and closely monitor the business. It helps if you have a seat on the board. Two, you make sure you have the right CEO in place, you support him – or her – and you let him do his job. You can't interfere. Three, you help define the company's mission and approve the strategies to reach its objectives. Four, you promote the highest standards of ethics and integrity. And you do that by setting the right example. No taking advantage of your control position, no nepotism, no crazy and unjustified compensation schemes, none of that. And finally, five, you make sure the board acts in the interest of *all* shareholders, not just the ones with control ... Actually, I'd go further than that: decisions should be made in the interest of all the company's *stakeholders*."

"So, wait, what do you mean when you say, 'you can't interfere' with the CEO?" I ask.

"Well, you put a guy in charge and then you leave him alone."

I understand the importance of not interfering and letting a CEO fulfill his mandate, but I can also see how a forceful CEO – one who completely dominates – can take advantage of his position if his power is unchecked.

Mistaking my silence for confusion, Eric continues his explanation. "If you're the owner, and not the CEO, you've got to let your CEO do his job. You give him objectives and you give him principles, but you leave him alone to execute on them. You watch, you evaluate, but you don't interfere."

"But what if he's ruining the place?" I blurt out.

"That's when you step in," Eric replies logically. "But, to a certain extent, you have to tolerate people's mistakes. That's how they learn, and that's how you can evaluate them and their team. You see how they handle their mistakes, manage accountability, and take corrective action."

I admire Eric's self-restraint (and make a mental note to try it next time I'm tempted to resolve a problem that doesn't belong to me). Still, I ask, "Didn't you ever just want to jump in and take charge?"

"I was only the boss once in my career. It was in 1973. They put me in charge of the Ontario division. It was one of my biggest promotions: president of Molson Brewery Ontario."

❧

Thirty-six-year-old Eric Molson sat at his Toronto desk, working on his first speech as president of the Ontario brewery. He pensively read over a quote by Einstein, one of his scientist-heroes (and another introvert). He took out scissors and a glue stick, cut out the paragraph, and pasted it on the first page of his notebook:

> Strange is our situation here upon earth. Each comes for a short visit, not knowing why, yet seeming to divine a purpose. There is one thing we do know: Man is here for the sake of other men – above all, for those upon whose well-being our happiness depends ... and for the countless unknown souls with whose fate we are connected by a bond of sympathy.

Eric felt a deep sense of responsibility in his new role, not just to his bosses and shareholders in Montreal but to the full scope of the stakeholders impacted by the enterprise his family controlled, including employees, customers, suppliers, unions, government agencies, and local communities where they operated.

A few months earlier in June 1973, a series of promotions were made at Molson. Bud Willmot was named deputy chairman of the board after five years as CEO, and James T. Black succeeded him as president and CEO of The Molson Companies Limited. (The company was now

In the main boardroom of the Notre Dame brewery, 1974 (*left to right*), Donald G. "Bud" Willmot, deputy chairman; Jim T. Black, president; and Senator Hartland Molson, chairman of the board. Molson Coors Brewing Company collection.

TMCL, as "Molson Industries" was thought to wrongly imply activities like mining, steel, shipbuilding, or heavy machinery manufacturing.) Jim Black was a Molson "lifer." A chartered accountant, he started his career at McDonald Currie (now PWC) as an auditor of Molson. Soon thereafter, the brewery poached him, and in 1953 he became Molson's assistant treasurer. He built his reputation as being fair, well organized, and results oriented and worked his way up to become president of Molson Breweries in 1968.

Over the years, Jim earned Tom's trust, to the point that Tom asked him to become Eric's "godfather" – the person at Molson who oversaw his career path. So when it was time to give Eric his first leadership role as head of the Ontario division in 1973, Jim was behind the move. He thought Eric was ready.

Nonetheless, when Jim made the offer, Eric hesitated. He wanted to make sure the promotion was based on merit and not his last name. "Don't you have anyone better than me? I'm not all that experienced."

Jim insisted. "You're the right man for the job. You've worked out West, you've been our brewmaster in Montreal, you've led cross-functional teams on a number of major initiatives. This is right for you. You'll be responsible for a full P&L – both profits and losses – an entire business. It's a natural progression."

"Let me think about it. But before I say yes, I want to make sure I'll be evaluated on objective criteria and results, just like any other division leader."

"You will be. Trust me."

That night over dinner, Eric spoke to Jane about Black's offer. Their relationship had deepened into an all-encompassing partnership, one that extended beyond their three boys. She was his companion, confidante, and most trusted advisor. The two were complementary. Whereas Eric was shy and introverted, Jane had drive and a contagious *joie de vivre*. Often she was the one urging, "Come on Eric, let's go for it!"

So they did. They accepted the job offer, and the young family got ready to head to Toronto.

The logistics of the move were mainly left to Jane. She put their Wood Avenue house up for sale and looked for a new place in Toronto. After one visit, she chose a home in the quiet, tree-lined neighbourhood of Rosedale. Once the papers were signed, she took Eric over to see their new place.

"It's the red brick one," she told Eric. Up and down the street they went, but no red brick.

"Are you sure it's the right street?" asked Eric.

"Yes, Whitney Avenue. I'm just not sure of the number … Keep looking for red brick."

Jane laughs now: "I was sure it was a red brick house. It ended up being grey." Oops. "It was a busy time. The kids were two, four, and five years old, we were travelling a lot for Eric's work, and we had all these social obligations. I guess the colour of the house wasn't the most important thing on my mind!"

For the young family, it was a new start. "We felt free and independent for the first time," she says. "We could be ourselves and establish the way we wanted to lead our lives. In Montreal, back then, there was just so much of 'one does this' and 'one doesn't do that.'" In private, Jane and Eric used to laugh at the snooty ladies in white gloves, but when she went out to run errands or take the babies for a stroll, Jane still felt the need to dress smartly and behave a certain way. "We could just be ourselves in Toronto," she says. The new city also offered the couple the opportunity to broaden their social circle. Although they loved their chums in Montreal (many would remain close throughout their lives), they were mostly family friends or people with whom they had gone to school. They had none of these ties in Toronto.

They could make their own choices based on their values. For their boys' educations, for example, they weren't constrained to send them to a traditional, all-boys private school like Selwyn House just because Eric and previous generations of Molsons had gone there. They chose Toronto French School, only ten years old and considered highly innovative, because it gave their sons a strong connection to French language and culture, even in the centre of English Canada. Jane and Eric wanted Andrew, Justin, and Geoff to become fully bilingual Canadians, not just good "Anglos."

🍁

In September 1973, Eric stood up in front of the Ontario brewery personnel for the first time. "One of my objectives as president of the division is to make sure that Molson is, for all employees, the best place to work in Toronto," he said. "We want to be known as a company that makes great beers, *and* has great people in it, a really *human* company, not a cold corporation of machines ... We're giving highest priority to the human needs of those who work for Molson, because only by listening to their needs, understanding them, and in many cases doing something to satisfy those needs, can we really make Molson the best place to work."

For Eric, the Toronto brewery on Fleet Street *was* the best place to work. To his surprise, he enjoyed being the boss. He had a great team. They all worked well together. And they were "coining it" – making more money per bottle than any other brewery in Molson's history.

Senior operating management team of TMCL's brewing group, 1975. *Front, left to right*: J.R. Taylor, VP marketing; Eric H. Molson, president, Molson Ontario; Norm M. Seagram, VP planning and personnel; G.M. Winer, president, Molson Newfoundland; Peter B. Stewart, SVP and president, Molson Breweries Canada; John P. Rogers, president, Molson Quebec. *Back, left to right*: R.J.D. Martin, VP production; Hollis H. Brace, president, Molson Western Breweries; C.R. Cook, VP finance and controller. Molson Coors Brewing Company collection.

"We were going up and up and up in those years – sales, market share, profits – all going up! Everyone was doing their job extremely well … hard for me to make a mistake. It was very exciting."

It was also a freeing experience for him. At the Notre Dame brewery in Montreal, he felt he had to watch himself. Whatever he did, his father and uncle were close behind, looking for something to criticize, some detail to nit-pick. Now his boss Peter Stewart, president of the entire brewing division, was 500 kilometres away in Montreal. "Peter never bugged me. I only talked to him about once a month to go over our results, and he just let me work."

Eric flourished. As his confidence grew, he started putting his brand of management into place. "What I did in the Toronto brewery was give them democracy."

All employees now entered the brewery through the same door. "It doesn't matter if you're a big shot, if you're just starting out, if you're in the union, or not in the union. We're all going in through the same door, hanging our coats in the same locker room and getting to work." There was resistance from some managers who felt they'd earned the right to separate facilities, but Eric persisted.

He put in place Molson's Communications Round Table. The committee, made up of employees from all levels and all functions, regularly met to discuss business issues and ways to make Molson a better place to work. He wanted to get all employees, staff and union, to voice their opinions. Only with their collective input did he feel they could improve.

"I made sure my managers thought and talked. I would ask them, 'What do you think we should do? What about you? What do you think?' And I would go around the table." It was the same approach he would use years later as Molson's chairman – a *modus operandi* that worked best when all the players around the table had the same goals in mind and weren't driven by an ulterior motive.

"I wanted to know what my managers felt and I wanted them to listen to each other," explains Eric, having lived through the nefarious effects of a siloed organization in Quebec. "That way they were involved in each other's areas. So the marketing people, for example, knew what the sales guys were up to, and the sales guys knew the challenges the production people were having, and so on." A scientist at heart, Eric approached the situation methodically: Mix the ingredients, sit back, observe the reaction, and only then draw your conclusions.

As a manager, Eric empowered his employees. He encouraged their self-development and put process improvement in their hands – not something that was standard practice in the 1970s. At the round tables, he reminded workers that "the best ideas for operations improvements and cost reductions come from the company employees themselves, and not from an outsider such as an efficiency expert." He tried to stimulate brainstorming and creative thinking "to help them put good ideas into practice." Quoting Thomas Edison, he urged, "There is always a better way. Let's find it."

Sometimes a little lubricant was needed to get the discussion going. Eric would bring in a beer cooler to the small boardroom where they all met. John Rogers explains: "Rather than send memos from department to department, Eric urged us to meet … and why not have a beer? We came up with a slogan to eliminate memo-writing: 'You get more ideas from a bottle of beer than you do from a bottle of ink.' He got people mingling and talking together." And he listened.

Eric attributes the success of the Ontario division during his time as president entirely to his team: "I was president. I never asked for it, but I did it. And we delivered huge profits. It was all because I had a gem of a team around me. Fred Mann was a terrific production guy, John Osterman a great marketing man, Bain McCastle a talented accountant, Gordon Bourne an excellent HR manager … I had all the important ingredients."

Just as he had years before when he first worked at the Capilano brewery in British Columbia, Eric felt these men taught him the Molson enterprise. "I learned more about the company from guys like Fred and Gordon than I ever did from my own father and uncle. They showed me how Molson worked and all the principles that were required to be successful." Three in particular resonated.

First, quality. The way to success is through quality products and quality people. "A marketing guy once told me, 'Give me something fizzy and brown and I can sell it,'" Eric remembers. "Nonsense. Pure horseshit. In our business, it's essential to consistently produce a high-quality liquid. That's how you build trust with your customers." It was a principle he shared with other great brewers around the world, like the Coors family.

Integrity. "It's a basic," Eric says. "In our business we're tough, but we are fair and we are honest and straightforward. You can't buy integrity. It's hard to get, takes years to build, and you can blow it overnight."

Hard work, already deeply ingrained by Tom: "Brewing good products, packaging them well, distributing them intelligently, increasing market share, and doing it cost effectively, doesn't just *happen*. You need hard work."

There were times in those early Toronto days, however, when Eric felt unsure. "It's always good to be in a little over your head," he now recognizes. "It's the best way to test yourself and grow." For example, he had never dealt with government officials before. The chairman of Ontario's liquor commission in the early 1970s was Major-General George Kitching, who had begun his career with the British army. Sophisticated and worldly, he could be intimidating. Eric put on his "most English suit" to visit him on courtesy calls and from time to time to negotiate price increases. It turned out that what Eric lacked in experience, he made up for with his forthright approach.

"I went in and gave it to him straight. He liked that. Our competitors weren't beer-style people. They had cigarette money" – tobacco giant Philip Morris Inc. had bought Miller Brewing Company a few years before, in 1970 – "and they'd come to meetings in fancy, expensive cars. I would go in with my 'frayed collar' approach and I'd never ask for more than what was necessary."

Eric eventually came to be trusted on questions as sensitive as pricing. "They would ask, 'What do you really need in order to proceed?' I would give them the real number, one that gave us room to manoeuvre and was politically acceptable, and that's the one they used."

His honesty paid off.

🍁

"What I like about you, Mr Molson, is that you come in the front door. You announce what you're about to do and you do exactly that. You and your team are straightforward guys."

Dorian Parker, the mayor of Barrie, Ontario, was speaking at the brewery on 21 August 1974. Molson had just purchased the Formosa Spring Brewery in Barrie from Philip Morris that summer for $27.7 million.

A few months earlier, Peter Stewart called Eric from Montreal, saying, "I think we should buy Formosa."

"Formosa? Do we really need the extra capacity?" Eric asked. The Barrie facility was close to Molson's existing Fleet Street brewery (which was also being expanded). Unless their export business to the

United States exploded, surely they wouldn't need the extra volume from another brewery.

"Why don't you look at it and let me know what you think?" Stewart said.

Eric and his team analyzed Formosa and built a business case based on demand and production forecasts that assumed a thriving Molson business in northern United States. Before making a final recommendation, Eric and production manager Fred Mann went to visit the brewery. They had to be discreet, not wanting to start any rumours. The two men drove around the Barrie premises a few times and Eric turned to Fred. "We don't need to go inside. Look at the layout of this place. Our research shows it's a good facility, the quality of the beer that comes out of here is first grade, and besides, it's all been built up with tobacco money. They always put in the best equipment – everything the consultants recommend. Let's go for it."

Their due diligence was done.

"We made a handshake agreement with the Philip Morris people," says Eric, "which they honoured right to the end. At one point they were tempted to listen to Labatt, who had heard talk of our deal and asked them, 'Why sell to Molson? We'll give you a few million dollars more.'" But the vendors kept their word.

When the Molson specialists finally went to inspect the premises, they discovered Eric's assessment had been accurate. "We realized we had bought a lot more than we anticipated," Eric says. "It had all sorts of extra tanks and equipment, all stainless steel, first class from tobacco money going into beer ... Overbuilt and all the best."

But what Eric found most thrilling was neither closing the deal with Philip Morris nor being right about the state of the Formosa plant. For him, it was getting the chemistry right. He would only deem the acquisition a success once a Molson product brewed there tasted just like a Molson should.

"I sent John Peasley up to Barrie from our Toronto plant to brew our first batch," he says. "I told him, 'We're going to make a Molson beer here for the first time and we want it *exactly* like what we have in Toronto and Montreal.' He came in and the team did it perfectly.

Completely on specs. We didn't have to blend it or anything. It was one of the greatest excitements in my life … A perfect beer right from the start."

For Eric, a "perfect Molson" meant that he was surrounded by talented people and that all employees – whether ex-Formosa or Molson – were working together. No silos. It was the only way to get flawless execution and a condition for the chemistry to work. The purchase of Formosa was a win.

❦

Even as he took on his new leadership role, the plant expansions, the acquisition, and the added responsibilities, the technical aspect of brewing remained Eric's priority and passion. Like Tom, he kept up to date with the latest advances and exchanged best practices with other brewers from around the world. He did so informally but also in the structured, annual meetings of the International Brewing Consortium with brewers from North America, Europe, and Asia. Members included Molson of Montreal, Falstaff of St Louis, Stroh's of Detroit, Coors of Golden, Amstel of Amsterdam, Kronenbourg of Strasbourg, Courage of London, and Asahi, Sapporo, and Kirin of Tokyo. "It was sharing the science and engineering of beer out of respect for the liquid," says Eric. "We were dealing with top-notch technology people from different parts of the world, and regardless of our culture, we were all compatible."

For Eric, however, these meetings went beyond developing his technical know-how. Talking with brewers from different parts of the world sparked what would eventually become his vision for Molson. In those years, it was more of a dream, really: what if Molson were to become a global brewer?

It was not a romantic notion based on Eric's desire to share the awesomeness of Molson beer with the world ("although it would have been nice to get the beer brand everywhere," he admits). Rather, his vision was for the endurance of Molson as an institution, and it was driven by necessity. Early on, he realized that "the beer business is like any other: If you don't go up, you get killed." And "going up" meant conquering new frontiers. With the blocking of the Hamm deal, Molson had been denied the opportunity to straddle the Canada-US border. Eric wanted Molson "to keep growing … not only in North America, but around the world."

The consortium fed his budding ambition. As he talked to brewery owners from different countries, their conversations would eventually lead to his asking, "Why don't we do something together?" He imagined all forms of partnership and expansion scenarios for Molson. "I would come home with all these ideas: Mutzig could have been ours, and we almost got Amstel," he recalls. "But Peter Stewart and the other bureaucrats in charge of Molson would dismiss my proposals. They were good people, very capable, but far too conservative." Eric, however, saw these impasses as temporary glitches. He remained convinced that if he kept at it, he would one day find a way to scale Molson globally.

In the meantime, he thoroughly enjoyed his Ontario experience. "Under Eric's presidency, the Ontario operation ran like clockwork," praises John Rogers, who went on to run it when Eric left. Unfortunately, that kind of unqualified approval would never come from the one person who could best give it: Tom. "My father would never tell me if he was proud of me or my success. I'm sure he was pleased, but he wouldn't say it to me."

Never an effusive man, Tom Molson did, however, keep close watch on Eric's progress, and in 1974 he decided his son was ready for the next step: Molson's board of directors. Setting off a chain of appointments that summer, Hartland replaced Tom as honorary chairman. Bud Willmot became chairman, and Eric was elected to the board.

With this appointment, Eric crossed the threshold into a new world, one with new protocols, new acronyms, and a whole new level of egos. He was not impressed. "The big shot stuff is not always all it's built up to be. Right away, you start running into some pretty obnoxious people."

He remembers his first Molson board meeting. He came in from Toronto and sat in the boardroom with fifteen other men. They were all older, more experienced, and seemed to have a rapport with one another that Eric did not share. Even John Aird and Frank Covert, who joined the board at the same time as he did, talked easily with most people around the table. Eric stayed quiet and observed.

"My father told me, 'Sit at the end of the table and keep your trap shut for the first ten years.' So I didn't say much. I was sitting there as a brewer because my father stuck me there. I didn't really feel like I belonged, but I listened and learned how a board of directors worked."

Besides heeding his father's advice, this approach was endemic to Eric's style: observe attentively, thoroughly digest information, scrupulously analyze the options, and only then, act. Eric is the first to acknowledge that his way is not very glamorous. It is, however, powerful. His idol, Albert Einstein, had a similar manner. The consummate physicist once said, "It's not that I'm so smart. It's that I stay with problems longer."

"Eric was persistent, but he was not aggressive in putting forward his thoughts," says John Rogers, who worked closely with him. "Whereas Tom and Hartland were very verbal, Eric listened carefully. He would sort out the good from the bad and then come to his own conclusion. But it must have been stressful for him when he first joined the Molson board … Tom and Hartland were a hard act to follow."

Jane concurs. "When Eric first went on the board, he probably didn't say a word. He likes to learn the facts and consider all angles before taking a position. Whereas I can easily make a decision based on gut feeling, and sometimes I've made mistakes – Eric waits."

Behind Eric's quiet demeanour, however, was a closeted determination that would one day surprise people.

🍁

By the mid-1970s, the Molson Companies was in full diversification mode. Besides brewing, it had a retail merchandising division made up of home-improvement stores (now Home Depot Canada), a commercial branch producing business furniture and equipment, and multiple smaller ventures in other areas.

By then the popularity of diversified companies was starting to wane with Bay Street analysts, but the verdict on Molson was still positive. A *Globe and Mail* article of 21 June 1974 called Molson "an exception to the financial experts' recent conclusion that Canadian corporations diversified badly."

"We are no longer just a beer company," Eric was quoted as saying. And back then, he was okay with that, or at least he said he was. Besides, he didn't feel he could influence the firm's strategic direction even if he wanted to. Those matters were left mainly to Tom and Hartland, chairman Bud Willmot, and CEO Jim Black. Eric's focus remained in brewing, where his development continued at a rapid clip. Only two years after becoming president of the Ontario division, he was offered the national role of executive vice-president (EVP) of Molson Breweries of Canada Ltd.

The promotion was bittersweet. Eric was interested in the role, yet he didn't want to leave his Ontario team. His sense of duty, however, made him accept the offer. At the April 1975 sales convention, he introduced his replacement, John Rogers, as the new president of the Ontario division and expressed his "regret having to leave, for I have thoroughly enjoyed my work here."

"I think he *was* very sorry to leave," says John Rogers. "They loved him there too. Eric opened the bar and the reception room at the brewery on Fleet Street, and that's where he liked to mingle with the working man. He really enjoyed it, and they enjoyed him."

CEO Jim Black, looking over Eric's professional evolution, championed the latest promotion. He thought Eric, now thirty-seven, should assume broader, pan-Canadian responsibilities, but he didn't think he was ready yet to take on the presidency of the entire brewing operation. He gave that job to Morgan McCammon and had Eric report to him.

"Jim was right to do that," acknowledges Eric. "I was weak in certain things. I wasn't the person to go out and glad-hand and do the more administrative stuff. I knew the brewery people and production, so I was in charge of operations, and Morgan was the boss."

Morgan McCammon was a corporate lawyer who had transitioned into a business role at Steinberg before joining Molson in 1958. "He was a very smart man," says Eric, "smart and organized." After a brief pause, he leans in and adds, "But he didn't have much vision and he wasn't very exciting."

Two categories of leaders were forming in Eric's mind: bureaucrats and visionaries. So far, most of his bosses – Jim Black, Peter Stewart, Morgan McCammon – fell in the first group. They were all capable and intelligent, but not very inspired. Later Eric would learn that those in the second category – the unbridled, visionary leaders – also had their limits.

🍁

A year after Eric assumed his new role, he and Jane decided to move the family back to Montreal. Their stay in Toronto had been a great experience. They had made new friends and flourished in the freedom they enjoyed, but it was time to come back home.

In the fall of 1976, however, they were returning to a very different Montreal and a very different Quebec. The city had just hosted the 1976 Summer Olympic Games, where fourteen-year-old, triple gold-medalist Nadia Comăneci and American decathlon winner Bruce Jenner had become household names. The pride that Montrealers felt at hosting the first Olympic Games in Canada was almost equal to the embarrassment of extraordinary cost overruns and construction delays of the stadium built for the occasion. The combination of political corruption, labour disputes, and mismanagement almost resulted in the Olympic Stadium not being delivered in time and inflated the city's initial $310 million budget to over $1.5 billion. (The stadium went from being referred to as "The Big O" for its oval shape to "The Big Owe" for its astronomical bill that took almost thirty years to pay off.) In the face of impending disaster, the Quebec government led by Liberal Premier Robert Bourassa intervened to contain the damages, and the 1976 Montreal Olympic Games proceeded as planned.

Thinking he could ride on the public favour generated from having "rescued" the Olympic Games, Bourassa called for an early election soon thereafter. (He was only three years into a five-year term.) He underestimated, however, both voters' disillusion with his ruling Liberal Party and the rising appeal of René Lévesque's separatist Parti Québécois. The PQ ran a powerful campaign that year, focused on providing "good government" for Quebec and steering clear of the thornier issue of sovereignty.

The vote was held on 15 November 1976. While the polls were open, and as many nervous Anglophones contemplated moving out of Quebec, Jane, Andrew, Justin, and Geoffrey were on a train leaving Toronto's Union Station to return to Montreal. On their arrival they learned the news: a solid victory for the PQ. With one of the highest voter participation rates in Quebec history, the sovereignists defeated the incumbent Liberal Party with 41 per cent of the popular vote. That night at the Paul Sauvé Arena in Rosemont, René Lévesque pledged, "We want and we will work with all our strength to make of Quebec a country that will more than ever be the country of all Québécois who live here and love it."

It was a time of effervescence. After generations of systemic and cultural prejudice – oppression by both the English-speaking ruling class and the Roman Catholic Church – the Québécois finally had one of their own, a sovereigntist, in power.

But what held promise to some represented instability to others. Some felt the PQ's separatist agenda and stringent pro-French laws encroached on their fundamental rights. The election of René Lévesque accelerated what became the "great exodus," a movement that started in the 1960s and culminated in nearly 20 per cent of the Anglo population leaving Quebec. The migration would forever change the profile of Montreal. Once known as Canada's business capital, the city went through a financial downturn as it lost head offices, decision-making centres, private investments, and some of its wealthiest and best educated people.

Some opted to stay, the Molsons among them. On 27 June 1977 Senator Hartland de Montarville Molson affirmed the family's loyalty in a speech he made to the Senate. Standing in the Red Chamber, speaking in French, he proclaimed himself a Québécois:

Why do I claim to be Québécois? The answer is obvious. It is just on two hundred years ago that my family gave up all other allegiance and made its home here. In the years since, six generations with a seventh generation approaching maturity, have participated in the development of Quebec, including some of the original ventures in steam navigation, railways, banking, manufacturing, water and light services, schools, hospitals, universities, the arts and research. This recital is not to seek recognition, but to substantiate the claim that our roots are very deep indeed in the soil of Quebec.

Eric too was deeply attached to his native Quebec and to Montreal in particular. In addition to his strong heritage, he moved back to Quebec because he believed in a bilingual, bicultural Canada. It was a vision he felt could only be realized if the two cultures continued to live side by side, learning from each other and growing together. He recorded his thoughts in his workbook on 26 August 1977, the day the Charter of the French Language was enacted – a key piece of PQ legislation making French the official language of Quebec, and regulating matters such as the language of education and of commerce. In his small, meticulous script, Eric wrote:

- We agree with the objective of preserving the French culture and language in Quebec and that French should be the dominant language.
- Having said that, democracy must prevail and be protected, as should our freedoms: Our freedom of press, personal freedoms, and human rights.
- Understanding the language is not enough. To know a culture, you need to know more than just the language.
- Too few really know the culture of the other. The combined French and English culture gives us our greatest strength.
- Politics is a personal matter; it is a private matter; it is not for a corporation to be involved in.
- All must be aboveboard. There should be no threats, no scare tactics, only talk of goodwill.

Eric put his convictions into practice. He hired a French tutor to strengthen his mastery of the language and enrolled his children in French schools. As Tom had years before, he spoke to the brewery workers in French; he gave speeches – to employees, suppliers, and customers – in French. He influenced the promotion of Francophones to the highest echelons of Molson's management. He participated in community initiatives that benefited both the French and English communities.

Eric *chose* Quebec.

As Quebec was in a period of tumult, so too was TMCL. President and CEO Jim Black led a restructuring charge, buying and selling businesses while reshaping the company's strategy. He limited the conglomerate to a few significant businesses that had predictable growth and earnings: brewing, specialty retail hardware, office and educational products, and possibly one more. He got rid of the rest.

On 17 February 1978, Black announced that "the next acquisition will be a big, substantial one, likely in the United States, that complements our strengths in distribution and marketing." What he didn't say was that TMCL already had a target (one where there was no US antitrust issue) in the specialty chemicals industry. It was called Diversey.

Diversey Corporation was a cleaning and sanitizing company founded in Chicago in 1923 by Herbert W. Kochs and his father. Their main competitor, Ecolab, had a stranglehold on the American market, so the pair focused on developing the business in other English-speaking countries. They began in Canada, an obvious first choice, and by the time Black started thinking of buying the company in 1977, Diversey had customers in more than one hundred countries and plants in thirty. It was a thriving business, and Black saw it as having great growth potential – especially in its US home market, where sales were marginal.

"We knew Diversey," says Eric. "Most breweries around the world did. We used their product Diversol all the time to clean our equipment. It was a pink chlorine powder – basically, chlorinated tri-sodium phosphate." Laughing, he adds, "Sometimes, we would even sprinkle a little bit on the floor before the boss walked in to show him we were keeping things clean!"

Discussions to buy Diversey began in early 1977. Over the next few months, and with the help of Diversey's chairman, Herbert Kochs, Molson bought over 10 per cent of the company's shares. The negotiations continued, and in April 1978, Black and his team made an offer for the balance of the stock at $28 a share. (It was trading at $22.37 on the American Stock Exchange.) It didn't work. The Diversey team got cold feet and said they would look for another buyer. "It happens all the time in these negotiations," says Eric. "They were told by their investment bankers that our offer wasn't high enough and that they could get a better price." When the Diversey management team and its board of directors rejected TMCL's offer, the takeover turned hostile. The TMCL team led by Black bypassed them, went directly to Diversey's shareholders, and upped the ante to $30 a share. The revised price was accepted, and on 30 June 1978, TMCL owned Diversey.

Eric viewed it as an enormous add-on to TMCL. He was excited by the company's global reach and international sales force. "The Diversey sales people were British-trained, intelligent world travellers who could put together a program to sell more and more cleaning solutions and services. They were great." And even though he knew it was unlikely, he mused, "Perhaps Diversey's international sales force could be used to sell Molson beer one day." Eric's international dream – turning Molson into a global brewer – was never far behind.

Jim Black did not share Eric's vision for the beer business. "Jim was a wonderful man, honest, hard-working, but he lacked imagination," says Eric regretfully. Soon after, the CEO made another decision that caused Eric consternation. He chose to move the Diversey head offices from Chicago, Illinois, to Mississauga, Ontario.

"Leave it in Chicago!" Eric urged. "You can access the world from Chicago. O'Hare serves airports all over the globe … Why would you move Diversey to a place where more than half of our employees don't even have passports?"

Black explained that they couldn't stay in Chicago because they wanted to merge the units and there were issues with employee fringe benefits, pension plans, and so on. "All administrative reasons," Eric summarizes. "Nothing to do with selling chemicals to the world."

In the end, Eric backed down. Just because his name was Molson didn't mean he had any more influence than any other employee or director. His was a voice amongst others. Black was the company CEO, and it was his decision to make. Ironically, years later, the fate of Diversey would make Eric take a stand against another CEO, but in that instance he wouldn't back down.

❦

As the company streamlined its activities, things were changing for Eric on a personal level. When he, Jane, and the boys moved back to Montreal in 1976, their newly purchased house was being renovated, so they temporarily went to live with Tom and Auntie Bea in Eric's childhood home on Ramezay Road. It was then that Eric witnessed firsthand his father's deteriorating condition. Tom had become a recluse and spent most of his time in his room.

When he was a young adult, before marrying Celia, Tom had been a bon vivant; he loved to sail, travel, play hockey, golf, and spend time with the ladies. That changed, however, soon after his twenty-ninth birthday. Perhaps it was because he watched the ravages of the Great Depression or because he had simply matured, but after that, he focused on work. Days, evenings, weekends, the brewery became the main concern of his life. In retirement, however, he seemed to stop living at all. Having lost his sense of purpose, he avoided contact with the outside world. His companions became his books, newspapers and, sadly, the bottle.

"I think alcohol probably got the better of him," Jane says. "He just checked out. He didn't seem to want to make an effort any more ... I was always a bit nervous around him, you know. He was a bit gruff. Tough on Eric, tough on Stephen. But he did have a softer side. When we were living at Ramezay Road, he once said to me: 'You know, Jane, you're doing a good job with your three boys' ... That was very nice. It meant something to me." It seemed that despite his stern exterior, Tom did care after all.

A few months later, Eric, Jane, and the boys moved in to their new home at 348 Wood Avenue. Like their previous Montreal residence a block up the street, it was a townhouse on a lane where neighbourhood kids congregated and played. For Andrew, Justin, and Geoff, the best part of the house was the basement. As part of the renovations, it was converted into a mock hockey rink, complete with steel cages around the ceiling light bulbs, two small nets on both ends, and a wood floor painted with a red centre line, two blue lines, and face-off circles. Soon after the family settled in, the house turned into a boisterous place, with kids coming in and out of the back door, alternating hockey games between the basement and the lane outside.

The lively mood at 348 Wood was a sharp contrast to the sombre quiet of Ramezay Road. Tom's condition was deteriorating. A lifetime of smoking had him gasping for breath, and his worsening arthritis was debilitating. With an oxygen tank at his side, he spent his days drinking Scotch, smoking British Consols, reading military history books, or watching hockey on the bulky, oversized TV atop of which stood a small Stanley Cup replica for 1968 – the last year Tom co-owned the team with Hartland, when the Canadiens swept the series against the St Louis Blues in four straight games. Soon, he was completely bedridden. Sadly, the lung cancer diagnosis did not come as a surprise.

In the afternoon of 3 April 1978, Eric drove from the brewery to the Montreal General Hospital where Tom was being treated. The next day he would be leaving for Edmonton to give a speech to Molson employees on quality control. Before going, he wanted to see his father. He stared painfully at the frail seventy-six-year-old in the bed, hooked up to oxygen, IV tubes, and monitors. The beeping of the machines and the wheezing of his father's laboured breathing was overwhelming. Here was the man he had worked so hard to impress all his life. A man he at times feared and resented because of his undemonstrative ways, but had always looked up to, respected, and loved deeply.

He wasn't going to make it, Eric thought. There was no way he could leave for Edmonton.

The doctors assured him: "Don't worry, he's in good hands. Go to Alberta." Eric acquiesced. Besides, he figured Tom would have expected him to go and do his job, no matter what.

The call came as he walked into the Edmonton brewery. It was Stephen. "Eric, Daddy's passed away."

Eric placed the phone back in its cradle. He handed his speech to Zoltan Vallyi, his trusted Hungarian colleague, and said, "Please do this for me, Zol. The production team is waiting." Eric sat down. A steady, swelling heartache overtook him. He could barely breathe. Tom

The Molson mausoleum was built in 1863 in the Mount Royal Cemetery. It consists of this lighthouse-shaped monument on which the family logo is inscribed and two large adjacent vaults (not pictured here). A third vault is located lower down the slope. Photo by Michel de la Chenelière, 2017.

was dead. He had known it was coming, but the pain was worse than he'd ever imagined.

Events unfolded rapidly. Eric took the next flight back to Montreal. Auntie Bea, Tom's widow, shared the news with friends and relatives. Deirdre and Cynthia took care of all the funeral arrangements. Stephen contacted the people at Royal Trust to start organizing Tom's succession.

"Everything comes to you at once when someone dies. There are a lot of responsibilities, *and* you have to hold your family together. Hopefully, you have a rational family. And we do. Deirdre, Cynthia, Stephen, they were all wonderful." Eric's voice catches as he speaks of his siblings, "They all did so much to help."

Tom was cremated on Friday, 7 April 1978. All of the brewery's old-timers joined the family to say goodbye. Tom's ashes were placed in one of the three large vaults of the Molson mausoleum near the summit of the Mount Royal.

As the ceremony drew to an end, Eric's attention turned to the family coat of arms engraved on the towering lighthouse-shaped structure built in memory of John Molson at the entrance of the stately burial chambers. Eric contemplated the motto chosen by his forefathers, *Industria et Spe* – "By industry and hope." Did it portray Tom? He had certainly mastered the *industria* part of the equation, Eric reflected, but the *spe*? … Tom could have used more hope in his life, especially in his later years.

Eric's thoughts then turned to how he would fare in the role he had to assume with Tom's death. He was now head of the Molson family.

❦

The mood was solemn in the boardroom of the Notre Dame brewery. Eric, Stephen, Deirdre, and Cynthia sat quietly around the large table waiting for Hartland and the Royal Trust executors to arrive for the reading of Tom's will.

"I was surprised. Everyone was surprised when they read the will," says Eric. "Tom left us a big block of Molson shares. We couldn't believe the number. Plus, they were voting shares. It was huge."

The other person taken aback by Tom's will was Hartland. First, there were the amounts. Forgetting Tom's frugal lifestyle, Hartland was surprised that his older brother had amassed so much wealth in his lifetime. (It is sad to think of Tom unable to enjoy his "golden years" after all the hard work he put into the brewery.) More vexing to Hartland, however, was the disposition of the TMCL class B voting shares: to have such a large control block go to Tom's children, Eric in particular, was unfathomable. How could someone like Eric, an introvert who hardly spoke up at board meetings, end up in control of the corporation? Perhaps he could convince his nephew to put Tom's shares in the Molson Foundation.

Twenty years earlier, on 28 November 1958, Tom and Hartland had created and funded the Molson Foundation by using a portion of their Molson shares. Before transferring the voting shares to the new charitable foundation, they addressed a series of issues: how to safeguard control of the company, how to make the transfer tax efficient, and how to provide for their successors. Their solution was to create a holding company in which they placed the Molson voting shares and did what is known as a "freeze" on their value. This asset management strategy allowed them to have the capital needed to fund the Molson Foundation, and it "protected" that portion of the Molson voting shares from the likes of corporate raider E.P. Taylor – an important consideration for maintaining long-term control of Molson. "They had to make sure that one of these vultures didn't come in and snap the thing up," explains Eric.

At the time of the freeze, Tom bequeathed a portion of the growth from those shares to his children as part of his estate planning, whereas Hartland chose not to. And when Tom's will was read, Hartland discovered the impact of that decision. The growth from the original shares in Tom and Hartland's holding company was substantial, and Tom's children now collectively held a major control stake in TMCL.

This new reality did not sit well with Hartland. "After Tom's will was read," Eric recalls, "Hartland seemed both surprised and upset. A few days later, he offered to take Stephen and me to lunch at the Mount Royal Club. We would rather have met him at the local tavern – more our style – but we went." They were ushered to Hartland's usual table in a quiet corner of the opulent dining area, and as soon as the white-gloved waiters discreetly stepped away to fill their order, Hartland broached the subject of Tom's will. "Hartland did a number on us at that lunch," says Eric. "He tried to get us to throw our control shares back into the foundation. He said things like, 'Your father would want you to do this,' or 'That was our plan, when Tom and I created the foundation' … Stephen and I just listened. We said we would think about it and get back to him."

Hartland, however, was not going to let this one go. He turned to his lawyer, William E. Stavert, and asked him to take care of it. Stavert organized a number of meetings with Eric and Stephen and always steered the conversation back to the same question. "Don't you think your father would have wanted those shares to go back to the foundation?" Or another time, "You know Eric, it was only this morning while I was shaving that I remembered a conversation I had with your father. He would have wanted you to give those shares back." Eric and Stephen struggled with Stavert's suggestions. They wondered, "Is this guy trying to do a con job on us?" They stayed noncommittal and Eric told him, "Bill, we need a bit more time to think about this."

As always, when Eric made an important decision, he was diligent. He took his time, considered all angles, and consulted with trusted advisors. This time, he turned to Benny Parsons.

Raymond E. "Benny" Parsons was an English-trained barrister who practised law at the prominent firm McCarthy Tétrault. (In the mid-1970s it went by the interminable name of Laing, Weldon, Courtois, Clarkson, Parsons, Gonthier and Tétrault.) Benny came from a family of lawyers; his grandfather, Eugène Lafleur, was a founder of McCarthy's and one of the most prominent appellate lawyers in Canadian history. But besides his admirable background and his impressive roster of blue-chip "old Westmount" clientele, Eric felt he could be trusted. He was, in Eric's terms, a "silver fox."

"You always need a silver fox as an advisor," says Eric. "You know, someone who's intelligent, trustworthy, sees the big picture, gets along with everyone … And that's what Benny was. He was admired by me, Stephen, *and* my sisters, so he could help me with all the family stuff."

When Eric asked Benny what he thought of the pressure he was getting from Hartland and Stavert, the lawyer said, "Don't do it, Eric. Those shares belong to you. Tom's instructions are clear. He wanted you and Stephen to have those voting shares. You own them and you shouldn't give them up. As you know, they're very valuable and control the company to a certain extent. Besides, you never know what will happen … One day you may need those votes."

So Eric stood his ground. Gently but firmly, he rebuffed his uncle's advances, kept the voting shares, and, as a compromise, agreed to donate money to the foundation. "Once we found proof that Tom intended for us to have the shares, I asked Stephen to negotiate a deal to offset the shares Hartland said were supposed to go into the foundation," Eric says. "Stephen and I ended up donating a fixed amount to the foundation for nearly fifteen years, which was actually good, as it made the foundation bigger. But we kept the class B shares."

Eric's determination and resolve was often masked by his quiet exterior. As much as he believed in not interfering and giving people room to make their choices, when it came to matters that were squarely his responsibility – in this case, the long-term, sustainable future of the Tom Molson branch of the family – he was tenacious. For that was the duty Eric took on when Tom passed away. He was not only the primary beneficiary of the estate (he got three-sevenths of the whole, Stephen two-sevenths, and the girls one-seventh each); he was also its trustee and the new patriarch.

Eric shies away from taking credit for keeping the siblings – the "Tom Molson gang," he calls it – united. "My sisters were wonderful and so was my brother, Stephen. We all worked well together." Nonetheless, for nearly twenty-five years, Eric managed his sisters' trusts pro bono and was the guiding hand that stewarded the Molson legacy.

Close to a month after Tom's funeral in Montreal, Eric went to Massawippi for the weekend with Jane and the boys. It was late spring and the poppies along the path leading to the barn were in full bloom. Their red petals looked like snippets of crinkled silk swaying in the wind. As Eric admired his favourite perennial, he was reminded of the famous line in Lieutenant Colonel John McCrae's poem "In Flanders Fields": "To you from failing hands we throw the torch; be yours to hold it high."

The only way to live up to the legacy of his predecessors and to pass the baton onto the next generation, Eric thought, was to act honourably: choose service over self-interest at every opportunity.

5 Buying Back the Canadiens

We are our choices.

JEAN-PAUL SARTRE (1905–1980)

"Hi, Andy, hi, Helen," Eric greets us as we walk in the back door. He holds up his iPad. "Have you seen this?"

Andrew takes off his jacket. "I'm not sure, Dad. The screen's gone blank."

"Right." Eric fiddles with the device. "You have to watch. It's amazing."

We are in Jane and Eric's country home in Massawippi. It's early October. The setting sun's last rays highlight the fiery colours of the leaves still clinging to their branches. It is the close of one of those glorious Indian Summer days that occasionally punctuate the fall and make me grateful to be alive.

Jane stands at the stove, stirring one of her soups. The aroma of spices, tomatoes, and sherry is mouth-watering.

"Hello, you two," she says. "Are you staying for dinner?"

I reply for both of us, a little too eagerly. "That would be great."

"Listen. Watch." Eric holds up his screen. He motions for us to sit down and pay attention.

Luciano Pavarotti's voice, interpreting Puccini's "Nessun Dorma," fills the kitchen in a potent crescendo. On the screen a succession of powerful hockey images from the Montreal Canadiens unfurls to the music. Each time a Habs player comes up, Eric mutters his name, "Big

Jean … The Rocket … Dryden … Carbonneau … Lafleur …" He's enthralled. We all are.

At the end of the three-minute, sixteen-second clip, Pavarotti singing the final "*Vincerò!*" (I will win!), the four of us are carried away by images of big goals and big wins, players and fans alike celebrating victory.

"Excellent!" says Eric. "Goose-pimple stuff. Just what you need to get the troops going."

"It's really good," Andrew agrees. "When was it made?"

"It was the show before a Leafs game a few years ago, I think 2013. We should do more of it … You know, combine opera or classical pieces with hockey. It's a great way to expose our fans to all sorts of music, not just the regular stuff."

He puts down his tablet next to his glass of Molson Ex and reaches for the TV remote. Saturday night, 6:55 p.m. *Hockey Night in Canada* is about to begin.

✹

Mid-summer 1978, close to midnight: the ringing phone pierced the quiet in the bedroom. Eric groggily picked up the receiver and listened to the thick, slurred voice. "Eric, you've got to do something … Labatt's … it's not good. They're here at the Ritz celebrating, drinking champagne … They say they've got the team!"

It was a call that changed the course of Habs history.

The 1977–78 hockey season was memorable for many reasons. The Montreal Canadiens, victorious in fifty-nine out of eighty games, were season champions. They topped that off by winning the Stanley Cup for the third year in a row – repeating their previous spring's triumph over their arch-rivals, the Boston Bruins. The final match on Thursday, 25 May 1978, took place at the Boston Garden. Even Bruins coach Don Cherry conceded, "They are worthy champions. They deserved everything they got. They beat us in our own building." Habs players Guy Lafleur, Larry Robinson, Bob Gainey, and Ken Dryden won more than half of the NHL's individual trophies that year. It was a glorious time to be a fan.

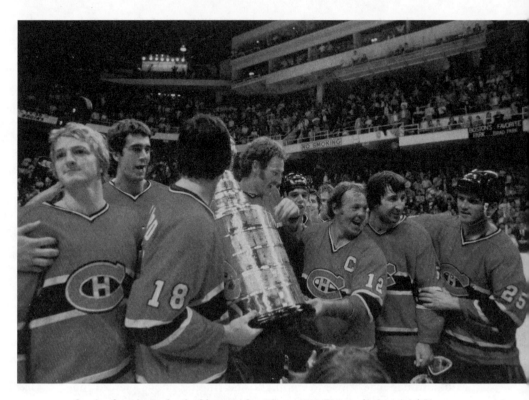

Stanley Cup victory for the Montreal Canadiens, 1978. Players (*left to right*) Pierre Mondou, Gilles Lupien, Serge Savard, Larry Robinson, Yvan Cournoyer, Guy Lapointe, Jacques Lemaire. Courtesy Club de hockey Canadien, Inc.

For owners Edward and Peter Bronfman, it was their fourth Stanley Cup since Carena-Bancorp Inc., the conglomerate they controlled, bought the team from David, William, and Peter Molson seven years earlier. It was an incredible stream of wins. Today, Eric acknowledges, "Edward and Peter ran the team very well. I liked Edward; he was a friend and a gentleman. He and his brother were good owners."

But soon after the last "Go Habs Go" cheer from the Stanley Cup parade resounded through Montreal's downtown core, rumours of a sale started circulating.

"As soon as I got the call, I phoned Morgan McCammon and asked him to get the show on the road," says Eric. "'Speak to the Bronfmans, talk to Jacques Courtois, meet with Sammy Pollock ... do what you have to do.' We just couldn't lose the team to Labatt."

Labatt Brewery, which became a public company the same year Molson did in 1945, was inching ahead in the Canadian beer market-share race. By 1978, the Ontario-based brewer held 38 per cent of the market compared to Molson's 36 per cent. Molson, however, was still the dominant player in Quebec, a position that could be compromised if Labatt bought the Canadiens. It was bad enough that third-place Carling O'Keefe was narrowing the gap through its ownership of the Quebec Nordiques. There was no way Molson could let Labatt get its hands on the Habs, one of the most powerful advertising vehicles in Quebec.

On 1 August 1978, Labatt's president Don J. McDougall confirmed the rumours to the *Globe and Mail*. "We've had discussions about buying the franchise with officials of Carena-Bancorp. And, yes, if the owners indicated that, yes, they want to sell, we will be able to react fairly quickly."

But the Molson people were faster. "Morgan McCammon knew how to close a deal," says Eric. "He managed to get his hands on the Labatt offer – it was a big, fat, three-inch book – and he basically added a dollar to the bottom line and got the team back." It was a major coup … and a close call.

"Labatt was really upset," says Eric. "But we couldn't let them near the team. It would have destroyed us. Everyone in the streets would have started drinking their beer instead of ours!" Moreover, with Molson Breweries being a major sponsor of the *Hockey Night in Canada* telecasts and radio broadcasts of NHL games, it was a natural extension for the brewery to own the local franchise.

It was the third time since the team was founded in 1909 that it would come under Molson ownership: twice by groups of individuals – Tom and Hartland, then their three nephews David, Peter, and Billy – and now by Molson Breweries of Canada, a subsidiary of TMCL. With every transfer, the price shot to new levels.

"Tom and Hartland bought the team for like $2 a share, they sold it to our cousins for almost nothing, and then Molson bought it back from the Bronfmans at something close to $55 a share," says Eric. "I think the brewery paid close to $20 million cash for the team (the sale didn't include the Forum). But that's *peanuts* compared to what we paid for it in 2009!"

LE CANADIEN ERRANT — ENTRE MOLSON ET LABATT

Editorial cartoon in *La Presse*, Friday, 4 August 1978 (A4), the morning Morgan McCammon was about to announce the purchase of the Canadiens by Molson. The French title reads, "Le Canadien errant entre Molson et Labatt" (Canadiens wandering between Molson and Labatt). Published by permission.

On 4 August 1978, Morgan McCammon stood in front of a roomful of reporters and read a bilingual message in his serious monotone. "Ladies and gentlemen, it is with considerable pleasure that I announce the purchase of the Montreal Canadiens Hockey Club by Molson Breweries of Canada Ltd. *Mesdames et messieurs, c'est avec grand plaisir ...*"

After the press conference, Eric turned to McCammon. "Morgan, you *do* realize that you didn't just buy a hockey team, right? In Quebec it's a lot more than that. It's an institution ... a unifying force for our society. You have to treat it delicately and with respect."

"You're right. We just bought an incredible sports team."

"Actually, you just bought an *entertainment* business. The hockey team is one of your 'acts.' It's like a ballet troupe ... it's delicate, you want them to dance well and you want them to win. But there's more. You can do concerts, you can do shows, events ... it's all about entertainment."

Again, Morgan signalled his agreement, but Eric wasn't really sure he got it.

✤

With the Montreal Canadiens secured, next on Eric's list of priorities was global expansion. The idea had germinated for ten years out of the conversations he'd had at meetings of the International Brewing Consortium. It was now Eric's vision for Molson. And given the brewery's previous attempts to grow beyond Canada, he felt that in order to make it, the brewery needed both a dedicated organization and a leader tasked with this mission. CEO Jim Black eventually agreed with Eric's proposal. On 24 July 1979, he created Molson Breweries International and named H. Hollis Brace as its president. The new group reported directly to Eric, then EVP of the entire brewing organization.

Hollis and Eric worked in tandem. They first looked to build the market potential south of the border. With beer sales in Canada stagnating, exporting to the United States seemed like a promising course of action. And for a while it worked. "We had an agent who knew how

Molson advertisement, 1981, highlighting its position as the number-two importer of beer to the United States. Molson Coors Brewing Company collection.

From left to right, Hollis Brace, Eric Molson, and Dan Pleshoyano at The Swan pub in Moulton, England, Tuesday, 24 July 1984, where they had gone to introduce Molson beer to the United Kingdom. Moulton, Lincolnshire, was the birthplace of John Molson, who set off to Canada in 1782 at eighteen years of age in search of a business opportunity. Molson Coors Brewing Company collection.

to sell imported beer down in the States," explains Eric. "They took our brand, Golden, and really did well with it. There was a sort of mystique about it that caught on. So much so that we started running out. We had to build more bottling lines in Ontario to get more Golden into the United States." In 1979, Molson exported close to twenty-one million gallons to all major US markets (except for Louisiana, Texas, and Georgia). Labatt was only shipping seven million gallons.

Jim Black was delighted. Uncharacteristically, he boasted that Molson's growth in the United States was "the major success story in the Canadian brewing industry of the last decade." By December 1980, Molson was the second-largest beer importer in the United States with about 25 per cent of the American import market. It was second only to Heineken. Like his boss, Black, Eric was pleased, especially as

Heineken was a competitor he both admired for its international success and aspired to surpass one day.

Eric then turned his attention to other continents. He and Hollis Brace visited brewers in Europe, Japan, China, and Australia. Connecting with beer-makers from around the world was part of the job Eric cherished. His chemist's mind valued learning new techniques and exploring potential combinations and alliances with other brewers. He always seemed to be concocting some plan to buy, merge, or partner with this international brewery or that one. His colleagues in Canada thought he was a bit of a dreamer.

At his core, however, Eric was a realist. He knew that international expansion was critical to the long-term success of the company. He was open-minded and had a strong respect for growth – of perspectives, of understanding, of reach. His son Andrew says Eric encouraged his company, as he encouraged his children, to have an "openness towards the world, towards difference: different people, different backgrounds, different cultures." So when he tasked Hollis Brace with the objective of global expansion, he keenly wanted him to succeed, yet he was able to step back and let him do his job.

"I was the same way in terms of managing at Molson as I was with my boys' education," Eric says. "You give them guidance and then you let them be … It's okay if somebody makes a mistake. I've sometimes let it happen just to see how it unfolds. If you value a guy, it's the only way he'll learn."

🍁

Eric was never going to push Andrew, Justin, and Geoff the way Tom had pushed him. He was not going to mandate, for example, that one study physics, the other chemistry, and the third accounting.

"Eric wasn't like Tom with the boys," says Jane. "In fact, he was the total opposite: Eric had a lot of faith in his sons and he *showed* them that's how he felt. I'm sure that contributed to their sense of self-worth."

From relatively trivial choices like their after-school activities when they were younger to what they would major in college, Eric let his sons make up their own minds. All he asked was that they follow their passion, work hard, and finish what they started. "If you think of education as learning how to think, then it doesn't matter what you take. You can take religion or film or accounting … it doesn't make a difference. What matters is that you know how to define an issue, collect the information you need to understand it, think it through, test your understanding, and then put what you learn into action. That's it. Of course that requires common sense, hard work, and perseverance. But as long as you've got the basics, you'll be all right."

As soon as they were old enough, Eric allowed his children to choose their schools and exposed them to different options. Eleven-year-old Andrew was drawn to Collège de Montréal, a French high school in downtown Montreal, founded by the Catholic Sulpicians in 1767. It was a choice unheard of at the time among other Westmount families. Nonetheless, when Andrew started there in the fall of 1979 (the only "Anglo" in his class), he didn't think he was any different from the other kids. He did not imagine that his family name made him special, especially not in his schoolmates' eyes. Unfortunately, by the late 1970s the Francophone–Anglophone tensions prevalent on the streets of Montreal had filtered through into the school halls, and to some, the Molson name represented the loathed, English-speaking, ruling class – *les maudits Anglais.*

Parti Québécois Premier René Lévesque announced the referendum question on Quebec's independence three months after Andrew started at the Collège. The vote would be on 20 May 1980. The province's citizens mobilized to show their colours: pro-blue and anti-red campaign posters plastered the poles of every city, village, and township of Quebec. Families, friends, and neighbours, local TV and radio programs, passionately debated *Oui* (pro-separation) versus *Non* (anti-separation). Emotions ran high.

Partaking in the social discourse, Andrew proudly sported a pin that read "*Mon NON est Québécois*" (a play on words, literally meaning "My NO vote is Québécois" and phonetically, "My name is Québécois"). In the schoolyard, however, some saw this expression of inclusiveness from one of the "Anglo elite" as inflammatory. An older boy pounced on Andrew, beating him and shouting names at him in French. Kids rushed to see what was going on. A school monitor broke up the fight, the instigator was sent off for reprimand, and Andrew went home to look up the words "*capitaliste*" and "*fasciste*" in the dictionary.

"As soon as I got home from work that day, I knew something was up," says Eric. "Andrew told us what happened. He'd been bullied. We tried to reassure him. I said things like, 'Don't worry about it … This is our home … We're in a bilingual country.' But Jane and I were nervous. It wasn't just that he might get roughed up again at school. We were worried about Andrew being kidnapped. We kept close to him and we tried to make sure that he didn't have much identification with the name Molson on it. During the time of the revolution when Laporte was kidnapped, our name was cited as a target by those extremists. They said Molsons were pigs. The Bronfmans, the Steinbergs, the Molsons … we were all referred to as 'the pigs.' So when Andrew came home all scuffed up that day, Jane and I were worried."

Eric didn't share his trepidation with Andrew. Instead, he tried to explain some of the preconceptions evoked by the name Molson. Some were favourable (for example, when related to the family's philanthropy or community involvement), while others were clearly not. The perception of privilege and wealth created a rift in society that sometimes led to radical actions. As they spoke, Andrew resolved to himself not to worry about what people thought of his Molson surname; he would focus on becoming "Andrew" instead.

"Dad showed us an openness toward the world, a curiosity and an openness towards difference," he says. "He also encouraged me to discover whatever I was interested in. After I was attacked at school because I was a Molson, I wanted to discover my first name. I wanted to find out who Andrew was and not let the Molson part of my name take over … and Dad supported me in that."

When he was thirteen, Andrew asked if he could go away to school, preferably to a place where "Molson" was less well known. Eric took a broad-minded approach. "Let's organize a road trip and see what's out there." He, Jane, and Andrew visited eight New England schools.

"We went to Exeter, Andover, Choate, St Paul's, and a bunch of other prep schools," says Eric. "All great places. But I was most impressed with Phillips Exeter. Instead of a typical classroom with rows of seats, they had the kids in small groups, sitting around a table with their

Eric and Jane Molson with sons: *left to right*, Justin, Andrew, and Geoff, 1987. Molson family collection.

professor, discussing ideas, debating … Amazing! It's called the Harkness method (and I'm sure I could have benefited from something like that). But I didn't say anything to Andrew. I didn't want to influence him. We just walked around the campus and when we got back to the car, I asked him what he thought, just like I had with every other place."

Eric's approach required self-restraint and faith in his sons. He figured that he and Jane had taught the boys the principles they valued, so now it was up to them. "Mum and Dad let me choose," says Andrew. "But Dad made sure I thought about the implications of my decision – you know, take a long-term-minded approach to it. When you pick a school, it's a big decision that affects you in the long run. So he made me think about that."

Then he laughs, "And you know, Phillips Exeter had *two* rinks, one next to the other! I couldn't believe it. That was pretty cool for a thirteen-year-old obsessed with hockey. But it was way more than that. I loved the feel of the place, and I was lucky to get accepted."

❦

Mark Twain once said, "That's just the way with some people. They get down on a thing when they don't know nothing about it." The comment struck a chord with Eric. He thought of it when *Montreal Gazette* editorial writer Philippe Deane Gigantes did a profile of him soon after he was named president of Molson Breweries Canada in October 1980.

"The most remarkable thing about Eric Herbert Molson, 43, is how well he succeeds at being unremarkable," wrote Gigantes. "Eric Molson scarcely projects the image of an imaginative, creative mover and shaker … His appearance is not striking. Should he ever find himself in a police line-up, witnesses would have problems remembering him. He is handsome but only if one looks a second time. His clothes do not attract attention. He has his shoes rebuilt as many as three times at Tony's on Greene Ave." And so on.

A more self-absorbed person might have been upset with having the word "unremarkable" used to describe him, but Eric actually agreed with it. In fact, he often asserted (with some element of pride), "I am boring. I *like* boring." The value of "boring" would later become apparent. "Boring" is easy to underestimate.

But the writer also painted Eric and Jane in the caricatural light of uptight, privileged snobs. For example, describing Merrill Denison's 1955 book about the Molson family, *The Barley and the Stream*, Gigantes says, "The book reads as though it were written by a courtier about Louis XIV, with the king himself looking over the author's shoulder." It was an image that went completely against deeply held family values of inclusiveness, humility, and openness to diversity.

On the yellowed clipping I read the words Eric wrote in the margin back in 1980: "Very negative orientation / Unfair and distasteful account (I'm not in politics!) / Not 'beery' enough, not 'community' enough and not 'Molson' enough."

With a bit more prodding on my part, Eric says, "After that, I vowed never to trust journalists again." He shrugs. "What can you do?" At the time, though, he was thrown by it. He had just been promoted to the top job at the brewery, and he probably felt a little over his head. Presumably, he didn't want to attract more attention to himself than necessary, especially from the media. Like his father before him, he thought a man should be in the papers only three times in his life – when he is born, when he gets married, and when he dies. That was not to be Eric's fate.

In the fall of 1980, Eric had bigger preoccupations than how the media viewed him. Labatt had taken the unprecedented step of entering into a licensing agreement with American Anheuser-Busch. It got the rights to brew and sell Budweiser in Canada, and counted on Budweiser's high brand awareness (a spillover effect of US television reach) to drive sales. The bet paid off.

"Budweiser took off," Eric says. "I really didn't believe that Canadians were going to drink Budweiser. Why would they go with a non-Canadian brand? Our market research people even told us: 'Canadians don't like US beer. There's no way they'll go for it.' Well, they were wrong. I was wrong."

Labatt had a dream product on its hands. Budweiser was an immediate bestseller. It shifted the Canadian market paradigm and hardly cost anything to launch. There was a licence fee to pay for every bottle sold, but that was almost irrelevant given the high sales volume. Other Canadian brewers rushed to do similar licensing deals. All except for Molson: Molson continued putting its energy behind penetrating the United States and ended up being the last of the big Canadian brewers to add an American brand to its product line. It did so five years later with Coors.

Eric respects his competitors. He often says, "You need competition to keep yourself sharp." But he adds, using a double negative for emphasis: "Just don't give them *nothing*. It's like with the Boston Bruins – don't ever let them touch the puck." In the case of licensing an American beer, the competition had deked them out, and it stung.

The pressure on Eric, however, came not only from the beer side of the business. He was increasingly uneasy with the performance of the other enterprises under the TMCL umbrella. He continued to question the wisdom of conglomerates. Was the theory of owning a bunch of unrelated businesses to counter economic cycles and stabilize earnings effective in practice? Shouldn't the operations be more compatible? Did TMCL have the managerial skills and financial capacity to manage all this complexity?

"We're starting to miss the boat," Eric told Jane. "We're becoming too bureaucratic and too internally focused. Plus, it's really hard to tell if we're actually making money in all these other businesses. I know exactly how the brewery is doing, but I don't know how to measure all the other ones. I don't care about gross sales – which is all they talk about. I want to know about the bottom line!"

"Then why don't you speak with them?" asked Jane, losing patience with her husband's reluctance to intervene. "Go see Jim Black, tell him what you're thinking … Do something if you don't agree with what's going on!"

Eric thought: *What am I supposed to do? I'm not the boss of TMCL. I'm a Molson employee and shareholder like many others. Besides, the entire board is behind this strategy. It's actually one that was built in part by Bud Willmot, the chairman! Am I supposed to bang my fist on the table and ram my ideas down their throats? The last time I spoke to Bud about it and told him that we weren't measuring ourselves properly, he dismissed me. I have to find another way. Also, I don't want to pull the plug too early. I want to see how this strategy plays out.*

So he kept quiet.

Part of him believed in letting people (in this case Jim Black, CEO of TMCL) do their jobs, and the other part of him was unsure. He was not ready to take on Hartland and Bud Willmot. Besides, after what happened at the reading of Tom's will, Eric felt he had to be extra careful with his uncle. He sent Willmot and Hartland newspaper articles and editorials on how conglomerates were uncoupling and businesses were being streamlined. Otherwise, he kept an observer's stance and, like a scientist with his experiment, waited to see how things would unfold.

Eric was more proactive, however, when it came to overseeing the family's control block in the company. Hartland's response at the reading of Tom's will taught him the importance of holding onto Molson's class B voting shares. Benny Parsons's warning resonated: "You never know what will happen, Eric ... one day you may need those votes."

So on 25 October 1981, when he learned that Bud Willmot was thinking of selling his block of B shares, Eric kept a close eye on the matter. He knew Willmot needed capital. Kinghaven Farms, the thoroughbred horse racing stable he founded in King City, north of Toronto, was an expensive venture. "If you ever want to learn to lose money, Eric, I can show you," Willmot once joked, pointing to his horses on the other side of the fence as they toured the property.

Eric analyzed the situation. What if he were to buy Willmot's voting shares? On the plus side, it would shore up control with the Tom Molson branch of the family for one more generation and allow them to set the company's long-term direction while providing continuity and stability. On the negative side, it meant losing the flexibility that came with the class A shares (which could easily be sold on the market), as well as assuming the cost of the purchase.

Eric approached Willmot to do a deal.

The two men agreed to swap shares. Bud traded his voting B shares for an equivalent value of Eric's A shares. That way Bud got stock that could easily be sold, and Eric increased the family's control block. To this day, he is grateful to Willmot: "Bud was a gentleman. He could have turned around and made a deal with a tobacco company or some other party for those shares. Instead, he did the honourable thing and traded them back to us."

🍁

When to comment on management decisions and how much to intervene were questions Eric grappled with throughout his career. He knew the impact of his last name. An offhand remark by him would send the troops running: "Oh, Mr. *Molson* said we should do it this way." It could be very disruptive. Worse, if taken too far, it could stifle others' initiative and creativity – the entrepreneurial spirit would be lost. So he often chose to stand back and not say a word. At times it could be frustrating, especially when he felt that management was too bureaucratic, lacked vision, or wasn't close enough to the front line.

When the brewery bought the Montreal Canadiens from the Bronfmans in 1978, for example, he felt that Morgan McCammon did not fully understand the significance of the team to the people of Quebec. "You have to be careful," Eric warned him. "The Habs are a Quebec institution. They *belong* to the Québécois." But when McCammon hired Irving Grundman, an Anglophone owner of bowling alleys, to become the new general manager, Eric thought, "He just doesn't get it. Maybe we need someone who understands hockey, the players, *and* the people of Quebec." McCammon didn't seem to grasp the importance of being a "sidewalk man" – being close to the people and the "*pouls de la population*," the pulse of the community.

It happened again in the summer of 1980. The Canadiens were in the enviable position of picking first in the NHL draft. The people of Quebec, just recovering from the schismatic referendum on the future of the province, were united in their choice for the team's number-one pick: Denis Savard. Savard was fast, skated with flair, and was good with the puck. (He was later inducted in the Hockey Hall of Fame with 1,338 points in 1,196 games.) Most of all, he was a Montreal native, a Québécois phenom. McCammon and Grundman, however, refused to bow to local pressure. Instead, they chose to draft Doug Wickenheiser of Saskatchewan. One never knows how these things will turn out, but on 12 October 1980, when Savard first stepped on the ice of the Montreal Forum as a Chicago Blackhawk and got a standing ovation from the Habs fans, Eric once again thought, "We need someone who's more in touch with our fan base to run this team."

The man he thought of was Ronald Corey.

Corey first got involved with Molson in his early twenties as a producer for Radio-Canada. He would solicit the brewery to sponsor sporting events and, as the on-site announcer, helped with beer promotions. Zotique Lespérance, Molson's vice-president of sales, spotted his talent and liked his positive energy. Originally from Hochelaga-Maisonneuve, then a depressed Francophone district in the east end of Montreal, Corey had the drive of a self-made man. Lespérance convinced him to join Molson and, once at the brewery, he worked his way

Ronald Corey behind the bench of the Montreal Canadiens in the Forum, 25 October 1986. Eric Molson can be seen in the background. Courtesy Club de hockey Canadien, Inc.

up the company's sales and marketing departments. Seven years later, he walked into Eric's office and declared, "You know, I want to be the boss here one day."

Eric liked people with ambition. "Ronald was my kind of guy," he says. "He spoke both languages, he could rally the troops really well, he was at the office at 7:00 a.m. every day. He worked hard, stuck with it and had good principles." McCammon, however, was not prepared to give him the top job right away. Corey lost patience and left Molson. He took a senior position with Mister Muffler, a local company. And in 1980 he re-entered the beer world as president of the Quebec division of Carling O'Keefe, the third-largest brewery in Canada.

O'Keefe competed with Molson in both beer and hockey. Just as Molson owned the Montreal Canadiens, O'Keefe owned the Quebec Nordiques. The Canadiens at the time were showing signs of weakness. Following the Wickenheiser draft-pick incident, they were eliminated in the first round of the Stanley Cup playoffs for two consecutive years – the last one by the Quebec Nordiques. Disaster. Were the golden years of the team known as *les Glorieux* now over?

Eric turned to Dan Pleshoyano, then president of Molson Breweries, and said, "We've got to get Ronald Corey back."

"Eric, we can't," Pleshoyano replied. "He just became head of O'Keefe two years ago. He'll never accept."

"Just go speak to him." Eric knew he was interfering, but this was too important. He didn't want another Grundman-like incident.

Pleshoyano and Corey were both members of the MAA, an athletic club in downtown Montreal. After doing laps at the club's pool, Pleshoyano approached Corey and tried to suss out his interest in the Montreal Canadiens. It was not long before the men shook hands and the deal was done. On 12 November 1982, Ronald Corey replaced Morgan McCammon as president of the Montreal Canadiens Hockey Club.

"The morning I started with the Canadiens, I got a call from Senator Hartland," remembers Corey. "He told me, 'Ronald, welcome to the family.' That was very nice. I was touched that Hartland, who must have been seventy-six or seventy-seven back then, did that. Eric and Stephen did the same thing. They all took the time to come see me and wish me well. The Molsons are like that. They are inclusive and respectful people."

Corey knew that in his role as president of the Montreal Canadiens he would be under heavy scrutiny. Unlike Eric, he welcomed the exposure. He told a *Globe and Mail* journalist on 21 April 1983, "In Montreal, six million people watch you every day. We have fifty hours a week of open-line radio shows – that's more than two whole days. I think that's fabulous. It's the voice of the people."

Eric had found his "sidewalk man."

Four months after taking the job, and just days after the Canadiens made yet another early exit from the playoffs, Corey took action. He dismissed general manager Irving Grundman (his son, Howard

Grundman, resigned) and scout director Ron Caron and demoted unilingual coach Bob Berry. He started building a management team that reflected the people of Quebec. His first hire: Serge Savard as general manager.

Savard, who had won eight Stanley Cups as a Habs defenceman, was the first Francophone to become the team's GM since the late 1930s. He completed the management team by hiring coaches Jacques Lemaire and Jacques Laperrière. "We're building a winner here," Savard declared. "My goal is to have the Stanley Cup here in Montreal." It was not long before he reached his objective.

❦

In the early 1980s, Eric was *the* Molson at the company. Tom had passed away years before, Hartland was close to eighty, and Stephen was not interested in getting directly involved. It all fell on Eric.

In 1982, he once again heeded the call of duty and became deputy chairman of TMCL, the overarching parent company. The move was part of a larger, two-step plan. First, Eric would take the position of deputy chair, and Dan Pleshoyano would replace him as president of Molson Breweries. Then, a year later, in 1983, Jim Black would take over Bud Willmot's position as chairman – the "Jim-Eric/chair-deputy chair" combination was thought to be a good one. And in parallel, John Rogers would assume Black's place as TMCL's president and CEO. Eric agreed with the scheme, even though it meant leaving behind a hands-on role at the brewery.

"When I got out of operations, I worried that I would have nothing to do, that I would have a title only and no responsibilities," he says. "In the end, it turned out all right. I still worked on moving the company forward, but from a governance perspective. That meant I couldn't give orders like an executive or CEO, but that wasn't really my style anyway."

As deputy chairman, Eric had to hone his ability to ask pointed questions and develop his proficiency in the art of persuasion. He also had to give more public speeches. And although he was at ease addressing his colleagues at Molson, it was different with outsiders. Standing up in front of a group of strangers, especially businesspeople, made him deeply uncomfortable. "Poor Eric," says Jane. "He really disliked having to make speeches. He would quite literally be sick beforehand."

※

At 5:30 a.m. on 5 November 1985, heading out for his morning run, Eric visualized the speech he was to give to the Montreal Chamber of Commerce that afternoon. He liked his morning runs. They gave him a chance to think about his day. As he breathed in the cool fall air, jogging along his usual path, he told himself, "Remember, go slow. Use your hands; look around. It's just a speech. It's going to be fine." The talk would be entirely in French, in front of a roomful of eminent Montrealers, including businessmen, politicians, and reporters.

Eric steeled his nerves. When he faced the audience at noon, he spoke on two matters. He started with the one closest to his heart – his vision of growing Molson beyond the borders of Canada and making it a global player: "Le plus lourd défi de notre génération est de continuer d'étendre à l'échelle mondiale cette tradition d'excellence née à Montréal" (Our generation's biggest challenge is to continue expanding globally this tradition of excellence born in Montreal). Molson was already heading in that direction by exporting 20 per cent of the beer it produced in Quebec to the United States, but it had been slow in other regards. It had only recently acquired the license to produce Coors in Canada, whereas Labatt had been making Budweiser for close to five years already and was gaining market share.

The second issue Eric spoke to was the upcoming Free Trade Agreement between Canada and the United States. He favoured free trade. He thought it could do more for Canada's development, identity, and sense of purpose than staying shielded by a wall of protectionism. To get there, however, he had one request: give brewers in Canada time to adjust.

For years, Canadian brewing companies had been subject to interprovincial trade barriers requiring them to build a brewery in each province where they wanted to sell beer. These protectionist laws gave local brewers a virtual monopoly on beer sales, but they also caused a proliferation of small breweries across the country. Instead of having

Eric Molson speaking at the Montreal Chamber of Commerce, 5 November 1985. Courtesy Chamber of Commerce of Metropolitan Montreal.

large facilities that could serve vast regions like their US competitors, Canadian brewers were fragmented, with a smattering of provincial operations. This impacted both their efficiency and ability to be competitive on a North American scale. Molson had nine breweries in seven provinces, with a combined brewing capacity of ten million hectolitres. An American brewer like Coors, for example, handled the entire US market from a single brewery in Golden, Colorado, with a capacity of eighteen million hectolitres.

"The average US brewery is four to five times the size of the average Canadian brewery and, in our industry, economies of scale are very important," Eric told the room. "We need a suitable transition period that would permit us to develop East–West free trade here in Canada before we adopt North–South free trade."

Sanjib Choudhuri, TMCL's vice-president of strategic planning, describes the difference between the US and Canadian beer markets in stark terms: "The US brewing industry was so different to Canada's. I mean, anything that you saw in 'big-bucks' brewing in Canada, you multiplied it by ten to get to the US. It's just not comparable. In Canada, price was controlled, distribution was controlled, production was controlled. In the US, it was a totally different ballgame. You found your own distributors, set whatever price you wanted, sold in whatever size you chose ... no comparison. So Molson would have had limited exposure to the ruthlessness of US brewing. It was a gentlemen's club compared to US brewing."

Canadian brewers would eventually get the exemption they lobbied for regarding the Canada-US Free Trade Agreement. But in terms of making Molson the global player Eric aspired to, they were starting with a handicap.

The brewery's two-hundredth anniversary – a monumental milestone by anyone's estimation – was in 1986. As part of the commemorations, Eric travelled to all of Molson's installations in Canada. "I met with employees across the country and talked shop with them, which I enjoyed. I made speeches about the values behind our success for two centuries. Things like hard work, honesty, integrity, commitment to excellence, basic stuff. So basic that people tend to forget about them, especially when greed and short-term appetites take over."

Molson organized public-relations events from Vancouver to St John's, and everywhere in between. The reception across the country was warm and effusive. As a show of gratitude to communities for their continued support, Molson refurbished the Montreal Botanical Garden, commissioned a sculpture for Toronto's Harbourfront, developed an arts plaza in Edmonton, and constructed a nineteen-kilometre jogging path in Vancouver. The slogan for the year was "Cheers for 200 Years!" (Eric murmurs to me, "Slightly cheesy, don't you think?")

Governor General Madame Jeanne Sauvé marked the milestone by holding a celebratory cocktail gathering at Rideau Hall in Ottawa on 20 May 1986. It was a formal, protocolary affair (not really Eric's style) attended by cabinet ministers, senators, MPs, senior civil servants, TMCL's board of directors, and Molson family members. "I had to make a speech, so I was pretty nervous," Eric says. "Plus, we were

As part of the brewery's two-hundredth anniversary celebrations, Molson opened a new brewhouse and reception facilities in Montreal. At the inauguration on 4 June 1986, a commemorative plaque was unveiled by (*left to right*) Jacques Allard, president, Molson Breweries Quebec; Prime Minister Brian Mulroney; Quebec Premier Robert Bourassa; Eric Molson, deputy chairman of TMCL; and Montreal Mayor Jean Drapeau. Molson Coors Brewing Company collection.

all kind of distracted because there was a game going on!" That night, back at the Forum, the Montreal Canadiens were facing the Calgary Flames for game three of the Stanley Cup Finals. The first two playoff matches were held in Calgary, and the series was tied. As soon as the speeches were over, some of Eric's relatives piled into Hartland's car and drove back to Montreal. It was a wet, stormy night, but the Molson crew made it in time for the last period of the game. The Habs beat the Flames 5–3.

The Canadiens won the Stanley Cup that year, without a doubt the perfect culmination to Molson's 1986 bicentennial celebrations. It was the Habs' twenty-third NHL playoff trophy and, with it they overtook the New York Yankees as winners of the most championships by any North American professional sports team. It was a thrilling series. Patrick Roy, the twenty-year-old goalie from Quebec City, became a star

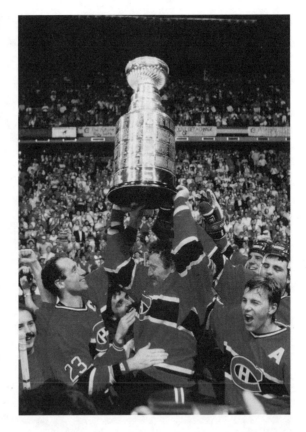

Larry Robinson and Bob Gainey hoist the Stanley Cup after beating the Calgary Flames on Saturday, 24 May 1986. Courtesy Club de hockey Canadien, Inc.

and earned the nickname "St Patrick." He was the youngest player ever to win the Conn Smythe Trophy as playoff MVP.

"I won the bet on the Stanley Cup that year," says Eric, smiling. "I still have the ten-dollar bill framed in my office. Guys like Big Jean [Béliveau], Toe Blake, Floyd Curry, Réjan Houle, Doug Kinnear [the team doctor], Stephen ... we would meet once a month to talk hockey and drink beer. We called them our 'Summit meetings.' Every year we'd bet on who would win the series, and the winner would have to buy the rounds of beer that day. I always picked the Montreal Canadiens. But when we won in '86, there was no way I was going to cash in that ten-dollar bill. Instead, I got all the Summit guys to sign it and kept it."

For Eric, and all the Molson employees, the Canadiens win was one of the emotional highlights of the anniversary year. Business woes could wait for another day.

Eric's 1986 playoff pool picks and the $10 he won as a result. He had both signed some of the Summit people (Stephen Molson, Hector Toe Blake, Red Carroll, Floyd Curry, Bill Powers, Zoltan Vallyi, Fred Steere, Rolland Péloquin, John Osterman and Jean Béliveau) and laminated. It has hung in Eric's office, behind his desk, since 1986. Photo by Michel de la Chenelière, 2017.

PART TWO

THE NEW
WORLD

6 Crossing the Threshold

Life is an ongoing process of choosing between safety (out of
fear and need for defence) and risk (for the sake of progress and
growth). Make the growth choice a dozen times a day.
ABRAHAM H. MASLOW (1908–1970)

Thursday morning, 8:50 a.m. I'm early. The front door is unlocked, so I
walk in. And that's when I hear the music, the beautiful piano playing.
I stop to listen. In all my years of knowing Eric, I've hardly heard him
play. I am enchanted by the sweet, wistful sound coming from the next
room. I know that if I make the slightest noise, he will stop.

I enter the living room quietly and sit down. My thoughts wander as
the melody flutters in the background. What else did Eric give up? He
stepped away from music, from the peace and quiet of a chemistry lab;
what else did he abnegate to fulfill the charge bestowed on him? Did
he *enjoy* becoming head of Molson? Was he a good leader? Can you
be a quiet, nice guy like Eric and still make it in business or as head of
a dynasty like Molson? Don't "blowhards" (Eric's term) and ruthless
egoists usually come out on top?

I just finished reading Walter Isaacson's book on Steve Jobs the night
before and was left with the impression that to be successful, you have
to be an intransigent asshole. And yet there is Eric – quiet, unassuming, selfless.

Daniel Colson, a one-time Molson board member, once told me,
"Eric is a very nice guy. He's a true gentleman and an honest guy, but believe me, you would never get him confused with General MacArthur."

Right, I think as the tuneful air persists, Eric is not arrogant and he doesn't bark orders like an army general. Does that mean he's not a good leader? He is certainly not aggressive, but he is assertive. He observes, listens, and evaluates – which can be misconstrued for in-action – and draws his own conclusions. He also has the courage to make tough decisions and act on them – but perhaps not always as quickly as some would want.

Eric interrupts my thoughts. "I didn't hear you come in."

"Sorry, the door was open. I let myself in."

"That's fine," he says, slipping off the piano bench.

"Eric, what do you think of the saying 'Nice guys finish last'?"

"That's a tough one." He smiles as he sits in the chair across from me. "Nice guys *do* often end up being losers unfortunately. It's tricky. Can you be a nice guy, do everything right, and still win? It happens. Not often, but it happens."

"What about you?"

"Well, I *think* I'm a nice guy. I *try* to be a nice guy. But when you have to get a job done, you have to get it done. For example, when a company keeps on a lot of extra people who are inferior, you have to take action and do the painful layoffs. Or when you have to share news with people that they don't want to hear, you just have to do it. It's not comfortable, but you grin and bear it and do it as humanely as possible. When you have to fire someone, for example, you never look forward to it, and you worry about it. It helps to be prepared. I always made notes. I would lay it out ahead of time so I'd get it right when I was face to face with them."

There is a strong resolve to Eric. Even if it's hard for him, when something falls in his realm of responsibility, he trudges on and gets it done.

"The key to delivering a difficult message is to be tough *and* humane at the same time," he concludes.

I realize that's how Eric dealt with all challenging situations – whether in relation to his sons, close collaborators, or even his mentors. Tough but humane.

By 1988, Eric could no longer hold back his exasperation. While Molson was stuck in a morass of internal bureaucracy, its competitors were taking bold actions. Elders IXL Ltd, the aggressive Australian conglomerate that owned Foster's Lager, for example, had just bought Carling O'Keefe Ltd, Canada's third-largest brewer. When the deal closed, a representative of Rothmans, the tobacco company that sold Carling, said, "It was just one of those lucky opportunities. It came along very, very quickly, and we jumped on it."

Meanwhile, whenever Eric raised the possibility of doing a deal with another brewer, he met with resistance. "I would visit breweries in different parts of the world and talk real turkey with the owners," he says. "Once, for instance, I was in Amsterdam with the Heineken people. They were ready to sell Amstel to us, so I was pretty excited. I came home and started working on a 'let's buy Amstel' proposal. But it wasn't long before I got shot down by management. They had no vision."

Eric worried that the inertia of the current administration was going to destroy the company. "We used the word 'clones' in those days," he says. "We kept replacing the CEO with a clone of the previous CEO, so we got nowhere. And if you keep doing that long enough, your company sinks down the tube, and you're finished. TMCL was run by financially oriented, bureaucratic people who weren't looking to expand the beer business; and beer was actually the only business we knew really well. Instead, they would do anything else – stationery stores, construction scaffolding – anything else, as long as the finance guys said it was good."

	1968	1978	1985
Chief executive officer (CEO)	Donald G. Willmot	James T. Black	John P. Rogers
Chairman of the board	Hartland de M. Molson	Donald G. Willmot	James T. Black
Honorary chairman of the board	Thomas H.P. Molson	Hartland de M. Molson	Donald G. Willmot

Between 1968 and 1985, the company had three CEOs: Bud Willmot, Jim Black, and John Rogers.

Willmot introduced Molson to diversification by buying companies in upward-trending industries. TMCL's strategist Sanjib Choudhuri explains. "Bud Willmot was the driving force behind the conglomerate. That was before my time. He started by buying up small businesses in growing industries – mainly in tertiary, industrial manufacturing – then built them up. And when he got the capacity to be strategic, he focused on the do-it-yourself and specialty chemicals industries. But once Bud stepped down as CEO, the businesses he had brought together remained the only pieces of TMCL. There was really no common thread to these pieces."

Jim Black, who succeeded Willmot as CEO in 1978, was from the more conservative, brewing side of TMCL. He focused on expanding the businesses acquired under Willmot's reign, while minimizing risks. Choudhuri says, "When Jim was CEO, the idea was that we still had to play the cards we had dealt ourselves under Bud Willmot. People were saying, 'We haven't played out all the expansion possibilities.' So Jim's time would have been continuing a legacy that Bud had left behind by expanding retail merchandising – Beaver Lumber – and growing specialty chemicals – Diversey." Then in 1985 Black became the company chairman, and John Rogers took over as CEO. According to Choudhuri, "John knew he was there because the family trusted him, so he just wanted to make sure TMCL didn't go off the rails under his watch. He kept the same approach as Jim Black had before him."

As Eric witnessed opportunities in the brewing world being passed up and the other businesses stagnate, he knew he had to act. Although he neither wanted nor felt qualified to take on the role of CEO, he was ready to work with his board to find the right man to replace John Rogers as the company's chief executive. But before this step could be taken, Jim Black had to be replaced. It was time for Eric to assume the chairmanship of the company.

"There was no one else around," he explains. "Tom was dead. Hartland had phased himself out earlier. My brother didn't want anything to do with it. And we owned the joint. We had the controlling shares. I had to do something."

Jim T. Black, chairman of the board and CEO of TMCL, and John P. Rogers, president and COO, 1984. Rogers would take over as CEO in 1985. Molson Coors Brewing Company collection.

Eric, however, dreaded the conversation with Black. "Jim was not only the chairman, he was my mentor. He always looked after me well. Over the years he made sure I was working in an area where I was developing, training with people who would help me grow, all while giving me a good idea of what was coming next."

What's more, Black had been loyal to Molson for many years. He had started at the company right after the Second World War in the accounting department, moved up through the ranks to become president and CEO, and after ten years in that role, transitioned to chairman of the board. Above all, Eric considered Black to be a gentleman. His grace and dignity was never more apparent than in spring 1988 when Eric met him at his office in Toronto to talk about his succession.

Eric sat down across from him and started in what he hoped was the right tone. "You know, Jim, Tom stuck me with control of this company when he passed away. You've helped me so much since I first started here twenty-eight years ago. You watched over my progress and gave me amazing opportunities. I will always be grateful to you for that. But there is so much happening right now, and I'm up to my neck in all this stuff. I've been deputy chairman now for five years. I think it's time for me to step in."

Black took a deep breath. "You're right, Eric. The time has come. You should take over as chairman. You're ready and you'll do just fine."

Eric was touched by Black's faith in him. He shook his mentor's hand.

"Jim was such a great guy. He was always there to help me. I was sorry to have to tell him that his time was over."

Jim Black graciously stepped aside, likely having anticipated and prepared for the inevitable transition.

Although Eric believed he was ready, he still felt some trepidation. It wasn't the "hard" responsibilities like risk oversight and strategic planning that worried him. He was more concerned about the "soft" issues like boardroom dynamics and personality conflicts.

CEO John Rogers made the official announcement at the annual shareholders' meeting in Toronto on 29 June 1988. Rogers first spoke of TMCL's performance in each of its four divisions (brewing, chemicals, retail merchandising, and sports) and then introduced Eric as the company's new chairman. Taking the podium, Eric thanked Black for his "enormous contribution to Molson's success in the past thirty-nine years" and spoke of the "honour and privilege" he felt in assuming his new role. He welcomed "the responsibility of stewardship as it applied to both the company and the family name," and made a pledge to two goals as chairman: "First, the name Molson will always be associated with the finest in the world: finest people, finest products, and finest services. And second, the Molson heritage of business integrity and vision, achievement of continued growth for our shareholders, and dedication to our communities and customers, will continue to be the standard by which we measure ourselves in the future."

Eric's confidence in assuming the role of chairman was bolstered by his sense of being well surrounded – not only by top-tier advisors and loyal employees but also by family. Stephen was named a director of TMCL at the same time as Eric became its chairman. Although Stephen was never interested in working at Molson, when Eric asked him to join the board, he said yes. "Stephen would have accepted out of a sense of duty," says Eric. "He would have done it because he's my brother, because we controlled the joint, and because we're in this together."

Eric and Stephen Molson working together in Eric's office, March 1987. Photo by Bob Fisher. Courtesy Club de hockey Canadien, Inc.

Eric's first move as TMCL's chairman was to find a new chief executive officer.

Unbeknownst to then CEO John Rogers, he formed a small search committee of board members and asked John B. Aird to head it up. A prominent Toronto lawyer, former lieutenant governor of Ontario, and onetime Liberal bagman, Aird had been a Molson director since 1985. He also had Eric's trust. The headhunting firm came up with a list of CEO candidates, but Aird was not satisfied. "There's no one really outstanding here, is there?" After a few seconds, he offered, "Have you considered Mickey Cohen?"

"The Reichmanns' guy who used to be in government?" asked Eric. "Do you really think there's a chance we can get him?"

At fifty-three, Marshall A. Cohen was already onto his third career: president and chief operating officer of Olympia & York Enterprises Ltd, the holding company of Toronto's Reichmann brothers. Like Aird, Cohen was a lawyer; his specialty was tax. He made a name for himself, however, in government, as deputy minister of three different departments: industry, energy, and finance. In the early 1980s, Cohen was one of Canada's most powerful civil servants.

"I knew him when I was in the Senate," Aird went on. "He's a guy who is used to managing across a wide range of activities. He has the kind of skill set TMCL needs right now."

"Okay. Let's add his name to the list and continue with the process," replied Eric.

The committee worked through a grid with the names of candidates down one side and the hiring criteria across the top. The scientist in Eric appreciated the methodic approach. At the end of the process, the name that came out with the most check marks was Cohen's.

Mickey Cohen was nothing like Molson's previous CEOs, who had been family members, loyal company men promoted from within, or shareholders of the business like Bud Willmot. Cohen was from the outside. Gregarious and outgoing, he was polished, charming, and incredibly well connected. His impressive intellect was matched by his drive and personal ambition. At over six feet tall, he was a big man. "Larger than life" was how some people described him.

His detractors, on the other hand, were quick to point out that he could be "obnoxious," "full of himself," and "like Teflon, immune to criticism." Even Marc Lalonde, who was Cohen's boss first as Canada's minister of energy and then as finance minister, once said (to the *Toronto Star*, on 12 November 1989) of his deputy minister that he was "like an eel. You can't grab him. He always slips between your fingers." An example of Cohen's elusiveness transpired at the end of his time in public service. It was suggested that, before leaving to join Olympia & York, he manoeuvred to get significant tax breaks for the Reichmanns when they purchased Gulf Canada Corp. Cohen scoffed at the insinuation. He told reporters that his department was involved in the deal "both above me and below me," but that he wasn't personally implicated in it. Like Teflon.

In 1988, Eric ignored the naysayers. "I was very excited about hiring Mickey. He ran the country's economy for a while and did it for *both* parties – the Liberals *and* the Conservatives!" Indeed, Cohen worked under four Canadian prime ministers: two Liberals (Trudeau and Turner) and two Progressive Conservatives (Clark and Mulroney). Eric liked Cohen's versatility and ability to navigate in different political waters. And despite his years in government, he was not a typical bureaucrat. He had the reputation of expediting files and getting things done. Eric felt his appointment would be a move away from the cautious, unadventurous leadership style of TMCL's recent chiefs to one that was more visionary and action-packed.

The TMCL search committee asked to interview Cohen. The recruiter contacted the Olympia & York executive, and the response was favourable. Cohen was intrigued. He says, "I knew the Reichmanns situation wasn't going to be long term for me. I wasn't a member of the family and I didn't really have a *job* job there. So when the opportunity for a *real* CEO job came along at TMCL – not a COO job (which is what I was at Olympia & York) – a real CEO job of a great Canadian institution, I couldn't pass it up."

Before accepting the board's invitation, however, Cohen made his own request. He wanted to meet Eric in a more informal setting. "There is too much chemistry in this stuff," he told Molson's headhunter. "I want to know who I'm dealing with."

"Fine, but it can't be in public," the recruiter said. "We need to keep this confidential."

"Of course. Why don't you have Eric come over to my house for a drink?"

At 7 p.m., Eric Molson rang the doorbell of Mickey Cohen's home on Roxborough Drive in the heart of Toronto's affluent Rosedale neighbourhood. Mickey greeted Eric at the door, his warm smile welcoming. As much as Eric was drawn to his affable host, he kept his usual subdued demeanour. Cohen was thrown off. He expected the controlling shareholder of a major public corporation like TMCL to be dynamic and outspoken – someone more like him.

They sat down, and Cohen offered Eric a drink.

"I'll have a beer," said Eric.

Cohen panicked, saying to himself, "Crap, what was I thinking? Of course Eric Molson would ask for a beer. I don't know if we have one in the house!"

He went into the kitchen and told his butler, Michael, "I need beer. Go to the store, do something … I need a beer for our guest. Do we have any?"

Michael remained calm. "Of course you do. Your children have beer hidden under their beds."

"Okay, Michael, quick! I want it on a tray, in a tall, frosted glass," Cohen instructed. "I'm trying to impress here!"

About ten minutes later, Michael appeared in the living room with a silver tray, a chilled glass, and a bottle of Labatt's *Blue*.

Eric looked at the Labatt bottle, stony-faced.

For once, Cohen was at a loss for words. He thought, if we get through the next five minutes, this is going to be fine.

"Eric was terrific," Cohen recalls. "I apologized over and over. He told me not to worry about it and never mentioned it again … I'm not sure if he actually drank the beer, though."

🍁

After meeting with Eric, Cohen was introduced to the other directors of TMCL and to some Molson family members.

Jane expressed misgivings. "I just didn't take to Mickey Cohen as a person. There's no doubt he's very clever, but he didn't seem trustworthy. The whole thing made me nervous."

Stephen shared similar reservations. "Eric, I'm not sure Cohen is a good fit for us."

"I know he's not what we're used to at the brewery," Eric argued, "but we need a guy like him. This company needs a powerful deal-maker who can shake things up right now."

Cohen's big, brash personality didn't appeal to Eric's sisters either. "Don't you think he's a little too flashy for us?" Cynthia asked.

Despite these apprehensions, Eric gave Mickey his support. Sanjib Choudhuri, TMCL's senior vice-president of corporate development and strategic planning, explains it this way: "Mickey was a sophisticated guy with great credentials. Not only was he the federal government guy but he was the right-hand man for the Reichmanns – and they were doing all those *deals*! That's what got Eric. Eric wanted a guy who could do deals. The only problem is that I don't think the Reichmanns relied on Mickey to negotiate their deals. I think they were doing that themselves. That's a personal view. And the interesting thing is that – unlike Bud Willmot, unlike the Reichmanns, and unlike the Molsons – I don't think Mickey ever spent a penny of his own money investing in any of those businesses. So he always dealt in other people's money."

Cohen's candidacy went to the TMCL board, and the directors fully endorsed the search committee's recommendation. Mickey Cohen was unanimously approved as the company's new CEO.

Before he could start, however, John Rogers had to go.

In some ways, this step was even harder on Eric than when he told Jim Black he was replacing him. It's not that he cared more about one man or the other. It was just that Black had probably anticipated that Eric would take over as chairman one day, whereas Rogers would be taken by surprise. And Eric felt a strong kinship with Rogers. He had been a faithful Molson employee for forty-two years, almost part of the family. Together they had turned around the Quebec division in the early 1970s; Rogers succeeded Eric as president of the Ontario brewery in 1975, and they both went from working in the beer business (which they loved) to managing a conglomerate (which they didn't). But business was business, and the board was unanimous. Rogers's time was up.

With resolve but a heavy heart, Eric endorsed the decision. "John was a good man," he says. "In a way, we shafted him by having an organization that required a guy who was only good at finance at the top. That wasn't John. We should have kept the brewery separate from the conglomerate. Then we would have had two companies, one run by a solid beer man like Rogers, and a financial guy doing the conglomerate." But that wasn't the structure of TMCL in 1988, and, as Eric says, "We had to get on with the show."

As chairman, Eric should have been the one to tell Rogers. "But I got a pass on that one. The board felt that it was too early in my mandate as chairman to do it, so two senior directors were chosen to break the news to John." The task went to directors John Aird and Peter Gordon.

When they left Rogers's office, Eric stepped in to see how he was doing. "It was an awful scene. John had just learned he would no longer be our CEO. I felt terrible. He was distraught; he was crying. It was very hard ... and I couldn't do much to help him."

Eric vowed to himself never again to sidestep a difficult conversation. It was his responsibility, and if he did it himself, he could at least better manage the message. "I will be prepared and will communicate the tough messages with as much compassion as possible – otherwise, it can just become brutality."

Rogers now acknowledges that when he took over as CEO after Black, it was "a giant step for me. All of a sudden, I had all these other companies reporting to me that I knew nothing about. I had every confidence in my own ability in the brewing side, but I knew nothing about the other businesses. *And* finance was not my forte. Whatever a company does, finance is the common thread across every organization. It's especially important in a conglomerate, and that was not my strength."

Publicly, Molson announced that Rogers was "voluntarily stepping aside to become the company's deputy chairman," while Mickey Cohen took over as CEO. In theory, he was to take over the role freed up by Eric a few months earlier when he became chairman of the board. The reality of it was somewhat different. "I was named deputy chairman, which allowed me to have a cup of coffee on the house, but not much else," Rogers says. "Shortly after Mickey Cohen came on board, I was gone. I think I lasted one meeting with him." Rogers remained an honorary director of Molson until 2002.

🍁

The day after TMCL announced its new CEO, it was all over the papers. Headlines on 18 October 1988 read: "Molson Recruits President from Olympia & York"; "Mickey Cohen Leaves O & Y to Run Molson Co."; "Former Mandarin Departs Reichmann Empire to Run Brewer." According to multiple media profiles, TMCL had nabbed an "exceptional strategist," a "visionary," a man "who would lead the company into the 21st century" and do it with great élan. Still, people were surprised by Cohen's move.

Mickey Cohen, president and CEO of TMCL, with Eric Molson, chairman of the board of TMCL, 1989. Molson Coors Brewing Company collection.

"I had lot of authority here [at Olympia & York], but I've been a deputy one way or another for a long time," Cohen explained. "It was time to stop being a deputy and be a CEO."

Moreover, the nature of the work was similar. As he had at Olympia & York, Cohen would oversee a portfolio of businesses – brewing, chemical specialties, retail merchandising, and sports and entertainment. With revenues of $2.4 billion and profits of $79 million, it was a smaller conglomerate than O&Y, but that didn't matter. The important thing for Cohen was that he was now completely in charge. He was CEO, and Eric would give him far more leeway than he ever had with the ubiquitous Reichmanns.

From the start, Eric told Cohen, "I believe in letting people do their jobs." He was chairman and controlling shareholder, but he didn't rule with a heavy hand. Eric was "CEO-centric" (as he called it), a principle he applied throughout his career but which also had its limits. Certain circumstances warranted him to intervene. The struggle was to know when and to what extent to do so.

When Cohen joined TMCL, Eric was keen to let him take control. "Mickey was an exciting, strategic planner. He also had the reputation of being a good deal-maker, and that's what we needed. When he came in, we had been trying to buy Carling O'Keefe from Elders for months and getting nowhere. We needed someone like Mickey to shake things up and get deals done."

Perhaps Eric saw in Cohen traits he felt he lacked personally. Maybe that's why he was so high on him. Could it be that he thought a business leader needed these characteristics in order to be successful?

The differences between the two men ran deep. Whereas Eric knew he was good at one thing (beer), Cohen thought of himself "a professional manager" who could tackle almost all things. "I'm a generalist," explains Cohen. "I didn't know anything about brewing; I didn't know anything about small hardware stores; I didn't know anything about specialty chemicals businesses. And, least of all, I knew nothing about running a hockey team. But that's why they hired me: I'm an executive who can handle a variety of businesses.

"As for Eric," he continues, "I think he would have been very happy if he could have gone back into the brewery and been a brewer. But he left that, and he ended up in this big administrative morass of a public company, securities, boards, and businesses. These were all things he understood, but he never really cared for … His commitment was to beer. That's where his questions went. At every board meeting, that's what he wanted to talk about."

Mickey didn't even *like* beer. A few days after becoming head of Molson, he admitted, "I'm not much of a beer drinker … I like wine, actually."

"Wine?" Eric was incredulous. Had this guy forgotten he'd just been hired to run a brewery?

Eric and Mickey Cohen just weren't on the same wavelength. While Eric shunned the public light, Cohen embraced it. He mugged for the media smoking cigars and socialized in elite-filled gatherings. ("Blowhards are not my thing," says Eric.) He got himself a corporate jet – something Eric was adamantly against but could not convince his fellow board members to veto. ("We sell beer, not champagne!" he urged in vain.) Cohen joined the World Economic Forum at Davos, where top leaders in business, politics, and economics meet annually to discuss global issues. "Mickey did things like Davos because he wanted to be Mr Big," says Eric. "I never went close to Davos, because it's not my style and I had no business to conduct there. If it would have been good for the brewery, then I would have done it, but that wasn't the case."

As a new CEO, Cohen moved TMCL's head office from the outskirts of Toronto into the recently built Napoleon red granite Scotia Plaza on King Street, in the core of the financial district. He wanted to be "where the action was," and that didn't mean on the factory floor, as it did to Eric. Cohen told reporters, "I'm not going to visit the breweries or the factories much. What would I tell them? To keep the machines clean? I'm in New York, in London, in places where things are happening."

Mickey and his second wife, Judi Loeb Cohen, were dubbed a "power couple." Both enjoyed the prestige that came with the presidency of TMCL and regularly organized lavish gatherings for the *crème de la crème* of the Canadian business community. On one occasion, they flew everyone down to Boca Raton in Florida for a weekend of golf and entertainment. For the Saturday-night party, guests were summoned up the grand staircase to the main ballroom: "Dinner is served." The doors opened on cue. The band played. The flower-laden tables shimmered in candlelight. In the middle of it all stood Mickey and Judi, ready to greet their guests.

"The stories inside and out of Molson about the 'imperial reign' of Mickey Cohen are legion," says Jim Arnett, the corporate lawyer who would later become CEO of Molson. "He was out there trying to make a name for himself. That event at Boca Raton was a big deal. Everyone talked about it. He was doing all this kind of stuff. It's hard to imagine that it was helpful in any way in terms of his relationship with Eric."

It's true that Eric did not care for all that. He was, however, eager to get on with business, and he expected Cohen to stir things up and to do it fast.

✦

The year before Cohen's arrival, John Rogers had been approached by John Elliott, the forty-six-year-old chairman and CEO of Elders IXL Ltd, to do a deal with Molson Breweries in Canada. Elders IXL, the Australian conglomerate that owned Foster's, had just acquired Carling O'Keefe, and Elliott wanted to merge his stake in Carling with TMCL's brewing division to take control of the profitable Canadian beer market.

Rogers said that TMCL would only consider a deal with Elders IXL if Molson kept control of the merged Molson-Carling entity. He argued that Molson Breweries of Canada was far more profitable than Carling O'Keefe (it had $1.5 billion in revenue and $96 million in profit, versus Carling's $950 million sales and profit of $22 million) and had a much bigger market share (33 per cent versus Carling's 22 per cent).

The ambitious Elliott and his Elders IXL executives, however, didn't budge. "We're not *just* Carling," they argued. "We're Foster's. We're all over the world, and we're far more efficient than Molson. We're the ones who can take this somewhere, so *we* should be in control."

Back and forth the discussions went. TMCL and Elders IXL spent over a year at loggerheads. The debate was not about valuation; money was secondary. It was about control, and they'd reached a stalemate.

Cohen's first task as TMCL's CEO was to revive negotiations. "The deal was almost dead when I got there," he says. "If I hadn't arrived, it would have died. Why? Because I wasn't a brewer. I was running TMCL, the parent company of Molson. So for me it wasn't a blow if I didn't control the brewery. My predecessor was a brewer, so if he'd stayed in charge, the deal wouldn't have happened, and the debate would have gone on and on. Someone just had to step away. It was easy for me to step away. There was no part of my ego or reputation tied up in it."

Also, Cohen knew John Elliott from his Reichmann days when O&Y was competing with Elders IXL in trying to take over Hiram Walker's liquor operations. "So I had dealt with John Elliott before," says Cohen. "I had gotten to know him, and he was a wild character … a real Australian gunslinger."

With this insight, Cohen knew the merger with Carling would never get done if Molson insisted on keeping control of Molson-Carling. "I looked at the situation and I talked with John Elliott," says Cohen. "I also spoke with his people." The only way the Australians would agree to merge their Carling asset with Molson was if they kept 50 per cent control of the merged Canadian brewery.

Cohen thought this would be a problem for his chairman. "Eric was very sensitive about this issue of control. It's natural. It's his heritage. Think about it: when Eric comes down the stairs in the morning, he has all these portraits of ancestors staring down at him, and they're all waving their fingers at him as he walks by, saying, 'Don't screw up! We've been here for two hundred years, and we should be here for another two hundred.'"

Mickey Cohen at a press conference with Australian partner John Elliott of Elders IXL. After the transaction with Elliott in 1989, TMCL was left with only 50 per cent ownership of Molson Breweries. The Canadian Press, staff.

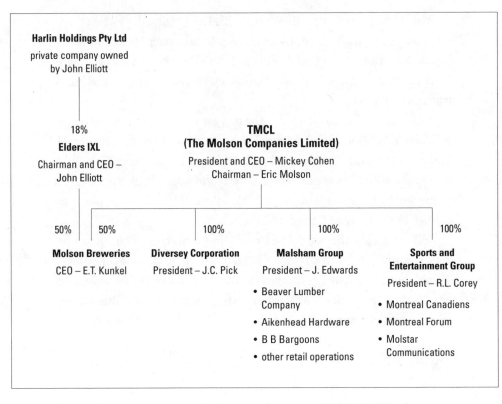

Harlin Holdings Pty Ltd
private company owned
by John Elliott

18%
Elders IXL
Chairman and CEO –
John Elliott

**TMCL
(The Molson Companies Limited)**
President and CEO – Mickey Cohen
Chairman – Eric Molson

50% 50% 100% 100% 100%

Molson Breweries
CEO – E.T. Kunkel

Diversey Corporation
President – J.C. Pick

Malsham Group
President – J. Edwards

• Beaver Lumber
  Company
• Aikenhead Hardware
• B B Bargoons
• other retail operations

**Sports and
Entertainment Group**
President – R.L. Corey

• Montreal Canadiens
• Montreal Forum
• Molstar
  Communications

Corporate diagram illustrating the structure of TMCL as of 31 March 1990, after
the merger of Molson Breweries of Canada Ltd and Carling O'Keefe Breweries of
Canada Ltd was approved by the Competition Bureau on 6 July 1989.

Despite the resistance he anticipated from Eric, Cohen went back to
the TMCL board with the only arrangement he believed could work: a
50–50 alliance with the Australians. "If you want the Molson-Carling
deal," he told the directors around the table, "the price you have to pay
is a 50–50 split in control [with Elders IXL]. We have to be equal partners. It's like we're getting married and there's no prenup."

Eric took a deep breath. Give up control of the brewery? Under his
watch? What would Tom say?

*Well, things have changed. Molson is not just a brewery any more, it's
a conglomerate, and that was Hartland's strategy. We are now TMCL,
and the brewery is just one of our assets – and not even the one with the
most promising future, given the maturity of the Canadian beer market.*

So if going to 50–50 with Elders is how we'll create opportunities for the company, for our employees, and for our shareholders, we have to do it. We need to move forward.

The more he thought about it, the firmer Eric's resolve became. He knew the risks. Molson Breweries would not survive the new era of deregulation and globalization if it didn't make a bold move. Although the beer industry had recently won a special exemption from the Canada–US Free Trade Agreement, it was temporary. Soon enough Canadian brewers would have to face more efficient and cheaper foreign competitors head on. Eric agreed with Cohen's prediction: "Before the year 2000, there's going to be a lot more beer coming into this country, and we have to get ready for that."

Eric and the other directors of TMCL approved the deal.

On Wednesday, 18 January 1989, Cohen announced that Molson Breweries and Carling O'Keefe were joining forces in a $1.6 billion merger. The new entity, equally owned by TMCL and Elders IXL, would be Canada's largest brewery, with an unprecedented 55 per cent market share. (In a surprising decision six months later, Canada's Bureau of Competition approved the merger without alteration, even though it essentially created a duopoly.) They named the new company Molson Breweries.

❧

On the day of the January 1989 announcement, John Elliott of Elders IXL set the tone. "The Canadian brewing industry is one of the most inefficient in the world. There is not one plant in Canada that is up to the minimum efficiency requirements to compete against the US."

Elliott appointed collaborator Edward T. Kunkel, a New Zealand native and a twenty-five-year beer industry veteran, to run Molson Breweries. (Mickey Cohen did not object.) Elliott's instructions were clear: Get the biggest synergies out of the deal in order to drive up the stock price.

Ted Kunkel executed. He closed seven of the sixteen breweries across Canada and cut nearly 1,400 jobs.

"It was tough. We had to close all these breweries, because after the merger we basically ended up with two in each province," says Eric. "At least we had Kunkel. He was a skilled brewer and a good manager. The brewing operations ended up being in good hands."

Patrick L. Kelley, senior vice-president of strategy at Molson's brewing division, was involved with the deal and had a different perspective on the new style of management at Molson Breweries. "After the merger, the Australians took over the brewery. They held most of the senior positions, and their approach was very downward directing. There was no talking to them; they weren't listening. Elliott and Kunkel were far more interested in giving orders."

Although the transition to the new leadership style was difficult for many Molson employees, the stock market lapped it up. TMCL's common stock bounced by more than $4 to the $32 range on the news of the merger and continued to inch up, peaking at $36.50 in May 1989.

"So Cohen did the merger with the Australians, and with that he managed to generate all this cash for TMCL," says Eric. "I think it was around $600 million. I don't remember how he did it, but he had all these sophisticated advisor-types around him, and through some financial engineering, they came up with $600 million."

This group of advisors was referred to by TMCL executives as Mickey's "shadow team." They counselled him on matters like potential acquisitions, mergers, and refinancings. They were financial types from Lazard Brothers and prominent corporate lawyers from firms such as Osler's – not Eric's coterie.

Here is a simplified explanation of how they came up with the $600 million for TMCL. At the time of the Molson-Carling merger, one estimate had the Molson brewing assets valued at $1 billion and Carling's at $600 million. To even out the $400 million difference and get to a 50–50 merger, Cohen's shadow team put in place a creative mechanism that generated twice that amount, while mitigating the tax consequences for both sides:

1 The newly created, merged Molson Breweries borrowed $400 million.

2 This amount was given to TMCL, which owned 50 per cent of the new brewery.

3 Molson Breweries then borrowed an additional $400 million. (It had enough cash to afford the interest on that kind of debt.)

4 This second loan was split between the two owners: $200 million to Elders IXL and $200 million to TMCL.

The end result was that TMCL got $600 million and Elders IXL $200 million – by all accounts a very clever scheme.

There were, however, strings attached. "In order to get this whole thing done, I had to promise that we would make a small investment in John Elliott's company," says Cohen. "That was part of the price of doing a deal with him." So TMCL invested about $134 million in Harlin Holdings Pty Ltd, the private company owned by Elliot. Harlin Holdings already had an 18 per cent stake in Elders IXL, but Elliott was trying to get enough capital to mount a takeover bid for the entire company.

Investing in a vehicle that aimed to buy Australia's second-largest enterprise seemed like a good investment. Unfortunately, the whole thing fell apart a little over a year later. Elliott's risky manoeuvres drove Elders IXL to the brink of bankruptcy. As a result, the Australian conglomerate sold all its assets, save for those in beer, and changed its name to Foster's Brewing Group Ltd. Elliott was forced to resign as chairman and CEO, and Harlin Holdings collapsed. By April 1991, TMCL's entire investment in Elliott's private company was written off, swallowing up most of TMCL's operating profit that year. Its bottom line in 1991 was an after-tax loss of $38.7 million, compared to a profit of $117.9 million a year earlier.

Eric was not impressed. Not only had they lost money but the very nature of the arrangements made him uncomfortable. "They were doing these financial gimmicks back then, with all these pieces of paper flying around. Mickey loved that kind of stuff. I didn't. He got along with Elliott and those guys. He loved their yachts, their houses in London … he told me about meetings he had with them on the French Riviera … not my style."

Although some of Cohen's schemes nettled Eric, he recognized that his CEO's shrewdness served the company well at times. For example, to navigate the occasional rough waters between shareholders with divergent interests, Cohen was able to find elegant solutions that worked for all.

Cohen explains: "What was most important to Eric and the Molson family was the beer business. The family was not money-driven. They were not lavish livers. Their concern was their heritage, their reputation, and the long-term success of the brewing business. That's what mattered to Eric ... which is not necessarily what mattered to the rest of the shareholders. Which is normal. There are some shareholders who care for the long run, and some which are just 'here today and gone tomorrow.' They only care about making a quick buck. If they buy the share at $40 and sell it at $60 twenty days later, they're thrilled! There are all kinds of extremes, and you have to find your way through it."

These differences were even more marked in companies like TMCL that had a dual-class share structure: non-voting class A shares held by the public, and voting class B shares, primarily owned by the family. When he started as CEO, Cohen knew that this dual-class structure somewhat hampered his ability to raise money in capital markets. Investors wanted equal treatment. In the event of a takeover, for example, they wanted to get the same premium that would go to the owners of the voting shares; otherwise they'd invest their money elsewhere. One option was to get rid of the two classes of shares outright.

But Cohen knew that Eric would never agree to that. He found another angle. Why not add a "coattail" provision to TMCL's class B shares? That way, if there was a change of control, holders of all classes of shares would get the same offer. Coattails were already obligatory for multiple-voting share companies listed after 1987, and although TMCL was exempt, Cohen recommended that it abide by that rule.

Eric agreed. "Let's do it." A clause to ensure that all shareholders, As and Bs, got the same upside if TMCL changed hands was consistent with Eric's values. In fact, he insisted, "If we don't share the benefits of control with all our shareholders, then we're not exercising our responsibilities wisely."

In July 1990, Cohen raised almost $300 million through a public of-
fering of TMCL shares and debentures. People inside and out of Molson (including Eric) expected him to use the money to expand the
company's brewing interests internationally. Different options circu-
lated: increase TMCL's stake in Harlin Holdings (this was before the
company went bust); take a direct stake in Foster's (Harlin's main asset
through Elders IXL); or even do something completely different and
invest in a brewery like Pilsner Urquell of Czechoslovakia. Cohen,
however, had another plan. He surprised everyone by using the cash to
expand TMCL's chemicals division.

TMCL was invested in the sanitizing and cleaning chemicals business through Diversey Corp. Diversey turned a profit of about $55
million on sales of $870 million, ran operations in thirty-five differ-
ent countries, employed over 6,600 people, and served clients such as
Coca-Cola Co. and H.J. Heinz Co. globally. Its primary weakness was
the United States.

"It was a great business, with great potential and a global reach,"
says Cohen. "From my point of view, this business could have been
as instrumental as the brewery for the overall success of TMCL ... Intellectually, it had all the opportunity to be a great, global company.
It was really well positioned everywhere in the world, except in the
United States. Ecolab owned the United States. We concluded that we
couldn't grow our business without getting a huge foothold in the
American market."

Cohen's solution to fill that gap was DuBois Chemicals Inc., the US
second-ranked producer of cleaners. So on 25 February 1991, he announced that TMCL was buying Dubois for $284 million, telling repor-
ters that the deal would "enhance Diversey's position as a world market
leader." His right-hand man and TMCL spokesperson, Hershell Ezrin,
underlined the importance of the acquisition: "We will be spending
a fair amount of management time and attention, as well as a large
amount of money, on this project."

Truer words could not have been spoken. Cohen and his team
ended up being consumed by Diversey. The deal with DuBois may
have made sense "intellectually," as Cohen said, but when it came to its

execution, it became a bottomless pit, eating up resources. The cultural chasm between DuBois and Diversey was too wide to bridge.

✤

"Was that Mickey I saw near the players' locker room between the second and third periods?" Jane asked as she and Eric got into a taxi outside the Forum after a Habs game.

"Yes. He was there to see Dr Lenczner."

"Really? He flew in from Toronto just for a check-up?"

Eric shrugged. "I don't know." He gave the cab driver their home address and stared out the window.

Mickey is always doing things for himself on the side. He just took the company jet to Montreal, went to the Forum, had the team's orthopaedic surgeon check his knee, and flew back to Toronto! He didn't even stay to the end of the third period! Imagine the value of that knee to the company … three hours of flying time at $3,500/hour to get his knee looked at.

Eric was increasingly unhappy with Cohen, thinking that he was taking advantage of his position. He also felt that his CEO was trying to elbow him out. "Every year Mickey would say the same thing to me: 'Eric, do you still want to stay on as chairman of the board?' You see, Mickey didn't want me around. He wanted to become chairman himself. He wanted to be CEO *and* chairman, just like the other big shots."

Jane noticed it as well. "Mickey had all his cronies around him and was trying to push Eric aside … It's true that Eric doesn't interfere, and he likes people to have the space they need to make their own decisions, but in this case, it looked like he was being brushed off."

Even people outside the company noticed. Daniel Colson, a Montreal lawyer and businessman who later became a Molson board member, says, "Mickey Cohen ran the company like it was his own. He basically told Eric what to do, what not to do, when to show up, when not to show up. It was a joke. He's the one that convinced Eric to grow Diversey in the US, and in the end that proved to be a disaster."

Cohen himself admits there were some people who probably thought he was pushing Eric to the side. "And I probably was. I was CEO. Eric was not hands-on running the company. Properly so – he was chairman. I used to call him to tell him what was going on, but he was hands-off, like a proper chairman ... until it got to the brewery. That's when Eric would get proactive."

And he did. He started noticing how profits from the beer business were increasingly being used to feed the other divisions of TMCL – an "asset-stripping operation," according to Pat Kelley. "Mickey Cohen stripped cash out of the brewery, and instead of ploughing it back into Molson Breweries for further international acquisitions, he used it to expand other areas of the conglomerate."

The brewery was still the company's most profitable subsidiary, but in September 1991, for the first time, the chemical business had a bigger top line than beer. In his notebook, Eric compared results of the two divisions for the first six months of 1991.

	Beer	Diversey	TMCL Total
Revenue	$474.9 million	$610.7 million	$1.5 billion
Profit	$110.7 million	$32.1 million	$148.1 million

Beneath the table, in his small neat script, Eric noted: "Beer is almost 75 per cent of company's profits ... but management continues to focus on the rest of TMCL. Change is needed."

As in the past, Eric decided to consult an advisor to substantiate his apprehensions and think through the different angles of the situation. He felt cut off from his own CEO and people within the company, so he opted to go outside. Who could he use? "Silver fox" Benny Parsons didn't have the right profile. Eric needed someone more connected to the ins and outs of TMCL's business. Someone he could trust (of course), but someone who knew more about the company's strategy and finances. He turned to Pat Kelley.

Kelley no longer worked at Molson. He had resigned soon after the merger with Carling O'Keefe and was now with Ernst & Young. Still, he kept in touch with Eric; the two men had developed a close relationship. They occasionally met after work at McKibbin's Pub on Bishop Street. Over a beer, they'd discuss the latest brewing techniques, global alliances shaping the industry, and potential international brewers with whom Molson could partner. Theirs was a bond based on beer, brewing, and mutual respect.

"Every week Pat Kelley would analyze these industry reports and update me on what was going on," Eric says. "He was very good ... He knew what the brewers around the world were up to. We visited a number of them together over the years."

One afternoon in May 1992, in Toronto at TMCL's head office, Eric called Kelley and asked to meet him after work. "I think we've done the wrong thing," he said. "I think this whole diversification strategy has been a mistake. We need to find a way to get back to beer."

Kelley thought Eric was probably right. "But how are you going to go about it?"

"I haven't spoken to Mickey and his team yet, but they're not interested. Every time I bring up the possibility of doing a deal in beer, they say we can't afford it or something. Yet they keep pouring money into Diversey. It looks like all the profits from beer are being siphoned into those other TMCL businesses ... If we keep going this way, we're going to lose it all."

"Do you have facts to back that up?"

"That's part of the problem. I don't trust their numbers." Eric paused to sip his beer. "You know what's worse? We're starting to miss the boat."

Consolidation was reshaping the brewing world. Eric worried that if Molson Breweries did not grow, it would be taken over. He kept looking at what Heineken had accomplished over the years, ballooning from a 3 per cent market share in Europe in the early 1970s to become the continent's number-one brewer twenty years later, and he couldn't help but think of all the opportunities Molson had missed. "Do you know how Freddy Heineken did it? He bought up all those small breweries around Europe, the same ones we looked at for Molson but the bureaucrats in charge decided to pass on."

In addition to missing out on buying opportunities, Eric bemoaned that TMCL management didn't put enough "muscle" behind Molson beer brands. The US experience was a good example. By the mid-1980s, Molson had lost its position as the number-two imported beer brand in the United States to Corona. "That's because we were busy using TMCL's money for everything else but beer. We even invested in B B Bargoons, a home-decorating business! What a waste."

"Why don't we put together a team to go through the finances and check all this out?" said Kelley. "I could ask one of my partners at Ernst & Young to help us."

Eric agreed. A few weeks later, he organized a meeting at the British-style Mount Royal Club on Montreal's Sherbrooke Street, known for privacy and discretion. Kelley arrived with Bob Long, a partner at Ernst & Young, and Herb Stoneham, a human-resources professional from TMCL whom they all trusted. Together they came up with a plan: Eric would ask Mickey for full disclosure on TMCL's operations and, in parallel, Kelley and his small team would run their own financial analysis based on available information.

From the start, Eric met with a wall of resistance. Cohen didn't respond to his request for more details on the bottom line. Instead, he sent Barry Joslin, vice-president of corporate affairs, to meet with him. Eric sensed that Joslin was there to appease him and throw him off his pursuit for information.

Kelley remembers Eric's reaction. "When you say no to Eric, he digs his heels in. He's actually quite stubborn when he makes up his mind about something. I thought it was a huge tactical error on Mickey's part to send somebody down to Montreal to essentially pat Eric on the head and tell him, 'We'll give you the information when we're ready.' Eric was not impressed."

🍁

On 17 December 1992, Eric met his brother Stephen and Kelley for lunch at the InterContinental Hotel near the brewery in Old Montreal. He waited while the club sandwiches and Export Ales were served. "Okay, Pat," he said, "tell us what you've found."

Kelley pulled out his report and started going over the numbers. "As you can see, it's not good. Diversey is bleeding cash, and if it continues this way, the whole company is going to go down with it."

The three men looked at each other in silence.

"That's it," said Eric. "We have to move. We need to get back to beer."

Stephen nodded.

"Beer is our heritage. It's our strongest asset," Eric continued. "Forget all the other crap. It's time for Molson to get back to beer. It's the only business we know well."

"All right! Let's put together a plan," said Kelley, invigorated by Eric's resolve.

"Simple," said Eric. "We need to do four things. One, get back control of the brewery – no more 50–50 with anyone. Two, stop the bleeding – we need to get rid of all the non-brewing assets … well, everything except for hockey, maybe. Three, we have to pursue an international strategy to grow our beer business. And four, we need to bring our head office back to Montreal."

Kelley wrote down the points. "We have our work cut out for us."

"But it's doable," said Eric. He raised his glass of Export and proposed a toast. "To going back to beer."

"To back to beer," Stephen and Kelly echoed, clinking glasses.

The "inside takeover" of TMCL was launched. Eric and his allies were taking Molson back. Of course, plans and actions are very different things. Plans, like yeast, take time to yield results.

7 Navigating the Road of Trials

There will always be rocks in the road ahead of us. They will be
stumbling blocks or stepping stones; it all depends on how you
use them.

Friedrich W. Nietzsche (1844–1900)

A deep freeze has conquered Toronto. It's 6:20 p.m., 26 February 2015,
and I think I'll lose an extremity to frostbite if I stay outside a minute
longer. It's not until I get to the twenty-third floor of the Ernst & Young
Tower in the Toronto-Dominion Centre that I feel the blood starting
to flow back to my fingertips.

I am here to audit a lecture by Mickey Cohen to law and MBA students as part of their course, "The Art of the Deal." A few months earlier, he suggested I sit in on the class (I may have inadvertently invited
myself), and I jumped on the opportunity. He was going to review
his tenure as Molson's CEO, and I was curious to hear how he would
present the story.

What facts would he emphasize? What deals would he focus on?
What mistakes would he admit to? One thing that became apparent to
me as I researched Eric's journey is that people build their own narra-
tives. The same set of circumstances, depending on perspective, results
in vastly different tales. I knew this before, but seeing it "live" with
every interview is fascinating to me.

There is a bustle and chatter around me in the lecture room as the
students greet each other and settle into their places. Once Cohen is
introduced, he takes off his jacket on which the Order of Canada is

pinned and leans on the lectern. He has gained weight since his early days at TMCL, and his hair is now fully white, but overall he looks good.

"Tonight, we're going to talk about my decade at Molson and the many deals I did during that time," he says in a low, throaty voice. "One of the reasons I wanted to do this lecture is that I realize that it's easy to get bogged down in all the technical stuff, all the rules and regulations of deal-making and lose track of the reality of what deals are really all about. And it's easy to come away from this class thinking that all deals are done by egomaniacs. Some deals are, but not all deals are done for people's egos. Nor should any of them be done for that reason. So, the first thing I want to drive home is that strategy should be what drives a deal." Cohen then describes the multiple phases of his career and the numerous transactions he did as a lawyer, civil servant, CEO, and corporate director. I can't help but speculate about how much ego played a role in his own wheeling and dealing over the years.

"Do you know what's the most important thing in deal-making?"

He answers his own question: "People. We have a tendency to think only about the numbers when we talk about deals. And while numbers and price are terribly important, *people* are far more important. The people you're going to exchange with and connect with as you do these transactions are key … Also, getting a deal done doesn't mean winning everything. People who try to win it all usually end up with no deal. Everyone needs to win from their own perspective."

As I listen to him, I wonder how someone so focused on building "win-win" scenarios fell so far from his chairman's goal to get back to beer. Of course, Cohen didn't just have Eric to think about; he had the other board members, the company's shareholders, and the market to grapple with. On top of that, he also had his own ambitions. Did Eric's back-to-beer objective lose out to those other interests?

Cohen is an engaging raconteur. As he details the deals he made with Foster's (and later Miller) in the beer business, Home Depot in the retail division, the Montreal Canadiens when he moved them from the Forum to the new Molson Centre, the students follow with rapt attention.

I find it interesting that in his three-hour talk, he mentions Diversey only in passing, first in terms of the types of transactions: "The deals involving Diversey were not as interesting as what we did in the brewery and what we did in the retail sector. So we'll come back to it if we have time, but for now I'll focus on the other sectors of TMLC." And then again later, in summary: "I had a lot of successes in my nine years at Molson, but Diversey was not one of them." That's it. He mentions Diversey twice.

I think, "Wow. He just skirted the entire issue. How could he do it and still feel like he told the whole story? Didn't Diversey taint his tenure as CEO? Wasn't its failure in the United States the reason for his downfall and why he left TMCL?"

🍁

"Eric, why don't *you* become CEO?" Peter Gordon, then honorary director of TMCL, asked when Eric shared his back-to-beer vision with him.

J. Peter George Gordon was once one of Molson's top directors, according to Eric. He served on the board from 1980 to 1991, witnessed the company go through CEOs Jim Black and John Rogers, and helped put Mickey Cohen in charge. Eric respected Gordon not only for his contributions as a director but also for all his accomplishments as chairman and CEO of Stelco, Canada's largest steel producer. It was also easier for Eric to speak openly to him now that he was no longer an active board member.

"I don't want the job," Eric replied. "You know the expression 'stick to your knittings'? Well, I know beer. I don't fully grasp all these other businesses we're in. All I know is that they're not performing, and we should get *rid* of them. We need to focus on beer."

Ever since the club sandwiches and Export Ales lunch with Pat Kelley and Stephen in December 1992, Eric had thought of little else. He realized he had three hurdles to overcome: (1) inertia – changing the course of TMCL would be like trying to alter the direction of a fifty-gallon barrel rolling down a hill; (2) competence – finding the right people to lead the transformation; and (3) leadership – unless something drastic happened, Mickey Cohen would continue steering the company away from beer.

In fact, at the same time as Eric, Stephen, and Kelley resolved to take the company back to beer, Cohen was working on selling off another piece of the brewery. In December 1992, he was in advanced discussions with Miller Brewing Company (owned by tobacco giant Philip Morris), the second-largest brewer in the United States, to sell them 20 per cent of Molson Breweries. If the Miller deal closed, the beer business that was once owned 100 per cent by TMCL would now have three owners: Miller (20 per cent), Foster's (40 per cent), and TMCL (40 per cent). Molson Breweries would no longer be Canadian.

"One of the things Eric always wanted was for Molson to go outside Canada and become a global brewer," says Cohen, justifying the sale. "We spent a lot of time deciding how to get into the US. It's a tough market to break into. It's a saturated market. We concluded with Foster's, our partner, that we had to do another merger. So we considered whether we should go with Miller or with Coors, and we ended up deciding to go with Miller."

Eric was uneasy. He always said the brewery had to find a way to penetrate the United States (especially with beer consumption shrinking in Canada), but Cohen's price was high. If we do this, Eric thought, we're not even going to own 50 per cent of our beer business.

He asked Cohen, "Do we really need to *sell* to Miller? Can't we do some other kind of deal with them?"

"We don't have to do this," Cohen said. "But if we want to break into the United States in a big way, this is it. Nothing comes for free."

Cohen now explains, "If we simply signed a distribution agreement with Miller, they might not have been as efficient in promoting our brands through their US distribution network. We needed something that would make Miller pay attention and put effort behind our brands. The only way we (and that includes Foster's) thought we could get that kind of commitment from Miller was if we pushed them into owning a piece of us. *We* were the ones who insisted that they put some skin in the game of our success and come in as a 20 per cent partner."

The TMCL board agreed with their CEO. Reluctantly, Eric followed suit.

On 14 January 1993, Cohen unveiled a $349 million deal to sell 20 per cent of Molson Breweries Canada to Miller. For an additional $20 million, Miller also bought Molson Breweries' US operations and the right to distribute Molson and Foster's brands in the States in exchange for royalty payments. "For the first time," Cohen proudly announced, "Canadian beer brewed in Canada will receive the support necessary to compete with major brands in the largest beer market in the world."

Not everyone shared Cohen's optimism. A reporter for the *Globe and Mail* bemoaned the sale to Miller: "The Molson Companies Ltd will allow its brewery – North America's oldest – to fall under foreign control for the first time in its 207-year history."

It was a grim period for Eric. He felt sidelined by Cohen, disconnected from the company's strategy and removed from what he loved most – brewing operations. He also struggled with internal conflict.

As non-executive chairman, I am CEO-*centric. It's one of my basic principles. But what do I do when the* CEO *is driven by his personal agenda and letting hubris cloud his better judgment? Do I step in? Do I find a way to go around him? They're using the beer business as a cash cow to fund all their other projects. They're wrecking the joint. I have to find a way to rein in Cohen and his crew.*

It would take Eric more than three years to navigate around Cohen to correct the situation. "When you're the non-executive chairman of the board, you can't really *do* much. You can only make suggestions, try to influence, and look for an opportunity to make a move. It can be frustrating." For the first time, Eric felt the limitations of the scientist-observer stance that had served him so well in the past. Besides, he still had to act through the board, and as long as TMCL's board of directors supported Cohen, he was limited in what he could do. So he stood back and grudgingly watched the Mickey experiment unfurl.

🍁

Aside from the sale to Miller, 1993 was also memorable for positive reasons. There was the Montreal Canadiens' Stanley Cup win. "That was fantastic!" recalls Eric. "We were playing the LA Kings in the finals. They had Wayne Gretzky, but we had Patrick Roy in nets. Carbo [Guy Carbonneau] was our captain and we were lucky. We won the series 4–1. But can you imagine? We went into overtime for three of those five games, and we won all three ... Even before, in the earlier rounds of the

Eric and Stephen Molson with Guy Carbonneau, captain of the Montreal Canadiens, holding the 1993 Stanley Cup. Courtesy Club de hockey Canadien, Inc.

series, we won in overtime seven times. We had a total of ten overtime wins in the playoffs. It was overtime magic!"

Hockey games were occasions for Molson family reunions. The 1993 Stanley Cup Finals were no exception. Eric, Stephen, Hartland, and their wives went to every match together (including to many "away" games). Hartland was now eighty-six, but he flew to Los Angeles with the rest of the family to watch the games on 5 and 7 June at the Great Western Forum. The family were back in Montreal on 9 June, and they all celebrated together as the Habs victoriously hoisted the Stanley Cup after beating the LA Kings 4 to 1.

That year also marked the beginning of the construction of the "new" Forum. Brian Mulroney performed what he termed his "last official function as Prime Minister of Canada": turning sod at the groundbreaking ceremony of the new arena on 22 June. The move had been announced four years earlier by Habs' president Ronald Corey. He said the team had to leave the Forum because it was too costly to expand the 17,000-seat hockey shrine. Montreal fans reacted emotionally. The Forum was the scene of twenty-four Stanley Cup victories and the home of hockey greats like Maurice Richard, Jean Béliveau, and Guy Lafleur. Even Corey admitted, "My first reaction was an emotional one. But my job is to look after the future of the Canadiens, and the Forum no longer suited their needs."

"Closing the Forum was like tearing the heart out of the people of Montreal," said Cohen. "It was an iconic facility, a treasure, but it wasn't big enough. We needed a better venue."

Eric agreed. Putting nostalgia aside (and some level of superstition – he was, after all, a huge fan), he acknowledged they had outgrown the old venue. "We would have gone broke if we stayed. Moving to the new location was the best bet, and the financials looked like they were going to work. As the league expanded and salaries went up, we needed a facility that would let us compete with LA, New York, and those kinds of places." Eric's scientific, rational side prevailed over his emotional inclination to stay put.

Finally, 1993 was significant to Eric, now fifty-six, for reasons unrelated to beer and hockey. Early in the year, Reginald K. Groome asked him to become chancellor of Concordia University. Just as he had back when Jim Black offered him increasingly senior positions at the brewery, Eric asked the chairman of Concordia's board of governors, "Reg, are you sure you don't have someone better suited for the role?"

"There's no one better," Groome assured him. The board wanted someone who could provide stability and guidance to help restore Concordia's tarnished reputation. Their unanimous choice was Eric.

Over the past year, Concordia had been in the newspapers for all the wrong reasons. On the afternoon of 24 August 1992, fifty-two-year-old Valery I. Fabrikant, an associate professor at the university, entered the downtown engineering building with three handguns and shot five people. Four of them, the department chair and three professors, died.

While Fabrikant was convicted of murder and sentenced to life in prison, the tragedy raised questions about the university's management practices. Could the terrible events have been prevented? Were there signs that Fabrikant was about to commit such violent acts? Rumours at the time (later confirmed by independent inquiries) were that, yes, something could have been done. Fabrikant had approached the administration with an application to carry a gun two months prior to the massacre; he could have been suspended at that time. University rector Patrick Kenniff, however, refused to act, citing insufficient proof of Fabrikant being a threat.

After his conversation with Groome, Eric told Jane over dinner, "They've asked me to become chancellor of Concordia."

"That's wonderful, Eric! Are you going to accept?"

There were many things Eric liked about Concordia, including its diversity, innovation, and connection to the real world. What he most appreciated, however, was that Concordia gave "people *access* to higher education, unlike those other elitist, ivory tower places." Still, he told Jane, he was unsure about becoming chancellor, especially with all the recent turmoil at the place.

"Maybe that's exactly why you should do it," said Jane. "Didn't Reg Groome tell you the board's decision was unanimous? They may see you as someone who can bring stability, resolve and a long-term perspective to the place."

"Maybe." After a long pause, Eric added, "You know, I think you're right. Why not? It would be good to serve a place like Concordia. I trust Groome, and I think I could work well with him. Maybe we can turn things around together. It's worth trying. It's a good way to contribute, and it fits with who we are."

He fell briefly silent, staring out the kitchen window into the darkness. "What is it?" Jane prompted.

"It's just that it's been a while since I've been engaged in something I care about. I find it so frustrating at the brewery … Well, it's not a brewery anymore, it's a conglomerate. But still. Every time I make a suggestion or try to get involved, Mickey finds a way to ignore it or push me aside. It's awful, really."

Six months earlier, Eric had resolved with Stephen and Pat Kelley to take the company back to beer. The mettle he felt at the time had fizzled out. With Cohen driving TMCL's strategy and the board behind him, there wasn't much he could do. He couldn't just fire the CEO. That was a board decision, and as long as the stock price stayed at a reasonable level, Cohen's place was secure. Eric would have to wait for a more opportune moment.

Jane got up to clear the table. "I don't know how you put up with it. Mickey may have done good things for the company as you say, but his attitude ..."

She thought back to the trip she and Eric had taken with Mickey and Judi to the former Soviet Union several years before. In September 1990, the Montreal Canadiens were playing a series of exhibition games overseas. Cohen proposed to Eric that they go watch the team play in Leningrad (now St Petersburg) and then Moscow.

Eric says his first reaction was, "Why go all the way to the USSR to watch the Habs play when I could see them here in Montreal? But then we organized meetings to try to export Molson beer to Russia. So then I was keen to go. Then there was a *real* reason to go."

Cohen describes the trip as "wonderful." The USSR was still a communist country, the iron curtain having only recently been lifted, so the Cohens and the Molsons stayed in a government state house. Hershell Ezrin, Mickey's "backroom wizard" or bagman, organized the entire expedition. Jane and Eric always enjoyed visiting new places and experiencing different cultures, so the trip was positive in that regard. However, Jane noticed Mickey systematically positioning himself ahead of Eric – whether in official ceremonies or private meetings. "It was funny. Mickey always organized the best hotel room for himself when we travelled with him. I would ask Eric, 'How come we have this hokey room, when Mickey has the grand suite?' Eric laughed it off. He didn't care about that stuff, nor did I. But it happened systematically, so it was hard not to notice."

🍁

On 21 May 1993, Concordia University announced Eric Molson as its new chancellor. "I'm looking forward to the experience," he told a journalist. "I'm excited about being here. I like the mix of the place." Just as he was a "sidewalk man," Eric saw Concordia as a "streetcar university." "If you want an education and are willing to work at it, all you have

Concordia chancellor Eric Molson being congratulated on 9 November 1993 by Patrick Kenniff (*left*), rector and vice-chancellor, and Reginald K. Groome, chairman of the board of governors. Concordia University Records Management and Archives.

to do is step off the streetcar and we'll get it for you. Education is for everyone. That's my kind of place."

Eric had first-hand knowledge of the Concordia style. When he started working at the brewery in the early 1960s, he took evening courses in accounting and economics at Sir George Williams University, the institution that merged with Loyola College in 1974 to form Concordia. Even back then, as a twenty-five-year-old student, Eric admired the school's diversity and mix of cultures. Thirty-one years later, that same admiration prompted him to choose "Strength in Diversity" as the theme for his installation speech as chancellor. To the graduates and their guests gathered for the ceremony on 9 November 1993 at Place des Arts, Montreal's major performing arts centre, Eric said, "Today, too few Canadians recognize the strength in our diversity, but I think it is inevitable that, in the years to come, more and more will come to recognize its importance, and work together to enjoy the many benefits we can derive from it."

He now says, "I linked Concordia with Canada because I believe in the great advantage we derive in Canada from our diversity, just like it's an asset for Concordia. It's what has helped us become a nation of tolerant, fair, understanding and compassionate people. Concordia is a great example of how well diversity works."

Once installed as Concordia's chancellor, however, Eric saw the internal chaos first hand. "We had to clean up the place." The effects of the 1992 Fabrikant killings were still being felt a year later, and the two independent committees investigating the tragedy were damning of the university's administration.

"Reg Groome and I decided to fire Patrick Kenniff. He was the rector and partly responsible for the chaos. We appointed an interim rector and set up a committee to find a new head of the university. We needed someone with integrity, someone who was highly qualified and who could rebuild the place."

They found Frederick Lowy, a sixty-two-year-old psychiatrist with impeccable credentials as both an academic and an administrator. Dr Lowy was named rector of Concordia in 1995. "Fred was a wonderful leader, the kind of guy I admire," says Eric. "He restored morale, brought people together and got things done. We were lucky to get him."

The feeling was mutual. Looking back on those years, Lowy says, "I was fortunate to have Eric as chancellor. He wasn't the most outspoken person on the board, but I gradually came to know him and appreciate him. He always gave me good advice ... He has a lot of the soft qualities that make for a good leader. There can be strength in softness too."

Eric adds, "You know, it was chaos when I got to Concordia, but the chaos was good because it allowed us to clean up the place, set things right for the future, and find a guy like Fred." He would later say something similar about the corporate world: no one likes it when the company is not performing and results are tanking, but it's in those times of chaos that changes can be made. That was how Eric eventually got re-engaged in Molson – "rolled up my sleeves and replaced Mickey Cohen."

❦

Meanwhile, at TMCL headquarters in Toronto, Cohen and his team were questioning the future of the company's retail merchandising division. It was created in 1971 when Bud Willmot bought Aikenhead

Hardware Ltd, a long-established company with nineteen Toronto-based hardware stores. It was turned into a pan-Canadian business after a few months with the addition of Beaver Lumber Company Ltd, a home-hardware chain with 262 outlets across the country. Eighteen years later, reviewing the division's performance, Cohen saw it was stagnating.

"Beaver Lumber wasn't losing money or anything, but it wasn't growing very fast, and there weren't a lot of opportunities for many more stores," Cohen says. "The real problem, however, was when we looked over to the south of the border. There was a giant tsunami forming in the US and it wasn't going to be long before it came to Canada. It was known as the Big Box Store or, more specifically, Home Depot. It was an innovative concept – a warehouse-style, one-stop shop for the do-it-yourself segment – and it worked … We realized that sooner or later these guys were going to come to Canada, and we were going to be eaten alive."

The Home Depot concept, built by founders Bernard (Bernie) Marcus and Arthur Blank in Atlanta, Georgia, ten years before, was indeed a powerful engine. Between 1979 and 1989, Marcus and Blank opened over a hundred stores across the United States: 120,000 square-foot premises (a typical Beaver Lumber outlet was only 25,000 square feet), with such a wide selection of products, excellent customer service, and so much throughput that suppliers dropped their prices to record lows just to be part of the enterprise.

"Cohen warned us about Home Depot," says Eric. "He was good at that kind of thing. He could see the big picture, spot the trends, and figure out the competitive landscape. So long as he used the right people to execute on an operational level, Mickey was good. He got things done. The other advantage with Mickey was that he had no emotional attachment to any of it. So he didn't feel like he had to hang onto something just because it had been part of our company for the past twenty – or even two hundred – years. This detachment could of course be a negative, as it was for the brewery, but in some cases it worked."

Says Cohen, "We didn't know quite what to do. We could either wait for the tsunami from the south and get bowled over, or we could get out of the market by selling Beaver Lumber to someone else – but there weren't any buyers. So instead, we decided that the best thing to do was to eat our own lunch before anyone else ate our lunch. We were going to put Beaver Lumber out of business ourselves instead of having someone else do it."

In January 1991, Cohen put his plan in motion. TMCL kept the Beaver Lumber retail chain and, in parallel, opened its own warehouse-style stores modelled on the US Home Depot formula. They were called Aikenhead's Home Improvement Centres. (The first one was launched in Toronto where the old Aikenhead banner still had high brand recognition.) The new stores were in the same business and direct competitors to TMCL's own Beaver Lumber outlets. Cohen, however, refused to transfer Beaver Lumber employees to the redesigned Aikenhead stores. Instead, he hired a whole new team. The two outfits, he argued, had such different cultures and dissimilar approaches to customer service that even though both sold hardware, their employees were not interchangeable. Besides, if Home Depot moved up to Canada, the result would be the same. TMCL was just pre-empting the inevitable.

Just as he felt about Cohen's financial engineering "gimmicks," Eric was uncomfortable with his approach to Aikenhead. It wasn't just the blatant disregard for Beaver Lumber employees. ("Couldn't we have trained them to adopt a new approach to customer service?") He was uneasy poaching and duplicating the Home Depot model.

"Mickey planned to make Aikenhead the Canadian Home Depot and then sell it to the Americans for a huge profit when they realized we had cornered all the good real estate up here," says Eric. "I understood the plan, but I didn't like it. I didn't like that we would copy Home Depot's storefronts, their colours, their themes, their retailing systems ... I was uncomfortable with the whole thing. We even hired this guy, a vice-president from Home Depot in Atlanta, to head up our new chain and make sure we duplicated everything just right. It felt like cheating somehow, a black mark on our integrity. So I tried to intervene, but I was told it was perfectly legal. I couldn't stop it ... I was not in charge, and everyone else was okay with it."

Cohen says, "It's true, we took the blueprint of what they had done in the US and copied it in Canada. There is no patent or copyright for this stuff, so if you walked into an Aikenhead store in Canada, it looked almost exactly like a Home Depot store in the US ... I knew that sooner or later Home Depot would call us to make us an offer for our Aikenhead warehouse stores. Home Depot still had a lot of ground to cover in the United States before coming to Canada, and by opening our own stores, we just accelerated things. We started occupying this space in Canada and getting the best sites for these stores. If they waited for another five years, we would have fifty Aikenhead stores and it would be much harder to buy us out."

Cohen's prediction materialized. Two and a half years after launching the revamped Aikenhead's in 1991, he got a call from Bernie Marcus asking to buy TMCL's Canadian stores. But Cohen didn't take the bait right away. He wanted to build the scope of Aikenhead. The two sides rekindled discussions in 1994, and by then TMCL had five warehouse stores running in Ontario (where it also closed fourteen Beaver Lumbers) and was about to open new ones in Vancouver, Edmonton, and Calgary. Meanwhile, Home Depot was operating 269 stores in twenty-three states across America. Cohen says, "It was like a heavyweight and a gnat being in the same ring together."

The deal was announced on 8 February 1994: TMCL would sell 75 per cent of its Aikenhead chain to Home Depot for $200 million. It was the creation of Home Depot Canada. Cohen explained to his board that TMCL would "do better with 25 per cent of a big, profitable pie than with 100 per cent of a competitive battle [in which] the margins get squeezed and everybody suffers." On the Home Depot side, Marcus shrugged and said the deal was a no-brainer: "We did this because the company is a clone of Home Depot. This is a slam-dunk for us. It would have taken us three years to get used to the [Canadian] market. Now we've got someone who has the systems and profits in place." By only selling three-quarters of Aikenhead to Home Depot, however, Cohen kept some of the upside that came with the chain's future expansion potential in Canada. There was an option in the deal that triggered the sale of TMCL's outstanding 25 per cent six years later at a price based on the number of Home Depot Canada stores then in operation.

"This was Mickey at his best," says Eric. "With his advisors from Osler's and those other firms – his 'shadow team' – he found a formula that helped us get full value for our investment. Sometimes these future-value deals can get tricky, but they figured it out. When we eventually exercised the option to sell in April 1998 (Cohen was no longer CEO), Home Depot paid $375 million for our remaining 25 per cent" – a steep increase from the $200 million the Americans paid for 75 per cent of the business only four years before.

Although he appreciated all these business manoeuvres on an intellectual level, Eric remained detached from it all. "Stationery stores? Home hardware? Do-it-yourself retail outlets? … What do I know (or care) about any of that? You know, I never really liked one moment of the whole time we were a diversified company. There was nothing I liked about it. So when I became chairman of this conglomerate, it was clear in my mind: I chaired a board that would oversee the affairs of the company, but it was the CEO's job to run it and I would let the CEO do his job. Sometimes it worked – like for our hardware business – and at other times it didn't – like for Diversey."

The job of a CEO is complex (to say the least). Not only do you need to excel at building the company's future through vision, strategy, deal-making, and capital allocation but you also have to manage its present success by handling multiple stakeholders, exercising outstanding team leadership, and ensuring the flawless execution of operations. And all this while instilling a customer-centric culture throughout the organization.

Cohen was skilled in the first part (i.e., clever deal-making and financial re-engineering), but he seemed less adept (and perhaps less interested) in straight operations. Besides, he considered himself responsible for the overall conglomerate and saw his division heads – whether in beer, chemicals, retail, or hockey – as accountable for the success of their own business. He had his job, they had theirs.

Unfortunately, it didn't quite work out that way.

In 1991, for instance, when Cohen decided to buy DuBois Chemicals as an add-on to Diversey, because chemicals were a "bigger growth business than the beer business," he hired Dr Derek Cornthwaite from England to run the division. A hard-charging executive, Cornthwaite was an engineer with a PhD from Cambridge University who had spent the previous twenty-five years at Imperial Chemical Industries PLC, a major British corporation. When he joined TMCL, his ambition matched Cohen's: turning TMCL into a global chemical company.

"Mickey picked Cornthwaite to run Diversey as a big, worldwide chemical cleaning company based in the US," says Eric. "It turned out to be a disaster. He wasn't the kind of guy who could change from one business to another and motivate the troops properly. His focus should have been the US, where Ecolab was the dominant player and where we needed to integrate DuBois, but he seemed to be more interested in socializing with the big shots." Within the first twenty months of joining the company, Cornthwaite visited twenty-nine of the thirty-nine countries where Diversey operated and hobnobbed with external stakeholders. A 1992 *Globe and Mail* article described one of Cornthwaite's trips to Zurich, "where he and Molson chief executive Mickey Cohen hosted a lunch for 50 top investment bankers, fund managers and stock analysts, and then to London where they schmoozed another 100."

All this activity did nothing to resolve Diversey's most pressing issue: the US market. The acquisition of DuBois was not turning out to be the magic bullet Cohen hoped for. Not only was it too small to have a substantial impact but its integration was not going smoothly. There were challenging operational issues and a cultural disconnect. An example was the different salary structures of the two companies: whereas Diversey employees were on a fixed salary, the DuBois sales force was 100 per cent commission based. Sanjib Choudhuri says, "As a DuBois sales guy, once you got your territory, you were like a foxhound. You would find a way to get that fox, one way or the other, out of every foxhole. One DuBois guy I knew had the Waldorf Astoria account. When he lost it to Ecolab, he literally chained himself to a pillar in the hotel's lobby and told the Waldorf Astoria manager, 'I won't tell you where the key is unless you give me back the account. I'm not leaving.' That's literally what he did! And he got the account back. It was a special place … DuBois was an entirely different beast than the rest of Diversey."

When the two sales forces were merged, accounts redistributed, and territories redefined, the inevitable frictions hurt Diversey's bottom line. By 31 March 1993, Diversey's poor results were affecting TMCL's overall performance. Shareholders expected strong results that year, especially with all the cash generated from the sale of 20 per cent of the beer business to Miller. Instead, most of those gains were wiped out by the lower profits from Diversey's North American operations. Cohen tried to reassure shareholders; he said the problems with DuBois's integration were being addressed and that Diversey was going to show gains in the upcoming year.

He was wrong. Problems at Diversey persisted. Ecolab continued to systematically win the large customer accounts, and the money pit that was Diversey US kept deepening. In March 1994, Cohen fired Cornthwaite, paid him a $2.7 million severance package (on top of his million-plus salary), and announced he would run Diversey himself until he could find a new CEO.

Eric watched from the sidelines in dismay. "What a waste. We could have had a world-class business with Diversey, but we put in the wrong guy, paid him a fortune, and ruined it. Cohen should have fired Cornthwaite earlier. Then again, I should have done the same thing. I should have gotten rid of Cohen earlier as well."

Three months later, TMCL's 1994 annual general meeting was tense. The company's profits were down 24 per cent from the year before, and the stock price was "unacceptably" low. Cohen tried to appease shareholders: "The Street is right to want to see hard evidence and to be impatient … No one is more impatient than me – but we must manage this company for the longer term." It had been three years since Cohen changed the company's strategic direction to invest in its chemical cleaning and sanitizing division with Dubois rather than expand the brewery globally. And for the past two of those three years, Diversey had run up losses, with no immediate prospects of becoming nearly as profitable as the brewery division. Despite this, Cohen remained suave and reassuring. He even joked with reporters that all the extra work he had with Diversey was cutting into his golf game.

Eric was not laughing. The only upside he could see was that it opened the door for reorganization. "When you're going downhill and there's chaos, you have an opportunity to make real change. You know, do something radical that can get you further ahead. We were really in the doldrums then, because Diversey was going down the tube. It turns out that that was my chance … I could do something. I'm not sure I could have gotten the brewery back if we hadn't messed up so badly."

Failure was one way to get rid of an imperial CEO like Mickey Cohen.

❦

At the same time, another storm was brewing at Molson over its 1993 partnership with Miller. Eight years before, on 11 October 1985, Molson Breweries had obtained the exclusive licence to brew and distribute Coors beer in Canada. As the relationship developed, Molson fostered the popularity of Coors locally, and, by 1993, Coors and Coors Light had 6 per cent of the Canadian beer market. Then in 1993, Cohen and his Foster's partner turned around and sold 20 per cent of Molson Breweries to Miller – Coors's archrival.

"Betrayal" was how Leo Kiely characterized the move. It was a predictable reaction from Coors's president and COO. Kiely and other Coors executives feared that now that Molson was partly owned by Miller, it would stop energetically promoting Coors Light in Canada. It would be much keener to push Miller products instead. Moreover, if TMCL was so determined to penetrate the United States that it was willing to sell a portion of its business to an American brewer, why didn't it make a deal with them instead of Miller? From Coors's perspective, there was only downside to Molson's new alliance.

Cohen anticipated the reaction. "They were pissed off. The Coors people were really angry, and I guess I didn't really blame them. But in the end, you can only have one winner at the table, and we chose Miller."

Hearing this, I can't help but wonder why he saw this issue in terms of winners and losers rather than trying to find a creative, win-win solution. After all, in the brewing world, there are all sorts of alliances where competitors are partners in one market and cutthroat rivals in another. Cohen justified his harsh attitude on the grounds of sound business judgment: "We were brewing Coors under licence in Canada, and Carling O'Keefe was brewing Miller under licence. When we did the deal with Elders IXL and bought Carling, we had both. We brewed and distributed both Miller and Coors Light here in Canada. So when the time came to decide who to partner with to have Molson penetrate the US, we had a choice – Miller or Coors. We studied both, and my judgment at the time was that Miller was the better play. To me, it looked like Coors was trapped behind the Rockies. We would have been two small players getting together. I thought we were better off trying to break into the US with Miller, who was owned at that point by Philip Morris. Also, Philip Morris was a tobacco company that was hands-off in its ownership style, so I felt we could do a better deal with Miller. And the board agreed."

Cohen tried to quell Coors's fears. "This is business; it's not personal," he told them. "We'll continue to promote Coors Light in Canada, you don't need to worry about that." But the Coors people were unconvinced. "How can we have our beer brewed in Canada by a company that's 20 per cent owned by Miller?" they asked.

Pete Coors, then CEO and vice-chairman of Coors, remembers meeting Cohen. "I went to visit Mickey in Toronto and found him to be quite full of himself. We went to some private club downtown … What a huge ego on that guy." He rolls his eyes. More than his personal reaction to Cohen, however, Pete Coors didn't like the deal with Miller. He agreed with his COO Kiely, who said, "In our mind it was clearly a betrayal when TMCL did the Miller thing. It meant that our growth prospects for Canada were diminished tremendously. Miller was our enemy, and Molson chose them as their sweetheart, so it was a betrayal."

A year later, on 30 March 1994, the Coors company sued both Miller (in a US Federal court for breach of antitrust regulations) and TMCL (via arbitration proceedings in Canada for breach of contract). Cohen brought in the lawyers from Osler's and asked them to assess the situation. What were Coors's chances of success in arbitration? The lawyers said they were very low. "We had like nine thousand legal opinions from Osler's telling us we hadn't breached our licensing agreement with Coors when we did the Miller deal," recalls Cohen. "We were feeling pretty comfortable about the whole thing." TMCL management coolly denied all wrongdoing, confident that the arbitrators would dismiss Coors's allegations.

When questions about the arbitration came up at the TMCL board, Cohen was sanguine. He informed the directors that it was a non-issue.

Besides, lawsuits were just a part of doing business. Over the years, for example, Molson and Labatt had taken each other to court countless times on claims of contractual violations, trademark and copyright infringements, or antitrust infractions. The situation with Coors was just a minor storm that would eventually die down. "They'll get over it," he said.

Coors COO Leo Kiely, however, was not prepared to let it go. It wasn't just that Miller had bought part of Molson Breweries. Something else was wrong. Kiely explains, "My team sat me down and showed me the facts. They showed me there was a discrepancy between what the management team up at Molson was telling us was going on in terms of Coors Light sales and what we actually saw happening ourselves. It wasn't a straight story. Something was off. So I said, 'Let's press it. Let's get all the figures right.'

"We suspected there was cheating going on, but we couldn't get the proof of it right away. We just suspected it. The numbers didn't make sense to us. Remember, when I joined Coors, it wasn't a company that was really sharp with business skills. It was conflict-avoidant as well … My sense was: something is not right, we just have to go find out what it is."

Arbitration hearings can take a while to set up, and it was no different in the Molson-Coors case. By the time three international arbitrators were found, agreed to, and hearing dates scheduled, almost a year had passed. It was during the evidence-gathering part of the proceedings, however, that Coors found what it needed: proof that Molson was cheating.

Cheating. It went against everything Eric stood for: his principles, his values, the way he chose to conduct his life. Here he was, someone who wouldn't even expense a meal to the company because he didn't want to be perceived as taking advantage of his position, now having the company his family controlled, which also bore his name, accused of cheating.

"It was horrible. It never should have happened. The image of Molson must always be protected. We are responsible for the integrity of our image and the integrity associated with our assets. You cannot buy integrity. You build it. You foster it. You protect it. It only takes one act like this for it to all fall apart. Cohen failed us."

Eric, however, didn't learn of the misdeed or miscalculation right away, nor did he learn of it from Cohen. He found out about it almost a year later on 18 October 1996 from Cohen's successor, Norm Seagram, when the arbitration ruling was rendered. "It was a complete surprise when Seagram called me with the news," says Eric. "Catastrophic. Somebody cheated Coors on the amount of money we owed them and was paying them less than we should have under our licensing agreement ... Cohen was CEO at the time. He should have known about it or had control mechanisms in place to prevent that kind of stuff."

After their initial denial, Cohen and his team tried to mitigate the damages and find legal arguments to lessen the impact of what the Coors team had uncovered. But it was over. The Osler lawyers representing TMCL, once so confident that they could win the arbitration hands down, knew there was no way to recover from this kind of proof.

"One of life's lessons is that you never know what's going to come up and bite you," says Cohen. "We ended up losing the arbitration, but it had nothing to do with the Miller contract like they said in the papers. We were paying Coors a franchise fee based on the volume of Coors beer we sold, and somewhere, deep down in the brewery, the calculation of that franchise fee was deliberately or accidentally mishandled. To this day I don't know how far up the ladder the knowledge of that went ... but once that was discovered, we were dead.

"It happens all the time in this world. The case is about X, but there is bad behaviour Y, so they ruled on the Y bad behaviour and not on the X facts ... I was sick about it. Someone way down in the bowels of the brewery had misbehaved, and it was probably deliberate. That's what led to the ruling against us."

"Down in the bowels of the brewery? Yeah, right," says Eric. "Mickey was the CEO. He must have known about it and if he didn't, he should have investigated it. It wasn't right, and it should never have happened. And then, instead of saying, 'Yes, we did something wrong' and adjusting it, we continued till they sued us. If I'd been in charge, I would have settled it right away with Bill Coors. I would have told him, 'This is very unfortunate; we haven't been paying the right amount. Let's correct it, settle it up, and get on with life.' It would have taken fifteen minutes. But I wasn't CEO." Eric looks down at his hands. I want to question him more, but I sense his deep discomfort. And then I tell myself that by the time Eric found out about this breach of ethics, the matter was already with the arbitrators. He couldn't intervene any more than he did. Nor could Cohen for that matter. Despite Eric's speculation, there was no proof he was aware of the misdeed until it was too late.

The dispute that started in April 1993 when Miller bought 20 per cent of Molson Breweries was settled in April 1997, six months after the arbitration ruling. Not only did it take close to four years to resolve but the settlement cost Molson Breweries $100 million.

"I actually got a plasticized copy of the $100 million cheque from Molson and kept it on my desk for a while," says Pete Coors. Leo Kiely did the same. It was a huge win for them. Kiely chuckles. "Remember, that amount was more than our total company profits that year. Well, it was at least bigger than our total profits for 1993, 1994, and 1995 … it just shows you how material it was for Coors. We never expected a cheque that big, but those things happen sometimes."

For Eric, the monetary loss was not what hurt the most. Once he learned of the underhanded behaviour – "Imagine, our *own* people doing that," he says incredulously – he wanted to find a way to rectify the situation and restore the integrity of Molson. The $100 million was a way to close a shameful chapter of the past, one that was ("thankfully," Eric says) kept entirely out of the public eye. An internal investigation was launched at the brewery. As a result, "a few people got lost abruptly" – Eric-speak for their being fired. Molson could now start the slow process of mending its relationship with Coors.

🍁

Eric always looked forward to the "Summit meetings." The camaraderie and lighthearted banter of these monthly luncheons provided a respite from the daily grind, especially when things weren't going well. The Summit people were a mixed group: ex-NHL players, Habs management people, team doctors, Eric and Stephen. They'd get together to talk beer and hockey and share a few pitchers ("*pichets*") of Molson Ex.

At first they met at Toe Blake's Tavern a few blocks from the Forum, but when Toe's closed in 1983, they migrated to the DQ – the "Dairy Queen," which is what they called La mère Clavet, a local tavern down by the brewery.

Today the group still meets, and their hockey pool remains active. Lunch is now at the Cage aux Sports in the Bell Centre, and there are new members, including Andrew, Justin, and Geoff. The essence, however, is the same: talk of beer and hockey over a couple of *grosses molles*.

On one of those occasions, Ronald Corey noticed Eric looking preoccupied. The Summit people were newly reunited after a three-month hiatus forced by the 1994–95 NHL lockout, and everyone was happy to re-engage in normal hockey talk and good-natured ribbing. But Eric was distracted. It was no longer Concordia that was troubling him. By that time Lowy was the university's rector. "Fred was someone I could delegate to," Eric says. "He also understood that I had things to take care of at Molson."

"Everything all right?" Corey asked as he and Eric put on their winter coats after lunch.

"Yes, thanks, Ronald. Everything is fine."

"Wait, I'll walk with you."

As the two men made their way to the brewery, they talked about the new Forum. It was one of Corey's most notable projects as president of the Canadiens – along with trying to win a third Stanley Cup. "Things are moving according to plan," he told Eric. "The roof and exterior facade should be done in the next six months, and then we'll start with the inside. Put in the ice, mount the seats, decorate the 135 loges, that kind of thing."

"That's good," said Eric. "When we finish construction, it will be good for Montreal. It will help develop another part of our city."

"What about you? Is everything all right?" Corey probed again.

Eric shrugged. "You know, Ronald, things aren't easy. We just went through a major hockey lockout. We've made this huge investment in the new Forum – which is good, but costly. We're converting our retail business to big-box Home Depot–type stores and getting rid of Beaver Lumber, which is also costing us a hell of a lot of money. Mickey says our future is in the cleaning and chemical business, so we've invested massively in Diversey, but we can't seem to make it work in the US. So that's more cash out the window. And to top it all off, we're neglecting the breweries. It's the only division of TMCL that's really profitable, and all we're doing is taking money from beer and pouring it into the other businesses … For the last two years I've been saying we should get back to beer. It's the only thing we know how to do well. But it seems Mickey's got his own agenda. I can't get through to him. To make things worse, our share price is tanking. Analysts and shareholders are pissed off. And they should be pissed off. I am!"

Although he knew all this already, Corey was surprised. In the twenty years he'd been with Eric, he had never heard him as open and voluble. Putting a hand on Eric's arm, he stopped him in his tracks. "You should talk to Luc Beauregard."

"Luc Beauregard? The head of that public relations firm – National? I hardly know him."

"He's the guy who organized all the PR for the 1990 Molson Indy in Vancouver."

Eric resumed his stride. "Sure, I remember. He put a real crackerjack on the file – Daniel Lamarre."

"Luc can help you. He knows business, he knows people, and he's savvy. Listen, he's advised many leaders in this province and in Canada who've had to manage crises. He's good at dealing with delicate situations. Plus, he's trustworthy. I'm sure he can help."

The two men walked silently side by side. Corey cued Eric: "Do you want me to organize a meeting? What do you have to lose?"

"Okay, let's do it." Eric's tone was purposeful. The time had come to ferment the back-to-beer revolution.

🍁

Eric and Luc Beauregard met for breakfast a few weeks later at the Paris Café in Montreal's Ritz-Carlton. They covered a range of topics: current affairs, politics, and National, the public relations firm founded by Beauregard in 1976. Eric appreciated Beauregard's colourful anecdotes about his experiences as a PR man, but he also respected his discretion. Beauregard spoke in general terms, never mentioned anyone's name, and avoided all references that might reveal his clients' identities.

From left to right, Eric and Jane Molson with Luc and Michelle Beauregard, 2007.
What started as a business relationship over the years turned into a strong, lasting
friendship. Molson family collection.

As they drank their coffee, Eric tentatively spoke about TMCL. The
night before he had summarized the company's 1994 year-end results
on his notepad, which he now pulled out of his breast pocket:

1 Brewing: 29 per cent of TMCL sales – 54 per cent of total profits
2 Diversey: 46 per cent of sales – 34 per cent of profits
3 Retailing: 22 per cent of sales – 8 per cent of profits
4 Hockey: 3 per cent of sales – 4 per cent of profits

Eric told Beauregard he was unhappy with TMCL's current focus.
He did not like the direction in which it was headed, and, as chairman
and controlling shareholder, he needed to steer the company back to
its core business. Otherwise its future would be compromised.

"Unfortunately I'm not sure I've got the full board behind me on
this. I *think* they are, but Mickey Cohen is very convincing. I'm sure I
need to work on persuading some of them, and that's not my strength."

Beauregard looked thoughtful. "Tell me, what would you change if you were CEO?"

"Simple. I'd turn TMCL into Molson. I would have us go back to our brewing roots so we could focus all our efforts into becoming an international brewer. That's it. That's how we'll survive for the long term." Eric elaborated. "Three things would have to happen. We'd need to do a few major transactions to get rid of all the non-beer businesses and buy back Foster's and Miller's shares of our brewery. We'd move the company's headquarters back to Montreal – the city is part of our DNA and it's where everything started. And we'd need to build the company's global platform, through acquisitions, mergers, partnerships – whatever works – so that Molson can prosper for another two hundred years."

By the end of their conversation, Eric's passion was evident: "You know, I'm not a real businessman. I don't like talking about finances or stock prices or the latest management fad … and I especially don't care for those who put on airs when they do. What I am is a scientist and a brewer. I know beer. I understand the beer industry, and I like beer people. And that's what the people at Molson are. They're good with beer, making it, marketing it, distributing it, selling it. We need go back to our core, back to what we know best."

❦

Mickey Cohen postponed TMCL's 1995 annual meeting in Toronto from June to mid-September, triggering questions and rumours. Why the delay? Was Cohen buying time? Making a big move? Changing strategies? Some institutional shareholders hoped he was working on selling Diversey. It was a loser, especially in the United States. Cohen, however, insisted Diversey was key to TMCL's future. He described it to journalists as a "business that we believe, and continue to believe, has lots of opportunity worldwide." Despite the fact that Ecolab dominated the American market, with a firm grip on over 80 per cent of the country's key accounts, Cohen insisted he could turn things around, given a little more time.

The numbers, however, didn't look good. In 1994, the losses of Diversey's US unit tripled to $37.7 million, pulling TMCL's overall profits down by 31 per cent from the year before. The company's share price reflected its poor performance: TMCL's class A shares dipped to $17 in 1995, down from $30 three years before.

TMCL's large institutional investors started speaking up. Claude Lamoureux, CEO of the Ontario Teachers' Pension Plan Board (one of Canada's largest pension plans, with $40.3 billion in assets) and one of TMCL's most important shareholders, said the company needed "focus." TMCL should stick to either beer or chemicals, but not both.

Finally, someone else was saying it! Maybe now, thought Eric, Mickey would start paying attention.

No chance. In September 1995, Cohen said he was committed to fixing Diversey's US business. "Besides," he said through a cloud of cigar smoke to the *Financial Post* journalist, "even if we were going to sell Diversey and become exclusively beer, this is not the right time to sell it." He admitted to feeling some pressure from shareholders, analysts, and his board, but that he was not going to succumb to it.

Eric's internal voice grew louder.

It's time for change. The diversification experiment is not working, and Mickey is not the right guy for the job anymore … The problem with Mickey is that what you see is not what you get. He wants to be a big shot and show everyone he's right. If he continues this way, he will ruin the company. And I'm not the only one who thinks so – the board and major shareholders agree.

It was around this time that Eric started being more open with his sons about business. Increasingly, he shared his views on TMCL, diversification, and the future of the brewing industry with Andrew and Geoff. (Justin was less keen on business-related matters.) Andrew, then twenty-seven, was a corporate lawyer working at the prominent Canadian firm McCarthy Tétrault, and Geoff, twenty-five, was completing his MBA at Babson College in Massachusetts. Eric felt heartened by his sons' interest and quick study. He talked to them about his back-to-beer goal for Molson. He discussed the changing landscape of the industry and worried that smaller beer companies were getting squeezed out by the moulding hands of globalization. In the summer of 1995, for example, while Cohen zeroed in on Diversey, Onex Corporation (Gerry Schwartz's private equity firm) had made a play for Labatt.

Forced to fight off the unwelcome takeover bid by Onex, Labatt looked for alternatives. Dutch brewer Heineken and Belgian Interbrew, maker of Stella Artois, both stepped in with counter-offers. Labatt was going to get bought out.

In Maine, early that summer, Eric spoke to Andrew. "We've got to get ready. Otherwise, they're going to come after us as well."

Andrew, who had been following the corporate manoeuvrings closely, agreed. "What's also interesting is that all three bidders – Onex, Heineken, and Interbrew – said they would get rid of Labatt's non-brewing assets if they got the company."

"You're right," said Eric. "Conglomerates are a thing of the past. Everyone is focusing on their core business ... if only I could get Mickey to agree that our core business is brewing and not cleaning products. At least our board is starting to see it that way."

Later that day, Eric sat down and wrote a letter to Geoff, then working for the summer at the head office of Marks & Spencer in London.

Dear Geoff,

Finally, I'm getting to writing a letter – it's so rare nowadays except business letters. I thought you might like to know what happened to Labatt. When you left, Onex had bid $24 for it and was planning to sell every part of Labatt except beer. The brewery would eventually be owned by the Bemberg family who have breweries in South and Central America.

Last week, Interbrew came in at $28.50 and it looks like this bid will win – that means that all the parts of Labatt except beer will be sold and that the beer will be owned by the two families that own Interbrew; both Belgian families (de Spoelberch & the Van Damme family that owns Piedboeuf beer).

The net result is the same – Labatt will be a brewery only, owned by a family (or families). This should help me achieve my objective as outlined to you and Andrew ...

Just a few minutes ago, in the last minute of the 3rd period, at 2–2, Claude Lemieux skated up the ice and blasted one from the blue line; and Hextall let it in – making it 3–2; and it's 3–2 in games for NJ – which is what I want. ...

After Jane added her own update to Geoff, Eric put in a PS: "Detroit eliminated Chicago in O/T last night."

✹

Interbrew ultimately won the battle and bought John Labatt Ltd for $2.7 billion. Molson's biggest competitor in Canada was now foreign owned.

Soon after, in the fall of 1995, Eric got a call from Ontario Teachers. TMCL's investor had already spoken out about the need for focus. They now wanted to meet Eric to go over the company's performance.

"All right," he said, "I'll tell our CEO, Mickey Cohen, and Stuart Hartley, our CFO, to get ready."

"No, Mr Molson, the request is that you come to this meeting alone. We want to speak to the chairman of the board."

Eric spent days preparing for the meeting. He flew to Toronto and steeled himself as he opened the conference-room door. "They had me on the carpet," he says. "Heather Hunter, their head of equities, was a real crackerjack. She knew her stuff. She met me with a few others and they essentially told me, 'We've got one piece of advice for you, Mr Molson. You've got to get rid of Mickey Cohen. He told us last year that he was going to put in a new value-based management system, and he's done nothing about it. His results are terrible. He's got to go.' They wanted me to dump Mickey. I didn't say, 'Yeah, he's gone.' No, I thanked them for their time and told them I would consider their remarks."

Eric left the meeting with new ammunition. The board could not ignore this kind of feedback. And while they wouldn't make a rash decision, it was clear that they could no longer stand behind Cohen.

"It's hard to get rid of a CEO," Eric says. "You've got to make sure he fails. You can't just go up and get rid of him, even if you're the chairman and controlling shareholder. There are many stakeholders to consider. In the case of Mickey, we had the market on our side because the business was failing under his watch. So the board started telling Mickey that things weren't going well. I only had to reinforce their message."

With the board's blessing, Eric arranged a face-to-face meeting with his CEO. He knew that telling Cohen his time was up would be a difficult conversation. He also wanted to have the right balance when he delivered his message: tough *and* humane. He called Luc Beauregard for help.

Beauregard agreed to go with Eric to Toronto. The whole time – on the flight, over dinner and for many hours thereafter – they went over what Eric was going to say to Cohen the next day. Until late into the night, Beauregard drilled Eric. "What if he says this, what will you reply? What if he asks for that?" And on and on. The only way Eric knew how to handle difficult situations was to get himself well prepared. Eventually, he said, "Okay, Luc, let's call it a night. I got it."

"Luc helped me put together the words," he says. "I'm not a good talker, so I had to pump myself up to speak to Mickey. I wanted to get it right, and in case I fumbled, I had my notes … A guy like Bill Clinton can just talk. That's not me. I don't ad lib. I like to be prepared. Firing Mickey was something I had to do, and I had to do it well."

He met Cohen the next morning in his Scotia Plaza office. Once again, he was struck by the grandeur of the place – the big spaces, the expensive furniture, secretaries buzzing around. He faced Mickey enthroned in his oversized leather chair, cleared his throat, and began. Point by point, he itemized the board's position: Cohen's performance was lacking, especially with respect to Diversey; his venture in the United States was a failure; and he'd run out of time to turn around TMCL as its CEO. Cohen went white.

"Getting fired was really damaging to poor Mickey's ego," says Eric.

Cohen, however, has a different version of events. "It was entirely my decision. It started to become clear to me that I had to go, so we did it. And we did it very peacefully and amicably … Six months later, I announced I was retiring."

Ultimately, it seems that both men were ready to end the relationship. Cohen explains, "Towards the end, I sensed that Eric turned from being a hands-off chairman to being more involved. He wanted to go back to being a beer company. He lost his taste or his patience with all the other stuff and he wanted to get back to beer … At that point, I stopped arguing with him, because Diversey wasn't going to be a big success. I could see that it was going to be another decade before we could do it. And I didn't have ten years left to do it, and I wasn't sure it could work anyway. And I wasn't going to end up in a battle with my major shareholder. It wasn't worth it."

Cohen had always known what was important to Eric; it just didn't coincide with the strategy he was spearheading for TMCL. He maintains, however, that over the years he has received a "bum rap" as the man who diversified and then dismantled Molson. "I didn't diversify that company one whit. I didn't take them into the cleaning and sanitizing business ... When I got there, they were already in the home-improvement business, cleaning and sanitizing, hockey, and brewing ... I inherited it and tried to make a go of it. But I couldn't."

Over the next six months, Molson began to clean house. Cohen was on his way out, the retail division was gradually unloaded, and investment bankers worked on selling Diversey. The sale was completed on 3 April 1996, although not at the price they'd hoped for.

The press was harsh, demanding to know why Cohen deserved a multi-million dollar salary, bonuses, and payout for "such lousy recent performance." An op-ed in the *Montreal Gazette* blasted him: "After years as the quick-witted adviser to ministers and corporate chieftains, Cohen's attempt at being top dog himself comes a cropper. He clearly doesn't have what it takes to be the ultimate decision-maker ... He spent too much time pondering grandiose theories and big-picture ideas in his executive aerie, or jetting to obscure global networking sessions, and not enough on the ground, dealing with the day-to-day reality of running a mid-size corporation."

Other journalists focused on TMCL's financial results to paint an equally dismal portrait. The *Financial Post*, for example, summarized that "during Cohen's seven years, from 1990 to 1996, Molson Cos. achieved just 75 per cent of the $411 million in profit it made during the previous seven-year reign of chief executive John Rogers. Long-term debt, meanwhile, soared from $159 million in 1989 to $907 million in 1996. The shares, once a buoyant $35, slipped to around $20."

Eric did not escape unscathed. The press was critical of him too. Journalists asked: Where was Mr Molson, chairman and controlling shareholder, while Cohen ran the corporation? Why didn't he take action earlier? How could Mr Molson allow TMCL to get derailed to such an extent? One writer even compared Eric to Rip Van Winkle, asleep at his desk for too many years and one day waking up to find himself head of a completely different company.

It is true that another type of chairman, one who was autocratic and didn't value his board's input or the role of a CEO, might have acted sooner and not given Cohen so much leeway. But that wasn't Eric's style and, besides, part of him believed in going to the end of an exercise, in this case diversification. Gradually, as he witnessed TMCL failing as a conglomerate, he became more assertive and persuaded his fellow board members to change the company's strategy: transform Molson into a global beer company.

This is where the Rip Van Winkle analogy takes on a deeper significance. The pattern of a long sleep that precedes an awakening is an age-old theme used in heroic journey-tales around the world: Rip Van Winkle, Sleeping Beauty, Snow White, Jonah asleep at the bottom of the boat, the Hindu King Muchukunda who slumbered until he was brought around by Krishna. Sleep represents a period when the hero is unaware of or ignores his true nature. By building his inner strength and individuality, the hero gets the courage to live a life congruent with his values and principles, a life where he is awake and fully conscious. American author and educator Parker Palmer tells us, "Our deepest calling is to grow into our own authentic self-hood, whether or not it conforms to some image of who we ought to be. As we do so, we will not only find the joy that every human being seeks – we will also find our path of authentic service in the world."

In his journey, Eric became chairman because he assumed the duty that befell him. During his first eight years in that role, many relied on his getting it right: his relatives, his ancestors, his successors, Molson's stakeholders. The list was long. And "getting it right" for Eric initially meant continuing on the conglomerate trajectory set by his predecessors who knew best. So despite nagging doubts about diversification, he followed their path and did what was expected of him – until one day he had enough.

By deciding to end the era of TMCL as a conglomerate and change CEOs, Eric put aside self-doubt and called up the courage to do what *he* thought was best. He gave himself permission to take the company in the direction he believed in and was passionate about. Some call it "following your bliss"; others talk about "finding your true purpose." For Eric, that thing was taking Molson back to its brewing roots.

At this juncture, he also realized that he did not need to hire his own exact opposite to run Molson. He didn't need to be a man of flash, dazzle, and charisma to do the job well. A more modest, reflective, and humble personality like his could also get results – especially when coupled with fierce determination. Heartened with this awareness and new vision for Molson, Eric became resolute. Rip Van Winkle had woken up a different man.

8 Welcoming Ian into the Fold

If you cannot get rid of the family skeleton, you may as well make it dance.

GEORGE BERNARD SHAW (1856–1950)

"I'd really like to interview Ian," I tell Andrew on our drive to Massa-wippi. It's Saturday morning; we've had a busy week; and, as always, our hour and a half car ride to the country is a good time to catch up and talk about our different projects.

Andrew keeps his eyes on the road. "I know. I'll try to arrange it. I'm just not sure he's going to want to talk about it … It was rough back then."

I stare out at the snow-covered hills of the Eastern Townships. "I hope he agrees to meet with me."

Ian is Eric's third cousin once removed. And even though the two men were once close collaborators, it's been over ten years since they last spoke.

"There's so much I want to ask him," I continue. "You know, like, what did he want when he first started working with your dad? Or how was it when he joined the board? Or when did he realize things were going badly? I don't know … I wonder how he feels about the way it all turned out."

True to his word, Andrew organizes a meeting: lunch, 8 April 2015, in London. Ian suggests Le Colombier, a small restaurant in Chelsea.

As soon as we arrive, Andrew and I are seated at a corner table next to the outdoor terrace. The waiter brings us menus. Unable to sit still, I glance through the list of traditional French dishes: *tranche de fois gras maison, feuilleté d'escargots, médaillon de lotte, coquilles saint Jacques à la provençale.* I fiddle with my cutlery, break off a piece of bread, take a sip of water, wipe crumbs from the white tablecloth. All the while, I keep glancing at the door to see if I can catch sight of Ian. Andrew puts his hand on mine as if to say, "Don't worry. He'll show up."

Just then, Ian walks in. He's a slight man, fair with blue eyes, and obviously known by the restaurant's personnel. He heads to our table.

"Sorry for being late," he says, his watchful eyes glancing at the other patrons in the restaurant.

"Not at all," replies Andrew. We both get up to greet him.

Ian's accent is not quite British, but the intonation reveals that he's been living in the UK for most of his adult life. From my research, I know Ian is well entrenched in the upper echelons of British society. His wife, Verena Brigid Molson, is part of England's aristocracy and, a Cayzer, from one of its more affluent families.

We make small talk. Ian tells us about his business interests, his three children, and their family summers in Métis-sur-Mer in Quebec. He describes how he's kept his children close to their Canadian roots and relatives, some of whom still live in Montreal. The Molson heritage is clearly important to him. In fact, as he reaches for the menu, I notice his wristwatch: a Molson Canadian promotional piece, its face adorned with the beer brand's maple leaf emblem and red and blue "Canadian" lettering. On his pinkie he wears a signet ring engraved with the Molson family crest and the "*Industria et Spe*" motto. I wonder if he's put them on for the occasion of our lunch or whether he always wears them.

Our conversation eventually turns to the brewing industry. Ian speaks of his close relationship with Charlene de Carvalho-Heineken (Freddy Heineken's daughter and only heir, with an estimated net worth of US$13.4 billion) and her husband Michel de Carvalho. Ian says he was Michel's flatmate for nearly five years when they were both bachelors and was best man at Michel's wedding to Charlene. He is godfather to one of their five children, Alexandre, and a board member of their holding company. He gets his point across: he has close ties to the Heineken dynasty.

As the waiters bring us our coffees, I think, "Lunch is almost over and we haven't even talked about the book! I'm going to miss my chance." I steel myself and ask timidly, "Ian, have you thought about doing an interview with me?"

Ian's demeanour changes. "I'm sorry, but I won't be able to do it," he says, looking down. "I respect the family too much, and I think time has a way of healing things …" His voice trails off, his cheeks flush.

"Eric and I have been through a lot," he continues. "We sort of had 'the best and the worst' together … And as much as I think I know exactly what happened, there is no merit in my telling the story. It's just going to bring pain and hurt and aggravation … It wouldn't be constructive. I'm sorry, I won't do it."

"I understand," says Andrew. "Thank you, Ian, for considering it. We appreciate it."

And with that, we say goodbye. So that's it, I think. I'm not going to get Ian's side of the story. I am left with a bittersweet feeling. I'm happy I got to meet him, but still, I would have liked to get his perspective. So far, everyone I've spoken to has been down on Ian; they say he was disloyal and greedy. But he has his own version of events, and as Spinoza said, "No matter how thin you slice it, there will always be two sides."

Andrew and I go over the lunchtime conversation as we walk up King's Road towards the Sloane Square tube station. He knows I'm crestfallen. "Helen, you can still tell Dad's story without interviewing Ian," he reminds me. "You have the facts; just be objective and fair. Besides, your story is about Eric and how he's dealt with the challenges he's had to face. It's not about Ian and some family feud."

I agree.

Perhaps some things are best left unsaid. I'm just not sure this is one of them.

Robert Ian Molson was born in Montreal in 1955 to Mary Elizabeth Lyall and William Molson. His father was the same Billy Molson who,

Ian Molson as he appears in the 2001 Molson Annual Report. Molson Coors Brewing Company collection.

with his brothers David and Peter, bought the Montreal Canadiens from Tom and Hartland in 1968 and then turned around and sold the team to the Bronfmans without offering their cousins the opportunity to buy it back first. This so-called "act of betrayal" transpired, however, when Ian was a teenager. And Eric didn't believe that the sins of the father should be laid upon the children.

There was an eighteen-year difference between Eric and Ian, enough for Eric to keep an eye on the younger Molson's development. He recognized Ian's potential early on as he saw him progress from Selwyn House to Milton Academy and then on to Harvard.

"Ian got interested in Molson at a young age," says Eric. "He wanted to be there. He worked at the brewery as a summer student and he'd come by to meet with Hartland and myself once in a while. Even back then I knew he was a sharp cookie."

Ian was good with numbers and particularly interested in finance. As soon as he graduated from Harvard, he joined Credit Suisse First Boston (CSFB), one of the leading investment banking firms, and moved to London, England. There he worked on a broad range of transactions – mergers, acquisitions, corporate finance deals. Eventually he was promoted to partner and managing director of the firm and later headed up CSFB's European investment banking department, a position of considerable scope. The whole time, however, he kept track of Molson.

In fact, the first time Mickey Cohen ever heard from Home Depot in 1993, it wasn't directly from co-founder Bernie Marcus. It was Ian Molson of CSFB who made the initial contact on behalf of his client, to see if TMCL was interested in selling the Aikenhead warehouse stores. Cohen remembers saying, "I'm very flattered, Ian, but I don't really talk to investment bankers. Why don't you have Mr Marcus call me directly?"

So even after Ian moved to London, married the elegant Verena Brigid Cayzer in 1985, and started a family there, he followed Molson's activities (and stock price) closely. He also kept in touch with Molson relatives and socialized with them when occasions arose.

Eric's nephew and godson, Eric Stevenson (son of Deirdre), spent time with Ian in London. "I was over there working in investment banking and I got to know him," he says. "Ian had a strong reputation as a banker. I think he was possibly one of the youngest-ever partners at CSFB. He had an impressive CV and a lot of cred in the investment banking world. He was a good banker."

Another one of Eric's nephews, Brian Baxter (son of Cynthia), is less generous in his description. "The first time I met Ian was in 1988 when I was living in London," he recalls. "I had just finished my master's in theatre. Eric and Jane happened to be in town at the same time as my birthday that year, and they were kind enough to invite me to join them for dinner to celebrate. They also invited two other couples: Eric Stevenson and his wife, and Ian Molson and Verena. When Ian arrived at the restaurant, he came in with a bowler hat, an umbrella over his arm, and a mid-Atlantic accent. I thought, 'What is this? This guy is a phoney' … But there must be a brilliant side to Ian, because Eric and Jane certainly seemed to be taken by him."

Eric saw in Ian characteristics that he felt complemented his own. His younger relative knew money matters and seemed to like mingling with the "fat cats" in the business world. "Ian could talk really well," says Eric, "especially finance. I mean, I understood finance and could work with it, but I certainly didn't like talking about it. And you need that in a business. Ian was a big-shot, London-based investment banker, and he was a strategic thinker when it came to money … and we didn't have that. So I felt he was the missing ingredient." The combination of Ian's financial savvy and Eric's intimate knowledge of the brewing industry held a lot of potential.

Ian gradually started talking to Eric about TMCL, its performance, and the Molsons' controlling stake in the company. Amongst other things, he suggested that the family would probably be better served if Eric, his siblings, and the Molson Foundation restructured their holdings and put all their shares (especially the class B voting shares) into a new corporate vehicle.

Eric was open. "It made sense."

In early December 1989, Ian flew to Montreal and met with Eric at the brewery. They discussed reorganizing the family's shares in TMCL into a new company he dubbed "Molson Holdings." Ian explained his rationale in a memorandum: The "main objective of such an exercise would be to coordinate control of TMCL from individual family hands into a corporate form." By putting a majority of TMCL's class B shares into Molson Holdings, it would "make the company safe from predators" and "would facilitate the family's control of TMCL into the foreseeable future. Instead of having to sell class B shares as and when liquidity is required, it would be possible to raise funds by diluting ownership of Molson Holdings rather than selling class B shares outright."

Eric felt there was merit to Ian's proposal. He liked the idea of protecting the company from predators by concentrating the shares into a single entity, and he knew other business families who were organized that way (Heineken, for example). But Eric never acted quickly on such matters. Instead, he took the time to reflect, consult with his siblings, and get the opinion of trusted advisors like "silver fox" Benny Parsons. Ian's plan would have to wait.

🍁

A few years later, in March 1996, the Canadiens' move from the seventy-two-year-old Forum to the newly built Molson Centre was all over the media. Some articles were nostalgic – "End of an Era: Hockey Shrine

The Molson Centre became the new home of the Montreal Canadiens in 1996. The multi-purpose sports and entertainment venue provided seating for 21,273 fans and was completely financed by private funds. Molson Coors Brewing Company collection.

Ribbon-cutting ceremony inaugurating the new Molson Centre on 16 March 1996. *Left to right*, Montreal Mayor Pierre Bourque, Quebec Premier Lucien Bouchard, (in background, an unidentified member of the Montreal police force), Canadian Prime Minister Jean Chrétien, unidentified person behind Mr Chrétien, Eric Molson, Ronald Corey, Mickey Cohen, André Tranchemontagne of Molson, and NHL Commissioner Gary Bettman. Photo by Bob Fisher. Courtesy Club de hockey Canadien, Inc.

Is Set to Close," or "Farewell to the Forum: The Mecca of Hockey Will Never Be Forgotten," while others focused on the future – "Molson Centre a Triumph: The Only Word to Describe New Arena Is Awesome," or "Rave Reviews for Rink: Players Love New Molson Centre."

Ronald Corey, in charge of the centre's construction, was very pleased. "We've been working on this project day and night for the past eight years," he told journalists touring the new edifice. "Right from the outset, we wanted a building that was designed precisely for hockey … We did not want one of those multi-function facilities where hockey is almost an afterthought. This place was designed by hockey people for hockey people."

.Eric also felt a sense of accomplishment: "The Molson Centre was not only good for us: it was also good for the city of Montreal." Unlike other sports venues in North America that are primarily financed by public funds, he said, "we built it without using one penny of taxpayers' money. And second, when we built it, you have to remember that the economy was in a slump and that it was the only construction project going on in downtown Montreal. I'm happy we contributed to our city that way."

After week-long celebrations to mark the move, the Canadiens inaugurated the Molson Centre on 16 March 1996 and won their first game there against the New York Rangers 4–2. The place was packed, all 21,273 seats occupied. Fans, ex-hockey players, stars, and politicians were in attendance. In the stands were Canadian Prime Minister Jean Chrétien and Quebec Premier Lucien Bouchard, who only four months earlier were engaged in a bitter feud over the future of Quebec and Canada. (The anti-separation side had won the province's second sovereignty referendum by a slim 50.58 per cent majority.)

Eric was also at that first Habs–Rangers game with his family. "Hockey has always been a unifying force here in Quebec," he says. "It's like that song by that hip-hop group, Loco Locass or something – you know, the anthem that goes on whenever we score. It's all about the Habs and how they bring together the people of our province." The name of the song Eric refers to is "Le but" (The Goal); it's an uplifting 2009 tune about the team: "*C'est ça qui nous ressemble. C'est ça qui nous rassemble: Anglo, franco, peu importe la couleur de ta peau*" (It's what looks like us. It's what makes us come together: Anglos, Francos, no matter the colour of your skin).

✦

The celebrations and fanfare for the opening of the new Molson Centre were a nice, albeit brief distraction. Eric remained preoccupied with two questions: Who was he going to hire as Mickey Cohen's replacement? Would he get buy-in for his back-to-beer plan?

Loyalty was now more important than ever to Eric. It became a quality he sought from people around him – not necessarily to him personally but rather loyalty to the vision of Molson as a global beer company. He knew the road from a diversified conglomerate to an international brewer was not going to be smooth, and he needed the support of people who shared his ambition to traverse the span.

Norman M. Seagram is seen here (*far right*) in 1987 when he was EVP Brewing Group of TMCL. The other TMCL executives around the table are (*left to right*) Peter Stewart, EVP Corporate Services; John Pick, EVP Chemical Specialties Group; Jim Black, chairman of the board; John Rogers, president and CEO; Eric Molson, deputy chairman of the board; John Lacey, EVP Retail Merchandising Group; Stuart Hartley, EVP Finance. Molson Coors Brewing Company collection.

With Cohen still in place for six months during the transition period, the search for a new CEO began. It resulted with a name familiar to Eric and to many others at Molson: Norman M. Seagram.

Seagram was then chairman and chief executive of the Canadian subsidiary of Air Liquide in Montreal. But before that, he had been an employee of TMCL for over twenty-four years. "We knew Norm. He had class," says Eric. "I don't really like that word, but Norm Seagram was a *dignified* businessman. More importantly, he knew the beer business, he knew Molson, he was ready to fit in, and he was loyal." In May 1996, Eric asked Seagram to meet with him.

"I was very surprised when I was invited to have a drink with Eric Molson," Seagram told a reporter that spring. "I thought it was just renewing old friendships. But then he approached me with the challenge, and I thought, 'I have never been afraid of a challenge, and this looks like a big one.'"

"We convinced Norm to leave Air Liquide and come back to run our company. He was going to turn it into a beer business," says Eric.

The announcement was made on 25 June 1996. Seagram would be Molson's new CEO after the annual meeting in September. Seagram, like Cohen, was in his early sixties (ironic, given that Cohen told the media he was retiring to make room for a younger CEO); yet Seagram differed from his predecessor in one important way. "I drink beer!" he proudly proclaimed.

A month later, with Cohen still in office, the company's year-end results were published: a loss of $305.5 million compared to the previous year. Cohen explained the steep decline by the costs related to the sale of Diversey. Analysts, however, were quick to point out that TMCL's operating profits were also down by 14 per cent that year. It was definitely time for Cohen to leave.

Despite these results, the Diversey sale left the company cash rich – almost $1 billion rich. Eric wanted to reinvest that money in the company and use it to buy an international brewer as part of the back-to-beer strategy. Other shareholders, however, were understandably mistrustful of recent management performance and wanted the money paid out directly to them through a share buyback or a special dividend.

"The vultures in the sky were slowly starting to circle," says Eric. "I could feel them. If they had a voice, they'd be hissing, 'Give us the Diversey money' … It sounds ridiculous, I know. But at the time the pressure was big, and it's not like our most recent track record demonstrated we were spending money wisely. And it wasn't only the Street. Some people within the company also thought we should do a share buyback. I refused. I was the only one who said no at the top. I had no choice – it was the best option for our long-term future."

Eric could have made a lot of money for himself and his family with either a share buyback or a special dividend, but he was more interested in building a thriving, sustainable, global brewery. That's where he saw lasting value for both the company and its stakeholders. "We had to find an opportunity to invest the Diversey money back in the beer business." If anything, Eric was consistent; whenever he was faced with the choice of either deriving personal gain from Molson payouts or allocating that capital to the growth of the enterprise, he chose the latter.

The issue dominated TMCL's 1996 annual shareholders' meeting that September. After introducing Seagram as the company's new president and CEO, Eric put the subject to rest with newfound assertiveness: "If we are unable to achieve our goal of investing further in the brewing industry, *then* we will consider other alternatives aimed at increasing shareholder value in the short term. Right now, however, we are *not* considering any form of special dividend … As for a share buy-back, the company will continue to keep it in mind. But right now, it is *not* on the table."

For Eric, that meeting marked a new era for the 210-year-old company: one focused exclusively on brewing. He publicly celebrated Seagram accepting "the challenge of returning TMCL to its brewing roots." And in private, he urged the new CEO to grow the business with an international venture that made sense.

At that pivotal meeting, Eric also gave TMCL's board a face-lift. Two new directors – both loyal and fully committed to the back-to-beer strategy – were elected: Jim Arnett and Ian Molson.

🍁

As one of Canada's oldest and most reputable companies, Molson always benefited from a "blue chip" board of directors. Heads of banks, chief executives of public companies, presidents of universities were all at different times members of the board. Until then, Eric had not been proactive in choosing these individuals. Some were appointed by Bud Willmot and Hartland, while others were close to Mickey Cohen; Eric had simply given his approval.

With the change in the company's direction and Cohen's departure, there were resignations from the board. Arthur S. Hara, a prominent Japanese-Canadian businessman from Vancouver, stepped down, as did Gordon F. Osbaldeston, an influential and legendary Canadian civil servant.

"Arthur and Gordon had a pact that they were going to quit together," says Eric. "So when Arthur left, so did Gordon. These things happen on boards. Maybe these guys were 'conglomerators,' and they didn't agree with me when I said we could only be good in one business. Maybe they didn't like the instability in the air. I'm not sure. All I know is that they quit suddenly on me, and I was on the ropes at the time. If we kept going in the same direction with Molson, we were going to get clobbered and the company would be gone."

E. James Arnett pictured here in the company's 1999 Annual Report. Molson Coors Brewing Company collection.

Others, like Ralph M. Barford (fifteen years on the board) and J. Edward (Ted) Newall (ten years) left because it was time for them to retire.

For Eric, these changes presented opportunity. He could now be strategic about the composition of the board. Although he did not want to fill it with yes-men, he did want directors who believed in the company's new direction and who could challenge the management team to get back to the core beer business quickly. That's when he thought of Jim Arnett.

E. James Arnett was a senior partner at the prestigious Canadian law firm Stikeman, Elliott. A graduate of Harvard Law School, he first practised corporate and commercial law in Toronto and went on to open Stikeman's offices in Washington, DC. Eric had known Jim for years. When Eric and Jane moved to Toronto in the early 1970s, the Arnetts lived a few blocks away in Rosedale – a happy coincidence for the Molsons, who were new in town. They had kids the same age, and Jane knew Jim's wife, Alix, from when they were boarders at King's Hall, the all-girls school in Quebec's Eastern Townships. Over the years, even after Jane and Eric moved back to Montreal, the two families kept in touch, exchanged Christmas cards, and occasionally got together.

In the summer of 1995, Jane and Eric were guests of the Arnetts at their daughter Shanley's wedding in Washington. It was a beautiful, weekend-long celebration. On the way home, Eric said to Jane, "You know, I think Jim could be a good candidate for us."

"A candidate for what?"

"For the Molson board. I've been thinking about it all weekend. He'd be a great fit. We know him; he's smart as hell; his entire career as a lawyer has been in mergers and acquisitions – which is what we have to do to get back to beer ... What do you think?"

It was almost a year later when Eric called Arnett. "Jim, the company's a mess," he said frankly. "I'm making some changes, and I'd like you to consider joining our board."

Arnett was surprised. The two men had never really talked business before, and Jim had no experience as a director. Trust, however, was high on Eric's list of priorities, and he and Jim had known each other for more than twenty years.

"I'd be honoured," Arnett told him.

❧

The summer of Shanley Arnett's 1995 wedding, Eric attended another family gathering: a Molson reunion. Family members from all parts of the country and around the world flew in to Montreal for the occasion, including Ian Molson and his wife, Verena, who came in from London. The celebrations extended over a three-day period in early July and culminated with a dinner at the brewery's main reception room on Notre Dame Street.

Amidst the festivities, Ian approached Eric. Had he thought about the proposal to restructure the family's shareholdings into a separate corporate entity? Since their first conversation in 1989, Ian had continued to raise the idea with Eric and, over time, a three-part plan had taken shape:

1 Ian would get more directly involved in TMCL. (At the time, Ian only had a very small number of class B voting shares.)

2 A joint family holding company, Molson Holdings, would be created, and Eric, his three siblings, and Ian would be its shareholders.

3 All participants would transfer their shares in TMCL (which together, represented control of the company) to this new entity in exchange for shares in Molson Holdings.

Besides the advantages they had already discussed, Ian now argued that Molson Holdings would be a tax-efficient way to expand and diversify the family's business interests. The borrowing powers of a company like Molson Holdings would offer the family the potential to increase its wealth significantly through investments and limit its exposure by building a sister company to TMCL. So, even though the overriding objective of Molson Holdings would be to remain the controlling shareholder of TMCL, it would develop additional sources of income through a separate and expanded asset base.

As he had back in 1989, Eric remained cautious. "Let's study it."

He did, however, carry out the first part of the plan. He recommended that Ian become a member of TMCL's board of directors. Ian was sharp, strategic, ambitious, and a skilful financier. "He'll be a good addition to the board," Eric told his fellow directors.

❧

Armed with a fresh strategy, a new CEO, and a reinvigorated board, Eric felt a boost of confidence: *We can pull this off! We can make Molson a great Canadian brewery once again!* It was the first time in years he allowed himself that kind of optimism.

But on Friday, 18 October 1996, came a setback. The arbitration panel initiated by Coors against Molson for breach of contract issued its ruling. It was a complete (though not public) lambasting of TMCL and its leaders. Once he got over the shock (and shame) of the news of cheating at Molson, Eric strove to correct the situation as fast as possible. He didn't want his new CEO distracted by it. The faster they reimbursed Coors, negotiated a new licensing agreement with them, and got rid of the guilty parties internally, the faster they could get on with the business of making TMCL a global brewer.

Newly minted CEO Norm Seagram, however, seemed stuck (some said "panicked") over the arbitration results.

"Seagram started in September, and in October there was the arbitration decision," remembers Jim Arnett. "We didn't know at that time what the dollar figure was going to be, but we did know that it was a big, BIG deal ... Norm Seagram had to deal with that straight out of the chute. But he got consumed with it and didn't seem to have the same sense of urgency about changing the company that Eric and the rest of the board felt."

Though the problem had not started with him, Seagram's handling of the arbitration ruling made Eric, Ian, and others question his abilities as CEO. The fact that it absorbed his attention to the point that he was unable to work on a back-to-beer plan troubled them.

"Eric and Ian really wanted to get moving, and Norm didn't have a game plan," says Arnett. "He was in the job, he was going to do stuff, but he was very ho-hum about getting the company back in the beer business. It was a problem."

The situation was aggravated by mounting pressure from the market. By the end of 1996, speculations were rampant that cash-rich Molson was a possible takeover target. Eric, who rarely addressed the media, felt compelled to issue a statement two days before Christmas to quell rumours. He said that the Molson family, had signed an agreement to maintain their class B voting shares and "not to sell or tender their shares in the event of a public offer for the company in a foreseeable future." Molson was not for sale.

Eric and Ian were united in their appraisal of the company. They agreed on the back-to-beer strategy, they wanted someone dynamic to steer the way forward, and they soon both realized that Seagram was not the right leader for that kind of transformation. "Norm was a great guy but he was slow to make decisions," says Eric. "It was very frustrating because there was so much to do, but he had no sense of urgency. Ian and I agreed he had to go."

Eric found that he and Ian made a good team. "Ian wanted performance, and so did I. If he sensed someone was not going to deliver, he had no problem moving on them." Ian was also at ease taking centre stage and speaking up, especially in a boardroom. Eventually, the two developed a board "routine" (as Eric calls it). Eric would tee up the agenda items as chairman, and Ian would step in to provide any complementary information required. It worked well.

It did, that is, until Ian left Eric hanging.

The first time was in January 1997. That night there was a blizzard in Montreal. The snow paralyzed the city's international airport, and a number of Molson directors called to say they could not make it to the board meeting. Nonetheless, quorum was obtained. Eric called to order the group gathered at the Mount Royal Club. He and Ian had agreed ahead of time on how to conduct the meeting: Eric would introduce the topic of Norm Seagram's performance, and Ian would then contend that the CEO had to be acted on quickly or the company risked failure.

Eric remembers Ian telling him, "Don't worry, Eric, you just start talking, and I'll take over."

Eric says, "I began with Norm's plans for the company, that they weren't bringing us any closer to being 100 per cent in beer, that we needed to move, and that maybe we needed a different CEO … But then Ian never cut in! He was supposed to take over and he didn't. I wasn't prepared with examples and details, because that's what Ian was supposed to talk about." Eric was left floundering.

The board members looked puzzled. "You can't replace Norm, Eric. We just got rid of Mickey!" one director said. Another piped up, "You're going through too many CEOs." Then a third, "You can't fire this guy as well, Eric. He just started."

Eric barely heard them. All he felt was Ian's betrayal. "Ian double-crossed me during that presentation. He was supposed to step in and he didn't. That was my first indication that he was unreliable."

In the end, the board agreed to give Seagram another six months. Six months to come back with a new plan on how to take the company back to beer – otherwise, he was out.

That night Eric made what he refers to as his "contemplative, long walk in the snow – just like Trudeau." It took him twenty-two minutes to go from the Mount Royal Club to his home in Westmount. He was so preoccupied and upset that he forgot his coat and overshoes at the club. Slogging down Sherbrooke Street through the storm, he thought of Ian. Why hadn't Ian backed him? He then remembered his brother's question a few nights before when they were having a beer after work. Stephen was president of the Molson Foundation, and his office was on the third floor of the Notre Dame Street building. "Ian is coming by the brewery more often these days, isn't he?" Stephen had said. "He's always stopping by for a chat. He seems like a nice enough guy … quite likeable, actually. I just wonder what his angle is. I just have this feeling, you know … can we trust him?"

As he made his way through the wintry Montreal night, Eric contemplated Stephen's words. The possibility that Ian could be duplicitous left him feeling cold and forlorn.

Norm Seagram took the allotted six months but didn't make much progress. "He came back to us with yet another proposal, and it was game over," says Eric. "The board realized, 'He can't even make a plan, we're not going anywhere with this guy.' We had to fire him. I had Ian and Matt Barrett on my side that time, so it was smooth sailing."

Matthew William Barrett was a banker and one of the more imposing figures on the Molson board. Originally from Ireland, he started working at eighteen as a teller in a London branch of the Bank of Montreal, was transferred to the bank's head office in Canada and, by age forty-five, became its chairman and chief executive officer. "He was a very influential director," Eric says. "If he said something, the board listened." In 1997, Barrett was categorical: Norm Seagram had to go.

It was the second time in less than a year that Eric had to fire someone. Eric called Seagram's secretary and arranged to see him. "I went to see Norm around 10 a.m.," he says. "When I walked in, he was putting his jacket on. He was sprucing himself up to greet me. Someone must have told him that I was coming down to give him the bad news, and so he got himself ready." Eric's voice catches. "Norm put on his jacket. He was a real gentleman. Then I fired him."

This situation was very different from the one with Cohen. Eric liked Seagram. "Norm Seagram was a great guy … but he wasn't getting the job done. The company was going downhill. I needed someone to turn it around and he couldn't do it. I realized that pretty quickly. Letting him go was rough."

✦

The question now became: Who would replace Seagram?

Eric had a plan. Once he got it approved by the other board members, he called Jim Arnett. ("I had to speak to the other directors behind Jim's back," explains Eric, "because he was also a director, and I needed their okay before making him an offer.") Flying to Toronto, he met Arnett at the Café Victoria in the historical King Edward Hotel.

Eric took in the ivory plasterwork, the crystal chandeliers, the old-world ambience. They would be able to have a private conversation here.

As the waiter left to fill their orders, Eric leaned back in his upholstered chair. "I did it, Jim. I told Norm his time was up."

Arnett raised his eyebrows. "You know the Street is going to go crazy when the news gets out. He's only been there seven months."

Eric nodded and shared the three options open to TMCL. Option A was to get back 100 per cent ownership of the Molson name by converting the partnerships with Foster's and Miller, as well as TMCL's non-core assets, into a global brewing business. Option B was to keep a modified brewing partnership and convert the non-beer assets into international brewing investments. And option C was to accept that the Foster-Miller-Molson partnership had limited potential and just liquidate the whole thing.

"Obviously we want option A," he concluded. "Route B is okay, but only if we get a good letter of comfort which gives us some hope for a decent long-term. And obviously C is extremely unattractive."

"I agree, Eric, but we need to move fast."

"Yes, and we've lost time with Seagram. To make things worse, he moved us along route C."

"So what are you thinking?"

Eric explained some of the changes he had already discussed with the rest of the board. Most urgently, they needed a new CEO, someone who could quickly get up to speed, talk with Foster's, Miller, and Coors and get to work on strategy A. They also had to replace TMCL's current CFO Stuart Hartley with "a highly skilled, fully bilingual financial guy who's qualified to become COO one day if necessary." The board had doubts about Hartley. And besides, Eric felt strongly that the new CEO, CFO, and the rest of the leadership team should all be based in Montreal. In fact, the company's head office should be scaled back and moved to its place of origin on Notre Dame Street. Finally, Eric described the changes they wanted make at the board level. They would create a new executive committee "to make sure the company is heading in the right direction and to oversee the progress of its transition to a pure-play brewer."

"It's ambitious," said Arnett. The conversation then turned to finding a new CEO. "Have *you* thought of taking the job, Eric?"

"No way," he replied categorically.

"What about Ian?"

"Ian is tied up in London. His family is there and so is his business." After a few seconds, Eric added, "Jim, what about you?"

Arnett was surprised. He later said it never crossed his mind that he would one day be CEO of a company, let alone a public corporation and a Canadian icon like Molson.

"Jim, it makes perfect sense. You know the company. You understand the strategy. Your whole professional life has been about making deals. You can handle complexity, you can lead intricate negotiations … you'd be perfect. We need someone who is going to sell off all those businesses, buy the right international brewing assets, and get Molson back to its roots. The board and I think that's you. Once that's done, you can hang up your skates and do something else. What do you say?"

After a few seconds of stunned silence, Arnett replied, "Wow, Eric, I didn't expect this. Thank you." He took a deep breath and grabbed the offer. "It's an amazing opportunity, Eric. I'd be honoured to do it."

Eric was delighted. He trusted Arnett, as did the TMCL board. Although they saw him was a stop-gap measure, an interim president to get the company back in the right direction, he could start putting things in motion right away. "You can't leave a company that is going downhill dangling," says Eric. "You need to act fast."

Jane remembers Eric breathing easier after the Toronto meeting. "When Eric went to ask Jim to be CEO, he was pretty desperate. He wanted loyalty. He needed it. And Jim was very loyal, very bright, and very capable."

With Arnett now secured as CEO, Eric continued with the next part of his plan: the reshaping of the company's board of directors. He created a new executive committee made up of Arnett, Matt Barrett, Ian, and himself. Putting aside his incipient unease with the younger Molson, he asked Ian to be its chair. Says Jim Arnett, "Ian was a young, smart, savvy, energetic guy who was just as excited about the idea of getting back to the beer business as Eric. So Eric got him involved and gave him a significant role."

Eric also worked to fill the vacant board positions. Three criteria were top of mind as he searched for candidates: competence, loyalty, and engagement with the company's back-to-beer goal. The first person he thought of was Luc Beauregard. "I decided to recommend that Luc join our board. Luc was like a psychologist. He knew what people were thinking and had good organizational empathy. I knew we needed those skills as we worked to transform the company, so I wanted Luc next to me."

Eric asked people close to him for other names. "Who do you think can help us get the company back?"

Ian recommended Michael von Clemm, chairman of Highmount Capital of Boston. Luc Beauregard put forward Dr Francesco Bellini, chief executive and co-founder of BioChem Pharma. Jim Arnett suggested Daniel W. Colson, a fellow Stikeman lawyer, who had become chief executive of the *Daily Telegraph* in London.

"The logic behind my Colson recommendation was that Eric was looking for suggestions for younger guys, smart guys that one of us could vouch for," says Arnett. "The interesting thing about Danny was not that he was involved with Conrad Black and Hollinger [the holding company that owned media interests worldwide, including the *Daily Telegraph*], but that he was based in London. He was a very intelligent businessman who knew a lot of people and knew the international scene, which was part of the story."

Eric was satisfied. "That was my gang – Colson, Bellini, and Beauregard." (Sadly, Michael von Clemm passed away suddenly soon after joining the board.) "With those guys as directors, Ian heading up the board's new executive committee, and Jim Arnett as CEO, I felt we could get the job done."

Arnett underlines the magnitude of Eric's undertaking: "What was going on was much more than just going back to beer. Eric was trying to regain control of his company. He'd almost lost it as a practical matter with Mickey Cohen ... Eric was trying to get control back of his family legacy."

❦

By May 1997, all the pieces were in place – new directors, new board structure, new CEO. Eric hoped this was enough to galvanize change. Nonetheless, there were roadblocks, and some were internal to TMCL. Head-office executives were aware that if the company got rid of all its non-beer assets, it would no longer need the elaborate TMCL headquarters. The brewery already had, for example, its own finance, HR, communications, and strategy people. Those in the Toronto Scotia Plaza would become redundant, and a whole organizational layer would naturally disappear.

Eric identifies two players as particularly resistant: Stuart L. Hartley, the company's CFO, and Brian H. Crombie, senior vice-president of corporate finance. "Hartley kept giving us information that would prevent us from making decisions. He would refuse to give any indication of why we should go fully back into the beer business. In fact, he kept showing us that we'd be fools to do it."

Arnett acknowledges that when he started in May 1997, the expectation was that he make a clean sweep in TMCL's top management. "Eric and the board probably thought the first thing I would do as CEO was fire Hartley. But I didn't. I kept Hartley for a year and a half after I started, because I needed him. He was really smart and he knew where all the bodies were buried. He understood the company and knew how to handle the financing and accounting issues in terms of selling off the stuff and winding it up. So I made the decision early on to use him. I'm not sure Eric thought that was the right decision, but it's what I chose to do."

Arnett and his chairman also differed on how quickly they thought the company's new strategic direction could be implemented. "'Get back to beer' sounds simple enough," says Arnett, "but remember, we owned only 40 per cent of Molson Breweries at the time. So even though my first objective was to get 100 per cent ownership of Molson Breweries, it wasn't at all clear that it was possible." As Brian Crombie told reporters at the time, referring to the 60 per cent of the brewery owned by Foster's and Miller, "Who knows whether it will be available, and who knows whether it will be available at an attractive price?"

In the meantime, the company still had an enormous cash pile from the sale of Diversey, so the pressure to do a share buy-back or give a special dividend remained constant. Arnett tried to buy time with analysts. "Trust me," he urged, before explaining the plan to buy back the brewery. The company's stock, however, was about 30 per cent lower than it was trading five years before. Time was running out.

Arnett reached out to Miller. They were open to sell their 20 per cent stake in Molson, but negotiations were complex. There was the sticky issue of price, and they also had to figure out how to continue licensing each other's products in their home markets. The latter was made more complicated by TMCL's ongoing discussions with Coors. TMCL had just paid them the $100 million arbitration penalty and wanted to sign a new licensing deal to continue selling Coors products in Canada. Unless it bought out Miller's part in Molson, however, a new Coors deal would need Miller's approval.

After initiating talks with Miller, Arnett approached Foster's to buy their 40 per cent of Molson Breweries. CEO Ted Kunkel was categorical: "No. Not interested." And just like that, the plan to buy back 100 per cent of the brewery came to a grinding halt.

"That's okay," Eric reassured Arnett. "They'll eventually sell it to us. We just have to be patient and look for another opportunity."

At the annual meeting of 10 September 1997, Arnett faced TMCL's shareholders for the first time as CEO. Standing at the lectern in Montreal's Windsor Ballroom, he gave an update. "At this point, the negotiations with Miller are at a very, very advanced stage." TMCL was set to buy back their 20 per cent by Christmas. As for Foster's refusal to negotiate, Arnett said, "It's not an enormous setback." It was a disappointment, but also an opportunity. Rather than pay for Foster's 40 per cent, TMCL could use its cash reserve to make a major acquisition in an established beer market outside North America.

"The vision always, certainly for Eric and Ian, was that we would get involved internationally," says Arnett. "I shared that vision in general terms, but I was first trying to get us back to *only* Molson. But then I didn't know how to do that when Foster's turned around and said they didn't want out. That's when Ian came to us with the Lion Nathan project."

Lion Nathan Ltd was a New Zealand-based brewery led by Arthur Douglas Myers (now Sir Arthur). In a fifteen-year span, Myers had grown the brewery from a small enterprise to a top player in the Australasian market, and by 1997 he decided it was time to sell. His banker was Ian Molson at CSFB.

Ian brought the opportunity to Eric and the board. Lion Nathan, Ian said, would be an excellent addition to Molson Breweries. Eric agreed. He flew to New Zealand to meet Myers and visit the brewery. "I liked what I saw. I felt we should buy this thing and use it to launch our business out in the Far East."

But Arnett was wary. Despite Eric and Ian's enthusiasm, he couldn't see how he would run a company twenty hours away. "I mean, we'd already had endless problems with partners – Foster's, Miller, Coors – and now we were going to go into a venture in New Zealand, with a new partner? … Forget it."

Eric knew it would be challenging but persisted. "I pushed for Lion Nathan because I wanted us to get going in the beer business and I wanted us to be international. Of course, we still had to organize things around Molson with Miller and Foster's, but I argued that we could grab Lion Nathan now and then put the pieces back together later, once we fixed our beer business in North America."

Arnett and his team spent the fall of 1997 working on the Lion Nathan opportunity. Multiple scenarios were reviewed by the board. Ultimately, Arnett put an end to it. "It was a big decision for the board," he says. "It was an important strategy decision, and I think Ian in particular really wanted to do the deal with Lion Nathan. He didn't want to lose the opportunity. But I basically put my job on the line and said, 'Look, I just think that the right thing to do here is to prioritize and focus on buying back Molson Breweries.' I thought once we got back control of Molson and fixed it, then we could work on an international transaction."

Eric felt frustrated. He had hoped that TMCL's management team could follow multiple leads at once – Lion Nathan, Miller, Coors, and eventually Foster's. He questioned whether Arnett and Hartley (also adamantly against the Lion Nathan deal) had enough of an international bent for the brewery. Nonetheless, he stood by his CEO. Today, with the benefit of hindsight, he says it was probably the right decision. The 45 per cent stake in Lion Nathan was eventually bought by Japan's Kirin Brewery for $1.33 billion – likely too rich and too risky for Molson.

"Eric and I had pretty straightforward discussions about Lion Nathan," Arnett recalls. "It's tricky, because we were friends – not close friends, but friends – and I went to work for him. So it changes the dynamic. As the CEO, it was difficult for me, because on the one hand I was totally loyal to him and the family, but I was also the guy that had to deal with the analysts and the media … So I was trying to do both: maintain credibility with them and maintain my relationship with Eric. Sometimes it wasn't that easy, but I think Eric and I respected each other."

🍁

"From the time I started as CEO, Ian was very present," recalls Arnett. Although based in London and leading CSFB's European Investment Banking group, the younger Molson regularly flew to Montreal (the Concorde supersonic jet did the Heathrow-JFK route in less than half the time of other airliners). He was so "hands-on" that Jim Arnett must have thought he had two Molsons as his boss instead of one. "Eric and Ian … I never really understood the dynamics between those two. At the time I was CEO, everything I saw was a collaboration between them. Whenever I advised them, I advised them together … My assumption was that Eric was bringing Ian in because he was a smart guy who was a family member, so he could trust him. You know, Eric doesn't trust a lot of people."

Although Eric had been let down by Ian at Seagram's performance review a few months before, he still felt his cousin could be trusted to do the right thing for Molson. Besides, he needed an ally who was as motivated as he was to transform the company and who was willing to get his hands dirty to make it happen.

"Eric was pushing to get the beer business back and move it to Montreal. Ian looked like he was going to help him do that," Stephen tells me. We are sitting in his study in Montreal. Amongst the many photographs laid out, I notice one of Stephen looking happy, fly fishing. His words draw me back to the present, "How could we have known that Ian would end up doing all that manoeuvring behind our backs? Still, he made me wonder. You never really knew what Ian was angling around for."

Ian's angle became evident soon enough: he wanted *in*. And even though he was a director, chaired the board's executive committee, and was given full access to TMCL, it wasn't enough. He wanted in as an owner and controlling shareholder. Ian's sightline turned to Hartland.

Senator Hartland Molson was then eighty-nine years old. He had done most of his succession planning, but was still contemplating what to do with his Molson voting shares. He had many options. He could leave them to his only child, Zoe; transfer or sell them to Eric and Stephen so as to consolidate the family's position in TMCL; or even give them to charity. That last option was Eric's suggestion. "At one point I told Uncle Hartland that he should start a foundation, one that was separate from the big one [Molson Foundation]. He could call it the Hartland de Montarville Molson Foundation and choose the things he liked to give money to. That way we would have some flexibility in terms of what we supported."

Now there was a fourth option: sell the shares to Ian.

Years earlier, it would have been an implausible proposition. The rift between Hartland's and Ian's sides of the family dated back to 1972 when Ian's father, Billy, and his brothers sold the hockey team to outsiders. Over time, however, Ian worked to mend the fissure between the two Molson branches. Eric's sister Cynthia explains that Hartland's daughter, Zoe, was the one who made the connection between Ian and her father. "Zoe lived in the UK, so she knew Ian. She thought he was the cat's meow and very well connected, so she made sure to introduce him to Hartland." The elder Molson saw in Ian the same qualities Eric did: smart, hard-working, ambitious, finance-savvy, and interested in the brewery. He decided Ian was different from his father.

Hartland sold his shares to Ian in tranches. The first was a block of 535,000 class Bs (around 4 per cent of the company's voting shares), transferred on 3 September 1997 for $13.6 million; the last was sold on 11 May 2002. In total, Ian purchased 2.3 million class B shares, which brought his holding to 10 per cent of Molson's voting stock.

The news of the sale reverberated throughout the family. Jane was thrown. "I couldn't understand how Hartland could sell his shares to Ian, especially after what his father did with the hockey team. Uncle Hartland let Eric down." Echoing similar feelings, Deirdre says, "Ian managed to hoodwink Hartland to get those shares. I was surprised. I don't know why he didn't transfer them to Eric and Stephen. Was he jealous of them because they were now in charge? Or was he jealous that his brother Tom was given a bigger stake in the company than he was? Perhaps Hartland wanted to have his own person in there? I don't know ... but he chose to sell those shares to Ian, and that was a surprise."

Eric was as stunned as his relatives. "Hartland could have sold his shares to Stephen and me in a transaction within the family, but we didn't even bring that up. He didn't have much use for us and I didn't see how I could influence him to do otherwise."

Remembering how Hartland had tried to pressure him and Stephen after the reading of Tom's will, Eric added, "Who knows, he may have woken up one morning and realized we were in charge and we had too many voting shares and that kind of stuff. So he decided to sell his shares to Ian." Moreover, he reasoned that what Hartland opted to do with his shares was his business, even though it probably would have been best to take a concerted family approach. So Eric went along with his uncle's decision to sell to Ian, although he had not forgotten Benny Parsons's warning back in 1978: "One day you may need those votes, Eric."

A month later, Ian left his job at CSFB in England to devote himself full time to Molson. He and Eric were now partners. And if Eric was the yeast that activated fermentation, Ian was the heat that powered the boiling of the wort and hops. Both are essential to beer-making, and if one is mishandled, the whole batch goes to waste.

9 Making Molson a Brewery Again

We are back to beer! We now own 100 per cent of two key elements
that bring together all Montrealers, all Quebecers, and almost all
Canadians: Great beer and hockey. It is a glorious and historic
moment for Molson and all its stakeholders.

ERIC H. MOLSON, 29 June 1998

It's a blustery winter day in Montreal. The wind lashes snow in my face
as I run down the street to the restaurant where the family has gathered. I walk in and spot Andrew sitting at a long table with Eric and
Jane, Justin and Julia, Stephen and Nancy. (Geoff and Kate are meeting
us later at the cathedral.) We're all getting together for a quick lunch
before heading across the street to Mary Queen of the World Cathedral for the funeral of Jean Béliveau. The Canadiens icon passed away
at his home eight days earlier on 2 December 2014.

Menus are laid out on the table, but no one is hungry. I sit down next
to Eric. The Molson Ex in front of him is untouched. He is quiet and
stares at the television screen mounted on the wall across from us. It's
a live coverage of the state funeral scheduled to start in an hour. Right
now, all we see are shots of the throngs of people gathering outside the
cathedral despite the near-blizzard.

"Big Jean ... he was a great," says Eric, almost to himself.

"An amazing hockey player," I agree, stating the obvious.

Eric nods, taking a sip of beer. "But he was so much more than that.
He may have gotten famous as Number 4 playing for the Canadiens,
but it's what he did off the ice that made him great."

Eric Molson and hockey legend Jean Béliveau walking to centre ice of the Montreal Forum for a ceremonial pre-game puck drop, 1992. Courtesy Club de hockey Canadien, Inc.

"Did you like working with him?" Jean Béliveau was a Molson employee in his early days as a player and then became a director of the company in 1978, serving on the board with Eric for almost twenty-five years.

"He was wonderful," Eric says smiling. "He was quiet on the board. But he was very loyal and he had stature and dignity."

He adds, "I'll never forget one of the first times I met him. It was when I first joined Molson in 1960. Big Jean and I both got a call from the brewery's Quebec president, John Kemp, asking us to say a few words at the opening of a new warehouse. So there we were, the following Friday, Jean and me, and the mayor and all the big shots on the stage for the ribbon cutting. I was *very* nervous. And, you know what? So was Jean! I couldn't believe it. Here was the guy who just a few years earlier was the first hockey player *ever* to be on the cover of *Sports Illustrated*, the guy who scored three goals in less than one minute during a single power play." (Power play rules had to be changed after that.)

Eric continues. "And there he was next to me, just as nervous as I was. Can you believe it? Jean made his speech, legs shaking, dripping like he just got off the ice. And then I made mine, legs shaking, sweating just as much, if not more. And right after the ceremony, I asked him, 'You're the star player of the Canadiens, you do this every day – how come you're nervous like me?' And he told me, 'Don't worry about being nervous, Eric, you'll do a better job at it if you're nervous. I've seen a lot of this, and the best ones are nervous.' So, you know, Jean helped me, ever since that first moment, when I was twenty-three years old. He must have been twenty-nine or something. I'll never forget it. Can you imagine how many Canadians he touched that way during his life?"

He doesn't wait for an answer. "Countless. And Jean always did it with such humility. He was a man with values. He understood what integrity meant, and he had respect for others. Big Jean used his fame in the best possible way – he set a good example."

🍁

Eric was invariably mindful of setting a good example. As chairman of the board, controlling shareholder, and head of the family, he saw an important part of his role was keeping his next of kin informed. Even though communication was not his forte, he organized regular meetings with the "Tom Molson gang." If scheduling conflicts prevented such meetings, he sent out written memos, as he did on 16 June 1997.

Dear members of Generations VI and VII, I cannot get enough of us together to have a meeting this week. So we will have one later when I have more to report. Here is briefly where we are in coded terms as most is very confidential:

(1) the new CEO [Arnett] and four new directors [Beauregard, Colson, Bellini, and Von Clemm] are strategic thinkers, very interested and very excited about the challenge;

(2) so far, no major breakthrough [i.e., to buy back 100 per cent of the brewery from Miller and Foster's], but progress is steady; the situation is extremely complicated;

(3) repatriation and small HQ [i.e., moving TMCL's headquarters back to Montreal] will happen, but it is a delicate issue right now;

(4) world-wide support and sympathy continues [i.e., to forge alliances with other brewers internationally];

(5) Foster's has announced its new scheme to buy out both its major owners (BHP and Asahi); Foster's is protected by the Australian government and no one from outside will be allowed to take it over; and

(6) keep thinking about the parent company idea as it does not seem to go away; we should prepare for a serious discussion on the positives and negatives, who wants in and who wants out, etc., as it may come to us rather abruptly.

Eric's last point on the "parent company" was a reference to the "Molson Holdings" scheme Ian first proposed back in 1989. The plan for family members to transfer their TMCL shares into a separate corporate entity had not gone away. It actually gained momentum as soon as Ian bought Hartland's voting shares.

The idea had evolved to include roles and responsibilities. If Molson Holdings was created, Ian would become its CEO, Eric chairman, and Stephen deputy chair. In a 1997 memorandum, Ian elaborated the fourfold mission of the company: first, to be proactive in its role as controlling shareholder of TMCL; second, to act as a wealth-creating vehicle by making investments largely outside Canada; third, to act as the deciding point of other Molson-family related activities and interests, such as the Molson Foundation; and fourth, to be run in a lean and cost-effective manner. Things were speeding up, and Ian was keen to put the new structure in place. Eric advocated for caution.

🍁

Progress was also being made on the TMCL front. On 27 November 1997, Arnett announced that TMCL and Foster's were buying out Miller's 20 per cent. The Canadians and Australians now owned Molson Breweries 50–50. A month later, Arnett followed up with a new licensing deal with Coors. It was for the manufacture, distribution, and sale of Coors products in Canada, but this time Coors owned 50.1 per cent of the partnership. "Of course, the Coors deal wasn't nearly as good as what we had before," Arnett admits, "but at least we had Coors." In the negotiations, the Americans used two points of leverage: the recent arbitration ruling and Coors Light's growing popularity in Canada.

Arnett's next move was to find a way to buy back the other 50 per cent of Molson Breweries. So far, Foster's had turned him down. In late December 1997, however, after a quarterly partnership review at Molson's Vancouver plant, Arnett detected an opening.

He was sitting alone with Foster's CEO, Ted Kunkel, overlooking Vancouver's False Creek. "Kunkel indicated to me that he could be prepared to talk about selling," he recalls. "It was very subtle, but it was there. That was my first hint from Ted that at the right price, Foster's was prepared to sell their interest in Molson."

Negotiations began in January 1998. Six months later, the deal was done. Mickey Cohen says the talks were made easier because of a clause he'd negotiated five years prior. In January 1993, when he and the Australians sold 20 per cent of the brewery to Miller, he was able to convince Foster's to give TMCL an option to buy them out. One of Eric's ground rules – one he learned when Tom and Hartland sold the Canadiens to their cousins without a right of first refusal – was to always consider the future and have a Plan B. So when TMCL's stake in the brewery went from 50 per cent down to 40 with the sale to Miller, Eric insisted on a buy-back option.

Cohen recalls: "When we sold the 20 per cent share to Miller, Eric was worried. I mean, it was one thing to be 50–50 with Foster's, but it was another thing to go down to 40 per cent and be in a three-way partnership. So to get this deal done, we extracted an option to buy back Foster's 40 per cent at a very robust price if we ever needed to. The public shareholders didn't really care about that very much. Eric cared about it because he could see that someday, perhaps five years from now, if they didn't have control and consensus broke down, Molson could lose the brewery. So we got the option. Many years later, after I was long gone, Molson exercised the option and bought back the whole brewery."

John Barnett, president and CEO of Molson Breweries, James Arnett, president and CEO of TMCL, and chairman Eric Molson raise a toast with glasses inscribed "100% Molson" after announcing the buy-back by TMCL of Foster's Brewing Group's 50 per cent stake in Molson Breweries. Photo by John Lehmann, 24 June 1998; licensed by the Canadian Press.

The *Financial Post* headline on 25 June 1998 read, "Molson All-Canadian Again: Lays out $1.1 Billion to Buy Back 50 Per Cent of Molson Breweries from Australia's Foster's."

Arnett smiles, remembering the feat. "That was the biggest thing I did for the company. We bought back Molson Breweries and took Foster's out of Canada. I believe to this day that if the Molson family wanted to be back in the beer business, they had to own Molson Breweries. And now they did."

"We're back to beer!" Eric announced at a celebratory reception held in the Molson Centre on 29 June 1998. "It is a glorious and historic moment for Molson, our employees, our clients, and our family." It had been five and a half years since the lunch with Stephen and Pat Kelley, but they'd done it. They had the brewery back. It was a huge accomplishment.

Privately, however, Eric cringed at the $1.1 billion price tag. "Arnett paid the Australians the whole buck. It's easy to buy something if you're willing to pay the seller whatever he's asking for."

In his defence, Arnett counters, "It's true, we had to pay a little more. We were going around telling everyone that our strategy was to go back to beer. In many respects that's a bad negotiating tactic. But on the other hand, we needed to say *something* to the Street. They were putting pressure on us to just go and wind up the goddamn company. They were saying, 'What is this company? It's nothing! It's just a hodge-podge of stuff. Sell it!' So we decided to announce our strategy, and that meant we had to pay up a little more."

Two days later, Arnett spoke to TMCL shareholders at the company's annual meeting about what came next: "Focus on rebuilding the brewery's dominant market share, expanding in the US, and finding solutions to the sports and entertainment division's problems."

While Arnett worked on the Miller, Coors, and Forster's deals, TMCL operations languished. Year-end results showed that the brewery's Canadian market share was down and Molson brands were not gaining much traction in the United States. The sports and entertainment division had a whopping 83 per cent profit drop compared to the year before. Moreover, there was still no buyer for Beaver Lumber, the last of the non-core assets. Completing the list, Eric added that the company's head office was still in Toronto, it was still overstaffed, and its CFO, Hartley, was still there. With mounting insistence, Eric pressed Arnett to address the gaps.

In the meantime, he had to deal with another critical matter. Ian's campaign to create Molson Holdings was escalating.

🍁

Whenever they discussed Molson Holdings, Eric told Ian he wanted to look at different ways to restructure the family's voting shares before going ahead with his plan. Eric's prudent nature saved him from getting caught up in a scheme unless he fully understood its implications. So although he respected Ian's financial expertise and saw merit in his proposal, he wanted to get a broader view on how to organize the family's affairs. He and Ian agreed to hire Guy Fortin, a top-notch corporate lawyer from Ogilvy Renault (now Norton Rose), to review alternative scenarios.

Ian, however, was eager to go forth with Molson Holdings. He hired Braehead, the management company of his cousin and personal advisor, Stuart Iversen, to set up the new holding company and deal with all related accounting, tax, and financial issues.

Eric balked. "I thought we had agreed to go slow on engaging Braehead at least until such time as we find out more about them and review alternatives," he wrote to Ian on 25 March 1998. "We must not extend this confidential project to Messrs. Iversen and Sutton until the Tom Molson family approves. We have approved Guy Fortin and Guy Fortin only."

Eric was mindful of "doing things right," be it in the governance of the corporation or in the management of family relations. He didn't want his siblings to think he would act on their behalf without their okay. Integrity was essential for healthy family dynamics and fostering an environment of trust.

"Thank you for your letter of 25th March," Ian wrote back. "I am sorry about any misunderstanding and I quite appreciate and agree with your concerns regarding the premature appointment of Braehead into any all-encompassing role." He went on to explain that all he wanted to do was "establish Molson Holdings as soon as practicable." Like Aesop's tortoise and hare, the two men advanced at different speeds.

Having halted Iversen's premature introduction to the file, Eric went back to study the Molson Holdings proposal. Back in 1989, when Ian first came up with the idea, Eric had not endorsed it because he had been counselled that it would not be beneficial for his sisters and their families. Now, however, things were different.

"What has changed," explained Eric in a letter to Stephen, Deirdre, and Cynthia dated 19 August 1998, "is that we now have a family shareholder who for the first time in generations has purchased a substantial number of shares in what can only be described as our under-performing company. Uncle Hartland has known and respected Ian for many years, and his decision to sell to Ian was his alone. Ian has a proven track record in business and has assisted us strongly to re-shape the board and to take the necessary steps to bring us back to our brewing roots, through a firm assertion of the family's voice on the board."

Eric reiterated the twofold objectives of Molson Holdings: first, to convert control of TMCL from individual family hands to corporate form so as to enable control to be safeguarded and exercised in a more concerted manner; and second, to act as a vehicle for the wealth creation of its shareholders. Eric concluded with the recommendation that the Tom Molson gang support Ian in his drive to create this new holding company and put him in charge.

The siblings discussed it amongst themselves and with their respective advisors, and they agreed. The plan made sense. The question then became one of money. If Ian's full-time work was to manage Molson Holdings, what would be his salary? In this respect, Eric and Ian were dissimilar.

"Ian's salary is becoming a serious issue," Eric told Stephen one afternoon that fall. "I've told him that I think salaries of family members ought to be nominal or modest, as they have been in the past."

"Did you tell him how much you were making?"

"I did. I also told him I haven't asked for a raise in all the years I've been at the company."

"Eric, look where he's coming from. I think his standards are a little different," said Stephen.

"I agree that he should be well paid for his work. But I also think that if he does a good job and grows the portfolio of Molson Holdings, he'll be rewarded through the appreciation of the capital."

Ian had a different perspective. On 5 November 1998, he sent Eric and Stephen a two-part remuneration proposal: $100,000 per annum, and an award of options to purchase 10 per cent of Molson Holdings at an exercise price equal to the fair market value of Molson Holdings on the date of its incorporation.

Eric discussed the matter with Jane over dinner. "It's not right," he told her. He explained that Ian wanted Stephen, Deirdre, Cynthia, and himself to put all their shares into Molson Holdings and that he would give them cash payouts from the growing value of those shares, but that he would pay himself with shares of the holding company.

"If Ian keeps doing that for ten years, he'll end up owning the whole company! It's like a creeping takeover."

Eric consulted his siblings and they all shared his concern. "Ian's proposal of paying himself in stock and the rest of us in cash was a mechanism that would ultimately result in him getting control of the whole thing!" says Deirdre's son, Eric Stevenson.

All November, Eric and Ian went back and forth. Ian kept coming back to his initial idea – options to buy more shares in Molson Holdings. Eric, however, was equally firm: no stock options. Ian's reward should be a modest salary and a 10 to 20 per cent preferred return on the wealth creation of Molson Holdings. So, if Molson Holdings was to create a capital gain of $10 million, then Ian would receive the first two million and the other shareholders of Molson Holdings would split the rest. That was it.

The debate led to a number of sleepless nights for Eric. Brian Baxter, Cynthia's son, noticed his uncle's preoccupation. "I remember one meeting with Eric in his office back then, and he was really distracted. I could see him wrestle. He would start down one train of thought, saying, 'You guys are grown-ups now; you should be involved and be comfortable with the idea of creating a family office or a holding company if we go that route.' And then he would switch to 'These trusts were only created as a fiction anyway, and Tom would have wanted us all to be working together.'" Tom Molson had created trusts for each of his four children and made Eric and Stephen responsible for those of his two daughters.

The discussions with Ian underlined the breadth of Eric's responsibility – to his own family, his siblings, Tom's wishes, TMCL, and the legacy of the Molson name. And, like Jean Béliveau, he wanted to do the right thing and set the right example.

In the end, Eric scrapped the Molson Holdings scheme. Ian's stratagem to be remunerated with stock options had turned everyone off. Eric explained his decision in a letter to Stephen on 3 December 1998:

While going through this planning process, I have come to the following conclusions: (1) Most, if not all of the Generations VI and VII want to keep the legacy shares intact and want to help create wealth with the proceeds of these shares; and (2) most are nervous about the Molson Holdings concept and about R. Ian Molson. These conclusions lead me to feel that we ought to change our course and go back to an earlier idea ... have a simpler and longer term shareholders agreement that votes the shares in TMCL regularly and keeps away the vultures.

Ian was upset with the family's decision. Eric remembers him saying, "You'll be sorry, Eric. This is a really good thing. Even if you don't do it right away, you should keep the file going ... Fortin did a lot of good work for us."

Eric advised Fortin of his decision, paid the lawyer's hefty bill, and closed the file.

✳

A summer party! The invitation was on heavy ecru cardstock denoting elegance and grandeur. R. Ian Molson and his wife, Verena, were hosting a black tie dinner and dance soirée on 11 June 1998 at Kingham Hill House, their country estate close to the village of Churchill in Oxfordshire, England.

Eric and Jane declined, but Jim and Alix Arnett flew to England for the occasion. It was "an incredible affair," according to Arnett – an English country estate party, complete with live entertainment and fireworks. Beyond the display of wealth and privilege, however, what struck Arnett most was Ian's posturing. "I remember a couple of Brits at the party asking me about Ian Molson," he says. "Their assumption was that Ian was *the* Mr Molson – you know, the controlling shareholder of the company. I remember hearing it here and there. It sounded like Ian was going around London telling people that he was the Molson who controlled the Molson Companies."

Board member Dan Colson, who lived in London, had noticed something similar. "I've known Ian forever," says Colson. "He worked for CSFB in London, which was about one hundred yards away from where I worked, and he belonged to the same squash club I did. We knew a lot of people in common. I think Ian is intrinsically smart. He is also very outspoken and reasonably articulate. But if you compare him to Eric, he is infinitely more assertive, infinitely more ambitious, and infinitely more treacherous. And his game plan from day one, as far as I'm concerned, was to take over the company and basically put Eric over to the side."

In those days, however, Ian's posturing was secondary for Eric. He was fixated on transforming TMCL.

With the Foster's buyout finalized, Eric urged Arnett to move the company headquarters back to Montreal. A year and a half had already passed since Eric first spoke of the change. Finally, on 28 October 1998, Arnett and TMCL's top management team relocated to the Notre Dame brewery in Montreal. The era of Mickey Cohen and the ornate Scotia Plaza offices on Toronto's King Street was over.

"We did it," Eric told Jane triumphantly over dinner. "We de-diversified the company, made it a brewer, and moved all the senior people to Montreal. It took us nearly six years, but we got it done." His relief was palpable.

"That's wonderful, honey. I'm so happy for you." After a brief pause, Jane added, "Now maybe Uncle Hartland will stop his criticism." A few months before the move was announced, Hartland had written two disgruntled letters to Eric complaining about the "depressing impression created" by the empty office space in Montreal where the brewery's headquarters once were.

"There's still lots left to do," Eric said. "We need to gain back market share. We've got to put more muscle behind our brands. We have to figure out the US and be more aggressive with our international strategy."

"How's Jim handling all that?"

"I'm not sure."

Eric wondered whether Jim had the right profile to do that kind of thing. He had many fine qualities, but he was not an operator. And now that they were back in beer, that's what they required. "We'll need someone with expertise in marketing and solid operational experience to get it done. I'll have to discuss it with the board."

Serving himself from the cheese plate on the table, Eric changed topics. "You know, we should organize a party, right before Christmas. We should invite everyone who worked with us to change the company's direction. We'll have them over at the house and thank them properly. What do you think?"

"That's great!" Jane said. Eric was not one for social gatherings. He was known as "Mr Nyet" when it came to parties, unless they were business related or for philanthropy like Concordia or the Montreal General Hospital. But this was different.

On 17 December 1998, Jane and Eric hosted a sit-down dinner at their home. Twenty-six people were there, mainly close friends and family, including the entire Tom Molson gang, plus Hartland and his spouse. There were no fireworks or musicians. After the main course, Eric stood and gave a heartfelt talk about three people he credited for bringing Molson back to its roots: Pat Kelley, Ronald Corey, and Luc Beauregard – men he characterized as having "gone to the wall" for him and for Molson. Ian was not among them.

Loyalty was the theme of the night. And as American author Elbert Hubbard once said, Eric felt that "If put to the pinch, an ounce of loyalty is worth a pound of cleverness." Eric described how the back-to-beer journey began in December 1992 over sandwiches and Export Ales at the Intercontinental Hotel. He spoke of Pat Kelley's indefatigable help, "on weekends and nights with his experience as a consultant, and knowledge of the people and operations at Molson." Ronald Corey offered his wisdom regularly: "He's like the 'Rocket' – the kind of player I want on my team. When we need a goal, he goes and gets it." And of Luc Beauregard, Eric recalled how the PR man offered his assistance "before I had even finished explaining the situation to him."

Eric concluded by describing Molson as a Canadian institution and thanking these three men for helping it survive:

Strong forces were working to eliminate us: not just the normal competitors of business but from within the company. We planned carefully and kept ourselves on track … Now, six years later, we have today a feeling that our family and the company will survive, and go on to do good things for the society of which we are blessed to be part, hopefully for another century or two …

It is not easy to understand Molson, for it is more than a company; it's an institution, with history, heritage, archives, Montreal

Eric Molson speaks about Molson going back to its roots at the Montreal Board of Trade luncheon, 2 February 1999, Queen Elizabeth Hotel. Courtesy Chamber of Commerce of Metropolitan Montreal.

roots, beer, hockey, a family. It's an icon for Canada, and we serve this country with dedication. Leacock wrote: "The name Molson is woven into the very fabric that is Canada," but once you begin to understand the institution called Molson, loyalty sets in, the good old-fashioned attribute of loyalty. I've seen it rarely, and it's lovely to see. I see it in Pat, Ron, and Luc. All three of you have worked to make sure we survive as a unique Canadian institution, and as a family. Thank you.

🍁

Eric began 1999 with another type of speaking engagement. He was scheduled to address (mostly in French) hundreds of businesspeople at the Montreal Board of Trade luncheon. He was nervous. "It was about the only public speech I ever made that was really important. It was to launch our new era." He practised for four weeks with one of the best trainers from the PR firm National.

On 2 February, as he walked up to the podium, Eric felt his heart race. He spoke about getting Molson back to beer, moving the head office to Montreal and making inroads on the international brewing scene. He also covered hockey. NHL clubs in Canada were facing hard times with the low Canadian dollar, high taxes, and soaring players' salaries. The Canadiens were no exception. "The company does not have an easy task trying to preserve shareholder value while putting on a good show for fans," Eric admitted. Nonetheless, he reassured the audience that, despite rumours to the contrary, there were no plans to sell the team. He concluded by proudly declaring Molson's devotion to the city: "Molson is to Montreal what Heineken is to Amsterdam, Miller is to Milwaukee and Foster's is to Melbourne."

The applause was lengthy. Concordia's Dr Fred Lowy, in the audience that day, sent Eric a note of congratulations: "I looked around the nearby tables as you spoke and I could see how much people appreciated your remarks. Your commitment to Montreal and its institutions came across loud and clear and it raised everyone's spirits." Eric's words were echoed in most major dailies, the *Gazette*, *Le Devoir*, *La Presse*, the *Globe and Mail* among them: not only had Molson survived but it was ready to take on the world.

CEO Jim Arnett was less exuberant. The president of Molson Breweries, John Barnett, had just resigned; the brewery was continuing to lose market share; the sports and entertainment division was in the red. Eric kept pushing him to go global, and Ian was becoming very (too) involved in the day-to-day operations.

When he was first named CEO, Arnett had accepted, even welcomed, Ian's counsel. Ian was, after all, chair of the board's executive committee and there to support Molson's overhaul. Yet from the time Ian bought the first block of Hartland's voting shares in November 1997 and resigned as managing director of CSFB, his involvement started to escalate and become burdensome. By early 1999, Arnett appeared frustrated with the situation.

Patrick Kelley recalls a couple of explosive exchanges between the two men. The first was after a meeting with the people at Bass Brewery in England. "Jim Arnett found out that Ian had gone with me to this meeting in the UK, and his reaction was horrible," Kelley remembers. "He called Ian and ripped a strip off of him. Then he ripped a strip off of me too, saying, 'He's *not* supposed to be involved in operations! … Why didn't you tell me Ian was going with you?'"

About two months later, Kelley witnessed another backlash. This time Arnett found out that Ian planned to meet with brewers in China. "Jim went bright red," recalls Kelley. "I told him that Ian was tagging along on this trip with Eric and me. He immediately called Ian, and they had an unbelievable conversation, just a huge temper tantrum. Arnett was yelling, 'You're interfering ... I'm the CEO, you should ask my permission.' It was an unending 'Piss off!' 'No, you piss off!' screaming match. That was the start of everything getting torn up. When people become undone, trust goes out the window."

Eric too felt the repercussions of Arnett's mounting insecurity. One time, for instance, Eric arranged to meet with a manager in Toronto to "talk beer" and get some insight on how the brewery's operations had evolved over time. When Arnett learned of the meeting, he quashed the initiative. "Eric, I have to say this puts me in a difficult, and embarrassing position," he wrote in an email. "I believe that any direct meetings with staff, certainly on important issues and with an agenda etc., should come through me."

Eric was taken aback. To Stephen, he wrote, "I should be able to talk to anyone, anywhere. I am a brewer and marketing-oriented. I want to know more about these important matters on which I have experience and interest." It was a question of balance. The CEO should have free rein to do his job; but as a controlling shareholder, Eric had the responsibility to be informed and knowledgeable about the business. Later, he wondered, "Why would Jim worry about me? I am the least threatening guy around."

Arnett probably didn't think of Eric as a threat, but he may have found his own position increasingly precarious. "When I started," he explains, "the board's executive committee was going to be more involved in the affairs of the company for a while, to get things shaken up. At the beginning, that was easy for me. It became more complicated later on. I would wonder, for example, what things do I decide on my own? What things do I discuss with the executive committee? What things do I discuss with Eric? Also, vis-à-vis the outside community, if every time I had to say, 'I have to check with head office,' then I would get, 'If *you*'re not head office, then why are we talking?' So it got a little complicated."

Arnett felt pressure from all sides, including the Street. Like most other board members, he assumed the company's stock price would bounce back after the announcement that TMCL owned 100 per cent of Molson Breweries. It hadn't budged. A consultant was hired to interview top institutional shareholders and ask them, "Why do you think TMCL's stock price isn't moving?" The response was clear: "None of the senior management of TMCL have any brewing experience. It's the same old guys that are there, so nothing is going to change."

Behind the scenes, however, there was movement. The board's executive committee had hired a head-hunting firm to find a new chief operating officer – someone who could eventually replace Arnett as CEO. "We were looking for a crackerjack, marketing-oriented businessman to be our new COO," says Eric. "And we were willing to pay a fortune for him. The board was behind the decision. We all agreed that we needed someone to take us to the next level."

The top name on the shortlist of candidates was Daniel James O'Neill. "He's a marketing whiz," said the head-hunter. "He's got all the qualifications to be a great COO and, in terms of succession, he could become the company's next chief executive officer."

Eric read the file in front of him. Dan O'Neill was a Canadian from Ottawa with a bachelor's degree from Carleton University and an MBA from Queen's. He began his career at Colgate Palmolive and ascended the echelons of corporate America by leapfrogging from Colgate to S.C. Johnson to Campbell Soup, and ultimately to H.J. Heinz, where he was executive vice-president. Eric was impressed by the breadth of O'Neill's experience and its global reach. He had worked in North America, Europe, and Latin America. "Let's interview him," he said.

A series of meetings was organized. The first was with Jim Arnett. It went well. The CEO came out of it thinking that O'Neill was the kind of "guy who could shake things up at the brewery."

The next was with director Matt Barrett. O'Neill remembers their lunch meeting at the Four Seasons' restaurant in Toronto: "I got there on time, but there was Barrett already sitting at a table, impeccably dressed with a tweed jacket and an ascot, sipping scotch." As with Arnett, it was a positive encounter.

At one point O'Neill leaned across the table, looking straight at Barrett. "To do what the company wants me to do, I'm going to get a lot of people upset with me."

"That's right."

"I've got to make sure the board hangs in there with me."

"We will. But now let me tell you something. You know when a plane takes off? You start the takeoff with the wheels on the ground and the whole plane is rattling and shaking and the wings are flapping. And then the wings get still, but the tires are still at it and it's still noisy. And then they put the wheels up, and it's clear sailing."

"So how long do you think it will take to get through all the rattling and the shaking?" O'Neill asked.

"Twelve to eighteen months. After that, it should be clear sailing," replied Barrett, who couldn't have predicted the trials to come.

O'Neill's next interview was with Ian Molson in New York City. They had scheduled two hours, but "it lasted close to seven. We talked about the company, the growth, the opportunities. Ian is a super-intense guy. Smart. Mathematically super smart and strategically smart as well … He has an attention to detail beyond belief. He will look for the hair on the gnat's back. No detail is too small to get into with him."

O'Neill's last meeting was with Eric. Whereas Ian got right into the minutiae of the business, Eric was much more a "big-picture kind of guy," says O'Neill. He was more like, 'I would like for you to get us there,' and he would describe the destination."

"We've lost a lot of time during this period of diversification," he told O'Neill. "We have to get back in there. Jim Arnett has managed to get us out of the different businesses we were in, but we have to start growing our market share if we're going to survive in beer. We need to rationalize our brand portfolio, move to a share-growth environment, and make Molson a prominent, global beer company. I don't want to be left behind. We have to move fast and make up for the time we lost during the diversification."

O'Neill tells me in retrospect that two things impressed him about Eric at their first meeting: his foresight and his passion. He explains

From left to right, Dan O'Neill, EVP and COO North American Brewing; Eric Molson, chairman of the board; James Arnett, president and CEO of Molson, 1999. Molson Coors Brewing Company collection.

that, "Back in 1999, the globalization of the beer industry was still in its infancy. Eric, however, knew it was the right direction for the company's long-term survival." As for Eric's fervour for beer, O'Neill says, "It just blew me away. It was incredible … I saw his intensity for beer-making and the brewery right away. I have to say that in all my years in the beer industry, and of all the beer people I met all over the world, Eric knew more about the beer business than any of them."

The last thing the two men talked about at that first meeting was the company's headquarters. They had to be in Montreal "because that's our culture and our base." Would O'Neill be willing to move to the city?

"It's actually perfect," O'Neill told Eric. "My wife is French-Canadian; she's from Aylmer, Quebec. We've lived in so many different cities around the world, it would be great to move back to Quebec, in Montreal."

So the deal was done. With a million stock options and a very rich salary, forty-seven-year-old O'Neill became TMCL's chief operating officer, North American brewing, on 1 April 1999. The understanding was that he would eventually become CEO of the entire company. First, however, he had to contain Molson's spiralling marketing costs and manage its over-capacity. It had seven breweries across the country, three in Quebec and Ontario, and none operating at full potential. The plane that Barrett referred to in his interview was taking off. The rattling was loud, and employee grumblings even louder. Synergies and plant closures were inevitable.

❦

"Reinvent" was the title of the corporation's 1999 annual report. It highlighted the company's reconfigured asset base, the return to its historical core business, and the forging of a new, going-forward strategy. It proudly declared: "We are operating brewers again ... We are reinventing Molson."

At that year's AGM, Eric announced that to reflect its "single focus on brewing," TMCL would become "Molson Inc." At the same shareholders meeting, Eric proposed that R. Ian Molson become deputy chairman of the board. "I promoted Ian and the board agreed," says Eric, "because he was doing well with all the strategic stuff." Even though Eric and his family had rejected Ian's plan to create Molson Holdings, he still viewed the younger Molson as the catalyst to accelerate the company's transformation.

"The pace of the company disturbs me," Eric wrote in a note dated 14 February 1999 to Stephen and Luc Beauregard recommending Ian's advancement. "I notice various degrees of impatience at the board level, so I know it is not just me. We have not rid ourselves of the bureaucratic approach to management left from our past. We need to show hunger, a sense of urgency, and a positive reaction to opportunity; meanwhile, I just hope the world does not leave us behind."

There are times in a company's existence when a board of directors needs to get more involved. Eric saw this as one of them. "Sorely lacking in the company is strategic planning, priority setting, and focus," he wrote. "The board will have to lead until we are sure our management knows where we want to go." Eric ended his message with a statement that became a precursor to the Molson Family Principles he would pen years later:

> Our family commitment to remaining as controlling shareholder and being a force for positive change is absolute and total. We will insist that every possible step be taken to ensure the regular and consistent creation of shareholder value in our company. We expect to be informed and knowledgeable about all material matters affecting the company and its shareholders. We intend to plan for family succession in a more concerted manner, and to this end, I will be proposing to the board that Ian be appointed as Deputy Chairman at the next shareholder's meeting and also that my son Geoffrey join the company in a marketing or strategic development capacity. I hope all this will be in accordance with the board's wishes and the best interests of the company.

Overall, Ian's appointment as deputy chairman was well accepted. He was seen as a complement to Eric, and together they made a good team. For CEO Jim Arnett, "it didn't really change things because Ian was already chair of the board's executive committee." To him, it was just a sign that perhaps Eric, now sixty-one, was getting ready to step down as chairman.

The board change that had a greater impact on Arnett was the addition of O'Neill as a director. Says Arnett, "When we hired O'Neill, we made a *very* rich deal with him, part of which was for him to go on the board. It made sense because the board also wanted to see him and get to know him if he was going to be the next CEO ... But for me, I now had Ian as deputy chairman, and O'Neill as CEO-in-waiting on the board, so it was starting to get a little crowded." Even fifteen years later, there is palpable frustration in his voice.

But according to O'Neill, Arnett's real point of contention was his pay. O'Neill explains that Arnett never knew what he was offered to take the job of COO. And when Arnett learned O'Neill was earning three times his salary and was granted five times more stock options, he was furious.

O'Neill remembers his CEO confronting him a few months into the job: "I was working on Saturday at my desk in Toronto. Jim comes walking in my office and says, 'You earn more than me and you have one million options. Is that correct?' I'm, like jeez, it's Saturday morning, 10:00 a.m., and my boss is asking me about my salary? I didn't know what to say. I said, 'I don't think you should talk to me about that … You should talk to Eric about that … or Ian. You should talk to them, not me.' He wouldn't leave my office. He just sat there in the chair and stared at me. It was nasty."

Eric says Arnett never complained to him. Even if he had, it's unlikely anything would have come of it. O'Neill was already delivering results for Molson, and that's what Eric cared about.

When Matt Barrett first interviewed O'Neill, the banker had asked him, "What do you think of the fact that Molson and Labatt have exactly the same sales revenue in Canada, but that Labatt makes $100 million more in terms of its bottom line?"

O'Neill replied matter of factly, "I think you need to close the gap. I'm sure there are lots of opportunities."

As soon as O'Neill started as COO of Molson, he tackled that $100-million profit gap. "Before O'Neill, we weren't making the decisions we needed to get the costs down at the brewery," Eric says. "There was a lot of resistance to change. O'Neill broke through all that."

The COO began chopping costs by centralizing the Ontario offices into a single location. "In Toronto alone there were *five* different offices," O'Neill says. "I pointed to each one and said, 'We're going to close down all these places and build office space for all of us in the brewery.' I probably offended way too many people because I was on this urgency thing. I was saying stuff like, 'We're going to get bought up! If we don't start performing, we're going to get swallowed up by someone else!'"

He went after further efficiencies and proposed closing the brewery in Barrie – the one Eric inaugurated as president of the Ontario division more than twenty-five years earlier. Eric challenged him. "We bought Barrie in '74 because we had huge plans to go into the US. What's changed?"

"We still want to be big in the US, but we'll never make the kind of volume we need to fill Montreal, Toronto, *and* Barrie," O'Neill replied.

"Can you guarantee that we won't have to open another brewery if we shut down Barrie?" asked Eric.

"I can't, but look: here are the current volumes and here are our projections."

Eric reviewed the numbers. He reflected that it was the first time in years that he was given such a clear, analytical breakdown of Molson's brewing operations. Barrie was running at a meagre 63 per cent capacity. If it was closed, the work would shift to the Toronto and Montreal breweries, raising their capacities from 78 per cent to close to 90 per cent. "You're right," he said, "we need to do it. But brace yourself: there'll be backlash."

🍁

It wasn't only arduous in brewing. Molson's hockey and entertainment group was also at a critical juncture. "When I took the job as CEO," Arnett recalls, "Eric said to me, 'Jim, don't get involved in the hockey team. It takes care of itself. Just get us back to the beer business.' And I said, 'Fine.'

"So I'd been in the job for a little over six months and [the team] wasn't making its numbers … The Street started raising hell because it wasn't making any money. So I *had* to get involved."

By 1999, the Montreal Canadiens and the new Molson Centre were hemorrhaging cash. The club was hit with an annual $9.6 million municipal tax bill, its operating costs were higher than ever, its players were paid in US dollars (the Loonie was at $0.62), and their wages were frothing over with no salary cap in place. On the ice, things were equally dismal. The Habs struggled through their worst season in over forty years, coming last in their division, and missing the playoffs.

In February 1999, Arnett publicly wondered "whether owning a hockey team is necessary to help sell beer." The comment set off a wave of speculations in the media. What did he mean? Was Molson planning to sell the team?

Denials were issued, but in the confines of the boardroom, the company directors decided to take action. The team was in the red, and prospects for a quick turnaround didn't look good. Their eyes turned to Ronald Corey.

The decision was very hard for Eric. Only months before at the Christmas dinner, Corey had been one of the three he singled out to thank for "going to the wall" for Molson. "I liked Ronald. He was loyal, he worked hard, and he was a practical businessman, a sidewalk man. We won two Stanley Cups with him, and he built the Molson Centre. But I think that after seventeen years and the way things were going, he must have felt it was time for him to go. He wasn't the right guy for the future."

Arnett spoke to Corey. It was a huge blow. It was also very public. Corey's sudden departure from the Canadiens was front-page news in Montreal. *La Presse* devoted its entire A1 page to the story, as did the *Gazette*. The news even made the cover of the more intellectual *Le Devoir*.

The months following Corey's departure were dubbed the "summer of speculation." Questions about Corey's successor fuelled newspaper sales. Familiar hockey names like Serge Savard, Pierre Lacroix, Marcel Aubut, Pierre Gauthier, and Bob Gainey were bandied about. The Molson board, however, wasn't just looking for a hockey man. They wanted someone who could reverse the division's bottom line. And on 2 September 1999 at the Molson Centre, businessman Pierre Boivin was introduced as the new president of the Montreal Canadiens. Fans and journalists alike were perplexed. Who was Boivin?

"Boivin was a talented businessman who fit our criteria," says Eric. "He'd had success as president of a large sport-equipment manufacturer and was good in the marketplace. He was good with government. And he was a good citizen. I told him that the team was not only important as a sports club but as a unifying institution in our society."

Boivin says that to this day he can't rationally explain why he ended up accepting the job. "I got seduced! Somewhere in the process, Eric in his quiet way obviously had an impact on me." He was impressed

Pierre Boivin accepting Habs jersey from Réjean Houle (*left*) and Alain Vigneault (*right*). The number 29 inscribed on it denotes the second day of the ninth month, 2 September 1999, the day he began his role as president of the Montreal Canadiens. *La Presse*, 3 September 1999, S1.

by Eric's modesty, reserved nature, and willingness to listen, but it was Eric's broad perspective and his vision that inspired him. For Eric, the team was not only a great sports franchise but a vehicle for social coalescence. And from the start, Boivin sensed that Eric was the kind of chairman who empowered his leaders to fulfill the mission they were entrusted with.

Before accepting, however, Boivin had one condition. "I told Jim Arnett that he had to swear to me that he was not going to sell the team. Otherwise I wouldn't take the job. The response I got was, 'Never. Never. Never will we sell the team.' I heard it from Jim, I heard it from Ian, and I heard it from Eric."

Boivin began working immediately to reverse the team's financial performance. "There was a real turnaround that had to happen. It was losing money fast. But the combination of having to do such a significant turnaround of such a public enterprise was daunting. I mean, you go in there knowing that it's going to take time and that you're probably not going to get it right the first time – or every time – and that you're going to be publicly scrutinized and criticized at every turn along the way ... That's why right up front I told Jim, 'To turn this around, you and I have to go a little distance together here.'" Arnett reassured Boivin that the Canadiens were not for sale.

They did, however, look into all other divestment possibilities, including selling the Molson Centre. Boivin tried. "It became obvious that the Molson Centre couldn't be sold on its own, not unless you wanted to make an incredible write-off. It just didn't have the cash flow yield for a real-estate company to buy it and give you the full value for it."

So within three months of starting in his new position, Boivin knew the status quo was untenable. "It became clear to me that while they were all sincere when they said they wouldn't sell the team, if they didn't do it, they would go from $5 million in losses to $10, $15, even $20 million in losses. They had to do something."

Eric did not want to sell the Canadiens. He thought of the team as a "heritage asset" to be safeguarded. Nonetheless, he sometimes got frustrated when board members spent more time talking about hockey rather than Molson's core business. O'Neill recalls, "The Molson directors would often go to a game the night before our board meeting. The next day they would spend all this time rehashing what trades should be made, which player should be on what line ... Eric found that extremely frustrating. He once turned to me and said, 'We can't keep these people focused on the brewery!' He loved hockey, but he wanted to focus on beer."

So, when it came down to strengthening the brewery versus keeping the team, Eric's choice became clear. His beloved Habs were "too expensive a treasure" for the company to own. "Also, the market kept telling us that a brewery shouldn't own a hockey team," he says. "An expert even illustrated that if we sold the team, our share price would automatically go up by $3. That meant something like an extra $300 million for the brewery."

At the 28 June 2000 annual shareholders' meeting, Eric made the difficult announcement. "As a publicly traded company, we have an obligation to those who invest in our company. Our shareholders have a right to expect a full return on their investment." The Montreal Canadiens and the Molson Centre were up for sale.

❦

It was a starkly revealing decision. People now understood that Molson's "reinvent" also meant the start of a new outlook: no more sacred cows.

In parallel to the changes in hockey, O'Neill continued to shake things up in brewing. Relentless in his drive for synergies, he slashed costs and streamlined the company's brand portfolio. Molson went from supporting fifty-five brands and thousands of individual product lines to seven: four value brands, Molson Canadian, Export Ale, Molson Dry, and Coors, plus three premium brands, Heineken, Corona, and Rickard's. O'Neill also restructured the organization, cutting headcount without flinching. Employees felt the changeover.

"It was tough going for a while," Eric says. O'Neill was ruffling a few feathers, but he was bringing the lustre back to Molson."

Analysts paid attention. They were impressed with O'Neill's resolve to make Molson competitive, to create shareholder value, and to reach specific targets. His commitment to close the $100-million profit gap with Labatt within three years was a clean break from some of the more vapid promises of the past. And O'Neill delivered. Molson's stock price began a steady climb.

Shareholders, including family members, looked favourably on all this activity. O'Neill was good at keeping the Tom Molson gang informed through regular updates, and the financial results helped with family dynamics. Brian Baxter, Cynthia's son, conveyed this in an email to O'Neill on 5 July 2000: "I have told you, and repeat again, how very pleased we all are to have you taking the helm and moving forward. It takes a toll, not only on our net worths but also on family dynamics, to have a company like Molson stagnating financially and drifting strategically. Especially for the 'non-Eric Molson' Molsons, whose future place within the company is ambiguous, there has been a great tension between wanting to support the legacy and watching our largest portfolio holding lose 30 per cent of its value while the general market rises by 300+ per cent. Seeing some positive and dynamic leadership, especially accompanied by a pleasant little stock run up, is a breath of fresh air for all."

As part of his sweep of changes, O'Neill challenged Molson's existing ad agency who'd had the account since 1957. "We need to revitalize the Molson Canadian brand," he told them. "Let's create a new ad campaign with an 'I am Canadian' theme." The advertisers resisted. "They told me they thought it was a terrible idea," says O'Neill, "that it would never work and that if that's what we wanted to do, they would resign. So I told them, 'Okay, why don't you? If you don't want to go along with this, then why are we working with you?'" For the first time in more than forty years, Molson opened the bidding process and invited three new firms to make proposals.

Bensimon Byrne, one of the contenders, came back with research showing that Canadians were proud of their heritage. "Look at all these people," the head of creative said, pointing to a video, "I started asking them questions about Canada, and they just started ranting!" That was the genesis of The Rant.

Switching ad agencies was a brilliant coup for Molson. With the brewery 100 per cent Canadian again, they hit marketing gold with a simple concept: I AM CANADIAN.

On 1 April 2000, the *Toronto Star* front page read: "It's taken Molson to revive the great Canadian identity by showing us the ways in which we aren't American. It delivers its message via a new commercial the company describes ominously as The Rant."

The campaign went viral, long before that term (or even the internet) became ubiquitous. In the ad, Joe – a Canadian everyman performed by actor Jeff Douglas – stands before a movie-theatre audience, politely but passionately ranting about being distinctively Canadian: "I don't live in an igloo ... I have a prime minister, not a president ... a toque is a hat, a chesterfield is a couch, and it's pronounced 'zed' not 'zee' ... Canada is the *second* largest land mass, the *first* nation of hockey, and the *best* part of North America! My name is Joe, and I AM CANADIAN! Thank you."

It caught the attention of the country and the world.

Molson executives were bombarded with calls. "The head of tourism in Canada was in Boston, and she asked me if she could use it,"

O'Neill recalls. "And the head of the Olympic Committee, who was from Sweden, said to me, 'I spent last night with your prime minister drinking Molson Canadian. Can I see this ad?'"

Arnett caught the wave of enthusiasm. "The Rant was a fabulous thing! I even got a letter from the premier of Ontario," he says, laughing. "I got a call from a friend saying, 'My kid is going to Israel to some youth camp. And he's supposed to take something to represent the country. Do you think I can get a copy of The Rant?'"

Arnett still gets goose-bumps remembering the first time he saw it. "I was so excited! It was unbelievable. I said, 'Can we do this? I mean, it's so emotive; and nationalistic! Will people like that or hold it against us?' Anyhow, we ran with it and it was a huge success. It was inspired. Really inspired."

Publicly, Dan O'Neill was a dynamic and engaging executive, a man on a mission who could almost do no wrong. However, there was a darker side to him. Stories started circulating within Molson about how he mistreated people, humiliated them in front of others, belittled them, and openly flirted with younger female staff.

Hearing this, Arnett approached the managers reporting directly to O'Neill and asked if they would be willing to answer questions about their boss. He prepared a summary based on their feedback, complete with statements about the COO's behaviour, and submitted it to the board.

"We had an issue on our hands," says Eric, "but it didn't go very far." The board confronted O'Neill with the report. The COO said he was not surprised by the comments in it, given that his employees didn't like what he was forcing them to do. "I'm being hard on the organization because it's what I need to do to break the old culture and create a new one."

The board accepted O'Neill's account, and the report almost backfired on Arnett. Several board members thought he was playing games, trying to turn the tables against O'Neill for his own benefit.

"Jim was starting to sell other people rather than O'Neill as the future CEO of the company," recalls Eric. "It started to look like he was doing it to stay on longer as CEO. When we first named Jim, it was clear that it would only be for an interim period of three years, but he didn't want to go in the end. He liked his position ... He tried all the tricks in the book. He would talk about how wonderful Boivin and others were, how it wouldn't work with O'Neill because he was too tough on people, and how we should get in a headhunting firm to conduct a new search for his successor."

The board's decision, however, was unanimous. Arnett's time as CEO was coming to an end. Molson made the announcement on 4 May 2000: Jim Arnett would be stepping down as CEO at the annual shareholders meeting on 27 June and would be replaced by Dan O'Neill.

Sandy Riley, who became a Molson board member in 1999 and is a good friend of Arnett's, describes it as a difficult transition. "I think there was an understanding that Jim had to get the company back together and that ultimately there would be a change of leadership. But I think what happened was that Jim kind of fell in love with the job of CEO and kind of forgot what the deal was. Others would say that Jim was probably the first guy that really caught onto Dan. If I look back on it, it was a little bit of both: Jim *did* like the job, but he *was* also concerned about what would happen if Dan took over. At the end of the day, the board and Eric felt that Molson needed an operator, and Jim's deal was that he step aside. But he didn't step aside as well as he should have and that led to friction."

Eric was uneasy. He was grateful for all Arnett had done. "He's the one who brought us back to our brewing roots and made us 100 per cent Canadian again," he says. At the same time, however, the company had to move forward, and that required a new type of leader. With a heavy heart, Eric took his pad from his shirt pocket and jotted down his thoughts: "Jim is very upset ... Alix [his wife] is saying we've booted him out ... very bitter ... very difficult."

Arnett, however, now looks back on that period with a positive perspective. "I felt good about how I left the company. Eric asked me to do something. I did it, put a bow around it, and said, 'Here it is.' So, as far as I was concerned, I'd done the job I was hired to do. At the end of the day, for me personally, it was a fantastic experience, and I will always be grateful to Eric for giving me that opportunity."

He pauses, looking at me intently through black-rimmed glasses. "But remember," he says, "after I left, we stopped talking ... Eric and I didn't talk for at least five years after that."

✦

The start of the twenty-first century was an exciting time for Molson. The stock was up, results were positive, and customers thirsted for its beer. Molson was "cool" once again.

"When you talked about Molson at the time, it was an organization that everyone wanted to join," says Robert Coallier from his office at Agropur Dairy Cooperative in Longueuil, Quebec, where he is now CEO. In May 2000, Coallier had just been hired as Molson's CFO. About his decision to take the job, he says, "The fact that the company was refocusing on its main business generated a momentum and excitement I found very appealing. Maybe it was also because I was this French-Canadian guy, born and raised in Montreal – so perhaps it was the aura of the Molson name that made me excited to join the company."

Part of Eric's ambition in getting Molson's head office back to Montreal was to have the company run by people who understood the history and social fabric that made the company unique, people connected to "the sidewalk," the "*pouls de la population*" – the public vibe.

By 2000, Eric saw his aspiration materialize. O'Neill had moved to Montreal, and the new leadership team under him included a number of bilingual Québécois. There was Robert Coallier, the new CFO; Marie Giguère, the new head of legal; Bernard Cormier, the head of human resources; Jean-Paul MacDonald, in charge of corporate communications; and Raynald Douin, responsible for the Quebec/Atlantic region. On the hockey front, there was Pierre Boivin. Eric felt Molson had a talented group of executives who "got it."

Nonetheless, there were inevitable tensions. Habs team president Pierre Boivin, for example, says: "Dan and I never got along. I know the good things he did for the company when he first started as COO, but he was a ruthless operating executive with zero people skills – a dangerous guy. In my book, a very dangerous guy."

Fortunately, the two men did not have to work together for long. "I started with Jim Arnett, and eight months later I was reporting to Dan," says Boivin. "But there was never any affinity with him, and it's clear that I never would have stayed under Dan. But it never came up, because the sales process for the team had already started." Right after the annual general shareholders' meeting in June 2000 when O'Neill was named CEO, he and Boivin held a press conference to announce that the Montreal Canadiens and the Molson Centre were up for sale. The CEO gave 31 December 2000 as the deadline for the transaction to be finalized.

O'Neill says that as soon as he finished answering the reporters' questions and got off the stage, his phone rang. It was George Gillett Jr, an American real-estate developer and serial entrepreneur with a roller-coaster career. (He had declared personal bankruptcy in 1992.) "I understand the Montreal Canadiens are for sale," he said. "I'm interested in buying the team. I've been a sports fanatic since childhood. I came close to buying the Colorado Avalanche. I looked at the Florida Panthers. I'm now looking at the Ottawa Senators ... but there is no other franchise that I would rather own than the Montreal Canadiens."

It turned out, however, that the price Molson was asking for was too high for Gillett. Besides, he said he didn't want to participate in an investment-bank led auction. Other potential buyers came forward, but they too eventually backed down. The price was too steep.

"We spent months trying to sell the team. It was really distracting," says O'Neill. "I went door to door, but when you're trying to sell a company that's losing $12 million a year, it's not easy. I went everywhere in Canada."

"Dan became really worried," recalls Boivin. "He started thinking that he might not be able to sell this thing and that he might have to hold onto it for another year or two. Remember, he had promised the Street that he would have the deal done by the end of the year, so the pressure was on."

Finally, an offer came in. It was approved by the board on 15 December 2000. "But then," says O'Neill, "the buyer called me immediately after the board meeting – he must have had some connection with the board, I don't know – and told me, 'The down payment I'm supposed to give you? I can only give you 30 per cent less than what we discussed. I don't have the money right now.' So I told him the deal was off."

O'Neill was forced to announce that Molson would miss its 31 December deadline. Analysts were critical, characterizing the delay as a "significant stumble" for the CEO – "the first time O'Neill has drawn a line in the sand but hasn't been able to make it."

Soon after, O'Neill left for a family Christmas holiday in Vail. Skiing, however, was not the only thing on his mind. As soon as he got off the plane, he called George Gillett, then based in Colorado. The next day they met in Gillett's office. Recalls O'Neill, "I walked into his board-room, and on the wall, he had every team in the NHL that was up for sale. There were about six teams that were for sale, and he had all their numbers and statistics up on his wall. So I showed him the deal for the Montreal Canadiens."

Gillett read the letter of intent, wrote a couple of notes on the back of the page modifying some of the terms, and said, "Here's the deal I'll do." The two men shook hands.

"Dan called me on New Year's Eve," says Robert Coallier, Molson's CFO. "I was at my cottage and he asked me, 'When can you get to Vail?' I said, 'Dan, it's New Year's Eve!' So he replied, 'Tomorrow is fine.'"

Due diligence started right away, and by the end of January 2001, the deal was announced. Gillett was the new owner of the Montreal Canadiens and would pay $275 million for 80.1 per cent of the team (Molson retained a 19.9 per cent interest in the hockey club) and 100 per cent of the Molson Centre. It was far less than the $325 million O'Neill hoped for. The arena alone had cost Molson $265 million to build five years before. Nonetheless, O'Neill justified the write-down by saying that Molson would no longer have to absorb annual losses of $10 to $12 million, as it had in each of the past three years.

Some said it was a sweetheart deal for Gillett. And in many ways it was. Given his credit history, the American businessman didn't have much borrowing power. He did, however, have tenacity and was dealing with an eager vendor. The sale announced in January didn't close until August 2001, and for those eight months, Gillett worked with O'Neill to get financing. They eventually convinced the Caisse de dépôt, Quebec's public pension fund, to lend Gillett close to $180 million. This opened the door to other investors for the balance of the price. The reason that the Caisse agreed to lend Gillett the money, however, was that the loan was guaranteed by Molson.

"If George was ever in default, Molson would buy back the team for the remainder of the value of the loan," explains Coallier, who helped put together the financing with the Caisse. "So it was a commitment to buy back the team if there was trouble, and then we would become the owners again. It served two purposes: one, to secure the Caisse that they wouldn't lose their money; and two, to secure us that a financial institution wouldn't sell the team to Labatt – which was our greatest concern."

Eric had left the negotiations to Molson executives. He had, however, two conditions: the team must stay in Montreal and it must not fall in the "wrong" hands (like Labatt's). With those two stipulations met, he firmly supported O'Neill, Coallier, and the rest team working on the deal.

Coallier was impressed by Eric's resolve. "I don't remember one day when Eric said, 'We shouldn't have sold the team.' Once the decision was taken, he stuck with it. That's something about Eric: when a decision was made, a decision was made. It maybe didn't happen overnight, but once it was made, the marching orders were very, very clear."

Determination was key to finalizing the sale to Gillett. As soon as it was announced that an American was buying the legendary Canadiens, the media's reaction was visceral. The *bleu, blanc, et rouge* would be owned by a *foreigner*? How could someone like Gillett even understand what the team meant to Montreal and Quebec?

The public debate got even more heated when the Caisse decided to finance the deal. Quebec Premier Bernard Landry felt obliged to stand in front of Quebec's National Assembly and argue that the government did not participate in the financing of the deal and that the Caisse had acted on its own accord.

What Eric remembers, however, was how Landry concluded his speech: "Et n'oublions pas que c'est une famille québécoise, profondément québécoise d'ailleurs par certains aspects, folkloriquement québécoise, la famille Molson, qui a pris la décision de vendre. Et la famille Molson est toujours dans le portrait et reprendra l'entreprise si jamais l'acheteur américain devenait à être défaillant" ("And let us not forget that it is a Quebec family, deeply Québécois in some respects, folklorically Québécois, the Molson family, who made the decision to sell. And the Molson family is still in the picture and will take over the business if ever the US buyer defaults"; 2nd session, 36th legislature, 8 May 2001).

To be called a "Québécois family," a "deeply Québécois family," even a "folkloric Québécois family" by a staunch sovereignist like Premier Landry was something Eric never thought he would hear in his lifetime. Although bittersweet given the circumstances, it made him proud. Perhaps all the efforts he and Jane had made over the years to learn French, send their kids to French school, and support francophone Quebec institutions were paying off. Perhaps his generation of Molsons were no longer *les maudits anglais* of the past.

❋

As much as Eric was concerned with the Molson identity and the company's long-term reputation, his CEO appeared obsessed with the firm's stock price and its every fluctuation. In this respect, Eric and Dan O'Neill were very different. Each up-tick seemed to bolster O'Neill to execute whatever initiative he was working on. It's called "driving shareholder value," and in many ways it's a good thing. That is, until the measures taken to drive up the stock price in the short term become detrimental to the corporation's long-term health.

O'Neill's ambition to grow the Molson's stock price was inextricably linked to his compensation and his one million stock options. In essence, every time he took the stock up one dollar, he made a million. Some say that it got to the point where "driving shareholder value" was almost code for "making Dan rich." O'Neill himself was unabashedly overt about his financial objectives. He spoke about it not only to his direct reports but to all other employees and even to clients.

Dave Perkins, a long-time Molson man and then president of the Ontario/West region, remembers how his boss used to speak to customers. "We took our biggest customers away each year with their wives on this thing called the President's Council. Dan would come and stand up in front of them and talk about how many options he had, how much money he'd made so far, and how much he was hoping to make. He wouldn't say, 'Thank you, I appreciate your business,' like you would expect. It was all about him, what he'd done, and how much money he'd made, and the customers used to laugh their heads off!"

Whatever his motivations, O'Neill continued to make positive moves as CEO. An example – one that was particularly important to Eric – involved Molson's business in the United States.

Since 1993, when Mickey Cohen sold Molson's US business to Foster's and Miller, sales in that country had fallen by 35 per cent, despite high growth for other imported beers. They had gone from being the second-largest selling import beer in the United States to the seventh in less than ten years.

Eric couldn't believe it. "We used to have a great export business into the US. We got into the US ahead of the other Canadian brewers and managed to grow our share of the total US import market from like 4 per cent in the early '70s to about 17 per cent in the mid-1980s. But then running a sales force in the States was a huge business, and we couldn't handle it. So Mickey Cohen decided to do it with someone else. It didn't work. We gave up control, and our brands became attention-deprived. We had to buy them back."

And that's what O'Neill did. For $200 million, Molson repurchased 100 per cent of its brands in the United States. "By reacquiring our brands, we are taking control of one of our major growth opportunities – the US market," O'Neill told the press. The day the deal was announced, the stock price went up by 6.2 per cent.

"When we bought the Molson brands back from Miller, they were badly damaged," says Dave Perkins who later went on to run Molson's US business. "There was double-digit decline, the brands were being discounted like crazy, and the portfolio was all messed up."

Knowing they couldn't turn around their US business on their own, Molson decided to find another partner. Coors was the natural choice. Molson already had a deal with them in Canada to distribute and sell their beer. Now they chose to do a mirror image of that arrangement, a partnership whereby Coors would distribute and sell Molson products south of the border. And unlike their previous arrangement with

Miller, Molson retained 50.1 per cent of the US partnership with Coors. Eric insisted, "We have to keep control of our brands."

With parallel arrangements on both sides of the border, the Molson and Coors teams met regularly for business reviews. Gradually, their two leaders, Dan O'Neill and Leo Kiely, got to know each other. "I met Dan O'Neill because he had our brands in Canada, and then we ended up with the Molson brands in the US," says Leo Kiely, then COO of Coors. "Dan is a very intense, very competitive, and hard-driven guy ... I'm different, I like to build teams. I like to empower the people to get things done. I can be very hands-on, but I tend to expect people to run their businesses. Dan is much more a top-down kind of character. It's okay – there are legitimately different ways to run a business."

O'Neill, however, was not the only one running Molson. Officially he was, but behind the scenes, Ian Molson continued to wield influence. His opinion carried a lot of weight.

"There was no doubt about it, Ian was very involved," says then CFO Robert Coallier. "He was on the phone and in contact with Dan all the time. He was more involved than any chairman or deputy chairman I've ever seen ... At the end of the day, this was Ian's full-time job. Think about it: deputy chairman as a full-time job? That's not normal."

Director Dan Colson contrasts Eric's collegial style with Ian's more directive approach. "I think Eric is a gentleman, and I think he's very smart, but he's not someone who leads from the front. He used to sit at board meetings and ask everyone what they thought. And I used to think, 'Well, Eric, you're the frigging chairman, and you've got more shares than anyone else. Why don't you decide and tell everybody what you think?' But that's not the way he is. It's exactly the way Ian is, though. Ian with hardly any shares was telling everyone what to do, what not to do, and basically running the joint."

In Colson's opinion, Ian's manoeuvrings became more cogent once O'Neill joined the company. "Ian completely took over O'Neill and brought him to his camp," he says. Soon, a pernicious "Ian–O'Neill–Eric" triangle was created. As Colson explains, this was facilitated by

O'Neill's nature: "Dan was one of these guys who was always trying to play both sides against the middle. He always pretended to Eric to be in his camp, when in fact he was constantly (in my view) conniving with Ian. He's one of these guys who thought he would line up with the heavy battalion. He thought that Ian was on some sort of irreversible march to take over the business, so he basically threw his hand in with Ian. They were basically in cahoots together."

It got to the point where some of the executives at the brewery quietly murmured that Ian was the actual CEO, with Dan as his COO. Ian had a hand in everything, from strategy to the company's talent pool. Dave Perkins says, "Ian operated at a depth and directiveness that was far beyond what was appropriate for his title of deputy chairman ... He was incredibly well briefed on operational aspects of the business. It went down to the level of people too." Perkins concludes: "There is no doubt that many people had the impression that Ian wanted to run the business and did as much as he could with Dan as his agent."

And just like O'Neill, Ian extolled one goal: the creation of shareholder value. But the question remains: shareholder value at what cost?

On 13 September 2000, O'Neill organized a long overdue company-wide, management off-site meeting. It was the first such gathering in eight years. Eric kicked it off. "We are in the process of remaking the ethic of individual responsibility a central facet of the way we do business," he said. He extolled the values of hard work, integrity, quality, innovation, customer focus, and accountability. These, he said, should "become the cornerstone of the way you individually do business for Molson."

Ian followed with his version of what mattered. "Be under no illusions, however, the raison d'être of Molson, our core mission, as employees of a public company, is the creation of shareholder value. Arguably, this should be the only objective of the company. All that we do should be in support of this objective, be it product quality, marketing, advertising, consumer satisfaction, financial management, even core values. There should be no confusion. Shareholder value is the objective, and all else is the means to this end."

In many ways, Ian was right. The creation of value for the shareholders has been the leitmotif of governance of public corporations for years, and Molson's recent history was not stellar in this regard. The danger in the drive for shareholder value, however, arises when it is done in an indiscriminate way, without consideration of the interests of the other stakeholders – including the sustainability of the enterprise itself. The potential for unabashed greed is high and can lead to disastrous results. (Think of the 2008 financial crisis.)

Eric's position was more nuanced. For him, corporate governance wasn't simply answering to the needs of Molson's capital providers. "You have to work for the benefit of *all* stakeholders. Not only your shareholders – although they are very important, but also your employees, creditors, suppliers, customers, and the communities where you operate … In this day and age, many companies are under enormous market pressure to deliver results in the short term, quarter after quarter. This short-term focus erodes their ability to plan for the long-term success of the company. The ultimate goal of your company decisions should be to maximize the long-term value of the corporation."

Therein lies the difference between Eric and Ian. Whereas Ian's position on what constitutes good governance is shareholder-focused (i.e., it's all about the Street – Bay Street or Wall Street – and what matters most is what the shareholders get out of the corporation), Eric's priority is the sustained health of the company. The shareholder, from Eric's standpoint, is only one of multiple stakeholders. And it's not that Eric is some superior, altruistic being. He simply takes a long-term view and thinks shareholders will do better in the long run if they continue to own stock in a company that is healthy and persists in doing well.

O'Neill was aware of Eric's vision for the company, even if his chairman was not forcefully vocal about it. "Eric is not the kind of person who bangs his fist on the table," says O'Neill, "but he knows what he wants to do. He knows it, he wants it done, and he expects you to get it done." He also understood that what energized Eric was not the same as what motivated Ian. "Some people, like Ian, are driven to maximize profitability, and others, like Eric, are driven to keep the company going and grow the long-term legacy. So what do you do? Do you maximize profitability? Get it up to a point and sell the company? But then that means your heritage is gone … A controlling family is really there as a legacy protector. They're going to protect it and make sure it's not tainted, it's not cheated, it's not taken away from. Eric was the protector of the Molson name."

On 13 September 2000, as the Molson managers listened to Ian and Eric's speeches, they agreed that the company's culture needed to evolve; some of the complacency entrenched years prior had not been completely cleared away. Still, as Ian spoke of shareholder value, some speculated that he was more concerned about his own pocketbook. Dave Perkins summarizes the sentiment: "I think the difficulty with Ian Molson is that people questioned his motives. They wondered: is he here to help build a stronger company for the future, or is there a stronger personal agenda at play?"

10 The Molson Family Principles

A people that values its privileges above its principles soon loses both.

DWIGHT D. EISENHOWER (1890–1969)

The Christmas 2015 celebrations are over and by 28 December, everyone is gone. Geoff, Kate, and their four kids are off to Massachusetts to visit other relatives. Justin, Julia, and their youngsters are headed back to Vermont. Andrew, our girls, and I are the only ones left in Massawippi with Eric and Jane.

"Headlights and taillights." Eric smiles as he adds wood to the small fireplace in the kitchen. "Two great holiday moments: the anticipation of seeing everyone as they arrive, and the quiet once they're gone." The fresh logs catch fire and crackle.

With three dogs, eight adults, and ten grandchildren (plus another on the way) chatting, opening presents, running around, laughing and playing games (with the occasional squabble, of course), the house has been busy. But I know that Eric and Jane love it. "I wouldn't have it any other way," says Jane. She also invites her siblings (Eric's are in Ivry) and friends who are alone or have no other plans to come for the traditional turkey dinner.

Eric pokes the fire one last time. Sitting at the kitchen table, he pulls his small pad of paper from his breast pocket and jots something down. Eric and his notes: I wonder if that's how he got through all he did, noticing, planning, writing. He always seems calm.

Was he like that back in the early 2000s? How did he confront the "Ian situation," risk losing everything, and remain unflappable? For Eric, 2003 to 2005 were gruelling years. Did he ever doubt himself? Was he scared? What was it like to be confronted by a whole bunch of bullies at once? Was he tempted to just let it go and let them have their way? How did he feel about walking away from all that money?

From my interviews, I've learned that Eric was driven by something larger. He never lost sight of what was most important to him – reinforcing the Molson legacy and transferring something greater than he'd received to the next generation. Perhaps it was this sense of stewardship that gave him the fortitude to overcome the setbacks on his path.

I've always admired the work of Austrian psychiatrist and Holocaust survivor, Viktor E. Frankl. In my opinion, his 1946 *Man's Search for Meaning* should be obligatory reading for all students. In his introduction to the 1992 edition, Frankl gives readers advice: "Don't aim at success – the more you aim at it and make it a target, the more you are going to miss it. For success, like happiness, cannot be pursued; it must ensue, and it only does so as the unintended side-effect of one's dedication to a cause greater than oneself or as the by-product of one's surrender to a person other than oneself."

I think that Eric, through his duality of purpose to the Molson legacy and to future generations, found such a cause. I also believe this higher purpose gave him a powerful fountainhead of inner strength and fortitude – easy to underestimate by those who went by appearances only.

❦

Things looked good at the company's AGM of June 2001. Results were positive, and the share value was up by 88 per cent from the year before – the best share price performance of all the major brewers globally that year. CEO Dan O'Neill was understandably upbeat. Standing in front of his shareholders, he boasted that Molson was one of the few breweries in the world that was growing. "Our opportunities outnumber our resources." His objective: to keep the corporation flourishing through international expansion.

Molson CEO Dan O'Neill responds to questions at a news conference after the annual general meeting on Wednesday, 27 June 2001. Photo: Paul Chiasson; licensed by the Canadian Press.

By then, Molson had already made its first foray outside North America. In December 2000, it penetrated Brazil with the purchase of Bavaria from Companhia de Bebidas das Américas, or AmBev, the largest beverage company in Latin America and the world's third-largest brewer by volume (behind Anheuser-Busch and Heineken). When the country's top two brewers, Antarctica and Brahma, wanted to merge to create AmBev, a condition for approval by Brazil's antitrust authorities was the sale of Bavaria. Molson grabbed the chance and bought it plus five other breweries in different parts of Brazil for what amounted to, with incentive payments, nearly $150 million.

Although Bavaria was Brazil's fourth-largest brand, it was not a premium beer and only had about 3.5 per cent of the local market. But O'Neill dismissed the naysayers, contending that it gave Molson an entry into one of the fastest-growing beer markets in the world. It was a part of the world that he understood, having worked in Brazil for a few years when he was with S.C. Johnson. He also thought it was a good test for Molson. "Bavaria was a little deal. We just got our toes in the water to see if we could manage before doing anything too crazy." Besides, when they negotiated the purchase, Molson mitigated some of the risk by arranging to keep using AmBev's distribution network for the next four years.

Ian Molson was also keen. "Ian loved Brazil," says O'Neill. "Strategically, it was right – the youth, the growth, the population. He just saw the potential."

An additional upside to Bavaria was the possibility to develop closer ties with AmBev. Four months after buying the brand, Ian flew with O'Neill to Rio de Janeiro to meet with Marcel Hermann Telles, then AmBev's co-chairman and CEO. The three men had dinner, talked business, and discussed future opportunities. Telles revealed that he and his partners were working on buying Quilmes, the leading brewer in Argentina, and that one day they were going to get their hands on Anheuser-Busch, the American giant. O'Neill now laughs as he remembers thinking, "Yeah, sure you will!" In 2008, however, AmBev did just that: they bought Anheuser-Busch and created AB InBev, the world's largest brewer.

"We greatly enjoyed our discussions," Ian wrote in a letter to Telles dated 27 April 2001, "and as I hope you have realized we are committed to developing a long-term and mutually advantageous relationship between Molson and AmBev ... As you pursue the Quilmes opportunity we would be more than pleased to consider working together with you if you ever concluded that you required a partner for any reason, financial or otherwise. The Bemberg family [owners of Quilmes] is well known to us and if we could make a contribution or lend any assistance, we would be more than pleased to do so." When Ian sensed an opportunity, he boldly seized it. It was a quality that Eric appreciated.

🍁

"The premise was 'We've got to get bigger,'" O'Neill says. "Eric kept telling me, 'We've got to get bigger or we'll be eaten up. And he was right. The industry was consolidating."

In his office, O'Neill had posted a series of charts showing where Molson was compared to the largest brewers in the world. "It was obvious that the distance between us and the big guys was getting bigger. They were growing faster. So even though we were getting bigger in absolute terms, we were smaller in relative terms, and that impacted our purchasing power and our world-wide leverage."

In January 2001, an enticing opportunity arose. Carling, the best-selling beer brand in the UK, was up for sale. Again, it was an antitrust situation: British regulators were forcing Interbrew, the Belgian brewer of Stella Artois and Labatt beers, to sell Carling after it increased its UK market share to 32 per cent with the purchase of Bass Brewers in August 2000. O'Neill raced to bid for it. He was not alone. Coors, Carlsberg, Heineken, Anheuser-Busch, and others also spoke up. With nearly one-fifth of the UK market, the second most profitable beer market in the world, Carling was a coveted asset.

The Molson team spent most of December in London that year working to win the deal. So did Coors. "Pete Coors literally stayed there over Christmas to get the deal done," recalls O'Neill.

Leo Kiely was also heavily involved in the negotiations on behalf of Coors. He remembers how the Molson and Coors teams regularly ran into each other during the due diligence process. "It felt like we were following the Molson people through London," he says.

In the end, Coors made the higher bid and won. The Carling sale closed on 23 December 2001 for US$1.7 billion. "We were shocked," recalls Robert Coallier. "We couldn't believe it when we saw the price Coors was prepared to pay." The business case just didn't make sense, according to O'Neill: "We were numbers-driven people, and we said this is how much we would pay for this kind of pay-out. Coors was willing to pay more, so we ended up being the number two bidder ... It was a lot of work to lose."

O'Neill was left grappling with familiar questions. What would be Molson's big, international acquisition? Where would it get its growth? The pressure mounted. Analysts grumbled that O'Neill's cost-cutting efforts, albeit effective, could only sustain the company's earnings growth for so long. Molson needed to expand, increase its revenue stream, or its options would quickly narrow to one: sell the business.

O'Neill's focus turned back to Brazil. Since the deal with AmBev a year prior, the Molson team realized it was impossible to make money in Brazil with a meagre 3.5 per cent market share. Coallier explains, "When we acquired Bavaria from AmBev, we thought we had done a fantastic deal because we had paid very little for it up front and we were supposed to pay the balance of the sale based on additional market share. What we didn't realize was that for AmBev, the brand was a write-off, and they didn't care about the balance of sale. They just wanted to show the competition bureau in Brazil that they got rid of their smallest brand. After the deal, they still owned like 80 per cent of the market. They were supposed to distribute Bavaria for us, and they were doing a lousy job of it."

According to Molson's chief legal officer at the time, Marie Giguère, "We knew that Brazil was very challenging in terms of distribution because of its poor infrastructure. Getting your product to the market there is complicated. I guess we were hoping that the agreement we had for AmBev to distribute Bavaria would work. But given that AmBev was the dominant player in Brazil, I don't think that was very realistic." On 8 November 2001, less than a year after its AmBev deal, Molson announced it was going to set up its own distribution network in Brazil to expedite the penetration of Bavaria.

Then Cervejarias Kaiser SA came up. Would Molson be interested in buying it?

Kaiser was the second-largest brewer in Brazil, owned by the Coca-Cola Bottlers of Brazil (75.5 per cent), Coca-Cola (10.3 per cent), and Heineken (14.2 per cent). By acquiring it, Molson would get an immediate 18 per cent of the Brazilian beer market, the fourth largest in the world and growing by an impressive 7 per cent per year. Ian Molson and Dan O'Neill agreed it was an excellent opportunity.

Says Coallier, "It made a lot of sense. It was a great organization. We also felt that being distributed by Coke and being their partner would be awesome."

Ian followed the opportunity closely and regularly travelled to Brazil with O'Neill to work on the transaction. A due-diligence team was put together, and the project was given a code name: "Project Do It."

Everyone knew there were risks involved, as with all business transactions. The most obvious danger was that even though Kaiser held the number-two position in Brazil, AmBev remained the market leader by far. And AmBev had the reputation of being ruthless. Still, O'Neill reassured the sceptics that the situation could be managed. Says Dave Perkins, "I remember Dan saying, 'I met with the AmBev guys; it's all going to work out.' He was implying that the AmBev guys were going to let us, you know, be in a 'cozy' market with them. And I'm sure they let Dan believe that, because that's how they operated."

The Molson team also took comfort in the fact that Heineken wanted to buy the business as well. Coallier explains: "Heineken owned like 15 per cent of Kaiser already, they were members of its board, they had been part-owners for like twenty years. We felt that they knew everything there was to know about what was going on. And they wanted to buy it. So we found that very reassuring."

In the end, Project Do It came to fruition. On 18 March 2002, Molson bought Kaiser for a whopping $1.2 billion. The transaction was approved by Molson's board of directors, despite its hefty price tag and all the risks linked with doing business in Brazil. "It certainly required a lot more convincing of the board than the Bavaria acquisition," says CLO Marie Giguère. "Kaiser was much bigger and a lot more complex. We had to make sure we aligned the interests of the Coca-Cola bottlers with ours because they were going to distribute our beer. So we had them keep a stake in the company for a while through cash and shares ... At the end of the day, Dan convinced the board. He was a very good salesman."

In 2002, the Molson board consisted of some pretty heavy hitters. They included:

- Matthew W. Barrett, group chief executive of Barclays Bank plc
- H. Sanford ("Sandy") Riley, president and CEO of Investors Group Inc.
- Dr Francesco Bellini, chairman of Picchio International Inc. and past chairman, CEO and co-founder of BioChem Pharma Inc.
- Daniel W. Colson, vice chairman of Hollinger Inc. and deputy chairman and CEO of Telegraph Group Ltd
- Donald G. Drapkin, vice chairman and director of MacAndrews & Forbes Holdings Inc.
- Luc Beauregard, founding chairman and CEO of National Public Relations
- Dr Lloyd I. Barber, president emeritus of the University of Regina
- The three Molsons: Eric, Stephen, and Ian
- CEO Daniel J. O'Neill

After the Kaiser transaction, three new directors were added to the roster: Luiz Otávio P. Gonçalves, founder and past CEO of Kaiser; Robert A. Ingram, COO and president, Pharmaceutical Operations of GlaxoSmithKline plc; and David P. O'Brien, chairman of Encana Corporation. It was "a talented group," according to Eric. "We had a good mix of insiders and independent directors. They were financially literate, they understood our business, supported our overall strategy, and they were willing to challenge each other and our management team while keeping a climate of open discussion and respect."

Colson recalls the board's exchange about Kaiser. "O'Neill recommended the Kaiser deal to the board. He said it was a wonderful idea, and he convinced everybody, including Eric, that it was a brilliant opportunity. Ian was also quite vocal and very keen on Brazil."

Eric was far less involved with the Kaiser transaction than Ian was. He agreed "it was a very exciting expansion … huge potential … lots of thirsty throats to drink beer in Brazil," but he allowed Ian to take the lead on it. "I never visited the breweries down there. Ian did. Ian would have been up to his neck in the Kaiser transaction. Brazil was his baby. He created a Brazil advisory board, recruited a couple of guys, and went down there many times. It was a separate group from the board

Molson
Daily Close, MOL.A - TSE

The Molson share price was on a steady nine-month climb and closed at $35.30 on 3 April 2002, two weeks after the Kaiser purchase was announced.

who oversaw the due diligence, and it included O'Neill and Ian … Ian worked well with O'Neill and took charge of that to a certain extent."

When they announced the Kaiser deal in March 2002, Heineken was "livid." "I mean, they were *livid*," emphasizes Robert Coallier. "That's when I turned to Dan and said, 'We don't need to own 100 per cent of Kaiser. Why don't we sell a portion of it to Heineken?' And we did." Molson combined Kaiser with its existing Bavaria operation and sold 20 per cent of it to Heineken on 17 April 2002. "Heineken paid a $200-million premium for it, so we were feeling pretty good about the whole thing."

The question then became who was going to run the Brazil operation. Straight away, O'Neill recommended Coallier. He argued that his forty-one-year-old CFO was bright, skilled in finance, and very reliable. "I had trust in Coallier," says O'Neill. "You need to have trust and confidence in your numbers when you're about to take on a new business. Ian felt the same way." They agreed that Coallier was the man Molson needed in Brazil.

There were, however, sceptics. Several board members pointed out that Coallier had never worked in a foreign jurisdiction. He was unfamiliar with Brazil's culture and local business practices and didn't speak Portuguese. But more importantly, they said that in order to face a competitor as fierce as AmBev, Molson needed a seasoned executive. Coallier had no hands-on operational experience.

"I told them you can't parachute in a guy to a new country and expect him to be the answer to your problems," recalls Colson. "You need to have local talent."

Eric agreed. "Don't get me wrong. I liked Coallier, but we hadn't had much luck with putting accountants in charge in the past, and Coallier was a Canadian who didn't know much more about South America than I did – and I didn't know much."

Coallier himself resisted the appointment initially. "Dan and I had a great relationship," he says. "He trusted me. But the first time he asked me to take the job in Brazil, I said, 'No, I won't go.'"

O'Neill urged Coallier to change his mind. Colson explains the CEO's insistence: "O'Neill couldn't delegate and he was a control freak. So he needed to get one of his acolytes to do the job. And that's how he decided to send down Coallier as CEO."

Ian backed O'Neill's choice. "After I said no to Dan," recalls Coallier, "Ian insisted a lot that I go down. He even told me that if I wanted a future in the company, I should seriously consider this opportunity. It was a strong incentive. Ian wanted someone who understood the finances of the operation. So, you know, they knew I was loyal to the organization, they wanted a Canadian, and I guess they thought I could do it."

On 16 May 2002, two years after joining Molson as CFO, Robert Coallier was named president and chief executive officer of Cervejarias Kaiser. He relocated to Brazil in August 2002. And though it was all new to him, he rapidly got up to speed. It only took him a few weeks on the inside to realize that there would be trouble ahead. By the end of September, he says, "I remember calling Dan and telling him, 'Dan, we'll never make the numbers we thought we'd get to in Brazil. Never.'"

Beyond Brazil, there were problems brewing closer to home. The co-hesion amongst the Molson directors was starting to come unglued.

Marie Giguère says that when she first became Molson's corporate secretary in August 1999, the board was healthy and participative. "Most board members had a position. Matt Barrett played an import-ant role; people respected and listened to him … Danny Colson also had a point of view on things, as did Don Drapkin. Lloyd Barber had been on the board for a long time, so he had seen quite a number of things. So I think different people played their own role on the board."

Like others, she credits Eric for making sure the directors could freely speak their mind. "There are two kinds of chairmen: there are the ones who have been CEO and think they're still CEO, and there are the ones who haven't been CEO and are playing their role as chair-man properly, letting the CEO do his job. Eric was the latter, and he made sure that everybody expressed their point of view on the board. He allowed for there to be an open discussion amongst directors."

Gradually, however, boardroom dynamics shifted with the growing influence of Ian Molson. As deputy chairman and the most vocal and forceful Molson family member on the board, his sway was undeniable. "The board listened to Ian," says Giguère, "probably because we were involved in a lot of M&A transactions, and Ian had some experience in that. So I think the other directors listened to him. And he also had very strong views about things, so he made his presence felt for sure."

Everyone noticed the change. Robert Coallier, who participated in most board meetings, watched Ian start "playing a more important role" and "taking a lot of space. Eric would lead the meeting, but he wouldn't necessarily get involved in the active conversation or debate. Eric is more of a listener. He analyzed what was going on, made his own opinion, but he wouldn't get into an argument."

Eric preferred that the board come up with its own recommenda-tions instead of imposing his will. He felt it was a more effective way to govern and use the talent around the table. He didn't care about being the first to speak or getting credit for ideas; his only concern was that opinions be tabled and openly discussed. While some recognized that this approach allowed him to have perspective and see the big picture, others viewed it as a weakness. Colson, for example, says that Ian with his more dynamic style was "running circles around Eric." Ian's authority, however, went beyond Molson's board. According to Colson, Ian got "involved in the day-to-day stuff with O'Neill" – a sharp contrast to Eric's CEO-centric approach. "Ian and O'Neill were buddy-buddy, so they would hatch all these wonderful plans together and present them to the board as some sort of great corporate strategy."

It gradually became apparent that Eric and Ian differed not only in style but also in values. "Ian is completely different from Eric," says director Francesco Bellini. "He was a manipulator, and Eric is nice. Eric is very much by the book, whereas with Ian, you never knew what he was doing behind your back. And Ian wanted power. He was young, and he wanted to take over the company."

At the time Eric didn't see it that way. He had even managed to put aside the disagreement he'd had with Ian four years earlier about Molson Holdings, and focused instead on the younger Molson's talents.

In a handwritten note dated 19 June 2001, Eric laid out his vision. He mapped out how the Molson chairmanship would go from him (EHM) to Ian (RIM) and eventually to his son Andrew (ATM) over the coming years.

	2002	2007	2012	2017	2022	2027	2032	2037
EHM (b. 1937)	65	70						
RIM (b. 1955)	47	52	57	62	67			
ATM (b. 1967)	35	40	45	50	55	60	65	70

"I let Ian in because he was a smart financial guy, a member of the family, eighteen years younger than me, and twelve years older than Andrew," says Eric. "So it fit age-wise." He thought his eldest son was qualified to eventually step in as the company's chairman. Andrew was a corporate lawyer who now worked as a public relations professional; he had just completed a master's in corporate governance and ethics at the University of London. If the rest of the board agreed, he could take over at the right time. And eventually, Eric thought, he could propose his youngest son, Geoff, who by then had been working at Molson in Toronto for two years, to take the role when he was ready. In the interim, Ian would bridge the gap.

Eric talked about it with Luc Beauregard. "What do you think?"

It made sense to Luc. He thought Andrew was a good choice. "I've seen him in action, and he's like you," Luc told Eric. "He listens, he considers all the options, and he's analytical. Andrew also has great intuition about people. As for Ian, he's a talented guy. The only thing you have to figure out is if you can trust him."

With Ian becoming a more commanding presence on the board, a line divided the Molson directors. On one side were those favouring Ian, and on the other were the Eric loyalists. Eric admits that, not being good with internal politics, he was slow to recognize the significance of the rift. At the time he viewed the divergence of opinions as a strength, one that could lead to more informed decisions. Even today he affirms "There's strength in diversity."

Colson saw it otherwise. "It was becoming increasingly obvious that there was a clique being formed with Ian and his little coterie of buddies – guys like Drapkin, and others. And then they slowly but surely co-opted some of the others. I could see it developing and see that they were up to no good. I mean, you had to be blind not to notice."

The clique Colson describes was partly a result of how new directors were selected. As Coallier says, "Ian had a lot of influence on who would join the board. Eric would obviously agree or disagree as the chairman, but sometimes I felt that the process was more led by Ian." Francesco Bellini is blunter. "Eric made a mistake. He let Ian bring his friends on the board." Perhaps that's true, but all the directors had a chance to voice their opinion during the director selection process. Still, it may have been difficult to speak up when the person making the recommendation was a Molson.

CEO Dan O'Neill was keenly aware of the two factions shaping the board. Like Eric, however, he initially thought the division provided a healthy tension. "There was one group that was more numeric and profit-driven – that would be Ian, Drapkin, and so on. They were fighting the numbers, driving the numbers, and asking a lot of questions about the numbers. And then there was the Eric side – Bellini,

Beauregard, etc. – who were more focused on the overall organization and the strategy going forward. It was good to have both sides. The combination of both kept me on my toes."

Before the Kaiser deal, when the company was performing well, the difference in approach was constructive. As results started faltering, however, it became a source of strain. "Eventually there were frictions between these two groups," says O'Neill. "Things started heating up between the 'quants guys' that Ian had brought in and the 'long-term guys' that Eric had. As CEO, I definitively noticed it. I had to manage both sides." Another way to describe the cleavage between the two groups was that one side focused on realizing immediate returns (buy low, sell high), the other on bolstering the intrinsic value of the enterprise for the long term.

Aside from the growing divide at the board level, there was an incident around Ian's remuneration that once again shook Eric's confidence in his cousin. In March 2002, the board approved a stock-option grant of Molson shares to Ian in addition to his $250,000 salary (40 per cent was for the "consulting" work Ian did for Molson, and the balance was for his role as deputy chairman). When Stephen reviewed the minutes of the meeting, however, he thought something was off. "There seemed to have been a slight adjustment or typo in the matter of the granting of options going Ian's way. It looked like the 340 options became 34,000, with extra zeros in the minutes. So we got Luc involved to ask whether there was a typo or something in the minutes. You can't accuse people of stuff like that. It's hard to prove."

Eric was also surprised by the figure. "I didn't remember much discussion on it. And I never saw what those options meant in terms of their value … but when I did, I was against it."

Once it was confirmed that the option grant was indeed for 34,000 shares, Eric and Stephen interceded. "We tried to persuade Ian to change his mind," says Eric. "We didn't feel it was right that a person in his position should ask the company for such a large block of options. It would have doubled his annual salary to $595,000." Eric didn't think it was appropriate for a Molson to receive more than half a million dollars a year as deputy chairman of the company. When he mentioned it to some of the other directors, they suggested that Eric raise his own remuneration as chairman to bring it up to Ian's level. They assumed Eric was upset because Ian's compensation would be higher than his.

"The solution is *not* to raise my salary," he grumbled. "Two wrongs don't make a right." In Eric's view, a family member serving on the Molson board should not get an excessively high pay.

At the next board meeting, on 24 June 2002, he spoke up. He pulled out the notes he had prepared the night before and read. "The Board should know that we have a long tradition of modest remuneration as members of the Molson family on the Board. As chairman, I consider myself as a service to the company and its shareholders; my mission is to help the company thrive. The previous Molsons were similar, and our efforts have been, and remain, for the long-term benefit of all shareholders."

To maintain the integrity of Molson's dual-class share structure, Eric said, the family could not be perceived as taking advantage of its position of control. "Three Molson family members on the Board control a very large public company with 11.5 per cent of the equity. It appears that our shareholders have accepted that fact. If they couple that fact with the remuneration disclosure paragraph of the management proxy circular, they know that we are not taking advantage of our position ... I feel it would not be right to start granting large option amounts to the family; the integrity of our family and company will be at stake, and we should not take that risk."

He concluded forcefully: "Governance is the biggest issue of the business world today, and we should make sure we do not make the mistake of granting large options to non-executive members of the Molson family." He could feel his heart pounding as he put away his notes.

This is common sense. Members of the family are on the board to steward the company on behalf of all its stakeholders. If shareholders start thinking we're not sharing the benefits of control with them, we will lose their trust and that will be the end of it ... Is Ian in this for himself? Is he another Mickey Cohen? I let that situation slide for too long. I won't repeat that.

Ian's annual stock option grant of 34,000 shares was not approved by the board.

As he had for years, Eric spent the summer months of 2002 going back and forth between Montreal and Kennebunkport, Maine, where he and Jane had a home. They both loved it there. They enjoyed the salty air, early morning walks on the beach with Baguette, their Jack Russell terrier, bike rides through town running errands. It was an idyllic reprieve from the pressures of Montreal. After only a few days, they both felt revitalized.

In 2002, however, Eric couldn't shake his "Montreal worries." Ian's recent grab left him wondering: Was Ian trustworthy? Whose interests was he looking out for, his own or the corporation's?

As he reflected on this, Eric's thoughts went to Elmer "Red" Carroll, a long-time Molson employee who had passed away nine months before. To Eric, this man (who always went by "Red Carroll of Molson") epitomized trust and loyalty. He was the driver who chauffeured Eric and his brother to school each morning when they were kids; he delivered the ultra-confidential documents to Hamm's in Saint Paul, Minnesota, when they tried to buy the brewery; he brought each of Eric's three boys home from the maternity ward of the Montreal General Hospital. Even after he retired from Molson in 1990, Red assisted Hartland and Eric's mother, Celia, until the end. Eric thought Red was a true Molson, regardless of his name. He now wondered, was Ian?

With all these questions about ethics and the family's role on the Molson board, Eric started reading up on corporate governance. He wasn't alone in this pursuit. Andrew, then thirty-five, was just as interested. The subject of his recent master's thesis was how, with proper governance, all shareholders can benefit from companies with a dual-class share structure.

That summer, father and son spent time discussing Ian's recent actions as deputy chairman, his immersion in the company's operations, and the cleavage forming at the board level. Andrew relished bonding with his father over this mutual interest in governance: "We shared information. We shared books. Corporate governance was the way we were communicating with each other .... It was a symbiotic moment when we were discovering something together."

One night after dinner, on the back porch in Maine looking out over the moonlit ocean, Andrew asked, "Dad, have you thought of writing down your principles? You know, make them explicit. Create a document that sets out how you think our family should fulfill its responsibility as a controlling shareholder of Molson. You can share it with Ian and even with the rest of your board. That way, everyone is clear on where you stand."

It was a task they undertook together. Editing and refining, they went through multiple versions until they produced a document they called the Molson Family Principles:

THE MOLSON FAMILY PRINCIPLES

All directors of a corporation should be acting in the best interests of its shareholders, *all* of its shareholders. Directors must act with a view to the best interests of the corporation: creating value for the shareholders, not representing particular constituencies.

Since the combined shareholdings of members of the Molson family can be defined as a "significant shareholder" and a "controlling shareholder," it is important to recognize certain principles and values that the family has followed over its long history in Canada. The family currently controls the Corporation with over 50 per cent of voting rights, although these combined holdings represent less than 15 per cent of the Corporation's total equity. All the more reason why members of the family involved must take care to practice sound principles of governance, and follow the family values and ethical behaviour that have brought the Corporation to this day. This family culture can be considered an important reason for the success of the Corporation.

As significant shareholders of Molson Inc., representatives of the family must wisely monitor the affairs of the Corporation in the interests of all shareholders. This can properly be achieved with a dedicated presence on the board of directors. These family members must exercise these responsibilities on the board for the benefit of *all* shareholders. The corporate structure will be efficient as long as the family acts in this manner.

If the family is not sharing the benefits of control with all shareholders, then it is not exercising its responsibilities wisely and it will lose the trust and confidence of the shareholders.

As a significant shareholder, the family must:

1 Understand the business.
2 Support and help motivate the CEO of the Corporation, and its management team, so they can fulfill their responsibilities to the best of their abilities.
3 Understand and approve the mission of the Corporation, including the related strategies required to achieve objectives.
4 Promote and encourage the highest standards of integrity and ethical behaviour throughout the Corporation.
5 Maintain and enhance all the best attributes of our history and tradition.
6 Make known to management that nepotism or favouritism will not be tolerated. Ensure that no personal benefits (such as unwarranted employment, donations, and/or business opportunities) are offered to friends, relatives and associates.
7 Ensure that compensation for any engagements by the Corporation, as stewards and monitors for all shareholders, does not exceed the norms of respected corporations, is in line with market standards and presents no private benefit to members of the family.

The Molson family ancestors have entrusted ensuing generations of the family to be guardians of wealth for the Corporation and its shareholders. While many generations have received the benefits of wealth, it is incumbent upon each generation to accept the resulting responsibilities and to conduct themselves in a manner to the benefit of Canada, which has provided the base of opportunity to the Corporation. Family descendants must strive to conduct themselves with the utmost integrity and the highest ethical standards. This is the family culture, as it is that of the Corporation.

The Molson family has a long history of good citizenship, creating wealth, and using it for the benefit of Canada. Members of the family in each generation have taken on responsibilities in the community and have worked hard to improve the lives of those around them. This tradition continues to this day.

The Corporation has also practiced good citizenship with a tradition of generosity towards charities across the country; a good example is the program as seen today ("Local Heroes"), where employees are encouraged to work in the communities for the benefits of others.

These are the principles, the ethics, and the values of the Molson family. This is the culture of Molson; both the family and the Corporation are committed to continued success, and a great tradition which we all must strive to preserve.

11 Facing Setbacks

Success is not final, failure is not fatal: It is the courage to continue that counts.

SIR WINSTON CHURCHILL (1874–1965)

The house in Massawippi is quiet as I wait for Eric to get me a drink. He does this every time. I tell him, "Don't worry about it. I can serve myself," but he insists. He goes to the next room to the cabinet, a unique piece of furniture hand-painted with the scene of a horse-drawn Molson delivery carriage from the late 1800s. But it has a twentieth-century secret: the drawers are refrigerated. I hear the clinking of bottles.

At the kitchen table, I take out my recorder and arrange my notes. Outside it's snowing. The fields are covered in a uniform coat of white. I can see Jane in the distance, walking the dog. Andrew is with our girls in the little house down the road. He has a fire going; there's smoke coming out of the chimney.

I'm overcome with a feeling of contentment and gratitude. I'm surrounded by people I love; they're all healthy, happy, and engaged in what they're doing; and I'm working on a project that I find fascinating. I don't always feel that way about the book. There are times I get nervous, especially when I worry, "What will Eric think? How will he react when he reads it?" But then, I tell myself, "Calm down, Helen. He explicitly told you to tell the story warts and all."

Eric pours me a glass of Bull's Head ginger ale and himself a Molson Ex. We pick up the conversation where we left it the night before.

"It's hard to find out if a person is a liar," he says. "Especially if they're skilled at it. They can cover their tracks pretty well. It's like trying to figure out when someone turns on you. Like Brutus – when did Caesar realize that his close friend had turned against him? Was it when he felt the knife in his back?"

I shrug. "But people warned you about Ian, right? Hadn't you already had a few difficult experiences with him? Like when you were working on Molson Holdings and he tried to get paid with options? Or during the board discussion about Norm Seagram when he left you hanging?"

"Yes, but those weren't really all that telling of a dishonest character. I mean, don't forget, I *wanted* Ian to be hands-on. We had to turn the company around. And he was helping me move things in that direction. It was hard to know that Ian was going to try to nail me. I didn't see it. No. I didn't see that he was going try to get rid of me till the very end. The thing is, I wasn't ready to go. I still had things to do. I had to make sure that Molson continued to exist. Molson had to become a global brewer, and Brazil wasn't going to be the answer."

🍁

Rio de Janeiro, Brazil. The view from the top of Morro da Urca, the 720-foot hill next to the more famous Pão de Açúcar (Sugarloaf Mountain), encompasses a myriad of images: the blue waters of Guanabara Bay dotted with boats entering the busy harbour, the long scalloped beaches of Copacabana and Ipanema, the city's white buildings crowding the valley between green hilltops, and in the distance, 2,300 feet above the city, the outstretched arms of the famed Cristo Redentor, Christ the Redeemer.

On the unseasonably cold, rainy evening of 29 January 2003, the view was eclipsed by heavy clouds. Molson had organized a giant Brazilian fiesta at the Morro to mark its investment in Latin America and to launch the export of Bavaria beer to Canada. Guests included Molson's board of directors, numerous company analysts and investors, its Brazilian partners, and local luminaries such as the mayor of Rio. Following a five-course meal, Eric was invited to speak on stage. Facing the crowd, he felt his stomach churn.

"There I was in my perfectly pressed suit, having practised all day, ready to deliver my speech, and I did it. I spoke in English and in Portuguese. But then, the next thing you know, somebody blows a loud whistle, and a whole bunch of Brazilian popsies come on stage with hardly any clothes on – just teeny-tiny bikinis! There I am, standing in the middle of it, and they start dancing all around me! On stage. With everybody watching! Jeez, I thought, this is really not up my alley. I wanted to get the hell out of there."

The comical image of the showgirls surrounding shy, awkward Eric was a profound metaphor for the growing divide bubbling under the surface at Molson: flash and trickery versus modesty and perseverance. On this night of samba and *merengue*, flash seemed to be winning.

The next day, Molson's directors met in a boardroom at the Copacabana Palace Hotel. Overall, the mood was elated. Perhaps it was the festivities of the night before, or O'Neill's upbeat presentation of the quarterly results (bolstered by the recent Kaiser acquisition), or his confidence that they could rectify the brewery's deteriorating market share in Canada. Whatever the reason, Molson seemed to be on an upswing.

Eric, however, was still preoccupied with the issue of governance. He'd recently finished the Molson Family Principles and planned to share them with the other board members. He felt they needed to be reminded of the family's role as a controlling shareholder of Molson. That afternoon in Rio, however, everyone was ready to end the meeting. The timing was not right.

He brought up the matter again at the next board meeting in March 2003. After sharing the Molson Family Principles, he asked the directors to approve a three-part corporate governance program: first, benchmark Molson's governance against best practices in Canada and the United States; second, survey all directors on questions related to the board's efficiency; and third, analyze the impact of the company's two-tier (voting/non-voting) capital structure.

By the time the program's results were presented to the board three months later, however, Molson had taken a turn for the worse. It was almost a complete reversal of fortune.

Eric doesn't remember exactly when he learned that Brazil was going badly. He was privy to the early warnings raised by Coallier. At first, he saw only small signs of trouble. For example, three months after Molson bought Kaiser, the value of the Brazilian real fell by 25 per cent against the Canadian dollar. Molson introduced a currency-hedging program and insulated itself from future fluctuations. Gradually, however, the reports of bad news became more frequent and not as easy to resolve. They mostly concerned product distribution.

In the beer business, distribution is key, especially in a country with poor infrastructure like Brazil. Knowing this, O'Neill arranged for the Brazilian Coke bottlers to continue delivering Kaiser (and Bavaria) after Molson bought the brewery from them in March 2002. He was proud of his coup at the time. "Think of where you have a Coke – in every bar, these little corner places – all of a sudden your brand is being brought to those places!" To make sure the bottlers kept their end of the bargain, he gave them 7.8 million Molson shares in the transaction. Unfortunately, that wasn't enough of an incentive. The bottlers made a lot more money distributing soft drinks than they did beer, so despite their shares, they didn't focus on Molson products.

The problem, according to Coallier, dated back to the due diligence on Kaiser. When the Molson team and its Brazil advisory board worked on the Kaiser transaction, they caught "deal fever." It's what happens when an organization goes from genuinely looking for an investment opportunity to "not wanting to lose the deal" at almost any cost. In this case, the fever's flames were fanned by many factors. They needed to find a way for Molson to grow; they had just lost Carling to Coors; they were running out of cost-cutting opportunities in Canada; assets like Kaiser didn't come up for sale very often; and Heineken was also very keen on buying the Brazilian brewery.

"On a few occasions, we almost pulled out, but then we went back in," says Coallier. "And I think that was the mistake. When we were about to pull out, we should have stayed out. We were prepared to take risks that were not necessarily to the level we thought. You know, in

Dave Perkins (*left*), a thirty-six-year Molson employee who held a number of leadership roles with the brewery throughout his career, stands with Robert Coallier, president and CEO of Molson's Kaiser operation in Brazil, 9 May 2005. Molson Coors Brewing Company collection.

Brazil, business ethics are very, very different. I think the Brazilians looked at us as naive, little Canadians and thought, 'We'll take them for a ride.' And, frankly, we were willing to go for a ride."

Dave Perkins also recalls the single-minded ambition to get the deal done: "I know several members of the due-diligence team that worked on Kaiser. To this day they maintain that they were strongly encouraged to remove findings that would have jeopardized closing that deal. People knew there were high risks around things like distribution, the competitive environment, the health of the brands ... but the environment was such that you couldn't be a whistleblower in those days."

Coallier remembers an incident that should have put a stop to it all. "At one point in the due diligence, we said we wanted to talk to the Coke bottlers. It was normal: they were going to be our distributors. We were told, 'No, you can't talk to them.' That should have been a clear reason to walk away. But we didn't. Dan had a friend who was the CFO or the manager of the Sao Paulo Coke bottlers. He had a side conversation with him, and they apparently settled the matter ... It turned out that the guy wasn't all that honest. Regardless, when they refused to let us talk to the Coke bottlers, we should have just walked away."

O'Neill, Ian Molson, and other members of Molson's Brazil advisory board, however, were eager to get their hands on Kaiser. (It was, after all, "Project Do It.") And shortly after they bought it, it became obvious that they had a serious issue. Despite their Molson shares, the Brazilian Coke bottlers were not focused on promoting Kaiser beer.

Nine months later, the situation deteriorated. On 23 December 2002, Molson's biggest Brazilian distributor, PanAmerican Beverages Inc. (Panamco) of Sao Paulo, got bought out by Coca-Cola Femsa for US$3.2 billion. Under the Femsa umbrella, the Molson business represented less than 1 per cent of their revenue. In contrast, the Sao Paulo distributor made up more than 30 per cent of Molson's Brazilian business. O'Neill tried to work out a new arrangement with Femsa, but the inconsequence of Molson products to Femsa's bottom line gave him little leverage.

"I believe to this day that Kaiser was the right purchase, but we executed really badly," O'Neill says. "There was one area – the state of Sao Paulo city – which was about 50 per cent of our business. We had a distributor there, Panamco, that was not working for us; they didn't execute well for us. And no matter what we'd do, it didn't work. It was the demise of the whole thing. In other parts of the country we were doing well, but in Sao Paulo we did crummy."

By summer 2003, Molson's market share in Brazil was down by nearly one-third. In one year it had fallen from 17.8 per cent to 12.7 per cent.

"Not only were we losing market share but the growth rate was not what we were told it would be," says Eric, "O'Neill said that Brazil's annual growth rate was something like 5 per cent. Then one day, he comes back and tells me it's now 1 per cent. You don't get that in the beer business. The market doesn't change that quickly. It got me upset and made me wonder about O'Neill."

Back in Canada, things were also slipping. O'Neill's public promise of 15 per cent year-on-year growth was taking a toll. He initially delivered on his commitment through relentless price increases and cost-cutting measures – steps that gave short-term jolts to Molson's stock price. But by late spring 2003, these actions were inimical to

Molson. Quality was compromised with shortened production cycle times and less-than-premium packaging. Executives complained that their hands were tied. "We're hurting our brands by always cutting marketing and selling costs to meet financial targets," they grumbled. Worse still, the company's future was put in peril as capital spending projects were brought to a halt.

"They were all focused on the stock market," Eric says. "They kept talking about metrics like EVA (economic value added), which has its merits, but when you don't account for the growth opportunities inherent in investment decisions, you can make the wrong choices. You can lose sight of both your customers and the long term. And that's what happened." Gradually, Molson's market share began to deteriorate.

As with past challenges, Eric gathered the facts, analyzed the situation, and consulted. This time he turned to Pat Kelley. By then, Kelley was back at Molson working for O'Neill as his senior vice-president in charge of the company's international brewing strategy. Behind the scenes, however, he briefed Eric on what was going on. They agreed that O'Neill's 15 per cent growth objective was unsustainable. Soon the company would miss the target. "When that happens and O'Neill fails to deliver," Kelley warned Eric, "it will be a very strong emotional negative for him … especially because it will impact his compensation. And we both know that's a huge issue for O'Neill."

Eric had seen firsthand what Kelley was talking about. "I remember once we had a board session to discuss O'Neill's pay increase with him. It was a terrible scene. O'Neill picked up all his books and threw them in the middle of the table. Then he stormed out. He didn't like what we were saying to him … You don't do that kind of thing, no matter how much strain you're under."

Eric started to question whether O'Neill was the right leader for Molson. "By the end, O'Neill started to contaminate everything because of the way he ran things. It wasn't just his focus on the short term; it wasn't just his outbursts. He was just not good with people. He would lash out at his subordinates. And he'd do very un-Molson-like things, like park in front of the fire hydrant or in the handicap spot, and then tear up the ticket. That's not Molson behaviour."

"Dan was churning through people," recalls Dave Perkins, who worked for him first as the head of Ontario and then as president of Molson USA. "By the time he left the company, of the two dozen most senior people who were there when he came in, almost none of them were there anymore ... and many of the positions had been quit two to three times! I was the *only* survivor. Which is bizarre, right? I mean, the churn was unbelievable, and the expectation for immediate results was craziness. He would bring in people to turn around Molson Canadian, for example, and if they couldn't do it in less than nine months, he would be like, 'Fire that person!'"

In 2003, Eric's son Geoff worked for Dave Perkins in Denver, Colorado, as a Molson USA key account sales manager. He joined the brewery a few months after O'Neill in 1999 and witnessed the CEO's evolution first hand. "Dan O'Neill was good at the beginning," Geoff says. "He turned the company around. He came in and cleaned it up really nicely and rebuilt the Molson brand. But, by the second half of his time there, he was starting to ruin the place." We are sitting at the round conference table in Geoff's Bell Centre office. There are Canadiens memorabilia everywhere. In a lower voice, he resumes, "Dan O'Neill was reporting that everything was going great, and it wasn't. It was all bullshit. It wasn't going right. I was in there and I could see it happening. The Canadian business was not growing – 80 per cent of our profits were coming from price increases. The Brazilian business was tanking. O'Neill was buying time ... I saw someone who was destroying the culture, someone who was bluffing his way through a difficult time to make the stock price go up."

At the 19 June 2003 Molson board meeting, a subdued O'Neill looked on as Robert Coallier reported on Brazil. Despite a 30 per cent price increase, the market remained flat. The Kaiser volume had dropped by 31 per cent since the beginning of the year. O'Neill said they were trying to revive the Panamco distribution system in Sao Paulo and negotiate a new deal with Femsa, but progress was slow. In the interim, they were working to build a Molson sales force. They eventually hired 1,200 Brazilians, outfitted them with motorcycles, and instructed them to visit individual accounts throughout the country to sell beer.

Too little, too late. "Brazil came off the rails quickly," says Eric. "We were getting killed on market share, and we weren't nursing our relationship with the Coca-Cola distributors whose trucks we were using. We started with a bang and then it fizzled ... When I learned about it from O'Neill and Coallier, we were losing our shirt. They should have warned us earlier."

With Brazil draining Molson's overall performance, tensions mounted. Marie Giguère says she witnessed the boardroom dynamics deteriorate. As they looked for solutions, the inevitable finger-pointing started. "I think Dan was more on the defensive," says Giguère. "He was no longer seen as the guy who was going to solve all the problems."

It was then that Eric decided "to get going again." The Mickey Cohen situation had taught him the importance of acting in a timely manner: "When there's a crisis, you have to roll up your sleeves and get in there." What made matters more complicated, however, was Ian's deep involvement in Brazil.

"Kaiser was Ian's thing. So at first I let him deal with it. He was on top of that Brazil board." But the Ian-Dan combination was no longer yielding results. Eric now had to handle both his CEO and his deputy chairman – far more complex than anything he'd attempted in the past.

❧

On 2 October 2003, Dan O'Neill phoned Pat Kelley. Although Kelley had retired from Molson four months earlier, O'Neill knew that he continued to have a privileged relationship with Eric. "Are you aware of the very serious problem between Eric and his cousin?" O'Neill asked.

"I have some inkling that there is an issue, yes."

"This is a very serious matter," O'Neill pressed. "Any open break between Eric and Ian is going to hurt this company in the market. There are a lot of people out there that see Ian as providing good help to Eric in running the company. A split isn't going to do anyone any good."

"Have you spoken to Eric about this?" Kelley asked.

"Yes, twice. But he just can't seem to get behind what the real issues are. This whole thing is going to come to a head soon in a very nasty way. We need to do something."

"I'm not sure what you're asking of me, Dan."

O'Neill continued. "I hope Eric isn't trying to get Ian off the board so he can put one of his sons on there instead."

Kelley was becoming irritated. "Why are you telling me all this?"

"I was just wondering if Eric's ever spoken to you about this. Maybe you could talk to him? We need to find a solution before this all goes too far."

"I know that Eric is working on the company's governance … so I think he *is* addressing the issue. I don't think there's much more I can do besides that." Kelley ended the conversation.

In the summer of 2003, Eric was deep into Molson's governance. The board had hired Egon Zehnder, a global leadership and executive search firm, to help conduct the three-part program approved at the March board meeting. When they produced a first report summarizing the results of questionnaires completed by the Molson directors, Eric was not surprised. They highlighted three points:

1 Issues around the "lack of potential successors to the CEO and the quality of the senior management team";
2 Confusion about what "constitutes the 'Molson family', its succession and its intentions";
3 Lack of clarity "about the mandate and expectations of the role of deputy chair … a number of board members questioned the need for the position."

Eric reread the last point. He wasn't the only one who thought Ian's role was unclear and that he was overstepping his position.

It was at that point that Sir George Adrian Hayhurst Cadbury entered Eric's life. Besides being one of the world's most eminent experts on corporate governance, and author of the renowned 1992 "Cadbury Report," Cadbury was chairman of his family's business, Cadbury Ltd (later Cadbury Schweppes) for twenty-four years before retiring in 1989.

Says Robert Swidler, Eric's primary advisor at Egon Zehnder, "Eric was fascinated with Adrian Cadbury because he had been the chairman of a long-held family consumer products, drinks, and confectionary manufacturer all these years. Eric asked me to make the introduction and I did. It was all his initiative, though. It wasn't me saying to Eric, 'You should really meet this guy.' No, he had decided on his own – or perhaps with Andrew's prompting – Andrew probably knew of Cadbury because of his governance studies – that he wanted to meet Sir Adrian."

On 26 August 2003, Eric left Kennebunkport and flew to London to meet with Cadbury. They had arranged to see each other in the offices of Egon Zehnder, adjacent to Green Park. The Englishman came into the city infrequently, and he greeted Eric in a borrowed office at the firm. He was impeccably dressed in a dark suit and a crested tie, yet despite the stiff upper lip, there was a twinkle in his eye. He reminded Eric of Benny Parsons, a "silver fox" who understood where he was coming from and what was important to him.

The two men talked about Molson's current governance practices, the Molson Family Principles, and the findings summarized in the recent Egon Zehnder report. Eric was candid about his growing concerns with Ian. "He walks around like he owns the joint," Eric told Cadbury. "That's not our kind of behaviour."

Following their discussion, Sir Adrian made a series of recommendations to Eric: (1) Create a corporate governance committee; (2) abolish the board's executive committee; (3) reduce the board size to ten to twelve members; (4) look for two new board members in finance and marketing; (5) establish parameters for attendance at meetings and report attendance to shareholders; (6) report all fees paid to directors, in addition to their director fees, regardless of their size; and (7) establish a principle that directors should be present in person and participate by telephone only as an exception.

The most noteworthy recommendation he made, however, was about Ian's position. "The key here is that the deputy chair must act as support to the chair in carrying out the chair's role," said Cadbury. "In this case, based on the interviews of your board members, the role is certainly not being performed or seen in this light."

Eric nodded. "I know."

"This leads to two different issues," continued Cadbury. "First, Ian is seen to be interacting very frequently with the CEO. And when he does, the board members wonder in what capacity he is doing so. Is it as a consultant? A board member? A major investor? Deputy chair? It's unclear."

"It's ambiguous," Eric agreed. "That's partly why I wrote the Molson Principles. This kind of interfering by Ian goes against our basic standard of letting the company's professional management team do its job. At first, I accepted – even welcomed – Ian's involvement, because we were in a crisis. We had to use all the talent around us to undo the conglomerate and get back to beer. But now that we're there, the CEO should be given the room he needs to do his job."

Cadbury nodded. "Now the second issue is that for some people, Ian's title as deputy chair is a sign that he is a designated alternative for your position. Is that the case? Is he to be your successor?"

Eric's pensive silence prompted Cadbury to continue. "The deputy chairman position would normally only be needed in three scenarios – if you wanted to designate your successor and groom him for your job; if you wanted to designate someone to act on your behalf in your absence; or if you had a specific role in mind for this person to play that would be enabled by providing him with this title. So, if you look back, what caused you to name Ian to this role?"

"Initially I thought Ian would be a good person to replace me as chairman. I saw him as a good transition between myself and either Andrew or Geoffrey (assuming either of them was qualified and approved by the board to be chairman). I mean, it made sense: Ian is the right age, he's a family member, he's an important shareholder, and he's qualified. That was my thinking. But it was all contingent on whether I could trust him. And now I'm not sure I can," Eric concluded.

"If that's the case," replied Cadbury cautiously, "perhaps it's best to eliminate the position of deputy chairman."

Eric knew that wouldn't be easy. Ian would resist. Nonetheless, Eric was determined to try. He would argue that abolishing the position was in line with best practices. And that "by following best practices, we won't have to worry that our dual-class structure will be challenged."

In a letter dated 15 September 2003, Eric brought Sir Adrian up to date. "I arrived back home with a clear mind and knew what I had to do.

Molson family's *Industria et Spe* emblem. Molson family collection.

The Corporate Governance Committee was formed at the next board meeting on September 10, with me as Chairman, Messrs. O'Brien and Cleghorn as members." (John E. Cleghorn, retired chairman and CEO of the Royal Bank of Canada, was appointed to the Molson board on 23 July 2003.) "Indeed, the 'show is on the road' and I can't thank you enough for your advice. We will soon be one of the best governed companies in the world."

On 20 November 2003, Eric wrote a second letter to Sir Adrian: "Most of the recommendations you and I settled on in London were accepted … The only serious issue I had was, as expected, the role and position of the Deputy Chairman. I had suggested that the position be eliminated in the interests of better governance, but the Board did not agree and decided we should try the route you and I had rejected, namely a change of behaviour. So we will now provide a detailed position description for this role and see how it goes."

Eric put down his pen and thought about how he had been unable to sway the board to eliminate Ian's position of deputy chairman. His mind went to the Molson motto: *Industria et Spe*, hard work and hope. "I guess this is where the 'hope' part comes in," he said to himself as he sealed his missive.

❦

In addition to his discomfort with Ian's hands-on involvement at Molson, two other incidents in the summer of 2003 undermined Eric's trust in his cousin.

The first was a book, *Crooks and Cronies: An Exposé of Corporate Corruption within the Law*. Self-published by Peter Teale, it described the rapid decline and eventual bankruptcy of Teale's employer, a UK-based dot.com company called Efdex Inc. Eric became interested in the paperback because "Ian Molson of Molson Breweries" featured prominently in its pages, including on its back cover, as a director of the failed enterprise.

Eric called Ian as soon as Andrew brought the book to his attention. "Ian, what's going on? This is very bad for our image and bad for our reputation."

"It's nothing," Ian assured him. He explained the context and continued his account in an email: "For good order's sake, I thought I should write to follow up on the discussion we had in August regarding my former directorship of a company called Efdex. In the wake of the company's bankruptcy, Peter Teale, a disgruntled ex-employee, attempted to sue on totally spurious grounds the former chairman and CEO of the company and threatened to write a defamatory book about the company and its board of Directors, which, of course, he duly did.

This book is grossly inaccurate, misleading, and, indeed, libellous ... The Board of Efdex made a mistake in not suing Peter Teale for having written such a defamatory and dishonest account."

Eric replied by return email. "I am still worried about the potential damage to our corporation and family." He then forwarded the exchange to two of his allies on the board, Daniel Colson and Luc Beauregard, saying, "I am going to keep going on this as I am worried about the Molson image. Ian's note is his opinion and that may not be reliable."

Eric's trust in Ian dropped to a new low in September 2003 after Eric met with Peter Buckley. Buckley was chairman of both Caledonia Investments plc, a UK-based conglomerate listed on the London Stock Exchange, and Cayzer Trust, the private family company that owned 49.6 per cent of Caledonia. He was also (through his mother) a Cayzer, one of Britain's most prosperous families, linked to Caledonia for generations. So was Ian's wife, Verena.

In the early 2000s, the Cayzers were divided. The feud was all over the British broadsheets and tabloids. The headlines were dramatic: "Cayzer Clan at War over Caledonia"; "Cayzer Trust Rallies against Rebel Cause"; "The Chairman, the Heir and a £10M Battle to Control a Family Fortune."

On one side was Buckley, a quiet private-investment manager and accountant who ran Caledonia, and on the other was Sir James Cayzer, a renowned *bon vivant* who sat on the boards of both Caledonia and the Cayzer Trust but took no active role in either until 2001. He criticized Buckley's management of the family fortune. He was also against the fact that family members could only sell their trust shares to other relatives at a discounted value. Ian Molson, presumably defending Verena's interests, got into the wrangle, siding with Sir James Cayzer and joining him in his attack on Buckley.

It was around then that Buckley phoned Eric. Introducing himself, he explained that Dan Colson, with whom he sat on the board of the Telegraph Group, had suggested they meet. The matter he wanted to discuss was personal, Buckley said. He wanted to meet face to face.

On 15 September 2003, Buckley flew from London to Montreal with another Caledonia director and family member, J. Cayzer-Colvin. The next morning the three men met at the Hilton Garden Inn near the Montreal Airport. "They came to see me because Ian and his camp were giving the Cayzer family lots of trouble," Eric recalls. "Buckley told me Ian was working with James Cayzer, a rebel cousin, and that they almost broke apart the Cayzer Trust ... They were trying to take over Caledonia."

Buckley asked about Eric's experience with Ian. At the end of their conversation, he delivered a stern warning to Eric. "He told me that Ian seemed to be devious and dishonest. He basically told me to watch out."

Colson, familiar with both the Molsons and the Cayzers, had a privileged vantage point. "Ian was trying to do at Caledonia the same thing he was trying to do at Molson," he says bluntly. "Ian was trying to arrange some sort of coup d'état. And in the end, it failed. Peter Buckley immediately put the screws on Ian, publicly disgraced him, and threw him out like a dead mouse ... The analogies and comparisons between Ian at Caledonia and Ian at Molson are hard not to notice. In both cases, he had no position of serious strength at all. His wife's shareholding in Caledonia was minimal, in the same way as his holding at Molson was minuscule – the only shares I'm aware that he owned were the ones he bought from the old senator ... At the end of the day, no one was more ambitious and more treacherous than Ian."

"Greed drove Ian," Eric concludes. "He was an insatiable man. It turns out that before he did all this skullduggery with us, he did it with his wife's family first ... Ian once told me, 'Eric, the one thing I want to do is make a lot of money.' His ambitions wouldn't have bothered me much if he was doing the right thing. But in the end he was dishonest, and that's what drove a wedge between us."

By the fall of 2003, the cleavage between the two Molsons was unmistakable. "Ian spent the better part of a year or longer trying to get everyone on his team," Colson recalls. "He was trying to make it increasingly clear that Eric was redundant and no longer necessary, and that he – Ian – was the answer to all of Molson's problems. Amazingly, some of these guys on the board actually believed it ... I mean, Ian went out of his way to impress upon everybody who was a director how he knew everything that was going on, how he was in charge, how he and O'Neill were going to solve this, and how Eric was past his sell-by date."

It was not exactly sabotage, more of a warlike "divide and conquer." Eric knew it. "Ian was stirring things up at the board, saying bad things about me. He was telling the board, 'Maybe you should get rid of Eric and put me in there.' Ian was working on them for a while."

Eric sensed that Ian might have enlisted Dan O'Neill as his ally. Marie Giguère, who had heard that "Ian was doing stuff in the background and playing games," says, "When things started going badly between Eric and Ian, with Eric knowing that Dan was close to Ian, that hurt Dan. Eric lost confidence in Dan's loyalty. And you know, loyalty is very important to Eric."

As the situation deteriorated, Eric knew he would have to act. In the meantime, he kept his thoughts to himself and his feelings in check. His cool silence further chilled the relationship. Stephen remembers Ian speaking to him about it. "Ian would pop by my office at the brewery all the time. He would tell me, 'I'm having trouble talking to Eric.' And I would say, 'I think you should try again. Perhaps he doesn't trust you too well.' I told Ian to get together with Eric, but I guess he couldn't do it. Then it all started to fall apart. By then you never really knew what Ian was up to."

Throughout it all, Eric remembered his old Princeton professor's surfing analogy. "You've got to get on a high wave and stay on it," The Turk used to say. For Eric, that meant he had to keep his eyes locked on the future, fixed on his vision for Molson, and not look down. If he did, and inadvertently got embroiled in Ian's machinations and politicking, everything would fall apart. Eric resolved not to get sucked in. He took a scientist's stance, observed the internal dynamics, and focused on his ultimate goal: make Molson a significant player in the rapidly consolidating, global brewing industry.

🍁

The landscape of the beer market was being reshaped by large, multi-geographic deals. Molson wasn't keeping up with the pace of consolidation. Despite having moved up from twenty-first to fifteenth in international volume ranking since 2000, the gap between Molson and the top four brewers in the world had increased from 60 to 90 million hectolitres. At a Molson investors' conference on 16 September 2003, O'Neill acknowledged that consolidation in the beer market was happening "much faster than we expected" and that "the gap between us and the four big guys has actually widened."

Eric worried. Not only were they not making progress on an international scale but Molson's existing assets were not performing. They were continuing to lose market share in Canada, going from 45.1 to 44.4 per cent in the past year – a significant loss, since Canada was Molson's profit engine and represented 94 per cent of earnings. Their investment in Brazil was turning sour: market share was down nearly one-third from the year before. And they were still struggling in the United States.

"We need a partner," Eric told Andrew. "To grow beyond our core, we need to get together with a brewer we can grow strong with, but not one that can swallow us." Eric did not want Molson marginalized, and he didn't want to sell out.

In 2003, the Molson board mandated the Boston Consulting Group (BCG), a worldwide management consulting firm, to study who could be Molson's partner going forward. "We had BCG look at all the possibilities for an international transaction," says Giguère, "but there was a sense that things were already predetermined. We knew there were some limits. One was that the family didn't want to put the company up for sale. Another was that we didn't have the scale nor the balance sheet to be the consolidator ... so that had to inform the work that BCG did."

BCG came back with two "priority" partner recommendations: Coors and Heineken.

"We knew early on that Coors was going to be one of the favourites," says Giguère. "There was also some talk about Heineken. Ian may have been predisposed in favour of Heineken, because he was close to the family. We all knew that. So I think there was some suspicion that Ian was going to try to arrange something with Heineken."

Ian didn't hesitate to let people know of his tight connection with Charlene de Carvalho-Heineken, owner of a 25 per cent controlling interest in the Dutch brewer. "I think Ian was the godfather to the kid of the daughter of Freddy Heineken," says Robert Coallier. "I'm sure there were discussions behind the scenes with them that I was not privy to. Dan may know more about that."

Dan O'Neill says, "The Heineken question was always muddling around. Ian is best friends with the daughter of Freddy Heineken, and they were godparents to each others' children … It looked like he wanted to do a deal with Heineken. I mean, I don't know for sure, but that's what it looked like."

One thing O'Neill did know for sure was Eric's position. "He felt that if we were ever purchased by someone like Heineken, it wouldn't end up being 'Molson-Heineken.' It would be 'Heineken.' And Eric didn't want to be swallowed up. He wanted to keep the name 'Molson' on whatever business we did going forward. He also wanted to have family members on the board. Eric made it very clear to me. He told me, 'I want us to continue to be in the beer business. We love it. It's our passion, our heritage, our family. I won't give up on it.'"

Molson had to survive.

12 Confronting Boardroom Politics

It does not do to leave a live dragon out of your calculations, if you live near him.

J.R.R. TOLKIEN (1892–1973)

The view from our room at the Excelsior in Dubrovnik is exquisite. Even though it's our third morning here, I'm still captivated by the scene from our balcony: the 180-degree vista of the deep blue Adriatic, bookended by the pine-clad island of Lokrum on the left and the Old City of Dubrovnik with its majestic medieval ramparts on the right. It's known as the "Pearl of the Adriatic," and for the past two days I've walked through its stone-lined lanes, explored its sights, and absorbed the quasi-spiritual feel of the place. It's no wonder that George Bernard Shaw once said, "Those who seek paradise on earth should come to Dubrovnik."

Meanwhile, Andrew has been in board meetings with the rest of the Molson Coors directors. Although they usually hold their gatherings closer to home in either Montreal or Denver, they've come to Croatia this September of 2015 to visit one of the nine Central European breweries the company bought as part of the StarBev LP acquisition in June 2012. That US$3.54 billion deal was another step in the expansion of Molson Coors outside its North American/UK base. With StarBev, Molson Coors gained a strong presence in Central and Eastern Europe and added Staropramen, a brand sold in over thirty countries

Peter Hanson Coors.
Molson Coors Brewing
Company collection.

worldwide, to its portfolio. The visit to Croatia was a chance for board members to see part of these operations first hand.

I don't usually accompany Andrew on business trips. In fact, this is the first time I've joined him for a Molson Coors board meeting. But I couldn't pass up on this opportunity. Pete Coors has finally agreed to sit down for an interview with me. It's been surprisingly complicated to organize. Besides the distance between Colorado and Quebec, when Andrew first approached Pete to set up a meeting, he was hesitant. He said he didn't know Eric well. Although they had been business partners and fellow board members for a number of years, he said they didn't have a close personal relationship. Nonetheless, Andrew convinced him. That's how I've ended up a tourist in Croatia, while Andrew sits in a boardroom.

My interview is scheduled to take place over breakfast on Saturday, 26 September 2015, the last day of our trip. Andrew and I arrive at the Excelsior's main restaurant around the same time as Pete Coors.

It's hard to miss him. Tall, broad-shouldered, with a full head of white hair, khaki chinos, a light-blue buttoned-down MillerCoors shirt, and an easy smile, he looks just like the man in the beer ads.

We exchange warm greetings and sit on the terrace overlooking the sea. The waiter comes to take our orders and, noticing Pete's shirt, asks whether he's from Miller.

"Coors, actually," replies Pete. "Miller is in Milwaukee, and we're based in Golden, Colorado."

And so our meeting begins.

Before sitting down with him, I had Googled Pete. He's the great-grandson of Adolph Coors, the German-American entrepreneur who founded the Coors brewery in 1873. A graduate of Phillips Exeter Academy, he has a degree in engineering from Cornell and an MBA from the University of Denver. He joined the family company in 1971 and climbed its echelons to become CEO in 1992. He's also interested in politics. In 2004, he made a run to become a United States senator of Colorado as the Republican candidate. Although his bid was unsuccessful, he is still a strong supporter of the GOP.

He and Andrew exchange stories about Exeter. Pete describes the summer jobs he held at the brewery since the age of fourteen. It seems to me that he's told these anecdotes before, but I can't help being drawn in. He describes how, when he was hired as a trainee in the company's waste-treatment plant, he had to take his clothes off in the garage when he came home at the end of the day. The smell was *that* bad, he says, chuckling.

It's all interesting and amusing. The engaging American raconteur is a contrast to Eric, the reserved Canadian brewmaster.

Pete starts off by explaining that he's not a brewmaster but that he knows "enough to be dangerous." He adds, "I've been around breweries a long time and can make intelligent conversation about beer-making and about the technology we use, but I am more into the marketing, sales, and management side of the business."

When I ask about his relationship with Eric, he tells me earnestly, "I didn't know Eric very much. He seemed particularly interested in the technical side of the business, which is what Jeff [Pete's older brother] took up ... Jeff and Eric used to meet at the International Technical Advisory Councils. So Jeff and Eric shared the technical side, but I don't know how well they knew each other."

Coors factory in Golden, Colorado. Molson Coors Brewing Company collection.

I'm surprised. "How did the two families get together, then?"

Pete corrects me. "The two *families* didn't get together. Jeff had a relationship with Eric, but that didn't influence the deal. Molson Coors was a business deal, strictly business. It was part of our international growth. We had to get bigger and grow, so we got together with Molson."

🍁

"What put Molson in play for us was Brazil," Leo Kiely says, sitting across the table from me on 4 November 2015. We are having dinner at a busy Italian restaurant in downtown Denver. "I think, fundamentally, Brazil was a terrible purchase for Molson that just got worse … but it opened up an opportunity for us." Speaking in a low, measured tone, he takes me back twelve years to describe the beginnings of the Molson-Coors merger.

On a Friday afternoon in the fall of 2003, Kiely, then CEO of Coors, sat in a Colorado boardroom with Dave Perkins, president of Molson USA, the Molson-Coors joint venture in the United States. The two met regularly to review the results of the JV, and as always the discussion was constructive. Any lingering bad blood between the breweries after the arbitration ruling six years before had long since dissipated.

That afternoon, Kiely brought up a topic they had touched on previously. "Can you pass along to your guys in Montreal that if they have any kind of serious interest in talking about a deal, we'd be open to it?"

"Sure, Leo. I'll speak with Dan," replied Perkins.

Kiely tells me there were multiple factors that prompted him to open the possibility of a merger. First, Molson was a very profitable business. "I remember the first time I saw the P&L [profit and loss statement] for Molson and Labatt," he says. "I thought, 'Wow! The Canadian beer business makes more than double our profits in the US on less than half the volume.'" Second, Molson was in a weakened position because of its investment in Brazil, so more likely to be open to a deal. According to Kiely, "Dan O'Neill ran into a buzz saw in Brazil." And third, the competitive landscape of global amalgamation was putting pressure on both Molson and Coors.

"Remember, that was when AmBev got its feet on the ground and went on a massive roll," Kiely says. "We both saw the world consolidating around us, and we knew it was going to pull away from us. The writing was on the wall that without more scale, both Molson and Coors were essentially going to be landlocked in North America against a very big competitor. Our belief was that together – and this has panned out, by the way – we'd have the scale and the expertise to really go out and credibly build a global business … That was the genesis of it. It was two country-bound family businesses looking at this and saying, 'We're going to be left behind.'"

Once Perkins passed on Kiely's message, O'Neill followed up with a phone call. "Eric won't move forward unless he can meet you and be confident we can do this together," he told Kiely. "There's got to be trust there."

"I understand trust," replied Kiely. If these two families were to join their legacies, trust was a prerequisite.

A meeting was organized at Molson's Montreal brewery for Monday, 8 December 2003. Eric took care of the menu: two smoked meat sandwiches (a "Montreal classic") and two Molson Export beers (another classic).

Kiely laughs. "Eric's lunches were the worst food I've ever eaten in my life! Smoked meat? How much of it can you pile into a sandwich? … It was a 'classic' all right! Here we were with these messy sandwiches, sitting in this little office at the brewery, talking about the future of Molson and Coors … it makes me laugh."

"Leo came to town and we had lunch," says Eric. "It was probably smoked meat. People love that stuff, so I must have ordered it, but I don't remember. I do remember that we talked about Molson and Coors and how it was maybe time to start getting more serious. We'd known the Coors people for many, many years, starting with Uncle Bill. They're highly creative, technical brewers … And by then, we were both around the same size, already working closely together, distributing each other's brands in our own country, and all the other brewers were getting together. We had to move."

They talked about how their prospects to perpetuate their businesses were a lot better together than alone, Kiely recalls. "I think the two families came at it sceptically at first. They had their two business guys – myself and O'Neill – saying, 'Hey, there's merit in this. We would like to have your approval to take a look at it.' We wouldn't do anything without Eric's or Pete's okay."

Soon after, a dinner was organized between the two principals. Eric and Pete met at the Hilton in Chicago's O'Hare airport. Eric says, "That's when I would have told Pete that I thought we should look at doing something and that we had a better long term facing us if we went at it together. Pete agreed."

❋

For Dan O'Neill, 2004 didn't start off well. His first public statement on 15 January was a downgrade of Molson's year-end profit forecast. While his target was to grow the business by 14.5 per cent from the previous year, he told reporters he didn't think it would get to more than 2 per cent because of the quagmire in Brazil. The next day, Molson's class A shares collapsed by nearly 14 per cent, their biggest one-day drop in nineteen years.

Eric saw his chance to do something. It was easier to take action when things were not going well. Besides, the pressure was on. "By then it was clear that if we kept going the way we were, Brazil would sink us. I couldn't count on O'Neill and Ian anymore. I had to go at it alone."

Although he had already planted a seed with Coors, he decided to meet other international brewers to get a better feel for the broader competitive landscape. "I wanted to get up to speed and find out for myself what was going on. I told O'Neill about my trip, but I also told him that I wanted to go alone. I said, 'Dan, I want to catch up. I'm chairman of the board. I've been cut off, and now I'm going to see these brewers.'"

On a five-day "European blitz" from 9 to 13 February, Eric met with Erik Hartwall, owner of Finland's leading beverage company, in Helsinki; Sir Brian Stewart, chairman of Scottish & Newcastle, in Edinburgh; Charlene de Carvalho-Heineken in London; and Povl Krogsgaard-Larsen, chairman of Carlsberg, in Copenhagen.

"I keep telling my boys that you have to do that sometimes, have one-on-one meetings with other owners," he says. "No witnesses. Find a time when you can say anything you want. Just talk turkey, when you can give them a couple of beers and have them start talking even more … One of our principles is to be an informed shareholder. My trip to Europe was just that. It was me, going alone, looking to find variations of what we could do for the future of the company. All the while, as I was talking to the Europeans, I knew we had Coors in the bag, because they were eager. This European blitz allowed me to get to know these other brewers better and allowed them to get to know us. When Ian found out about it, he blew his stack."

Ian expressed his displeasure by email. "I understand you were in London, Copenhagen, etc., last week," he wrote to Eric on 23 February, copying Dan O'Neill. "I heard back from a variety of sources about the meetings (which obviously I didn't know anything about) … I find it odd that you did not speak to me, if only as a matter of courtesy and good manners, prior to your meeting in London with Michel and Charlene. It is a bit strange to have learned of and be briefed about the contents of this meeting by them rather than by you, and to be asked my reaction to certain things you supposedly said. I am sure you must realize, good communication is a hallmark to any well run (and led) corporation."

Ian was mistaken. Eric's silence was not due to his lack of communication skills. There was a far more fundamental reason: Eric no longer trusted Ian.

As the two Molsons grew apart, their disunity was reflected on Molson's board. The two camps became more entrenched and disagreed about what to do next. "You could see clearly that the board was getting divided," says Francesco Bellini. "There were directors for Eric, and there were those for Ian." The ones with Eric thought that the best move for Molson was to merge with Coors. The two companies were already very close collaborators, they were around the same size, and the Molson and Coors families could find a way to govern the combined corporation jointly.

Ian and his supporters were against a Coors transaction. They thought there was a better deal out there.

"It was awful, but a lot of boards have big divisional things that happen," says O'Neill. "That's pretty normal. You're not always going to have board members who agree. You have different groups that think that one strategy is better than the other."

In this case, however, it more than a division over strategy. It was also about leadership. The two were inextricably linked. "Ian was clearly trying to replace Eric as chairman," says O'Neill. "He was clearly trying to demonstrate to the board that he knew more than everyone else. Personally, if Eric had been meaner and tougher, he would have cut it off with Ian way earlier. But Eric takes a lot of this stuff and keeps it inside."

The dissension between the two Molsons was not only evident to the directors of the company: senior executives saw it too. Robert Coallier, in charge of Brazil, says, "Eric was preoccupied with the sustainability of Molson. And for that reason, he was in favour of a deal with Coors. Ian was totally against the Coors transaction. He never wanted to do anything with Coors. He felt that the assets of Molson were much better than the assets of Coors … and that's when he started trying to push Eric aside."

❧

On 4 March 2004, another upheaval rocked the brewing world: the $18.3-billion union of Interbrew, the Belgian brewing giant (owner of Labatt) and Brazilian AmBev. The transaction was significant for Molson not just because it knocked Anheuser-Busch off its pedestal as the world's largest brewer, but because it created a common competitor for them in both Canada and Brazil. On the day the Belgian-Brazilian behemoth was announced, a Bear Stearns analyst said out loud what many thought privately: "This is terrible news for Molson. If Molson didn't have a bull's-eye on its back, it does now."

Eric felt the heat. "The consolidation parade was taking off. People started saying that we were a takeover target. The vultures were circling once again."

The last time Eric had used the vultures analogy was after the sale of Diversey, when the company was cash rich and short-sighted shareholders were demanding a share buy-back or a special dividend. As he did back then, he called Pat Kelley. "Have you looked outside yet? Do you see them? They're all around. The vultures are circling."

"I know," said Kelley. "The AmBev Interbrew deal has changed our world."

"The problem is not only outside. There are people in here, within the company, working to sell us out. I think Ian and O'Neill are trying to get something going with Heineken."

Kelley was already well aware of the tension between the two Molsons. Days before, on 8 March, a flustered O'Neill had phoned him. "Have you spoken to Eric in the past few days?" he asked.

"I spoke to him last week, but very briefly on some matters related to Concordia."

"Well, Patrick, I've got to tell you that I think Eric is going around the bend. He's very agitated. He thinks Ian is against him and he thinks

I'm working with Ian to sell the company from under him. Please talk to him and see if you can calm him down."

"I'm not sure what I can do, Dan," said Kelley. "This is between Ian and Eric. Besides, it isn't like Eric to be confrontational unless he's provoked."

"Patrick, just talk to him. See if you can calm him down. I don't need this shit."

Next day, at the Molson board meeting on 9 March, the directors discussed the company's going forward strategy. Matt Barrett picked up on the tension between Ian and Eric and asked to meet with them privately later that day.

"This is has got to stop," he told them. "The organization is going to blow up if you two keep going this way. You guys have got to collaborate. Otherwise, I'm going to bang your heads together and make sure you do!"

"Thank you, Matt," Eric replied. "Everything is fine. We'll work this out."

Eric now reflects on Barrett's "bang your heads together" sermon and says, "It was all BS. I wasn't in any 'family feud' with Ian. I know that's how Ian portrayed it to the press, but that's not how it was. I always treated Ian with civility. I just didn't trust him. Ian was devious, mischievous, and doing things on the side."

That night when Eric got home, Jane noticed he looked like the weight of the world was on his shoulders. "What's wrong, honey?" she asked. "How was the board meeting?"

Eric poured himself a Molson Ex and sat down at the kitchen table. "We have a problem."

Jane pulled out a chair and sat facing him.

"It's bad." he said. "I can't trust Ian. He's stirring things up, and it looks like he wants to take over. Also, he's got O'Neill on his side. I'm not sure what the two of them are up to."

"Do others see it?"

"I've spoken to Beauregard and Colson, and they say the same thing. I'm not sure about the rest. Matt Barrett took us aside today and said that we'd better get along or he'd bash our heads together. Can you imagine?"

Jane covered his hand with hers. "You've got to do something. I'm worried about you ... You haven't been sleeping."

"I'm fine."

"I'm serious, Eric. This can't continue."

"It's not that simple." He took a sip of beer. "I have a board to deal with, and Ian can be very convincing. He's on the phone with people all the time, scheming and making deals ... He's got a serious case of telephonitis. That's all he does."

"I thought you were going to abolish the deputy chairman role."

Eric shook his head. "It didn't fly. The board rejected it. Regardless, we have to find a way for Molson to survive long term. If we don't do something, we'll be swallowed up. Plus, Brazil is tanking. And O'Neill seems to be going through people faster than yesterday's news ... O'Neill, jeez, all he cares about are his stock options."

"What about Coors?"

"Coors would be a good partner for us. I don't think anything will work with the Europeans right away, but Coors could be a good match. They're like us – they're in it for the long term and they care about quality. Plus, they've got Leo Kiely. He'd be a great CEO for us. But Ian is against it. He says Coors is a sick company. That they're a 'one-brand' brewer and much weaker than us."

"You don't agree?"

"No. They have a huge distribution system in the US. They're very good technically, and Coors Light is a brand with legs. If we combined their strengths with ours, we could build a solid North-American platform. Then together we could add a third partner. We could add Femsa, for example. We could have a Canadian-American-Mexican partnership – a NAFTA-like brewing platform. Then we could go even further, talk to the Europeans or the Japanese and create a world-scale brewery." Eric was always more voluble in private with Jane than in any other context. She was his sounding board.

"Have you spoken to Stephen or your sisters about this?" she asked.

"Stephen knows what I want to do. But you're right – I should talk to Deirdre and Cynthia before any of this goes too far."

A week later, on 16 March 2004, O'Neill received a letter from Kiely. The Coors CEO wanted to organize a meeting with Eric and Pete Coors to explore how their two companies could work closer together:

> As we have previously discussed, while our situations are in many ways different, Molson and Coors share a dilemma. In a consolidating global beer business, neither of us, on our own, is in a favourable position to make further significant acquisitions and to thus become a major global brewer; this is less a question of financial resources than a lack of competitive synergies. In addition, there are few potential "partners" for either of us (though there may be potential buyers). In short, we each are likely to become more and more marginalized and risk being compelled, in not too many years' time to sell to maximize shareholder value.
>
> Together, on the other hand, we can form a major world brewing power with sufficient scope and earnings to remain independent and sufficient cash flow to look at and take advantage of further opportunities.

Kiely then outlined a number of options. Molson could buy Coors or, conversely, Coors could buy Molson. He immediately discarded these alternatives saying, "At this point, we are assuming that the Molson family wants to stay in the beer business and are not sellers. I know this is true for the Coors family."

The second option was a "merger of equals" – not a takeover or purchase by one company or the other. Instead, Kiely proposed a transaction in which both firms surrendered their shares and received securities issued by the newly merged entity. He acknowledged there would be challenges in doing this, like deciding on the board structure, stock listings, and headquarters location. Nonetheless, he wrote, "We believe that it all starts with cultural compatibility – whether the groups (as well as the respective management and employee groups) share the same values ... We think we know Molson well enough to believe that our values and cultures are suitably compatible."

Reading Kiely's letter, Eric kept going back to the words "merger of equals." He wondered if such a thing was realistic. He could think of at least one group of shareholders who would be against it: those who had invested in Molson with the hope of getting a big payout in case of a take-over. They would be opposed to any transaction that jeopardized their premium.

They'd cross that bridge when they got to it, Eric thought. "Let's look into this merger of equals idea."

In the meantime, he had to get his own family onside. He had not yet spoken to Cynthia, Deirdre, or their children, now adults in their forties. He didn't like saying too much while things were still tentative. There could be leaks or even interference by people who didn't know all the facts. They could also question his judgment. "Didn't you say just three years ago that Ian was the right person to take Molson to the next level?" they would ask.

Well, things change. He'd made a mistake.

He called a meeting of "Generations VI and VII" of the Tom Molson gang. He included Andrew (Geoff and Justin were both in the United States), Stephen, Deirdre, and Cynthia, and their children, David and Eric Stevenson and Colin, James, and Brian Baxter.

Eric was blunt. "It's falling apart with Ian. We need to find a way to move on."

Silence.

Says David Stevenson, "I think it was difficult for Eric to come to the family and say that Ian was no longer on our side. I remember my brother and I looking at each other, like, 'Wow!' But I was probably not that surprised, to be completely honest. I always thought Ian had an ulterior motive ... It's hard to say when things started going badly with Ian; it all happened quite quickly."

Eric Stevenson, David's brother and the eldest of the seventh generation, says, "I always thought you could see Ian coming. To me it was very obvious. He's a tough guy, a ruthless guy in many respects, and that was fairly obvious from the start. So we shouldn't have been surprised when Eric told us things were falling apart."

Brian Baxter, Cynthia's son, says, "Eric told us, 'We've got to be ready. There's going to be an attack coming from Ian.' It was clear that Eric felt he had a tiger by the tail and he wasn't too sure how to let it go."

Once over their initial shock, all the Molson family members present that day confirmed their support of Eric. Says David Stevenson, "When my uncle said, 'Ian has let me down and he's got to go', we were like, 'If that's the case, then what do you need us to do? We're with you.' We were not in the boardroom with the Molson directors, we were not in the meetings, so when it's time to make a change, we trust Eric that it's the right thing to do."

✸

The next day, Friday, 19 March, O'Neill put in another call to Patrick Kelley. Again, Kelley made notes, recording the conversation as soon as he hung up.

O'Neill started by thanking him for helping his daughter Jennifer with her application to Concordia. "She just got an email and a confirmation letter saying she was accepted. We're very pleased."

"That's great. It was nothing, really. I was happy to do it," Kelley replied.

"By the way, have you had a chance to speak to Eric?"

"I did, a couple of days ago."

"He's very distracted by the whole Ian thing. I'm telling you, he's lumped me in with Ian. He thinks Ian and I are trying to sell the company to Heineken."

"You mentioned that last time we spoke, but he hasn't said anything to me."

"What about Coors? Did he talk to you about it? They sent us a letter proposing a merger of equals a couple of days ago." Without waiting for an answer, O'Neill continued. "I'm not sure about Coors. Their performance in the US hasn't been great. In all honesty, Patrick, what would you rather? A merger of equals with Coors, or a great deal with Heineken for the Americas at 50–50? We'd put in our company and they would put in their entire business in the Americas … think about it."

"Sure, Dan. But then there's the whole question of preserving the Molson name. I don't think the family is ready to exit the beer business."

"Yeah, I know. Anyway, please speak to Eric and see if he'll talk to Coors. He's so withdrawn lately, I'm not sure where he's at."

Had O'Neill been able to engage Eric, he would have understood that his chairman remained preoccupied with Molson's long-term survival.

Eric felt he couldn't trust Ian or O'Neill to do what was right in that regard. Both seemed too driven by self-interest and short-term results. So despite their seeming preference for a Heineken transaction, Eric chose to explore Kiely's proposal for a merger of equals with Coors. "We needed to straddle the border with our own investment. We needed a good light beer like Coors Light. And I had to offset Ian, who had his sights on taking over the company for himself, or possibly for Heineken. I had to make sure I had a good deal coming our way."

Eric decided to speak with Pete Coors face-to-face. The two families had to meet before management got further involved.

✽

A dinner was organized for 15 April 2004. Pete flew to Montreal with his daughter Melissa and met with Stephen and Eric. In his jacket pocket, Eric had notes on the items he wanted to address:

1 Confirm intention of Molson family to remain in the beer business for the long term.
2 Determine Coors family objective: Do they want to create a world-scale brewer? What about Pete Coors's run for the US Senate (November 2004 Colorado election)?
3 Explore idea of three-step approach: (i) Start with Molson & Coors; (ii) then create a "true NAFTA brewer" by adding a third partner like Femsa; and (iii) finally go on to negotiate with a European/global brewer.
4 Consider different European brewers: Carlsberg have cleaned up their act and can now deal with North America; Scottish & Newcastle may be problematic in the UK (competition issue with Coors owning Carling); and Heineken would only be possible if they would agree to a minority position (unlikely).
5 Share Molson family view of governance: (i) we are CEO-centric – important to have professional management; (ii) as owners, we act strategically through the board; and (iii) only family members who are competent, have experience, the right credentials and who want to work in the business can eventually be employed by the business.

After touching on these topics over dinner, Eric urged Pete, "Let's do this together. We've got a continent to conquer and we have great breweries and superb talent. Let's get our teams to work on this."

They agreed in principle, and established a list of five "musts." A Molson-Coors deal must offer long term value for all shareholders, must be fair and in the best interests of all stakeholders, must maintain the heritage of each company, must keep brewing as the core of the business, and must allow each family to play a continued role in the combined company.

The following day, Eric and Jane flew to London for a week-long holiday planned months earlier. As they taxied on the tarmac at Montreal's Trudeau Airport, Eric told Jane that the meeting with Pete had gone well. "I have a good feeling about Coors."

"I hope so, Eric."

"Our next board meeting in May might be tough, though. I think Ian will make a move. We've got to be ready for it."

❧

On the eve of a board meeting, there is usually a dinner for Molson directors. The one on Tuesday, 4 May 2004, was held at the Mount Royal Club, the stately limestone building on the corner of Sherbrooke Street and Stanley. The fifteen board members, most of whom had flown in to Montreal, gathered in one of the private dining rooms. The setting, the service, and the food were flawless. It would have been a pleasant evening were it not for the heavy tension in the room.

As the main course was served, the talk turned to the future of Molson. Dan O'Neill brought up the merger of equals. The discussion that ensued highlighted the chasm on the board.

On the Eric side were those who thought it was a good opportunity. Molson and Coors knew each other well and had done business together for years. Both were led by families who cared about the long term. And they could jointly form a strong basis from which to conquer the world.

On the Ian side were the directors who viewed Coors as a one-brand company that had made a lot of mistakes in the past. For example, they had paid too much for Carling in the UK, which was now a drag on their results. Two weak players would not make a strong one.

Lively debate ensued. It was still going on as the plates were cleared and dessert was served. O'Neill turned the discussion to Brazil: Molson's business was improving, he said, and he was soon expecting to get back to double-digit growth. Eric noticed Luc Beauregard fidgeting. It was unlike him. As O'Neill spoke, he kept shifting his six-foot-two frame from one side to the other.

"Come on, Dan," he finally interrupted, "what do you take us for, fools?"

"I'm telling you, we're about to turn this thing around. I have it under control."

Beauregard, threw his napkin on his plate and muttered, loudly enough for everyone to hear, "Fuck off, Dan. This is bullshit!"

The table went quiet. It was an unprecedented insult to the CEO and a first for Luc. He always chose his words carefully.

Eric stood up. "This dinner is over. We'll see you all tomorrow morning at the brewery for the board meeting."

Later that evening, he called Luc. "You've got to go in there tomorrow and apologize."

"I know. I lost my cool. I just can't stand all these lies anymore. I think you're going to have to do something, Eric. Did you see the dynamics around the table tonight?"

"I did."

"Well, if you don't pull the plug on the Ian and Dan duo soon, they're going to find a way to steal the company from under you. Ian has been working against you for months. He's divided the board, rallied people around him, and has been saying to anyone who will listen that you're incompetent and should retire. As for Dan, he'll basically go with whoever he thinks will serve him best. So, if you don't do something, like tell Ian he won't be the next chairman or find a way to get rid of Dan as your CEO, they'll find a way to get rid of you."

"Yes, I know," Eric said. "I need to find the right time to do it."

"Okay. Just don't underestimate Ian," Luc said darkly. "I'm sure he's talking right now with Barrett or Drapkin or whoever else will listen to him."

Luc Beauregard might well have been looking through a spyglass at the scene taking place in the bar of the Ritz-Carlton Hotel across the street from the Mount Royal Club. After the board dinner, a small group of Molson directors had gathered there. As they polished off a bottle of Scotch, their conversation became more animated. The topic of discussion: who should be Molson's chairman?

Matt Barrett had been a board member for close to ten years. He had seen the company go through a number of phases: from conglomerate under Mickey Cohen, to back-to-beer under Jim Arnett, and now to global player under O'Neill. It was time for a new chairman. Eric was sixty-six. He'd been in the role since 1988. The company needed someone younger and more dynamic.

Moreover, the brewing industry was evolving. Gone were the days when it was governed by old, established families. It was now dominated by cutthroat private-equity firms. If Molson wanted to be part of the new world, it should be led by someone well-versed in corporate finance and deal-making. Eric was *passé*.

John Cleghorn sat pensively sipping his drink. He had been on the board for only a year and the difference between then and now was staggering. Back then, Eric had touted Ian as the future of Molson. Now they were at loggerheads. It was incredible how quickly the situation had deteriorated.

By the end of the night, the men around the table concluded it was time for a change. Ian was their man. It was all going to come to a head the next day.

Eric drove to the Notre Dame Street brewery at seven the following morning. He wanted to prepare for the board meeting scheduled to start two hours later. He took the elevator to the fourth floor, made a cup of coffee, and sat down to review his notes.

Unexpectedly, Ian walked into his office. His face was tense and slightly flushed. "Eric, is it true that you're not going to support me to become the next chairman?" he asked.

"Excuse me?"

"I'm asking you, have you changed your mind? Are you no longer going to support me to become the next chairman of the board?"

"Well, yes. You're right," Eric said. "It's not going to happen. Neither I nor my family will support you to be chairman. When the time comes, we're going to look elsewhere."

"How can you do this?" Ian's complexion became more florid with each passing second.

Furnace face. Peter Buckley had used the phrase a few months before when Eric met him to discuss Ian's plotting against Caledonia.

"It's simple, Ian," Eric said calmly. "It's not going to work because I don't trust you. I don't trust you and my family doesn't trust you. So, when the time comes, we are *not* going to recommend that you take over as chairman."

Ian turned and walked stiffly out of the office. He went to the boardroom, took out his fountain pen, and began to write furiously on the pad of paper in front of him.

Back in his office, Eric was relieved. He'd finally done it. He'd looked Ian in the eye and said out loud what he had been thinking for months. Ian was devious and untrustworthy, and he had finally told him. Eric picked up his papers and headed towards the boardroom where the other Molson directors were gathering. The meeting was about to start.

In the hallway, board member Don Drapkin stopped him in his tracks. Drapkin was a savvy, New York–based financier, corporate lawyer, close collaborator of billionaire Ronald Perelman (the two had a very public falling-out since then), and Ian's friend. "Eric, I wanted to ask you about Princeton," he said. "You know, my daughter goes there."

Eric was puzzled. He thought, "What's this guy doing talking to me about Princeton and his daughter right now? Is he trying to distract me?" He cut him off. "I'm sorry, Don, I don't have time right now. The board meeting is about to start and I have to get ready."

Walking away towards the boardroom, he thought to himself that he had never really liked Drapkin. His feeling dated back to when he first met the Wall Street deal-maker in New York after Ian recommended him as a Molson director. Maybe it was because during their entire interview Drapkin had kept his eyes glued to the stock market lighting up the computer screen on the side of his desk. Or maybe it was that Drapkin regularly called in to the Molson board meetings by phone rather than take the one-hour flight to Montreal. Either way, Eric didn't trust him. Taking his seat at the head of the table, he noticed Drapkin lean over to speak quietly to Ian before sitting down himself.

"They're up to something," he thought as he called the meeting to order.

Luc Beauregard spoke first. "Before we start, I would like to apologize for last night. My words were uncalled for and disrespectful towards Dan. I think we're all frustrated with the situation in Brazil, but I'm sure we can work through it and find a solution."

Acknowledging Beauregard's regrets, Eric tackled the meeting's agenda. After the routine approval of the minutes from the last meeting, O'Neill gave his business update. The CEO reported that the results for the past six months were poor but that he remained confident. He explained the various initiatives being taken in Brazil to prepare for future growth. As for Canada, O'Neil acknowledged that Alberta was becoming an important area of weakness because of competitors' discount pricing. To counter this, he said he was putting in place a new organization, one that would give national focus to Molson brands and drive more successful market development.

Despite O'Neill's assurances, there was scepticism in the room. Disbelief turned to dissension on the next item of the agenda: With whom should Molson develop a strategic alliance? Coors? Heineken? Another international brewer? Out of the corner of his eye, Eric saw Ian shaking his head, staring down at his notes, his face still flushed.

Given the cleavage on the board, the conversation rapidly evolved from who should be Molson's future partner to who should be the company's future chairman. "It was a very emotional meeting," says director Sandy Riley. "Very emotional. I wasn't happy at the time. I don't think anybody was. We were caught in the middle of this very tough family situation … Ian basically told us 'It's either Eric or me.' We had to choose."

Riley felt the breakdown between Eric and Ian was foreseeable and should have been managed between the two men privately, rather than come to a head as it did in on 5 May 2004. "I chastised both Ian and

Eric at the meeting. I told them both that they had the obligation to settle their issues on their own. It wasn't right for them to put us in a situation where we had to resolve something that they should have dealt with privately. This wasn't a business issue: it was a people issue. A family issue. It was clear that there was a whole bunch of family baggage that was being drawn into this. Eric and Ian may say it was *just* business, but to anybody watching as an outsider, it was *all* about family dynamics."

Eric remembers Riley's emotional outburst. "Sandy spoke up. He got all red in the face, started pounding his fist on the table. He was very upset. He basically told me that maybe it was time for me to go."

One by one, the directors who had gathered together the previous evening for their late night digestif spoke up.

Lloyd Barber said, "You're right, Sandy, this is untenable. The board needs a new chairman."

Donald Drapkin added that the board needed a chairman who was more communicative and engaged than Eric. To emphasize his point, he mentioned how Eric had brushed him off that very morning.

"Don, I didn't brush you off," Eric shot back. "I was trying to get my thoughts together before this meeting and you were chatting to me about Princeton and your daughter. I wasn't being rude. I had work to do!" He was incredulous. This was the man who'd kept his eyes locked on his computer throughout their entire first interview, and now he was calling him rude?

Matt Barrett was last to speak. "I know this must be hard for you, Eric," he said, "but maybe it's time for you to retire."

Eric looked over at Stephen. His younger brother, who'd always stood by his side, projected encouragement and support.

"Well, I'm not planning to go anywhere," Eric said. He turned to John Cleghorn, head of the board's corporate governance committee. "So tell us John, what do we do next?"

Cleghorn took a deep breath. "I recommend that we adjourn. We'll set up a separate session with just the independent directors to discuss the issue of succession."

The directors looked at their agendas and agreed to meet three days later on Saturday, 8 May, 11:00 a.m. at the Toronto Hilton airport hotel. Molson family members were not invited. The only topic on the agenda was who should be the next chairman of the board. Eric or Ian?

🍁

It was a long three days for Eric. After the board meeting, he left Montreal and went to the place where he always found peace and tranquility – Massawippi. On the drive down, he and Jane did not speak much. Both were exhausted, having stayed up late the night before going over different scenarios. If worse came to worst, Eric was ready to replace the entire Molson board with a new slate of directors. After all, he still had control of the company. He now acknowledges, "That would have been complete chaos."

"I can't believe how calm Eric was," Jane says. "He kept a lot of his stress to himself. There were people on the board who wanted to kick him out, but he stayed focused on Molson. He always wanted to do the right thing for the company. He was like, 'If you don't want me anymore, fine, but it can't be Ian.' He didn't believe that having Ian in charge was the right thing to do for Molson."

"I had done all I could. Now I just had to wait and hope," Eric recalls, unwittingly echoing the Molson "*Industria et Spe*" motto. "Jane saw me go through it. She was there for me." Quietly, he adds, "She's always been my best friend."

Eric reflected on how the vote would go. Molson's future and his family's legacy were in the hands of eight men: Beauregard, Bellini, Colson, Ingram, Riley, Cleghorn, O'Brien, and O'Neill. Board members Matt Barrett, Lloyd Barber, and Donald Drapkin had resigned from the board right after the 5 May meeting.

Eric knew he had the support of Beauregard, Bellini, and Colson. There was no doubt about that. Robert Ingram and Sandy Riley were solid directors, but with all that had been said a few days prior, he was unsure how they would vote. As for Cleghorn and O'Brien, he sensed he had lost their confidence. "Cleghorn couldn't believe I went from bringing in Ian as deputy chairman and my potential successor to wanting to get rid of him. He was unsure of me because I'd changed my mind." It was the same for O'Brien. "Both O'Brien and Cleghorn were very important directors, but they were like peas in a pod – what one did, the other did too. They were good, though. They loved Molson and they knew what we stood for." Still, he was apprehensive about which way they would vote that Saturday morning.

Dan Colson remembers the uncertainty. "Even guys who should have been intensely loyal to Eric, like John Cleghorn and David O'Brien, wavered. They could have gone either way … I remember seeing them that morning before the meeting at the Toronto airport. I had a chat with both of them independently. I wanted to make sure they didn't do anything stupid because Ian had been working them over pretty well."

Describing the 8 May meeting, Bellini recalls the division and tension in the room. "I was almost alone to fight for Eric's position and to fight for the merger with Coors. I had already told Ian I would never see him as chairman … I was surprised it came to that. In the back of my mind, I always knew that Eric had the voting shares, so he could throw out all the directors if he wanted to. But Eric didn't use that. Even though what happened at the board back then was a revolt! … At that Saturday morning meeting, Colson stayed with me. He was on Eric's side. So was Beauregard. O'Neill at the end was with me. Even if all along he had been siding with Ian, at the end he was on Eric's side."

The CEO had been so close to Ian over the years that Eric wouldn't have been surprised if O'Neill had sided with Ian. The two had collaborated tightly on everything from restructuring the corporation to investing in Brazil. But at the 5 May meeting when everything came to a head, Eric noticed O'Neill looking miserable. Perhaps he was having second thoughts? Even journalists picked up on it. They said the "normally enthusiastic CEO" sounded "down" and "depressed" while reviewing the company's fourth quarter and 2004 year-end results on the analysts' call following the board meeting. Reporters concluded that the industry rumours were true and that "Dan O'Neill may be on the way out as chief executive of Canada's largest brewer."

O'Neill describes it as a very stressful time. He felt pulled in two directions at once, with legitimate loyalties to both Ian and Eric. "You can't imagine how bad it was. I mean, a lot of boards have big divisional things happen, but this was awful. It was a major mutiny. I mean, I had a mom and dad who split and left the family when I was ten, and the arguments were awful, but this was way, way worse. I'd never seen anything like it in my entire life."

When Dan O'Neill prepared for that May 8th meeting in Toronto, he worried about the message he would deliver. He had put together a short presentation with the pros and cons of a transaction with Coors (synonymous for supporting Eric or not) and at the last minute decided to talk to Dave Perkins about it.

"That Friday night," recounts Perkins, "Dan pulled me aside and explained what was going on. I think Dan used me sometimes to process his thoughts. It was like he was practising with me. Anyhow, he was not conclusive as to where he would land, but I walked away with the impression that Coors was his preference. You see, I didn't see it as an Eric versus Ian issue back then, but rather as a Coors versus Heineken issue. So I walked away with the view that Dan was in the Coors camp."

As O'Neill talks about that meeting in Toronto, he becomes pensive. "We all met in this boardroom at Pearson. Everyone was expecting me to be on Ian's side. I wrote this four-page thing, and I said, 'I've talked to every one of you. Ian hired me. He was my mentor. But for the long term value of this brand and this company, I am going to support Eric.'"

The cynics on the board say O'Neill sided with Eric because he worked out that his own interests would be best served in a merger of equals with Coors, rather than a Heineken takeover. Perhaps he felt there would be a better role for him in a Molson Coors scenario? Maybe he hoped to become CEO of the new entity? That remains speculation. Nonetheless, O'Neill noted the surprise in the room when he announced his position. "The other directors at the meeting were all like, 'What? We thought you were going to support Ian!' And I said, 'No, I will only support Eric.' And after that, Ian has never spoken to me again … That was probably one of the worst things in my entire life – the tension, the impossible choice, the loss of friendship."

There were others who spoke up in favour of Eric. One was Sandy Riley. Although he had been critical a few days earlier of both Molsons for allowing family dynamics to penetrate the boardroom, he thought the situation "was largely driven by Ian." Riley is unequivocal in his assessment: "I really feel like Ian was the one who was really rushing the fences on this one and pushing things way beyond what it was his prerogative to do. Ian *way* overstepped the bounds of what he was entitled to do ... I also thought Eric may have been naive in some ways in bringing Ian in. He should have seen it coming. But at the end of the day, that's not a fatal flaw. That's just human nature."

Back and forth the discussion went between the directors who supported Eric and those who argued that Ian should step in. At a critical point, Luc Beauregard interrupted the debate. "Don't you all realize that Eric and his siblings own over 800,000 voting shares in the company?"

The room went quiet.

Beauregard had planned the move. Before boarding the plane for Pearson, he had called Eric and said, "Don't worry, Eric, I'm bringing the hydrogen bomb with me today." His weapon was Eric's control position in Molson.

Picking up on Beauregard's cue, Sandy Riley spoke. "We have to draw this to a conclusion, and I'm supporting Eric. He's the principal shareholder and he's the guy who's been the leader of the firm for the last few years. So if you're asking me to make a choice, I've made my choice. It's Eric."

Shortly thereafter, the other directors in the room voted on Molson's future chairman.

🍁

The phone rang in the house in Massawippi. Jane answered and passed it to Eric.

It was John Cleghorn. He got right to the point. "We've had our meeting. It's okay, Eric, you're staying on as chairman of the board. You've still got your job. Ian is out."

Eric sat down as a wave of relief washed over him. "What happened?"

"We discussed it and decided to support you. We're also recommending that Molson hire Citigroup to evaluate all options. We're going to ask them to consider everything – whether it's continuing with Molson's existing business strategy, doing a merger of equals, selling the company, converting it to an income trust, or even doing a series of smaller acquisitions and selling Brazil. It's going to be a full review."

"Okay, sounds good."

"Also, Sandy Riley will be calling you. He wants to apologize."

"All right. Thank you, John."

"Don't mention it, Eric. I'm sorry it had to come to this, but I think we're doing the right thing."

Eric put down the phone. Who had saved his bacon? Colson? Bellini? Beauregard? O'Neill? They probably all played a role. He took a deep breath. It had been a close call. But was it over? Would Ian just go away? "Not likely," he said under his breath.

He glanced down at the newspapers Jane had left on the kitchen table. At once the headline on front page of the *Globe and Mail* grabbed his attention: "Hollinger Lawsuit Now Seeks $1.2-Billion from Black." Eric scanned the update on the lawsuit against "media baron" Conrad Black. His heart sank when he got to the third paragraph: "Two new defendants – Lord Black's wife, Barbara Amiel, and his long-time colleague Daniel Colson – have been added to the suit."

"Shit," Eric muttered. He had been following the Conrad Black situation closely. A US$1.25-billion lawsuit had been filed in Chicago against Black and other Hollinger executives, alleging that Black and his crew had made unauthorized transfers of the company's cash to themselves. Eric saw it as an example of what could happen when a controlling shareholder of a corporation with a dual-class share structure took advantage of his dominant position. Now Colson, one of Eric's own loyal directors and Black's right-hand man, was named in the lawsuit.

"These charges against Danny are probably unfounded," thought Eric. "But it changes things."

Eric viewed Colson as someone trustworthy and intelligent, with excellent business acumen. At one point he'd even thought of asking him to take over as Molson's chairman if he was ever forced to step down. The company was now "in play," and all alternatives had to be explored. One of Colson's most admirable traits was his loyalty, but Eric now wondered. Was he *too* loyal? Maybe that's what had got him in trouble with Hollinger and Conrad Black. Perhaps his devotion to Black was too unequivocal? Or maybe he just got greedy.

Colson's name would later be cleared, but at the time, the only thing Eric was sure of was that his own troubles were far from over.

On 11 May, three days after the fateful meeting in Toronto, Eric received a letter from Ian announcing his resignation from the Molson board.

Dear Eric,

I am writing to confirm that I do not wish my name to be put forward for re-election to the Board of Directors of Molson at this year's Annual General Meeting on 22nd June, 2004.

Over the last 12–18 months, it has become clear to me, to our Chief Executive and to most of our Board members, that you are no longer able or willing to work with me in a professional and harmonious manner. This breakdown in our relationship and your refusal, notwithstanding explicit board instructions, to conduct yourself properly, has destabilized our Board and our management and has meant that, at this critical moment, the company is suffering from a lack of unified and coherent leadership.

In view of these circumstances, it is clear to me that it is not tenable for us both to continue to serve on the Board of Molson. Since you have refused to consider retiring, notwithstanding the advice you have received in this regard from some of our directors and in view of the fact that you have served for in excess of 20 years as Chairman or Deputy Chairman, I believe that the only responsible course of action is for me to leave the Board at this time.

Eric noticed that Ian had copied all the other Molson directors on this missive. "He's not going to let up," thought Eric. "He wants to make sure everyone hears his grievances against me once again. I may not be perfect, but nor is he." At no point did Ian seem to recognize that he might have contributed to the deterioration of the relationship and the breakdown in trust.

The next day Molson issued a press release announcing that it would seek to reduce the size of its board at the upcoming annual general meeting. The directors up for election were Luc Beauregard, Francesco Bellini, John Cleghorn, Dan Colson, Robert Ingram, Eric Molson, Stephen Molson, David O'Brien, Dan O'Neill, and Sandy Riley. Absent were Ian Molson and his allies.

"Things moved fast after that," says Eric. "The board completely changed, but perhaps it was for the best. As chairman/owner, you have to make sure you have some good directors around you. You know, people who ask the right questions and are savvy about business."

As Cleghorn had told Eric when he called him after the Toronto meeting, Molson hired Citigroup Global Markets to evaluate the company's options. O'Neill says this was done even though he and his management team had already conducted a thorough analysis. "The board felt they had to do their own study. I was like, 'Jeez, really?' Anyhow, that delayed us, but they wanted to do it … So the report came back, and their conclusions were the same as ours. In the end, the board did the work, management did the work, and the outcome was the same. And we went forward with Coors."

On 1 June 2004, Dan O'Neill met with Coors's Leo Kiely in Chicago to discuss guidelines for a potential transaction. Ten days later, they signed a confidentiality agreement. The Molson-Coors deal was underway. Due diligence was about to begin.

♦

A few weeks after Ian resigned from the board, Stephen received a letter from Bill Molson. Ian's brother, Frederick William Molson, the second of four boys in the family, was a Montreal-based stockbroker who followed Molson's stock performance but was never otherwise involved in the brewery. In his note to Stephen, Bill voiced his "dismay" and "indignation" over Ian's departure from the board.

"Ian's arrival on the board was the best thing that has happened to this company," Bill wrote. "Instead of thanking Ian and embracing him, you [Eric and Stephen] have engaged in a shameful series of actions resulting in Ian's departure. He has done absolutely nothing to deserve this. Your actions against Ian are based solely on your own insecurities and self interests and have no basis or foundation and have nothing to do with ensuring the continued growth and success of the company. History and the markets will judge your behaviour but let me stress your brother's behaviour is the antithesis of the Molson family 'values' he is so fond of referring to." The note continued in that vein for a few more paragraphs.

Stephen passed the letter on to Eric. "Wow," Eric muttered, "not embraced Ian? I made him deputy chairman." Rereading the sentence accusing him of not living up to the Molson family values, he shook his head.

He picked up a second letter on his desk. It was Cynthia's reply to Bill. Ian's brother had sent copies of his note to both Cynthia and Deirdre.

Cynthia dismissed Bill's attempt to drive a wedge between her and her brothers. "It is surely distressing for all family members to have ill-feelings generated by business matters, but unfortunately it isn't new," she wrote. "Certainly it has happened on several occasions over Molson's more than two centuries. No forbearers are going to be 'rolling in their graves.' Both my brothers are extremely conscientious stewards of the family brewing business, and both value highly the family history and their ties with family members near and far. If there has been a major split between or among Molson family board members, there may have been strong words spoken on both sides, but I think it neither helpful for those who know little or only one side of the disagreement to form hasty, uncompromising opinions, nor appropriate to wade in with angry, provocative statements."

Eric put down the letter and a wave of gratitude washed over him. "Thank God for Stephen, Deirdre, and Cynthia," he thought. "I could never get through this without their loyalty and support."

Leaning back in his chair, he stared up at his memorabilia-lined bookshelves. As he contemplated the different beer bottles and labels from the past, he wondered what the future would bring. Just as his predecessors had shaped Molson with their decisions, the merger of equals with Coors would be his defining move. He had undone the conglomerate and was about to partner with Coors to build a North American platform for Molson to grow. It had taken him twelve years – twelve years from that lunch when he raised his glass of Molson Ex and proposed his "going back to beer" toast.

Perhaps the challenges Eric faced over the years made him stronger. There was a time when, intimidated by the likes of Tom and Hartland, he didn't speak up. He let others take the lead. But maybe his struggles against greed and self-interested people pushed him to define his vision for Molson and elucidate his principles. It may be that, without the likes of Mickey Cohen or Ian, Eric would not have had the resilience to push forward his global brewery vision or his corporate governance ideal for Molson.

I can't help but think of the passage in William Shakespeare's *Twelfth Night*: "Be not afraid of greatness. Some are born great, some achieve greatness and some have greatness thrust upon them."

In his usual self-effacing way, Eric smiles and tells me he didn't do anything great. "There were times when I thought I wouldn't make it," he says. "But I was well surrounded. Jane, my boys, Stephen, my sisters, and our silver fox advisors … they all stood by me and had faith in me. I couldn't have done it without them."

PART THREE
THE RETURN

13 Taking the High Road

Are you not ashamed of caring so much for the making of money and for fame and prestige, when you neither think nor care about wisdom and truth and the improvement of your soul?

SOCRATES (470/469–399 BC)

It's an annual ritual. Every spring as the snow recedes and the ground starts to thaw, we gather in the family's sugar shack up the road from the house in Massawippi. The small wood structure stands in the middle of a maple forest. Each tree has a tin bucket hanging from the spout that was hammered gently into place a few days before. If you stand quietly, you can hear the plunk-plunk-plunk of the sap dripping into the pails. The kids tentatively dip their fingers in the clear liquid, hoping to taste some of the sweetness that will come once it's boiled.

The shack is in full operation. Its sliding doors are open, the coolers are stocked with Molson Ex and Molson Canadian, and smoke trails through the opening in the middle of the roof. On one side is the syrup-making equipment – stainless-steel boiling vats, evaporating pans, and filtering stations – and on the other a place for sampling. It's a large table on which trays of packed snow are laid out for the first pouring of hot syrup.

"Is it ready yet?" asks the youngest of Jane and Eric's grandchildren, holding up her popsicle stick.

Finally, it's time. The freshly boiled and filtered maple syrup is poured in strips on the beds of snow. Young and old reach in and eagerly roll up the cooled stickiness with their sticks into lollypop-like balls. Delicious.

Eric Molson in the doorway of the family's sugar shack in Massawippi, Quebec, 2009.
Molson family collection.

"Can I have some more?" asks my four-year-old.

"How do you ask?" prompts her father.

"Pleeeeeeaaase!"

The mood is festive. The kids are running around (fuelled by sugar), and the adults are engaged in lively conversation (fuelled by Molson).

Eric is not with the group. He's on the other side of the shack with Larry, who is in charge of the syrup-making operation. Larry has been doing this for years. As Eric holds up a vial of syrup to the window, the two men contemplate the colour and clarity of this year's production.

"What do you think?" asks Eric.

"Yup, looks good. Yup. Ah-hum," Larry nods.

Eric goes back to the evaporating pans, leans into the steam rising from the boiling sap, and takes in the aroma. He checks the temperature once again. This is Eric at his happiest. As a chemist, he is managing the transformation of one substance to another through a well-controlled process. As a lover of Canada, he is partaking in an activity that fully represents his heritage; few things are more Canadian than maple syrup. And as a family man, he is surrounded by the people he cherishes. To top it all off, he gets to sit with Larry, absorb the scene, and not talk much.

"I could do with a little less chaos," he says when I ask him how he's doing. Then he leans in and adds, "I actually love it." The smile on his face manifests how this place – so far removed from the machinations of boardroom politics – feeds his soul.

❦

"Family Feud Envelops Boardroom at Venerable Molson" was the headline on the front page of the *Globe and Mail* of 17 June 2004. Citing an "informed insider," the article by Derek DeCloet and Andrew Willis detailed the "struggle for power involving members of one of the country's most prominent families":

The cause of the tension appears to be Eric Molson's refusal to grant more responsibility to cousin Ian, a former Wall Street deal maker who is given much of the credit for the strategy that has improved the financial performance of the company …

Matthew Barrett, a Molson director and former chairman and chief executive officer of Bank of Montreal, told Eric Molson at a May board meeting that it was time for the chairman to step aside, said an insider familiar with the matter, speaking on condition of anonymity. Mr. Barrett could not be reached for comment.

Eric Molson is 66 and has been a director for about 30 years, more than 15 of them as chairman. Rather than quit, he is standing for re-election in his current post. He has effective control of the company because he owns the largest block of voting shares.

"[Eric] knew that the board . . . would have wanted Ian to succeed him as chairman of the board, and he wasn't going to let that happen," the insider said.

Similar stories were on the front pages of the *National Post, Toronto Star, Montreal Gazette, Calgary Herald,* and *Vancouver Sun.* Eric may have won the vote on 8 May, but Ian had not laid down his arms. "Ian did that to us," says Eric. "He was talking to the press, and you just don't do that if you can avoid it. Here we were, trying to do a deal with Coors, and every day there was stuff in the papers."

Dan Colson, deeply involved with the media and newspaper world for over eighteen years as CEO of London's Telegraph Group, confirms Eric's belief. "I discovered through my contacts that Ian was talking with this guy at the *Globe and Mail* … I ran into Ian about a month later in London at the squash club and I decided to confront him. 'Ian, I heard you were in Toronto having dinner with your good friend DeCloet.' Ian immediately went five shades of red, and he said, 'Oh, we were just talking about business.' Yeah, right. So I said, 'Funnily enough, he's never written about the beer business. That's not his beat.'"

Regardless of the source, the media strikes against Eric were constant. There were a few on 22 June 2004, the day of Molson's AGM. Sitting down for breakfast that morning, Eric grabbed the *Globe's* business section. The first piece he read covered the upcoming meeting: "When Molson chairman Eric Molson appears today at the brewer's annual meeting in Montreal, shareholders might want to ask him a question: Is it not time, sir, for you to retire to the beer garden before more damage is done?"

Already he loathed speaking in public, and now this. Putting away the paper, he took a deep breath. He had a long day ahead. First the (very public) AGM, then a board meeting, and later a family meeting to go over everything. As long as he stayed focused on the bigger picture, he thought, he could get through it. "It's not about me," he repeated to himself, "it's about doing what's right for Molson."

"Get on a high wave and stay on it," The Turk had told him. The beginning of a smile formed on Eric's lips as he remembered his professor's faith in him. He then thought of his father. Tom had often been harsh and critical, but ultimately, he'd entrusted him with the family's legacy. Tom believed in him too. The realization gave Eric strength.

The reception room at the brewery was packed. "It was a mob scene, full of reporters and journalists," Eric says. "We had to bring in extra security guards."

Molson AGMs were usually staid, formal affairs, strictly adhering to the rules of protocol, with a manageable group of stockholders politely listening to reports by the company's chairman and CEO. On 22 June 2004, however, not only was the room crammed but there was undeniable febrility in the air. How would they explain that five directors had resigned at once? Why was Ian Molson out? Was Eric Molson going to stay on as chairman? What about Dan O'Neill and his tanking investment in Brazil – would he be the next to go? Why was Dan Colson up for re-election as a director when he had just been named a defendant in the Conrad Black lawsuit with allegations of financial impropriety?

Eric kept his composure as he stood in front of the room and adjusted the microphone. At least he didn't have to face the media directly: the space constraints meant journalists were asked to watch the proceedings on television screens in another room.

Reading from his notes, Eric first gave thanks to the Molson directors who were not standing for re-election – Lloyd Barber, Matt Barrett, Donald Drapkin, and Luiz Otávio Gonçalves. Then: "Last, and certainly not least, R. Ian Molson, who has served on the board for the past eight years and as deputy chairman since 1999, has decided not to seek re-election to the board this year. Ian has served on several committees of the board, and with his investment banking background, has made an excellent contribution to the direction of this company

Eric Molson at the media-packed AGM on 22 June 2004. Photo: Ryan Remiorz; licensed by the Canadian Press.

showing strong personal commitment to its success. He remains an important shareholder." Eric hoped that would be enough. Journalists, however, were quick to point out that he did not directly thank Ian as he had the other directors.

He then went on to explain the corporate governance work the company had embarked on over the past year. How, for example, they had reduced the size of the board and eliminated the executive committee so that all directors could participate more fully in the board's decision-making.

Eric also touched on the company's dual-class share structure and what it meant to have a controlling shareholder like the Tom Molson family. "Decisions can be taken with a view to long-term growth. We do not have to take short-term measures simply to boost the value of our stock in the next quarter or to please those who like to flip companies."

Finally, he shared his vision for Molson and the four ground rules that drove all his decisions:

1 We are determined to be a pro-active player in the global brewing industry.

2 We are a company that is sensitive to its Canadian roots starting with the Montreal community where we began.

3 Our focus is NOT on short-term shareholders who invest for a quick profit.

4 Our focus IS on shareholders and indeed ALL our stakeholders who want to be part of a long-term successful and profitable Canadian brewer, including our employees, the communities we serve, and our business partners.

By the close of his speech, Eric felt emboldened. He intensely disliked the family feud stuff splashed all over the papers and the public airing of confidential board discussions, but he believed in what he was doing. He hoped it would be worth it in the end.

Next on the agenda was the election of company directors. The three-person slate representing Molson's class A shareholders – Dan Colson, John Cleghorn, and Robert Ingram – was problematic because of the controversy around Colson's involvement in the Conrad Black case. Some thought it made him unsuitable to be a director of Molson. AIM Funds Management, Molson's largest shareholder, for example, declared that anyone whose activities on Black's board were unclear had no business being a director of a major Canadian company. Others, including Jarislowsky Fraser Ltd and Amvescap plc, voiced similar concerns.

Eric was resolute. He told shareholders that Colson was under "severe pressure as a result of allegations that have yet to be proven" and that he was a "diligent board member" who had done important work for Molson since becoming a director seven years before. He then called for the vote on the Colson slate of directors.

"Any opposed?" He glanced quickly around the room. "Motion carried."

"Excuse me." Bill Molson, Ian's older brother, was in the audience, as was Ian. "What was the tally on the vote for the class A directors?"

About 20 per cent of the class A stockholders had withheld their votes, he was told – a high number given how, in the past, independent directors were usually voted in unanimously. The controversy surrounding Colson had taken its toll.

"Any other questions?" Eric asked.

Again, Bill Molson piped up. "It seems clear to a lot of people that Ian Molson's involvement has been good for the company. The CEO and several directors of Molson have told me on several occasions that they've found Ian's advice and guidance to have been invaluable. I would like to ask Eric Molson why, given that, he is not supporting Ian Molson to succeed him as chairman of the company."

And there it was: a public face-off.

Eric took a deep breath. "I think I've answered that question in my speech. Mr Ian Molson has done wonders for this company, but he has made his own decision not to seek re-election for personal reasons."

Bill Molson insisted, "Well, you have stated that you oppose Ian Molson succeeding you."

"I don't believe I've stated that," Eric replied.

The media and Molson shareholders waited quietly for a comeback. Ian looked straight ahead, stone-faced.

Thinking back on the exchange, Eric says, "All this was orchestrated ahead of time by Ian. He was at the meeting, but he wasn't saying anything. First he got his brother Bill to stand up and confront me in front of everyone. And then he got his aunt, Claire Faulkner, to make some other negative comments."

There was another challenge, this time from Bruce McNiven, a Montreal lawyer and close friend of Ian's. Should Eric still be chairman of the board at sixty-six years old?

Eric replied tersely. "The board chooses the chairman, and they're conscious of my age." He then deferred the question to the head of the corporate governance committee, John Cleghorn.

"It's fair to say that the independent directors have cast their vote in favour of Eric Molson as the chair," Cleghorn confirmed.

Marie Giguère remembers the ambiance in the room that day. "It was tense. Eric doesn't like annual meetings to begin with, and most of our annual meetings were *really* boring. I mean, there were usually *no* questions. Nothing. But this one, the room was absolutely packed. We had to bring in extra chairs. Then Bill, Ian's brother, raised his hand

and started asking some difficult questions. It was *very* tense. In the end, it was fine, but Eric was not a happy camper. This was not his kind of environment. Eric doesn't like confrontation. He *really* doesn't like confrontation."

Ultimately, the vote went as planned. According to the report filed with the Canadian securities regulators, 10.3 per cent of the class B shares – equivalent to the 2.3 million shares owned by Ian – voted against the directors representing the B shareholders, which included Eric and Stephen, and 20.2 per cent of the A shares withheld their vote for Colson and the other A directors.

When the meeting adjourned, Eric left the brewery without talking to the media. At least it was done. The second battle involving Ian, this time a very public one, was over.

Reporters scrambled to get a quote. Stephen had exited with Eric. Colson also ducked out, not wanting to draw any more attention to himself. When reporters approached Ian and asked him why he was not Molson's new chairman, his reply was terse: "That's not my decision."

Bill Molson was equally brief. "I just want what's best for the company, that's all. I want there to be a good leadership going forward."

Ian Molson speaks to shareholders after the 22 June 2004 AGM. *Globe and Mail*, 23 June 2004, B6. Photo by Christinne Muschi.

When asked about Ian's resignation, he said, "It's too bad. Ian's done a good job."

O'Neill was more loquacious in the post-AGM news conference. Of Eric staying on as chairman of the board, he said, "I totally am in agreement. The current chairman is the right person for the job." About Ian's departure, he said Ian was a talented individual who brought a lot of experience to the board. "I'm not saying Molson is better off without Ian on the board, but the balance is still within the board to function effectively."

The questions directed to the CEO, however, were mainly about the company's performance. Over the past year, Molson's sales volume in Brazil had plummeted by 17.5 per cent. Profitability and market share were also down. "Myself and the management team are not happy with the results," O'Neill told shareholders that morning. "We're all in angst about what's going on there." At the news conference, he announced that unless Kaiser's fortunes improved markedly by January 2005, the company would likely seek a buyer for its 80 per cent stake in the Brazilian business.

The press conference over, O'Neill joined the other Molson directors for their board meeting. The main item on the agenda was Coors. They discussed the broad terms of the proposed merger of equals and instructed Molson's management team to continue pursuing the opportunity. They also created an independent committee chaired by Sandy Riley to review the terms and conditions of the deal so as to make a recommendation to the rest of the board. The other members were Francesco Bellini, John Cleghorn, Daniel Colson, Robert Ingram, and David O'Brien.

"It was delicate," says Marie Giguère. "A controlling shareholder, as a shareholder, doesn't have a fiduciary duty per se. So that's why we had to have an independent committee without Eric or any other family member present. This committee had a lot on its shoulders. It had to decide whether the transaction we were about to do with Coors was fair to *all* shareholders."

The emphasis on independence was so high that the committee opted to hire its own separate financial advisors, Merrill Lynch, and lawyers, Fasken's and Shearman & Sterling, to help with the evaluation.

That meant that the brewery had its own counsel; Eric, Stephen, and their holding company, Pentland Securities (1981) Inc., had theirs; and Deirdre and Cynthia had a separate group of lawyers. It was a bonanza for professional services firms. Nonetheless, Eric felt it was important for everyone to be duly represented. They all had to make their own decision and not be influenced by the controlling shareholder.

Eric's last meeting was with Generations VI and VII of the family. It was the end of a long day, and he was exhausted. Still, he sat down with his siblings and nephews to give them an update on the plans going forward.

"Eric didn't say much, but he made it quite clear how he felt," says Cynthia. "We knew he really felt deeply betrayed by Ian, and he said that he was in the fight of his life to essentially save the brewery."

"One thing Eric's siblings will probably say about him," says Brian Baxter, Cynthia's son, "is that he's a lousy communicator. I mean, the sisters will get off the phone with him and ask, 'Why doesn't he just come out and say what he's trying to say!' But they have a great deal of respect for Eric's intelligence, his knowledge, and his integrity. So there's been a willingness to give him the benefit of the doubt and support what he's doing."

Eric tried to prepare his family for the storm about to be unleashed. Having failed to mount a public challenge at the AGM against Eric's chairmanship, Ian was likely to intensify his media attacks. Worse, he might launch a counterattack with a hostile bid for Molson. The Tom Molson gang had to stick together. Bill Molson had already tried to divide them with his letter to Stephen. And nothing prevented Ian from trying once again to turn Eric's siblings against their brother.

What Ian probably had not counted on was the Tom Molson gang's loyalty to each other. Brian says, "There's a sentiment by the siblings that 'Right or wrong, we're going to support the direction Eric takes.' In my mind, it would be almost inconceivable that they would come to a point of not supporting Eric."

❧

Ian launched his offensive a week later with a tell-all article on the front page of the *Wall Street Journal*. The 29 June 2004 piece by journalists

Robert Frank and Elena Cherney, "A Brewing Family Feud Poses Risks for Molson Beer Empire," was full of backroom details. Ian was quoted as saying "a succession plan should be put into place now and Eric should retire." The account revealed some of what had transpired:

> One morning in May, Ian Molson strode into the executive offices of Molson Inc. looking for his cousin Eric H. Molson, who had been chairman of their family's beer company for more than 16 years.
>
> Ian found his cousin in a hallway. "Is it true that you are opposed to my succeeding you as chairman?" Ian says he demanded to know. Eric confirmed he didn't want his cousin to take over, according to Ian …
>
> While Eric appears to have won the first round, the battle for control between the two cousins is likely to intensify now that Ian is leading a shareholder revolt against his cousin. Already, members of the board, shareholders and family members are taking sides …
>
> At a board meeting in Rio de Janeiro in January 2003, Eric surprised the board by announcing a broad review of Molson's corporate governance. In June, word leaked out to Ian that the study recommended eliminating Ian's position as deputy chairman. After hearing about the report's conclusions, Ian confronted his cousin. "Is there something from this governance report that you and I need to talk about?" he recalls asking. According to Ian, Eric said no, and shrugged his shoulders …
>
> The tensions boiled over in early May. At a dinner the night before a board meeting, directors including Messrs. Drapkin and Barrett lobbied for Eric Molson's ouster, according to several board members. Neither of the cousins were present.
>
> The next morning, Ian says he walked into his cousin's office and asked if he would ever be chairman, only to be shot down by Eric …
>
> Ian says the battle is just beginning. In his resignation letter he charged that Eric's 'refusal to conduct yourself properly … has destabilized our board and our management.' He's canvassing

shareholders to support a new chairman – even if it isn't him – and is lobbying family members to pool votes and blunt Eric's voting control.

"Ian was disloyal," says Eric Stevenson, Deirdre's eldest son. "Worse still, he went public. When we saw his picture on the front page of the *Wall Street Journal*, that's when we closed ranks."

Eric tried to ignore the "family feud" articles by concentrating on the brewery's long term. "Ian decided to speak to the media. I don't think that's the way to do things, but that was his choice. He did the same thing with his wife's family when he tried to break up Caledonia Investments with James Cayzer – at least that's what Peter Buckley told me … I knew the deal we were working on with Coors was what we needed for our future, so that's what I focused on. I also had a secret weapon – I had the next wave of successors ready to take over. Andrew and Geoff were coming through the ranks of their organizations and showing me that they had the right stuff. So I had that going for me. I had my boys."

Andrew was then working in public relations at National, and Geoff was in Denver at Molson USA. Both were closely following what was going on and giving updates to their father. Andrew had an external perspective, analyzing what was reported in the media and the financial community, while Geoff had an internal view, evaluating what was said by Molson employees and people in the beer industry.

🍁

The negotiations between Molson and Coors intensified in the first few weeks of July 2004. Meetings in Montreal and Denver often went late into the night. Both sides were working to find a mechanism whereby Molson and Coors shareholders would agree to surrender their shares in exchange for securities of the new company. They had to find an exchange ratio that reflected the value of each company and was consistent with the "merger of equals" notion.

Marie Giguère was deeply enmeshed in the talks. "It was intense. We had to find the right balance in order to keep it as a merger of equals … Remember, the shareholders of Molson were getting 55 per cent of the new company, because Molson was actually worth more than Coors. So it was almost equal in terms of the number of shares that each group got, and we wanted to keep that 55–45 per cent balance. That's how we were able to do a merger of equals and not have an acquisition premium. But if the balance tipped more in favour of one, so that one became the 'acquirer,' it would have meant a different treatment from an accounting point of view. And if you treated it differently from an accounting perspective, there would have been a psychological impact as well."

To make things more complicated (and distracting), while the Molson and Coors teams worked on the merger of equals, Ian was putting together his own deal. His efforts were depicted by Andrew Ross Sorkin, a financial columnist for the *New York Times*, on 25 July 2004: "Furious that his cousin, Eric Molson, the company's chairman, refused to step down in May and give him the top job, Ian Molson is scrambling to find backers to start a corporate coup d'état and scuttle the merger … So now, Ian is going around cup – er, make that beer mug – in hand, trying to raise the financing. He has been hitting up his old friends at First Boston's London office, his pal Ron Perelman (the Revlon chairman, who can't resist a good fight) and the Onex Corporation, a Canadian buyout firm that once went after John Labatt Ltd., among others. He has also reached out to Heineken."

Rumours that Ian was trying to sell Molson to Heineken were running rampant that July. Individual Molson directors received phone calls from "Ian and his surrogates," telling them, "You can't do this deal with Coors. You'll get more value if you put the company up for auction and let the Heineken guys get in on it."

Sandy Riley, then chair of the independent committee overseeing the Coors transaction, describes the inordinate pressure on him and Eric *not* to transact with the Coors family. "There was the feeling that if you sold to Heineken, you would get a much better price at the time than if you went with Coors. But with Coors, you had the chance to build something bigger, better, and more global, which could generate more value in the long term … Throughout that whole period, Eric was getting bombarded with people who were saying, 'You have to sell to Heineken.' And I was getting phone calls from investment bankers saying, 'You know, there are some pretty sharp guys out there who know how to put pressure on boards if you don't do the right thing.'"

Despite all this coercion, Eric remained steadfast.

Riley remembers saying to Eric, "Look, as long as you tell me, as chair of the independent committee, that a merger with Coors is the course of action you want to pursue, and as long as it's clear from the work that's being done here that the Coors transaction will create an enhancement in value for the shareholders and the stakeholders of the company, you make my job easier ... If you are firm in your conviction, we can be firm."

So when people came to Riley and said, "You can get a better price from the Heineken side," he would reply, "That may be the case, but the fact is that the controlling shareholder has a strong view on the best way to create value. And the merger with Coors *is* a fact sheet that will create additional value. It may take a bit longer than a short-term transaction with Heineken, but in the longer term it has the potential to create even *more* value. And, yes, there are execution risks, but this is what the major shareholder wants to do. There is no reason for us not to support this view, because it's not demonstrable that the value that will be created in a Heineken transaction, for example, is that much greater than the value of the transaction the major shareholder wants to do with Coors."

Meanwhile the Molson and Coors teams continued to work on the merger. What was the value of the synergies that could be generated by combining the operations of the two companies? Where would the new company's head office be located? On which exchange would the shares be listed? Who was going to be leading the combined operations? How was the new corporation going to be governed? What was the role of the Molson and Coors families in this new venture?

Then, on 18 July, there was a leak. Giguère remembers it well. "I guess there were starting to be a lot of people implicated by then. I mean, we had financial advisors, Coors had financial advisors, there were lots of lawyers involved, etc. And then one Sunday in the middle of July – I can't forget, because I had my whole family visiting up north and I had to come back to Montreal – we were all in the office working, and our head of communications gets a call at like 9 p.m. She doesn't look to see who's calling, she picks up the phone, and it's a journalist. Now how can you deny that something is going on when a journalist calls you at 9 p.m. on a Sunday night, in your office, in the middle of the summer, and you're there to answer the phone?"

The next day, Molson publicly acknowledged it was talking to Coors. "In response to reports published today in the public media," read the release, "Molson Inc. and Adolph Coors Company confirmed that they are in advanced discussions concerning a possible merger of equals between the two companies, the terms of which are still being discussed and are subject to final Board approvals. The parties confirmed that the terms being discussed include Eric Molson (currently Molson's chairman) becoming Chairman of the Board; Leo Kiely (currently Coors' CEO) becoming Chief Executive Officer ..."

The leak forced the Molson and Coors teams to double their efforts and close the deal before things unravelled. On 21 July, two days later, Molson's independent committee met to review the final terms of the deal. Leo Kiely presented his vision of Molson Coors as a merged entity. Experts from Merrill Lynch, advisors to the committee, intervened and said the transaction was fair to all shareholders from a financial perspective.

Then it was Eric's turn. He told the committee that he supported the merger and was "committed to staying involved as a shareholder of a major player in the global brewing industry for the long term." Molson Coors would be the fifth-largest brewer in the world. In the end, Eric emphasized that neither he nor Pentland (his holding company) had "any intention of selling their interests in Molson."

The directors of the independent committee listened to the three presentations. They reassessed the terms of the merger and voted on whether the deal was fair to *all* Molson shareholders. Their decision was a unanimous "yes."

The full Molson board meeting took place right after. With all directors present, they went through the details of the merger. Riley shared the independent committee's recommendation and asked them to approve the merger of equals.

Before endorsing the deal, however, the board had one last issue to contend with: Ian Molson. Earlier that day, Ian had couriered a letter to Riley as head of the independent committee. He also sent a copy to all the other Molson directors. His goal was to convince the board to back the deal he was trying to put together for Molson, rather than the one with Coors:

Dear Sandy,

Further to our recent correspondence, I wish to formally advise the Board of Directors of Molson Inc. and its Independent Committee that I lead a group of investors who wish to make an offer to acquire all the outstanding Class A shares and Class B shares of Molson for a cash consideration of $40 per share. Our offer envisages a strengthened relationship with the Adolph Coors Company and a continuance of Molson's commercial arrangements with Coors. We are confident that once the Board has an opportunity to review the details of our offer, the Directors will agree that it represents superior value for shareholders compared to the alternative transaction that has been discussed in the media.

As you know, I have entered into an arrangement with Onex Corporation to sponsor the offer. We have received term sheets from two banks for the necessary debt financing. The next step before presenting formally our offer to shareholders is to obtain the agreement and support of the Board of Directors and holders of a majority of Molson's Class B shares.

Since last Friday, July 16th, we have requested a number of times to meet with the Independent Committee or the Board of Directors to present our offer for the Board's consideration. We have not yet been accorded a meeting. We are concerned that the Board is intending to sign an alternative transaction that will diminish the value we are able to provide to shareholders or prevent them from having full and timely opportunity to consider our offer. Such an outcome would be ill advised, especially if a break-up fee were to be triggered by the offer we intend to make. Moreover, as you know, I intend to exercise my right under the Molson Family Shareholders Agreement to block a transaction that is not in the best interest of all shareholders.

Again, we request that until the Board has had an opportunity to consider our offer, it not make any commitment that limits shareholders' options or reduces the value that can be made available to them.

Powerful words. Not only was there a barely veiled threat that the Molson directors would be sued if they continued with the Molson-Coors merger but Ian also promised to use whatever means he had to block the deal. That included the 2001 shareholders agreement with Eric and Stephen – the one they'd entered into after rejecting Ian's Molson Holdings scheme.

Yet Ian was not actually offering an alternative option. Although he claimed he could buy all Molson shares for $40/share (about a 15.3 per cent premium on their market value), he didn't confirm he had secured the financing to do it. There was a vague reference to an arrangement with Onex but nothing concrete. Moreover, he didn't give any information about the structure or the other terms and conditions of any deal he was proposing. The independent committee talked with its advisors and concluded that the communication from Ian did not constitute a proper offer.

Most misleading, however, was Ian's claim that the relationship with Coors would not only continue but would be "strengthened" in his scenario. It was the exact opposite of what the Coors people had told the independent committee hours earlier. They said that if negotiations between Molson and Coors were delayed because of talks with Ian, Coors "could not provide any assurance that a Molson-Coors transaction would go forward on the same terms as those then being discussed between Molson and Coors, or at all."

They also said that if Molson was bought out by a competitor or any other party in a financial buyout (as Ian was proposing), Coors would exercise its right to terminate its partnership agreement with Molson. That meant Molson would lose Coors Light – a brand that represented nearly 20 per cent of Molson's volume (and a higher percentage of its profits) in Canada.

The risk of losing the Coors business and the conclusion of the independent committee that Ian's letter did not constitute an actual offer closed the debate. As for Ian's threat to block the Coors merger by using the shareholders agreement he had with Eric and Stephen, that was a battle for another day.

The Molson board unanimously agreed to go ahead with the merger of equals with Coors.

Looking back, Riley concludes: "I think negotiating the deal with the Coors family, in the face of what Ian was trying to do at the same time, took an awful lot of courage and real fortitude on Eric's part. It also required a step of confidence on the part of the family to put itself in the hands of a partner. Even though the Molson and Coors families are equal partners (each has in effect a veto on the other), the operations of the firm and the reputation of the families and of the beers they have historically brewed are now potentially in the hands of somebody else. The families went from having positive control to having negative control in their breweries. And that takes courage."

*

That afternoon Eric boarded a flight to New York City. Putting away his briefcase and buckling his seatbelt, he thought about the upcoming press conference. The next morning he would be facing journalists at the Palace Hotel on Madison Avenue. Pete Coors would be there with him. Pete had interrupted his US Senate campaign in Colorado for this event. They would be jointly announcing the Molson Coors merger of equals.

Again, Eric considered the merits of the deal. They could conquer the world together, he told himself. First consolidate their position in North America, and then go global – two families with great history, great heritage, and great brands, Molson Canadian (number 1 in Canada), Coors Light (number 7 worldwide), and Carling (number 1 in the UK). They had excellent breweries and very talented people.

Eric then thought of Leo Kiely. "We'll also get him as our CEO. He'll be great. He's honest. He's smart as hell. He can rally the troops. And he's good with both strategy and operations. He'll take our company to the next level."

Eric was not the only one who thought this way. Other directors like Sandy Riley agreed that Kiely was the right choice for CEO. "Leo had a better personality for this kind of thing," says Riley. "When you put two companies together, you need someone who's going to be generous and warm and connecting … especially in this particular case, where you're dealing with families."

As chairman, Eric had transitioned through four CEOs. First was Mickey Cohen, a strategist with the vision, drive, and connections to lead a multi-business conglomerate like TMCL. Cohen, however, wasn't close enough to day-to-day operations. Then there was Norm Seagram, a gentleman and a good manager but lacking the gumption needed to turn the company around. Next was Jim Arnett, an M&A guy, there on an interim basis to take the company back to beer. Once that was done, Arnett wasn't suited to run the brewery. And then came Dan O'Neill, a change agent, someone who could find synergies and execute on tough decisions, but Dan didn't drive top-line growth and lacked certain people skills.

"Not only is it hard to find the right CEO but it's just as hard to get rid of one," says Eric. "You've got to make sure he fails before you can make a move. With the Coors merger, I saw an opportunity to grow our company and put the right guy in charge. That was Leo Kiely. I wanted Leo to run our business, and I had the support of the other directors."

At a certain point, Eric took him aside and told him, "Look, Leo, you're going to run this thing."

Says Kiely, "I obviously didn't know him as well as I knew Pete back then, but I was very confident that Eric would support whatever we needed to do to get it done. And he did." Kiely felt confident that Eric was "the kind of guy I could do a good job for." He felt he could count on Eric's long-term perspective. "That was an absolute rock to me. I knew Eric would never take the business out from underneath my feet. So I had a platform that I could run after. It was really confidence-building for me … Eric may be a shy individual and he's conflict avoidant, but he's resolute. I mean, he's *very* resolute."

Giguère saw the same quality in her chairman. "Eric decided to go with the Coors family and not pursue other opportunities because, as the controlling shareholder, he didn't want to put the company up for sale, yet he still wanted to participate in the global consolidation in his own way. The fact that he hung on to that view very strongly, because he really believed that it was the best thing for the company, I think that showed a lot of resolve."

And according to Kiely, that view was one of the things that united Pete Coors and Eric. "They both fought for the independence of their businesses. And in putting them together, they did it in a way that they remained independent from anyone else ... To me, there was a warmth in working for people who were totally committed to the business and not their careers. I knew that Pete and Eric were totally committed to the success of their businesses. Eric gave everything to get the beer business back. Everything. That's resolute. That's incredible."

On the morning of 22 July 2004, Pete Coors and Eric Molson sat side by side before a roomful of reporters. Both wore small pins on their lapels: Pete, the American flag, and Eric, a red maple leaf. They presented the broad terms of the deal, gave it a compelling endorsement, and shook hands for the cameras. They were about to create the fifth-largest brewing company in the world.

Peter Coors and Eric Molson unveil the Molson-Coors merger plan at a press conference on 22 July 2004. Photo by Jeff Christensen/Reuters.

Name: Molson Coors Brewing Company.

Size: Combined volume of beer sold: 60 million hectolitres (51 million US barrels); net sales of US$6 billion; EBITDA of US$1 billion; and free cash flow of US$707 million.

Market share: 43 per cent in Canada, 21 per cent in the UK, 11 per cent in the US and Brazil.

Expected synergies: US$175 million.

Leadership: Eric H. Molson, chairman of the board; Dan J. O'Neill, vice-chairman, synergies and integration; W. Leo Kiely III, CEO.

Governance: Fifteen-member board of directors (nine of them independent of management and the controlling shareholders) – five nominated by the Molson family, five by the Coors family, three elected by the company's non-voting shareholders, plus Leo Kiely and Dan O'Neill.

Family voting shares: Molson and Coors families entering into a voting agreement, combining their shares into a single block with 62 per cent voting control (each owning half) and agreeing not to seek an alternative offer to this one.

Break-up fee: If one pulled out, it would have to pay the other US$75 million.

At the end of the press conference, Eric repeated his vision. "We are not interested in exiting the beer business. The family wants to play a role in building a major global brewer and driving greater value for all our shareholders."

It wasn't a done deal – far from it. The Molson and Coors shareholders still had to give their endorsement, and the bar was high. The deal needed approval by two-thirds of both the voting *and* non-voting classes of Molson shareholders. The vote was to take place before the end of 2004.

Leo Kiely and Dan O'Neill put together a "road show" to sell the Molson Coors combination. They spoke to investors in Montreal, Toronto, New York, Los Angeles, Memphis, and Boston. But everywhere they went, they were met with resistance. Some didn't like it because it was a merger of equals and not a takeover. That meant they wouldn't

W. Leo Kiely III
depicted here as
CEO of newly created
Molson Coors. Molson
Coors Brewing
Company collection.

get the cash premium that usually came when one company bought another. In a merger of equals, shareholders essentially exchanged their existing shares for new ones in the merged company – no extra gravy for anyone.

"A merger of equals is a very hard sell," says Kiely. "Canadian institutional investors didn't want to do it. Some of the US hedge funds didn't want to do it. It was tough. These investors had bought into the stock based on an exit strategy that would have valued the company for a premium. But a merger of equals is a *zero*-premium deal."

This is where it makes a difference to have a long-term-minded shareholder control the business. As Kiely says, "That's what's really interesting about family businesses. They're not in it for the short-term gain. No matter how big the premium, Coors or Molson could just say, 'No, I'm not going to sell it.' And that made the financial guys really *crazy*! The families have an awful lot of control, and if they didn't think the deal was good for the company in the long term, no matter how big the premium, they could just say no. The question about the premium is whether you're invested in the short term or in the long term. Molson and Coors took a long-term view on their businesses."

It was gruelling. They were repeatedly confronted with investors' Jerry Maguire–like "show me the money" (or the premium) reactions. Meanwhile, Ian and his allies were trying to mount a hostile takeover. And there were those who wanted to turn Molson into an income trust. "It was all over the papers," says Eric. "All they wanted was to get money out of the company without any consideration for its long-term viability."

An income trust was essentially a tax scheme (abolished by the Canadian government in 2011) whereby a company paid out all of its earnings to investors on a tax-advantageous basis rather than reinvest it back into the company. For companies like Molson that needed the capital to thrive and grow (through acquisitions, innovation, etc.), this mechanism would ultimately lead to asphyxiation. At least that was Eric's position – even though, of all shareholders, he stood to personally benefit the most from turning the company into an income trust.

It turns out that not everyone is motivated by how much money they can make for themselves in their lifetime. "You need money for three things," Eric once said. "Health, housing, education – those are the important things. The rest is superfluous. I don't need to drive around in a Lamborghini; I don't need to eat crêpes Suzette every night; and I don't need to own a yacht. You don't want to just make a pile of money and that's it – what's the sense in that? Once you have the basics covered, there are far more significant things to work for in your life."

Philosopher Adam Smith famously said: "Two different characters are presented to our emulation; the one, of proud ambition and ostentatious avidity. The other, of humble modesty and equitable justice. Two different models, two different pictures, are held out to us, according to which we may fashion our own character and behaviour; the one more gaudy and glittering in its colouring; the other more correct and more exquisitely beautiful in its outline."

I have always admired the latter profile. And maybe that's why I've been drawn to Eric and his story.

The period leading up the shareholders' vote was difficult and uncertain – a time of crisis. In Chinese, the word "crisis" – 危机 – is composed of two characters. One (危) means danger, the other (机) opportunity. The danger here was of Ian succeeding in having Molson taken over by a third party, while the opportunity was international expansion. For Eric, however, the deal presented another opening: to introduce the next generation of Molsons to the new board of directors.

If the merger was approved, Eric planned to make Andrew one of the five people proposed by the Molson family to serve on the new board. The other four would be Sandy Riley, David O'Brien, Francesco Bellini, and Eric. Stephen Molson, Luc Beauregard, and Dan Colson would be stepping down.

"I don't think it means that I will be chairman," Andrew told reporters in August 2004 when asked the question. "My brother Geoff is extremely competent, understands the beer business, and I hope that one day he will be on the board with me."

Andrew was thirty-six. He had transitioned from practising corporate law at McCarthy Tétrault to public relations at Canada's largest PR firm, National. At both places, he worked on Molson-related files. Andrew says he never thought of working at Molson as "an operator – you know, like what Dad did. I got interested in the business by following the company's transactions. When I was young, I would hear Dad talk about them, and then I started reading about them in the papers. Later, I got involved as an advisor when I was at McCarthy's and then at National. But it's when I learned more about corporate governance that I decided I wanted to get into it. I wasn't going to work *in* Molson. Geoff was already doing that. I wanted to contribute by participating in the oversight of Molson, at the governance level, perhaps by becoming a board member one day. So I decided to get a degree in corporate governance."

In 2000 when Andrew made that decision, corporate governance was a new field. There weren't many programs available, so Andrew did his own research. "Robert Monks is a corporate governance guru, and I was fascinated by him. He's this blueblood, waspy American from Boston who decided to take on the establishment and become a shareholder activist. There's a book about him by Hilary Rosenberg, *A Traitor to His Class*. So after turning into a shareholder activist, he became a leading thinker on corporate governance in the US. I emailed him and asked, 'Where can a working stiff like me go to study corporate governance for a short period of time and then get back to work?' So thanks to him, I found this master's of science in corporate governance and ethics at Birkbeck, part of the University of London. It's not a well-known school or anything, but I applied and got in. There were six of us in the class."

The experience was a turning point for Andrew. Among other things, it allowed him to crystallize his thoughts on dual-class companies. In his thesis, "The *Juste Milieu*: Sharing the Benefits of Control," he illustrates that these corporations outperform the ones with a single class of shares if certain conditions are met; namely that the privileged shareholder "is not incompetent at the board level," "is responsive to other shareholders' concerns," and "does not expropriate from them." With these prerequisites in place, Andrew argues, a dual-class allows for knowledgeable, committed, and long-term-minded shareholders to sit on the board of directors and act in the best interest of the corporation and *all* its shareholders. It favours long-term investment decisions instead of ones driven by quarterly results. And it can also be an effective takeover defence against opportunistic acquirers.

When Eric read the thesis, he was impressed by his son's reasoning. As Andrew progressed from commercial law to public relations to corporate governance, Eric increasingly sought his point of view. Their business partnership was cemented in the summer of 2003 when they worked together on the Molson Family Principles. From that point on, Eric systematically consulted Andrew on strategic decisions, boardroom dynamics, and shareholder relations.

Eric also talked business with Geoff, but more from an operational perspective. The two went over matters related to sales, marketing, customer satisfaction, and employee morale – the "inside scoop," as Eric calls it. By 2004, Geoff had worked at Molson for six years.

"I remember after O'Neil arrived, I called my father and said, 'Dad, it's now my chance to come work at Molson,'" says Geoff. "Because for years he kept telling me 'Geoff, go out there and show what you can do. We'll hire you when the company sees value in you. We're not just going to hire you for who you are.' My dad wanted me to get my experience elsewhere and prove myself. It was the best thing he ever did for me because, if it was up to me, I would have been at Molson from the time I was twenty-one. I would have been a lifer beer guy. Instead, I got great outside experience."

Geoff spent a year when he was twenty-four working for the Coca-Cola Company in media services before enrolling in Babson College for his MBA. After graduating, he became a management consultant with the Kalchas Group in New York. Two years later, he joined Molson. Dave Perkins hired him to work with the sales team in Toronto.

"When I started there, I was very careful about the conversations I would have with my dad," Geoff says. "Eric never wants to interfere. Also, I didn't want to lose the trust of the people I worked with. So I would never go to Eric with gossip or complaints from employees – never. Eric taught me to be careful. But I did speak up and talk to him when things started going badly.

"When this whole thing with Ian was going on, I was in Denver. I would call Eric and give my input. I would tell him, 'Dad, be strong. You're doing the right thing.' That kind of stuff. It was an emotional time for Eric. It was very stressful. I don't stress out too much (unless it involves my kids), but I stressed out about this one. I was wondering whether we were doing the right thing. The politics on the board were bad. I was worried about my dad. Remember, Ian was against the merger, and he was feeding the media with all these stories. It was ugly."

Throughout this period of upheaval, however, Eric continued calmly planning his succession. Andrew would join him on the Molson Coors board and Geoff would move back to Montreal from Colorado to work in the brewery's Canadian operations. "It's all about the siblings working well together and carving out a role that's suited to their skills," says Eric. Like him and Stephen, and before that, Tom and Hartland, Andrew and Geoff would be strong partners and allies.

Eric saw Justin having an important role as well. His middle son was never keen on business; he preferred science and nature and delved into landscape design, agriculture, and cooking. He is also a very private person. He chose to live away from Montreal, in the Vermont countryside, raising his children far from the attention drawn by the

Molson name. Eric respects Justin for following his passion and being "a great family man."

Says Eric, "Andrew and Geoff will have to sort out the business issues as they come up later on. But they're not going to fight, and they're not going to get greedy. They're just going to sort it out. I *think* that's how it will work, but you never know. Justin is the sleeper in there, because he's the one who's going to keep them all calm. If something happens, he'll get them to sit down and he'll cook up some great chili. He'll be there, and if it's needed, he's going to help."

Eric's main supporter, however, throughout the 2004 crisis was Jane. Even though she maintains that she "knows nothing about business," especially this kind, with hostile takeovers, poison pills, leveraged buy-outs, and other corporate stratagems, she knows people. "Jane understands what motivates folks better than I do," he says. "I rely on her for that and for many other things. She saw me go through that whole period with Ian and was a constant source of support to me. Jane is actually the Rock of Gibraltar of our family. She raised our three boys to be good, solid citizens – to contribute to their communities, to be respectful of all cultures, and to uphold the values we have as a family."

The feeling is mutual. Jane's love and admiration of Eric comes through clearly. "Once Eric took on the responsibility of being the head of the family, he took it very, very seriously. Things haven't always worked out exactly as he wished – nothing's perfect, and he's had disappointments along the way. But Eric has a tough side to him, and he's stuck with his commitments, and I admire him for that.

"Another thing Eric has done very nicely is help the children take over. He never had that himself, neither from Tom nor from Uncle Hartland. He was never given much confidence by either of them. But he did it very nicely with his sons. He showed them that he trusted them, and when the time came, he stepped aside and let them take over."

An important step in that transition came the summer Eric proposed Andrew as a director of Molson Coors. The merger, however, still had to be approved by a majority of shareholders, and the road to consent was contorted and full of obstacles.

The first setback was on Friday, 17 September 2004. At 7:19 p.m., Molson and Coors filed their preliminary proxy statement with the Securities and Exchange Commission. In it they laid out the terms of their agreement.

Right away, journalists saw the timing as suspect. "Rule No. 1 in public relations: If you have to drop some bad news, do it as late as you can on a Friday afternoon," wrote Derek DeCloet on the front page of the *Globe and Mail*. "Fewer people will notice, and your antagonists will have the entire weekend to cool off before they call on Monday morning to yell at you. So when Molson and Adolph Coors filed a 790-page document with the U.S. Securities and Exchange Commission just as most of Bay Street was hitting the pubs last week, investors had reason to be suspicious. Sure enough, there were a few nasty surprises lurking inside."

One "nasty surprise" for shareholders was that Molson executives with stock options could vote on the deal. They were granted this right even though they didn't own stock per se. Not only that, but once the deal was done, their options would vest and become exercisable. Some saw this as a hidden incentive for these company leaders to vote in favour of the deal in order to get an immediate payout. To make matters worse, actual Molson investors – those who owned real shares, not just options – would get no premium if the deal was approved. They'd only get to swap their Molson shares for ones in the new company.

To top off shareholders' indignation, Dan O'Neill stood to make more than $7.3 million if the deal went through. Of that, $3 million was the result of his demotion. Given that O'Neill was not going to be the future CEO of Molson Coors, a clause in his contract was triggered that gave him three years of salary, even though he continued to be employed at the brewery. Another $1.7 million was from the vesting of his share units. The performance conditions attached to these units disappeared with the merger. And the final $2.6 million was from the 400,000 stock options O'Neill was given two years earlier. These options were only supposed to kick in if Molson's stock doubled to $61.32

by 2007, but with the merger, they vested right away. (The shares were at $34 at the time.)

One by one, investors reacted.

Henri-Paul Rousseau, CEO of the Caisse de dépôt et placement du Québec (the powerful Quebec pension fund with $90 billion in overall holdings), expressed his "concern" that option holders could vote on the deal. He also pointed out that some Molson senior executives stood to get "very advantageous bonuses" if the merger was approved, even though these same officers stood to be employed in the new company. "Such double remuneration," he wrote in a carefully crafted letter to Eric about what O'Neill stood to gain if the merger went through, "would appear to be excessive."

Claude Lamoureux, CEO of the $75 billion Ontario Teachers' Pension Plan, said that option holders, being executives and directors of the company, "have totally different interests" from other public investors in Molson. He then warned that Teachers would take legal action to block the deal if they could vote on the merger.

Stephen Jarislowsky, chairman of Jarislowsky Fraser Ltd, whose firm owned more than four million Molson shares, told the press: "They [option holders] don't own the shares yet. They haven't paid for them. I think it must be a desperate measure which is in absolute opposition to good governance … What this shows, if this can be done, is that the Canadian laws protecting shareholders are non-existent."

According to Molson's lawyers, the proposed terms of the deal (including having option holders vote) were legal. The Canadian Business Corporations Act gave all security holders the right to vote in transactions where their rights stood to change. "The reality of it was that that's what the law provided for," says Marie Giguère. "The CBCA said that in such an arrangement, option holders could vote. It was perfectly legal and we were doing things by the book, but investors went ballistic. And we didn't control the message. Not at all. It also didn't help that a lot of us in management stood to make a fair amount of money with this transaction. So it became a big issue."

The way it used to work was that if shareholders weren't happy, they would vote with their feet and walk away by selling their shares. But in 2004, after the corporate scandals of Enron, Worldcom, and Tyco, shareholders were much more vocal. Sylvain Cossette, one of Eric and Stephen's lawyers at Davies Ward and Beck, said there was "nothing technically wrong" with the vote by option holders, "but in 2004 we are living in a world of shareholder activism."

Unfortunately, Eric only became aware of the issue once shareholders started speaking out. "I wasn't very involved with the ins and outs of the transaction. I should have been. I was never good at that kind of stuff, so I let the professionals do it. I was more into the strategy and the broad strokes of the deal. I knew I wanted Leo as our CEO; I wanted us to have joint control with the Coors family; I wanted us to be incorporated in Delaware where they had progressive corporate laws to protect our assets; and I tried to protect Montreal as best I could. But I didn't go into the details. That was my mistake." His regret is palpable.

"I wouldn't have allowed that option holders thing had I known about it. It wasn't right and it was bad for our image. I didn't catch it. And the board approved it. We did it as a board and we shouldn't have. Otherwise, you could print all sorts of options and control your company. You could really take advantage of your position ... It was a bad decision."

I wonder whether I should probe any deeper. I'm uneasy with Eric's discomfort.

But he continues: "I understand Stephen Jarislowsky's position on this." Then his tone turns fiery. "But he let me down. He should have come to see me about the option holders' vote before going public with his criticism. He was working for us, you know. He was managing my family's investment portfolios. So why didn't he send someone to see me and tell me about it?" Jarislowsky Fraser was not only a Molson shareholder – the firm also handled Eric's and his family's private investment accounts.

Eric's disappointment in Jarislowsky is understandable but, as in most situations, there are two sides. Perhaps things would have turned out differently if Eric had spoken to Jarislowsky personally about why he favoured the Molson Coors merger. Maybe then the financier would have told him what he didn't like about the deal, instead of going public.

Eric had sent O'Neill to speak to investors. "It was O'Neill's job as CEO to sell the merits of the deal." But by delegating to O'Neill, Eric missed an opportunity to have a shareholder-to-shareholder conversation with the likes of Jarislowsky. Andrew surmises, "If Eric had gone himself to visit major investors like Jarislowsky instead of sending a hired gun who stood to pocket a huge bonus if the deal went through, he may have persuaded them of the benefits of the merger." O'Neill's meeting with Jarislowsky on 21 September lasted less than an hour. When he came back to the brewery, he told Eric that the investor was against the deal.

"I put all my assets with Jarislowsky. He is a very capable money manager," says Eric. "But then he came out publicly against the merger without talking to me. I had no choice. I had to fire him. He was standing in the way of our future."

As soon as he learned of Eric's decision, Jarislowsky wrote a letter to thank him "for past patronage" and to express "trust that our friendship will not be marred by the fact that we have a major business difference." Jarislowsky disagreed with Eric's vision that Molson Coors could be a significant player in the global brewing scene. "I have always defended your family's resolve to retain a family company in the past," he wrote, "but the present and future rationally and unemotionally indicate that this is no longer feasible unless you're the size of Anheuser-Busch and you can go worldwide alone." This was not the case for Molson, according to Jarislowsky, even if it merged with Coors. As for giving option holders the right to vote, he wrote, "To have options vote, especially since once the merger is done, these options will immediately be in the money seems in conflict with the rights of the "A" [non-voting] shareholders with whom you want to group these votes ... Options should not vote other than as a class apart or not at all ... A fair fight is a fair fight and acceptable. A loading of the dice is *not*, and truly does no one proud. It undermines the high regard which the Molson name has in our community."

Eric says, "I didn't agree with Jarislowsky's view on the future of the beer industry. And now we've all seen what happened to Anheuser-Busch. But on his point about the option holders' vote, he was right. It was a mistake. Even if it was legal, it wasn't the right thing to do. They should have been voting as a separate class, on a specific issue or not at all … It could have become a black mark on our reputation if it wasn't corrected."

The criticism continued. On 29 September, ex-directors Donald Drapkin, Matt Barrett, and Lloyd Barber all spoke out against the vote by option holders. Eric wasn't surprised by Drapkin's comments, as he had "always been an ally of Ian's," but the other two were a disappointment. Barrett had been on the Molson board for more than ten years and Barber for twenty-five. They had gone to hockey games together and been guests at each others' homes. So when they announced that giving option holders the right to vote was "unnecessary" and not "a particularly classy move," Eric wondered, "Why didn't either of them voice their concerns to me directly instead of going to the media?"

He took steps to rectify the situation. He asked the Molson team to speak with the big shareholder groups, like the Caisse and Teachers, about the more sensitive points of the deal. And on 30 September, he met with Molson's directors and advisors to discuss possible solutions.

"Garth Girvan, our lawyer from McCarthy's, told us there was nothing wrong with the option holders' vote," says Eric. "There may have been nothing wrong technically, but I had to explain that it wasn't right for *us* and it wasn't right for our image. It was contrary to our principles of being honest, straightforward people. Even if it was legal, we had to correct it."

On 14 October, Molson announced it was changing the terms of the transaction. Option holders would *not* be entitled to vote on the merits of the merger. Instead, they could only vote on the issue of converting their Molson options into options of the combined company. O'Neill would *not* be getting a payout at the time of the change of control. He would only be entitled to it if he left the company within twenty-four months of the merger (instead of severance). Finally, O'Neill's performance-based options and restricted share units would *not* vest immediately. They would be converted to Molson Coors ones and be subject to similar performance-based triggers.

With these changes, Ontario Teachers said the corporate governance issues were resolved. The Caisse also found the new proposal "acceptable." Jarislowsky, however, continued to be opposed to the merger. "I can't see what two guys with the same profile are going to achieve," he told the press. "For the moment they're staving off the idea of not being a family firm by being half pregnant. But what does it do in the long run if market forces are favouring [larger global brewers]? What does it do except make it more difficult the next time to get the thing done, because it takes two to agree instead of one? ... I don't think Coors or Molson are growth companies in the beer business, and I don't think they'll become growth companies by this device. It doesn't solve the issues. It leaves the wolves right in front of the door."

It also didn't solve the issue that a merger of equals between Molson and Coors was a no-premium deal. To some shareholders, that was unacceptable. The wolves were hungry.

In the fall of 2004, Ian contrived to pull together a counter-offer for Molson. He had already secured $1 billion from Onex and was looking for other partners. Many insiders assumed he was going to collaborate with Heineken. The two companies already had ties in Brazil, Molson distributed Heineken beer in Canada, and Ian always alluded to his close relationship with the family. A few weeks earlier, however, a Heineken executive publicly refuted the rumours. Heineken, he said, was not interested in Molson.

By mid-September, there was talk that SABMiller plc, the world's third-largest brewer by volume, would jump in to make a joint hostile bid for Molson with Ian and Onex. It was an appealing proposition to shareholders hoping for a cash payout. There were, however, a few hang-ups.

One was the Coors Light business. If Molson wound up in "enemy" hands like SABMiller, Coors claimed it would pull the plug on Coors Light in Canada. Given that it was Canada's best-selling light beer, with an 8.5 per cent market share and growing, the threat was a strong deterrent. Analysts viewed it as an effective poison pill. Then there was the US$75 million break-up fee. If Molson broke up the merger of equals to go with SABMiller, for example, it would have to pay that sum to Coors – not a negligible amount.

On 23 September, when reporters asked SABMiller's CFO, Malcolm Wyman, about the rumours, he acknowledged that theirs was an "acquisitive business in a consolidating industry," but he declined to comment on reports that it was planning a rival, hostile bid for Molson. Ultimately, SABMiller took a "wait and see" approach.

In addition to fending off a hostile bid mounted by Ian, the more personal obstacle for Eric was the family voting pact. Ian had referred to it in his letter to the Molson board on 21 July 2004 when he said he intended to use it to block the deal with Coors. Back in 2001, Eric and Stephen's holding company Pentland Securities and Ian's Swiftshure Trust had entered into a five-year shareholders agreement after the Molson Holdings scheme fell apart. In it, they combined their respective 44.69 per cent and 10.3 per cent stakes in Molson's voting class B shares and pledged not to transfer them except under certain conditions. It was essentially a blocking mechanism designed to deter unwanted takeover bids through the family's combined control position. Ian, however, was now using it to veto the merger of equals with Coors.

The only way out was for Eric to get more class B shares. If Pentland owned more that 50.1 per cent of the Bs, it could exit the arrangement. At 44.69 per cent, he wasn't far from the threshold, but because the B shares were traded in such low numbers, it would be impossible for him to buy the balance on the open market. The obvious solution was to solicit the help of his sisters.

Deirdre and Cynthia had inherited 2.4 million class B shares (or 10.8 per cent of the class) from Tom. Their shares were held in a family trust, of which Eric was a designated trustee. Given this position, he could easily have ordered that the shares be sold to Pentland. Alternatively, he could unilaterally have converted their Bs into non-voting As to raise his percentage ownership of the Bs above the 50.1 per cent bar. But to think that Eric would have coerced his sisters instead of allowing them to make their own decision about their inheritance was to confuse him for one of the bullies he disliked so much growing up.

Eric took his fiduciary duty towards his sisters as trustee of their father's estate very seriously. Stephen, also a trustee, felt the same way. They asked Deirdre and Cynthia to decide for themselves. Eric met with them and their adult children to explain the implications of the shareholders agreement between Pentland and Swiftshure. He organized for them to have an in-depth presentation of the merger of equals by Molson's management team. He also urged them to hire their own lawyers and advisors to get an unbiased opinion on their best course of action. Brian Baxter, Cynthia's middle son, said Eric and Stephen were "extra-scrupulous" in making sure their sisters got independent advice. "Because of the potential for perceived conflict of interest, they felt it was critical that not just the sisters but their five sons be unanimously in favour of it."

With the approval and support of the Stevensons and Baxters, Eric engaged in a three-step process to exit the 2001 family voting pact with Ian. First, Deirdre and Cynthia's trusts sold 18,000 class B shares to Pentland. Then, they converted the remaining 95 per cent of their voting class B shares into non-voting A shares. The overall number of Molson voting shares (i.e., the denominator) thus shrank, and Pentland's stake in class B shares rose from 44.7 per cent to 50.7 per cent. This allowed Eric and Stephen (i.e., Pentland) to go over the 50.1 per cent bar they needed. Ian could no longer block the Coors transaction.

"It probably came as a shock to Ian that my sisters helped me the way they did," Eric muses. "He had been trying to convince them both to do otherwise. But my sisters were on my side. They said, 'Eric, we trust you,' and together we got it done."

I am impressed by the level-headedness of Eric and his siblings. I come from a Greek background, and whenever we have to settle a family matter, there tends to be a lot of hand-waving and vociferous opinions thrown about. We get there eventually, but it's messy. I ask Eric if it was at all like that for him in 2004. "There wasn't any drama," he replies, smiling. "Remember, we're Anglo-Saxons. We don't blow our stacks. But in the end we were lucky – Ian was the only greedy one from his generation. The rest of us stuck together."

"I know Uncle Eric has always been grateful for what we did, but there was never any question that we wouldn't do it," says David Stevenson. We were like, 'Yeah, we'll do that to help our family. Tell us where to sign' … That was the difference between our group and Ian. As far as I know, Ian was just trying to sell the company or do whatever he needed for his own personal gain."

The only thing Eric's nephews asked for in return was that he and Stephen step down as trustees over their mothers' portions of Tom's estate. Brian Baxter explains: "One of the ancillary benefits of converting our shares and no longer being part of the voting block was that we no longer needed to have Eric and Stephen as trustees for Cynthia and Deirdre's trusts. Ultimately, that's a much more healthy and appropriate relationship between Eric and his sisters." David adds that it made no sense for them to continue as trustees because the sisters would then "be tied to whatever was going on with Molson Coors in the future without having control." Eric and Stephen agreed and recused themselves as trustees.

In a handwritten note dated 18 January 2006, Deirdre expressed her gratitude for Eric's diligence on her and Cynthia's behalf over the twenty-six years since Tom's death:

My dear Eric,

For many years you have been a trustee of my investment company, THPM Estate ... You have advised me and Cynthia, held meetings for us with the Trust company (whichever one it may have been, Royal or National) and discharged your duties without charging a penny which would have been your due, and even provided lunch. All this with patience and equanimity even during times of conflict and difficulty within the Molson companies, and times when you were more than busy with other pressing duties.

For this, your loyal diligence to our affairs, I thank you from the bottom of my heart. It has been a comfort to me to know that you have guarded our interests since Daddy died, and that I could always rely on you and your steady advice ...

With much love as always,
Deirdre

Although he cleared these significant hurdles, Eric still had to win the shareholders' vote. The merger of equals needed to be approved by at least two-thirds of Molson's class As and Bs for it to go through. It would be tight.

Dan O'Neill and Leo Kiely met with all major investors and used their full powers of persuasion to sell them on the merger's merits. Still, without a premium, it didn't look like they would get the support they needed. They had to find a way to make the deal more appealing while keeping the merger of equals balance. One solution was to make a one-time payment to Molson shareholders from the company's treasury – a special dividend.

Initially, the Coors side resisted. Giguère says, "The Coors people weren't happy about the special dividend, but they were told, 'This deal isn't going to happen unless you rebalance things in some way.' And, remember, the Coors people needed the deal too. They were also a medium-sized company, and they realized that if they wanted to be one of the five global brewing companies of the world, they had to do it. So they eventually agreed in order to get the deal done."

On Wednesday, 3 November, the Molson board met to discuss how to "sweeten" the deal. "We've been talking with Coors," O'Neill told the Molson directors. "We can offer shareholders a special dividend of $3 per share for a total of around $350 million, to be paid out once the merger goes through."

The directors discussed the pros and cons of making this kind of payout to boost support for the merger. After a while, Eric interrupted the debate. "If we go ahead with this special dividend, Stephen and I will forego it. Pentland will not take a special dividend. I don't want there to be any confusion about why we want to do this deal. This merger of equals is in the best interest of our company and its long-term future. It will bring significant value to our shareholders for years to come. For us, it's not about getting a payout, and I don't want anyone to think it is. So we won't take the dividend. You can put the money that was to come to us back in the pot for the rest of the shareholders."

With Eric and Stephen foregoing payment for their class B shares, the amount owed to the remaining Molson shareholders increased from $3 to $3.26 per share. The proposal was approved by both the Molson and the Coors boards.

"I thought Eric not taking the special dividend was a very gracious thing to do," says Dan Colson. "It was typical of Eric. It avoided all discussion. I mean, no one was going to complain about the fact that he *didn't* take the money. He was worried about the optics of it. He didn't want people like Jarislowsky to accuse him of featherbedding or anything like that. But why shouldn't he get the special dividend? He was entitled to it like everyone else! I remember telling Eric that. But his mind was made up, and he didn't want anything to get in the way of the merger with Coors. He wanted that deal."

Eric recalls, "Danny told me I should have taken that extra dividend. Stephen and I coughed it up anyway. We let the money go back to the other shareholders. I thought it was a pretty good move. We didn't need the money, and more importantly, we were solving other issues. There was our future: the dividend was going to help get the merger with Coors approved. There was the Molson Foundation: even though we weren't getting it, the foundation was, and that meant a lot more money for charity and for Canada. And, finally, there were my sisters: they would get it, and that made things fair somehow."

On the last point, the conversations about exiting the voting pact with Ian were taking place at the same time as the allocation of the special dividend. Eric felt some comfort knowing that although he was asking his sisters to convert their B shares to As so Pentland could get out of the agreement with Ian's Swiftshure, they would at least benefit from the special dividend like everyone else.

Thinking back on that decision, Deirdre's son Eric Stevenson says, "When we learned that Eric and Stephen were going to forego the special dividend, that's when it became very clear to us. It actually made it all right for them to ask us to convert our shares so they could use our voting position to get out of the agreement with Ian. To me, foregoing the special dividend said Eric and Stephen are prepared to do what it takes to back the deal. So, good for them. If they're prepared to back it that hard, we'll support them."

In all these decisions, Eric and Stephen stuck together. "Stephen was my partner through all this stuff," Eric says. "During all the tensions with Ian and the board and the demand for my resignation, Stephen was there. And when the time came to decide about the special dividend, I would have said, 'We don't need it, Stephen. Let's just get this deal done and have a good long-term future with Molson Coors.' Stephen would have gone along with my advice. He's a great partner that way. Not greedy. He just says, 'I'm in,' and does it."

Still, there were others to convince. In addition to shareholders and family members, there were also Molson employees to consider. Geoff and other executives told Eric that they were getting contradictory messages about the merger. The uncertainty around the deal was starting to affect morale within the company. Eric decided to pen a personal memorandum to employees.

"I strongly believe that this proposed merger provides the best business solution for Molson and its employees in the rapidly changing global beer market," he wrote. His long-term view, he reminded them, was to establish Molson's "global presence." He then became more intimate. "My commitment to this transaction is very personal. I have demonstrated it in two very concrete forms: First, Pentland Securities, the corporate entity that owns the family shares, is giving up absolute control for the first time because I believe strongly that this merger is in the best interest of the company and its shareholders. We are diluting our own voting interest in the merged company to 33 per cent compared to the 51 per cent of Molson that we hold today. For their part, the Coors family is reducing their voting interest to 33 per cent as well, down from 100 per cent of Coors today. Second, Pentland has agreed to waive any participation in the special dividend of $3.26 per share that will be paid as part of the merger to provide shareholders with additional consideration. This decision will cost the Molson family several tens of millions of dollars, all of which will go to Molson shareholders. This was a costly decision; however, I believe that the ultimate gains that all shareholders will reap from the merger with Coors will more than offset this short-term loss."

The memorandum had its desired effect. People at Molson understood that Eric and his family wanted the merger to allow Molson to survive in the global marketplace. It wasn't for their personal benefit. It wasn't a takeover by the Americans. It wasn't a cop-out. And although Eric couldn't guarantee their jobs, at least they had a better chance as part of an enterprise in charge of its destiny rather than in one that sat like bait, waiting to be taken over by a brewing giant.

From the time the merger of equals was announced in July 2004, the deal team faced and overcame multiple hurdles. On 14 October, the proposal was modified to remove its less palatable terms, such as stock-option holders' right to vote and O'Neill's multi-million-dollar bonus. Three weeks later, on 5 November, Molson and Coors declared a special dividend of $3.26 per share to Molson shareholders if the merger was accepted. Five days after that, Pentland announced it had amassed enough shares to break the voting pact with Ian. Finally, a week later on 16 November, Ian's rival investor group said it wouldn't bid for Molson unless the brewery's shareholders first voted down the company's proposed merger with Coors. It looked like everything was in place for the vote in mid-December.

Despite all this, shareholders remained unconvinced. "If you want our vote," they said, "you'll need to do better than $3.26."

"People saw an opening, and greed took off," Eric says. "There was a lot of that."

As the teams worked to revise the special dividend, it became clear that they wouldn't be able to meet their original December deadline. They opted to postpone the shareholders' vote to 19 January 2005. They figured it would give them time to revisit their major investors and work out the "right" number for the special dividend. In the meantime, they hired the securities arm of the Bank of Montreal as additional arsenal to persuade shareholders to back the deal.

A tracking mechanism of the top thirty shareholders was put in place. In the weeks and days leading up to the vote, tensions mounted as proponents of both sides took position:

- *Anti*: On 20 December, Jarislowsky Fraser said it was against the deal because of governance concerns; on 3 January, Burgundy Asset Management (another Canadian investment manager) said it was also against it, claiming the deal didn't value the brewer's profitable Canadian business enough.
- *Pro*: On 4 January, Canada's leading proxy advisory firm Fair-vest said it "weighed the economic parameters and strategic rationale of the deal with corporate governance issues" and recommended that shareholders vote in favour of the merger; on 5 January, Glass Lewis & Co., another proxy advisory firm of San Francisco, also came out in favour of the deal.

- *Anti*: On 7 January, portfolio managers at AGF Management and TAL Global Asset Management said they would cast their shares against the merger.
- *Undecided*: AIM Funds Management, Molson's largest shareholder with close to sixteen million class A shares, did not announce its position; it remained the "wild card."
- *Anti*: On 11 January, Ian Molson gave his first public statement about the merger. From his London office, he said, "Molson should not be afraid of the future. I have evaluated the Molson/Coors proposal carefully and have concluded that this is a bad transaction for Molson shareholders. The status quo is a better option. Molson shareholders are not being paid for the change of control nor the disappearance of the institution called Molson that they are being asked to facilitate."
- *Pro*: Dan O'Neill came out with a public rebuttal to Ian's missive. "Shareholders need to consider that the real difference between a standalone Molson and a merged Molson Coors is access to an estimated US$175 million in potential synergies, increased investment behind key brands in the Canadian market and the operating and financial scale to participate in the consolidating brewing industry. These are all advantages that are otherwise unavailable to Molson shareholders."
- *Pro*: On the same day, the Ontario Teachers' Pension Plan, holder of 1.6 million class A Molson shares, said it planned to vote in favour of the merger.
- *Anti*: On 12 January, SABMiller came out to encourage Molson shareholders to turn down the merger by saying it would be interested in making a bid for Molson if the $3.4 billion merger with Coors fell through. It said, "A Molson transaction would both have strategic merit and could be value enhancing to SABMiller."

It was 6:15 a.m. on Wednesday, 12 January 2005. The sky was still dark. Montreal winter days are short – so short, dark, and cold that even its most resilient residents want to hibernate at times. Sleep, however, was the furthest thing from Eric's mind as he went through his morning routine. He filled the coffee mill with dark, oily beans, pressed the switch three times (short bursts so as not to overheat the mix), and waited for the water to boil. He stared pensively at copies of the statements from London issued just hours earlier – Ian's and the latest from SABMiller. The ticking of the clock punctuated the silence of the kitchen. He thought about the shareholders' vote in seven days. Many claimed it was going to be "razor-thin." Of course, Ian's ongoing campaign against the deal and statements like SABMiller's didn't help.

Eric's advisors had urged him to retaliate. They said he should go public and explain why the merger with Coors was the best business opportunity for Molson. So the night before, he spent hours penning a press release to that effect. He planned to have it issued that day under his name: "Statement by Eric H. Molson, Controlling shareholder of Molson Inc." It would be a first for him. In his forty-five years with Molson, he had never made such an open declaration.

He poured the boiled water into the cafetière and then reread what he had written.

As the January 19 vote approaches, I want to reiterate to our shareholders our fervent belief that the merger of equals be-tween Molson and Coors, as proposed in the shareholder proxy, is the right transaction with the right partner and it is fair to shareholders in the short, medium and long term …

Indeed, as controlling shareholders, we have made two signifi-cant gestures to other Molson shareholders to demonstrate how strongly we believe in this deal. As a result of this transaction, our voting interest will fall from 51 per cent to 33 per cent of the new firm. We have agreed to reduce our position because we strongly believe that the benefits of the deal will more than offset the smaller ownership position.

We have also agreed to waive any participation in the special dividend of $3.26 per share that is being paid as part of the merger to provide shareholders with additional consideration. This latter discussion will cost us tens of millions of dollars in the short term; however, if it leads to the successful conclusion of the merger with Coors, then it is a decision well-taken.

Molson shareholders should not be misled into thinking there is an alternative transaction in any form that will provide the same opportunities as the Molson Coors merger. And shareholders should not be misled into thinking that we would agree to any such alternative transactions.

We will not trade away our medium-and-long term growth prospects in favour of short-term payoffs or limited growth solutions like transforming the company into an income trust … Nor will we sell to other groups for the sake of short-term financial gain. We will continue to put the company ahead of our own interests, even if it means further dilution of our equity position in the company through the addition of a third partner within the new Molson-Coors global platform ….

We are committed to creating wealth for our shareholders by growing our business – not selling it. This company is not for sale and the merger of equals with Coors is the only option on the table on January 19th.

Pat Palozzi, vice-president of the Canadian investment firm Beutel Goodman (who continue to be shareholders, since 1998), remembers seeing Eric's statement on the newswire. "It came out on January 12th at 6:02 pm, after the close of markets. I read it and realized that it wasn't a Molson press release but that it was directly from Eric. I was like, 'Wow, I've never seen that.' It seemed unusual. In most deals like this, communications go through the company or its board and follow a certain protocol. This was more personal. It came directly from Eric. And he was firm. Read the last line of his statement: 'This company is not for sale and the merger of equals with Coors is the only option on the table.' It's pretty clear."

That same day, Eric met with Dan O'Neill and other members of the deal team. O'Neill had just flown back from a meeting with Kiely in Golden, Colorado, where they worked on how to overcome the opposition to the merger. They too worried that the negative statements by some of the institutional shareholders would sway the vote. The two CEOs agreed that they had to improve the economics of the transaction.

"What did the Coors people say?" Eric asked O'Neill.

"It looks like they're prepared to allow us to pay an additional $2 per share."

Eric called Kiely directly. He wanted to make sure that Coors was okay with raising the special dividend to $5 per share. If they thought Molson shareholders (including the family) were getting too much, they might back out of the deal.

"Leo says they're having a little trouble with the $5 dividend over there," he told Stephen after hanging up with Kiely. "Some of the Coors people think it stinks."

Privately, the two Molson brothers again discussed whether or not to accept the larger special dividend. Based on their number of shares, it would amount to $51 million. "Not chicken feed," Eric pointed out. Also, as Colson had said earlier, they were entitled to the payout just like any other Molson shareholder. Still, Eric maintained his earlier position.

"We'll let the $51 million go to the other shareholders and get this deal done. Molson needs this merger." Stephen agreed.

Remembering his telephone conversation with Eric years later, Kiely gets uncomfortable. "I did speak to Eric about not taking that special dividend. He asked me if I thought it was important for him to give it up, and I said, 'Yes, it might be important' ... To this day I feel bad about it. In retrospect, I actually don't think Eric had to do it. But I remember believing back then that it was going to be important in order to get the deal done. There were so many different interests swirling in the air at the time ... I figured if he was going to take it, it would muck stuff up. But Eric was very graceful about it. He said he would give it up and he didn't make a big deal over it. I wasn't surprised, because that's who Eric was."

Sandy Riley acknowledges it was "a significant give-up on the part of the family in order to get the transaction with Coors done." But he also says, "It was a smart thing for Eric to do. It allowed the family to go forward in a situation where it continued to maintain its control and its involvement in a beer company that was no longer landlocked in Canada."

"Besides," says Eric, "Stephen and I are not greedy. We were not recommending this deal with Coors just to make a pile of cash for ourselves. As shareholders, we're not speculators, we're investors. We focus on the intrinsic value of a company and are in it for the long haul." He regrets that businesses now seem to be run exclusively on the basis of quarterly results. "It's gone too far. Shareholders expect immediate returns, and executives are motivated by compensation packages tied to the stock price. The risk is that greed takes over and everything else falls by the wayside."

As the controlling shareholder of a corporation with a dual-class share structure, Eric feels his role is to counterbalance this kind of short-termism. Like Warren Buffett who famously said, "Our favourite holding period for a stock is forever," Eric focuses on growing the company's real underlying value rather than benefiting from short-term fluctuations based on "whatever the market's spinning."

He and Stephen wanted Molson to remain active on the global brewing stage which was actively morphing. Only four months earlier, on 27 August 2004, the world's largest brewer InBev was created when Belgian brewer Interbrew SA merged with Brazil's Cia. de Bebidas das Americas SA (Ambev). Weighing all these considerations, the brothers relinquished the $51 million special dividend.

I pause my handheld recorder and look pensively at Eric sitting across from me. I wonder: What would I have done had I been in his shoes? Would I have given up all that money?

🍁

On Thursday, 13 January 2005, Molson and Coors announced the increase of the special dividend. With Eric and Stephen renouncing their part, the amount going to the other shareholders was $5.44 per share instead of $5.

Molson director Francesco Bellini maintains that Eric's decision not to take the special dividend was a mistake. "A big mistake!" He shakes his head. "But again, that's his style. He didn't want people to think he took advantage of his position. He was like that. We all told him to take it. I would have taken it! But I respect Eric for what he did."

"Forfeiting the dividend looked like a major sacrifice in everyone's mind," says Eric, "but not if you're thinking of your stakeholders, not if you're thinking of your family, and not if you're thinking of the long-term health of the company. Besides, the market wanted something more from us ... Renouncing the dividend sewed up the deal. It made it more acceptable for the shareholders."

"Most people would have taken the money," says Stephen. "About 90 per cent, I bet. But we didn't, and that's why I feel we're something special – one of the oldest companies around. We are proud of it, and we wanted it to stay that way, even if it meant sharing control with another like-minded family."

David Stevenson says, "There was the special dividend, and Eric and Stephen said, 'No, we don't want it.' There's not a CEO in the world who would do that. But that's what those two guys did. It's pretty impressive, and it shows where their allegiance and interests lie. They're working for their shareholders. It's a nice thing to see in this crazy world we live in, in this world where bankers are getting ridiculous fees and all that. Today all you see in the world is take-take-take. To me, Eric and Stephen's position was unique. To just say, 'Leave $51 million in the company' is pretty cool. It sums up Eric's personality right there. He's someone who sees the bigger picture."

As Molson announced the increased special dividend, it also informed the public that the vote on the merger, planned for 19 January, would be rescheduled to 28 January 2005. In the interim, the sweetened premium had its desired effect. One by one, investors revised their positions: AIM Funds Management now said they would support the deal, as did AGF Management and Burgundy Asset Management. There were still some dissenters, including Jarislowsky Fraser and Highfields Capital Management, but the tide was turning.

"It was a bit hairy," admits Stephen. "Right to the end, we didn't know how things were going to turn out."

"We had a team of people going over the lists of shareholders, counting the votes, checking if we had the right number," says Eric. "It was a very tense time."

Friday, 28 January, was a typical Montreal winter day: minus 21 degrees Celsius (minus 30 with the wind chill), partly cloudy and grey. The roads were snow-covered. Eric managed to avoid traffic on the drive with Jane to the Queen Elizabeth Hotel. The special shareholders' meeting was at 9 a.m., and he wanted to get there early. Walking into the Marquette Room, he saw a number of familiar faces, but noticed there was no Ian, no one from Highfields, and no one from Jarislowsky Fraser. The most vocal critics of the deal were absent. Good, he thought, they voted by proxy.

The meeting was called to order and the room quietened. At 9:17 a.m., after the usual introductions and formalities, the final tally was read out:

- Class A non-voting shares in favour of the merger, 80.2 per cent; 19.8 per cent against. A total of 88,411,157 votes were cast, representing 81.9 per cent of outstanding class A shares.
- Class B common shares in favour of the merger, 84.3 per cent; 15.7 per cent against it. A total of 15,540,418 votes were cast, representing 78.2 per cent of outstanding class B shares.

Eric let out his breath. It was done. The Molson Coors merger of equals was approved. He walked to the podium and asked the room of shareholders: "Are there any questions?"

More than three hundred people were present. After all the drama, bitter debates, and shareholder unrest of the previous months, the room was strangely quiet.

Eric cleared his throat and congratulated everyone. "This transaction marks a new and important chapter in Molson's history. This merger builds on the strategic and cultural fit between our two companies and creates a global brewer with the operating scale, resources and geographic coverage necessary to compete in today's consolidating brewing industry ... This has been a long process, and I am thankful that our shareholders have supported us and have understood the strategic and economic value of this transaction."

The Molson Coors merger, approved 28 January 2005, marked the start of a new era of international expansion. Cover of the Molson Coors 2006 Annual Report.

The audience broke into applause.

Dan O'Neill clapped with everyone else. Thank God it was over.

Looking back, he says, "That whole year was really hard. Right to the very end – hard. I remember we didn't know how the vote would go right to the end. The night before, we stayed up till midnight and we still didn't know the vote. We got the vote in the morning ... After Eric did his speech, I had to go up and do my presentation. When it was over, I was like, thank God I don't have to do this anymore ... I got off the stage. I walked away and I said, 'No interviews. I'm not talking to anyone.'

"There were reporters everywhere. I went down to my car and there were these two female reporters with microphones who said, 'Come on, we want to talk to you. We know you didn't talk in there, but it's just us.' And I said, 'No, I don't have to do this anymore.' And the papers the next day said, 'The guy who never said no to a microphone refused to talk.' I couldn't do it anymore. I just went to my farm and, for like a month, I just cut wood and didn't talk to anyone."

The episode left scars. The day after the vote, Geoff wrote to Ian. In his letter, he spoke of his father's dedication and life-long commitment to Molson, giving as an example his forgoing of the special dividend. He then contrasted Ian's conduct to Eric's and concluded that, "judging from your actions, you clearly did not inherit the commitment and loyalty genes." Geoff's words were tough and his ire deeply rooted, but he never sent the message. He didn't see what good would come of it and predicted that Ian's "false attempts to publicly harm the reputation of my father will be forgotten very shortly."

Eric put the Ian chapter behind him. Even though his cousin's schemes and attempts to take over were aggressive, they weren't illegal. He chose instead to focus on the future. "Right after the passing of the vote, of course I felt some relief. But I also knew that it was going to be a major challenge to merge these two organizations. I went right to thinking, 'Can the Molson and Coors cultures work together based on what they agree with?' We do have many compatibilities with Coors in terms of technology, focus on excellence, high-quality products ... But integrating two companies like that takes a lot of work, and there are risks." It was all worth it according to Eric. As Molson Coors, they were now players in the global arena. They owned great brands like Molson Canadian and Coors Light. And Andrew would be a member of the board, and he would be good; he had a long-term view and knew what was going on. Soon Geoff would be there too.

Tears of pride well in Eric's eyes as he speaks of the transfer to his sons. It's like the passage from "In Flanders Fields" displayed above the dressing-room stalls of the Canadiens: "To you from failing hands we throw the torch. Be yours to hold it high." Eric had passed the torch to the seventh generation, and it looked like it was going to keep burning bright.

14 Relaying the Elixir to Generation VII

There are only two or three human stories, and they go on repeating themselves as fiercely as if they had never happened before.

WILLA S. CATHER (1873–1947)

"And they want me to make a speech?" Eric puts down his glass of cold beer, shaking his head. "Andy, I hung up my skates years ago. I don't do that kind of stuff anymore."

Andrew is once again trying to persuade his father to go to the 2016 Gala des Grands bâtisseurs (great builders) of Quebec's economy. It's a biennial affair, and this year the organizers want to honour Eric. So far, it doesn't look like Andrew's getting anywhere with his father ("Mr Nyet" is being true to himself).

"I know, Dad, but this is a good one," he says. "It's organized by the IGOPP."

"The what?"

"The Institute for Governance of Private and Public Organizations. It's the group that does research and policy papers on governance issues, chaired by Yvan Allaire."

"Oh, yes, the think tank on governance," Eric says. "You're right, I've read their material. They do good work."

"Also, I talked to them and they've agreed to honour the entire Molson family, not just you."

When Andrew spoke with Allaire a few days earlier, he told him that if the IGOPP wanted to pay tribute to Eric personally, his father would probably decline. He suggested that maybe it could work if they focused on the entire Molson family. I look at Eric (who still doesn't seem won over) and reflect on his unwavering humility. Will he ever take credit for a job well done?

"Plus," Andrew continues, "this year they're celebrating people who've used their business success to benefit society as a whole. So it's right up our alley. And the best part is that you'd be honoured alongside André Chagnon. Think of it, Chagnon and Molson, Franco and Anglo, business success and social commitment. All winning combinations."

"You're right, they are," Eric agrees. "And André Chagnon is a great. Imagine, he built up Videotron, made it one of Canada's biggest tele-communications companies, sold it, and then used the money to create the largest charitable foundation of our country ... Think of the thousands of families the Chagnon Foundation has helped with all the work they do to counter poverty."

It looks like Eric has turned the corner. "Okay, let's do it," he says. "Let's get Stephen, Deirdre, and Cynthia to come. We'll go together as a family."

So on Thursday, 19 May 2016, we're all at the Windsor Ballroom in downtown Montreal to celebrate André Chagnon and the Molson family. About four hundred people are in the room, mostly business leaders, and some politicians including the premier of Quebec, Philippe Couillard, and the mayor of Montreal, Denis Coderre. It's a joyous occasion, and despite Eric's initial reluctance, he seems to be enjoying himself.

"Are you ready?" I ask as we walk towards our tables.

"No," Eric says, and grins. "Don't I have to be somewhere else?"

"You'll be great."

The speeches begin. Yvan Allaire sets the theme for the evening with a quote by Pope Frances, who in 2014 told Davos participants, "Business is, in fact, a vocation, and a noble vocation, provided that those engaged in it see themselves challenged by a greater meaning in life ... I ask you to ensure that humanity is served by wealth and not ruled by it."

Then it is Eric's turn. The crowd applauds as he makes his way up the stairs with Andrew, Justin, and Geoff right behind him. The crowd

Eric Molson at the podium of the IGOPP gala dinner for Builders of the Quebec Economy, May 2016, with sons Geoff, Justin, and Andrew behind him. Courtesy Institute for Governance of Private and Public Organizations.

is still clapping loudly as Eric stands slightly awkwardly at the podium. He clears his throat as if to say, "Okay, thanks gang, that's enough." The applause eventually dies down. In a clear voice, Eric acknowledges the warm welcome. He's speaking in French and chooses his words carefully. "Almost two and a half centuries, 234 years. Three sons." He pauses. "It is now time to delegate a speech like this to one of my sons. That's what John Molson, our founder and builder – a real *bâtisseur* – did with his sons and the generations that followed. He delegated well. So now I'm going to ask ... Andrew? ... Geoffrey? Who's coming up here?" The crowd breaks into laughter and starts cheering again.

And that's it. Eric ends his speech in less than thirty seconds. I smile and think, "He warned us! He told us he'd hung up his skates." I realize, however, that the image is not quite accurate. Eric may have passed the puck to the next generation, but his quiet, rink-side presence as coach and advisor makes his younger teammates better players than they ever would be on their own.

According to Eric, it's all about teamwork. As Babe Ruth once said, "You may have the greatest bunch of individual stars in the world, but if they don't play together, the club won't be worth a dime." Whenever asked about achievements under his watch, Eric always credits the combined talents and efforts of the people around him. His role was to set the overall vision, pick the right CEO for the times, and embody the Molson Family Principles.

On 9 May 2005, three months after the creation of the Molson Coors Brewing Company, Eric held a dinner at the brewery to thank and pay tribute to the loyal team players who accompanied him on his journey. When the plates were cleared, he told his audience, "As you know, we have seen a lot of short-term thinking in the last year. Stories about us surfaced from unattributed sources. We were exposed to tabloid-style financial press, and some unsavoury characters. So 2004 was a horrible year from that point of view." However, he said, it was also the year that the company took a significant step with Coors to be part of the global

Eric Molson with part of the Molson team who helped pull together the Molson Coors merger of equals at the 9 May 2005 dinner. *From left to right*, Stephen Molson, Raynald H. Douin, SVP Strategy; Marie Giguère, CLO; Eric Molson; Luc Beauregard, corporate director; Brian Burden, CFO; and Daniel W. Colson, corporate director. Molson family collection.

Eric and Jane Molson with Stephen and his wife, Nancy Molson, at the thank-you dinner of 9 May 2005 (Molson family collection). In his speech that night, Eric said: "Many times in the recent past, Tom Molson's children have banded together as a family, and now we have done it again. I want to thank them for their loyalty, their vision and their courage in the face of great adversity last year: the Baxter family, the Stevenson family, my own family, and my brother Stephen."

beer scene. And this was only possible with the help of colleagues and family "who share the culture of this Molson institution ... loyalty, integrity, respect for history, hard work, community involvement, and our continued optimism for the future."

🍁

Like the companies that preceded it, Molson Coors is a corporation with a dual-class share structure. It is jointly controlled by the Molson and Coors families. With the merger, each brought down their respective voting interests to 33 per cent and entered into an agreement to combine their voting powers. According to Leo Kiely, it's a structure that has allowed both families to have "a significant amount of control of our destiny on an ongoing basis."

The only challenge with the arrangement is that the two families have to agree on all major decisions. Otherwise, it can lead to a stalemate. This risk is highlighted in the corporation's public filings: "If Pentland [Eric Molson] and the Coors Trust [Pete Coors] do not agree on a matter submitted to stockholders, generally the matter will not be approved, even if beneficial to the Company or favoured by other stockholders." But so far, so good: more than a decade since the merger, the two families have been aligned. Their partnership is working.

In 2005, however, business journalists did not focus on the families' shared control. They said the merger of equals was essentially a takeover of the Canadian brewery by the Americans. And this despite the fact that control is shared 50–50, that both families have the same number of representatives on the board, and that there are dual headquarters in Montreal and Denver. What the press zeroed in on was that Molson Coors's command centre is in Colorado. The CEO and the leadership team are based there, so that made it an American takeover.

"There's no such thing in business as a merger of equals," says Dan Colson. "Otherwise you wouldn't merge. There's got to be a dominant partner." Robert Coallier, who left as Molson's CFO soon after the merger, also says, "I think the family missed an opportunity when Eric was chairman after the merger to do a better balance of power with Coors. Today, the leadership team is in Denver, but it could have been different. It could have been a real split head office … Eric was the first chairman of Molson Coors, and he probably could have better managed the balance of power. But Eric had also just fought the battle of his life with Ian and getting the deal through. So I'm not sure he was ready to fight another battle."

Leo Kiely disagrees. "You could argue that it was a Coors takeover because I became the CEO and many functions were based in Denver. But it wasn't. In truth, in the governance of the company, it *is* a merger of equals. Nobody holds the upper hand. There may be economic differences – Coors was bigger and Molson was more profitable – but nobody is on top."

Sandy Riley echoes the sentiment: "It's a real partnership. I sit on the board and that's how it's governed. Look at the board composition and look at the disclosure on the shareholder agreements, and you will see that this thing is a partnership between the Molson and the Coors families and that's how it's run. The one difference was that Leo Kiely was chosen to run the company rather than Dan O'Neill, and that was the correct choice. So, naturally, the main head office went to Denver, and that's what the press picked up on."

Eric says he can see why some people would say that the merger of equals was a camouflaged takeover, but he doesn't agree. Yes, the executive leadership team was going to be in Denver; that's where Leo Kiely was. "But I *wanted* Leo as our CEO," he says. "We never had someone like him before. He was a great beer leader, he was a strategic thinker, and he was excellent with operations. We finally had someone who could run both sides of the border. He could take the company to the next level."

Giving another perspective, Andrew explains how Molson led the way in terms of governance. With thirty years more experience as a public corporation (Molson did its IPO in 1945 and Coors in 1975), Molson had developed practices that influenced the way Molson Coors is now governed. One was having independent directors on the board. "We had a mechanism where we allowed for three directors to be voted independently by the non-family shareholders every year," explains Andrew. "Coors didn't have that in their structure. So when we merged in 2005, that got tacked on."

Another Molson innovation was voting shares with coattail provisions. These ensure that all shareholders, voting or not, are treated equally if an offer is made to buy the shares of the controlling shareholder. "Molson installed coattails in the 1980s," says Andrew. "But Coors didn't have them when we merged. Without them, you can really take advantage of your position of control. But with a coattail, if someone approaches us as a family to buy our shares, all the shareholders have to be offered the same deal. When we merged with Coors, we brought the coattail to Molson Coors."

The most significant corporate governance practice adopted by Molson Coors, however, was Eric's longstanding CEO-centric approach. "Our two companies had a different level of experience with professional management," says Andrew. "Molson has had a non-family member CEO for many, many years. I think the last time a Molson was CEO was in the mid-1960s. So by the time the merger happened, we had a professional outsider as our CEO for close to forty years. Coors, on the other hand, had a family member as CEO until very recently. Leo Kiely joined Coors in the early 1990s as president and COO, but Pete Coors was the company's CEO until just a couple of years before the merger. So that mentality in terms of having outside professionals manage the business was a bit different between Molson and Coors. But we're both still learning and growing."

For Eric, a personally gratifying change that came with Molson Coors was the involvement of the next generation in the company's governance. Andrew was now his fellow director. "I've often been asked whether I wanted my boys to join the business. I would always reply, 'Not necessarily, no.' You have to let them choose … As a father, you watch your kids very carefully. You watch for jealousy and greed, but you also watch for them working hard, getting along, and thinking of the people around them.

"At the time of the Coors deal, I felt confident because I knew I had talent behind me in the next generation. Andrew was ready to step in as a board member. I had seen him in action, and he had the right stuff. Geoffrey was also coming along very nicely. He was working his way up through the ranks. Neither of them had that 'don't you realize who I am' kind of attitude. And Justin brought a good external perspective to it all. So I believed in the next wave of successors. I had that going for me. I had my boys."

Sandy Riley witnessed the integration of Andrew and Geoff into the board of Molson Coors. "The transition from Eric to his sons has worked really, really well. I mean, I know Eric is still involved in the background. A person like that doesn't step away 100 per cent. But when the decision was made that Andrew and later Geoff would go on the board, he stepped back and let them find their own way. He's let them be themselves. Over time, they've both gotten more comfortable and more confident – although Andrew came in sort of wise, because he knew a lot about governance and had learned a lot from Luc Beauregard along the way. They've both shown the same kind of respect for management and for independent directors that Eric had.

They're finding their own way on their own terms. And that's a wonderful gift for Eric to have given his sons."

✻

On the business side, Molson Coors experienced unmistakable growing pains after the 2005 merger. Leo Kiely describes it as a two-year "shit storm."

"Everything went wrong. The US business was in the tank. Bud lowered its prices and took all the fun out of it. The Canadian business lost control of the small brewers and started losing market share to some of the underbelly brewers. And Brazil was in free fall. So, within weeks after we merged, our stock price fell by 20 per cent. We got killed … It was really, really hard."

He tackled the issues one by one. In terms of Brazil, Kiely announced soon after the merger that he was "unwilling to make further cash investments in Kaiser without greater certainty that it is a viable, long-term platform to compete effectively in Brazil." He opted to operate it on a cash break-even basis until he found a solution. On 13 January 2006, Molson Coors sold a 68 per cent equity interest in Kaiser to Femsa, the Mexican beverage company, for US$68 million in cash and debt. It was nearly ten times less than what O'Neill had paid for it four years earlier.

One thing Kiely says he could count on during those difficult, post-merger years was the backing of his chairman. "Eric and I would sit down regularly, talk about everything going on … and by the end of our conversation, I felt everything was going to be all right. For example, when the Molson Coors board was first put together, he watched me beat my head against it. I had board members on both the Coors and Molson sides that I had to convert. But the whole time, Eric would coach me on it, always in a very, very supportive way."

Eric stood by his CEO even when critics on the Street got vicious. Kiely was reassured in the knowledge that "nobody was going to try to sell the business from under us no matter how bad it got." He explains: "Our controlling shareholders never took a short-term outlook. Another board would have fired us in a heartbeat for that kind of performance. But they stuck with us."

On 9 February 2007, Ian Molson added his voice to the fault-finders. "My enduring emotion is one of sadness," he commented from London. "In fact, this was nothing short of a takeover, and Molson shareholders weren't paid for it. Worse, it did nothing for the fundamental value of their equity."

Within a few months, however, Ian was proven wrong. The merger's benefits started to kick in, and the Molson Coors stock buoyed up. While it was trading at under US$65/share in October 2006, by April 2007 it went up to US$97/share. On 2 August 2007, the company announced a two-for-one stock split of both its A and B shares in order to keep the stock at an accessible price. Business columnist Peter Hadekel of the *Montreal Gazette* acknowledged the turnaround: "It's sweet vindication for Kiely, who has been preaching patience after encountering a host of problems in the early going."

"By the end of 2007, things were pretty good," says Kiely. "We couldn't have done it without committed controlling shareholders like Pete and Eric ... I thought Eric was a great chairman. He gave everybody a lot of space to do their job, and he was absolutely committed. It was his final years in that job. By then he had gotten the beer business back, he had consolidated all the pieces and owned the whole thing, and he made it a sustainable business. That's why I believed in him. His behaviour showed me that I could count on him. On that rock, we could build a great company."

🍁

In Eric's mind, the merger of equals with Coors was the first of a multistep plan. He always envisioned that after they got together, Molson Coors would join forces with other brewers to create a world-scale company. Kiely and his team explored different international options, with Femsa in Mexico, for example, but they didn't pan out. They then decided to act closer to home. Anheuser-Busch controlled over 50 per cent of the US market; they needed a partner to counter the "King of Beers."

One possibility was SABMiller. "I kept bugging Pete about it," says Eric. "I would tell him, 'Let's get together with Miller in the United States. We need their strength and tonnage to catch up to Anheuser-Busch. It's the only thing to do.'"

The problem was that SABMiller and Coors had been embroiled in cutthroat competition in the United States for years. Some of the dog-eat-dog tactics by both sides had left scars. "Coors and Miller was just like us and Labatt, or like us and the Nordiques," says Eric. "It was intense competition. So it was hard to convince Coors to enter into a deal with SABMiller for the US. Pete was against it. They had been fighting all their lives. If you have hatred there, it stands in the way of rational decisions."

Kiely agrees that SABMiller was Coors's "archenemy" in those days. He wasn't surprised that Pete Coors refused to do a deal with them when he heard of the idea in 2007. "Why would we want to do this?" Pete balked. "We've just had our best year ever!"

"Yeah, Pete," Leo said, "we just had our best year ever by gaining a half a share point. That means that in ten years, we might gain five share points if we have our 'best year ever' back-to-back-to-back for ten years! What do you think the chances of that are?"

Pete Coors eventually agreed with the rest of the board to do a transaction.

On 30 June 2008, SABMiller and Molson Coors combined their US and Puerto Rico operations to create a joint venture called "Miller-Coors." And while SABMiller held 58 per cent of the equity in the new entity, the voting control was split equally between the two partners. MillerCoors had annual sales of US$6.6 billion and 30 per cent of the US market; it became the second-largest player in the United States behind Anheuser-Busch.

As to who would run MillerCoors, Pete Coors was against putting in someone from SABMiller, and the people from Molson Coors didn't want to lose Kiely. Eric, however, saw things differently. Says Kiely, "Early on, Eric took me aside and he told me, 'Look, if we pull this thing off, why don't you just go run it? You become CEO. Appoint yourself a talented COO and have a blast. You deserve it, Leo. Just go do it' ... And that's exactly what I did."

A few weeks after the deal closed, Eric presented MillerCoors to the top fifty leaders of Molson Coors at a conference in Texas. "Our decision to join with SABMiller to take on Anheuser-Busch is a big deal, and it will quickly have a positive impact on our company. This new joint venture in the US will make us stronger and will give us the resources not only to do bigger deals globally but also to ensure our independence as a large global brewer well into the future."

Eric's prediction turned out to be true. In the very short term, the MillerCoors JV helped them face the new brewing behemoth in the works. While Molson Coors worked on its US partnership with SABMiller, InBev was making a run at Anheuser-Busch. The Belgian-Brazilian giant offered $65/share for the American brewer in June 2008 (a premium of 24 per cent compared to the share price a month before). Shareholders were excited with the unsolicited bid, and Warren Buffett, Anheuser-Busch's second-largest shareholder with almost thirty-six million shares, backed it. Anheuser-Busch resisted, as did the Busch family. Their efforts and limited shareholdings, however, were no match for the determined InBev CEO, Carlos Brito, and his investors. On 11 July, InBev raised its bid to $70/share, making it a US$52 billion offer, and it was game over. Two days later, on a Sunday night, Anheuser-Busch agreed to sell itself to InBev, and a few months after that, AB InBev was created. It was one of the top five consumer companies in the world with close to 50 per cent of the US beer market – a formidable competitor. "But imagine where we'd be if we had not combined our US assets with SABMiller's," Eric says. "They could have crushed us."

Eight years later, Eric's prognostication fully materialized. The strategy he championed to combine the US operations of Molson Coors with those of SABMiller became the "company-maker" in 2016. When the joint venture was created in 2008, however, it was far from sure that things would turn out that way. Director Sandy Riley describes the risks: "The problem was that when we did the MillerCoors JV, we kind of landlocked ourselves from the point of view of being able to do anything strategic with our US assets. We were a minority partner in this joint venture with all these joint venture restrictions, so our hands were tied. *But* our one path to glory was if the Brazilians [AB InBev] took a run at SABMiller. That was always somewhere in the background as a possibility. Because if that happened, we'd have the ability to catch the whole US business."

That's exactly what transpired in 2016. Some call it a lucky break, or "rolling triple sixes," but as the Roman philosopher Seneca tells us, "Luck is what happens when preparation meets opportunity." In this case, the opportunity came when global leader AB InBev made an offer to buy its closest rival, SABMiller, for US$107 billion. The move triggered a change-of-control clause in the MillerCoors joint venture agreement which said that if there was ever a change of control of SAB-Miller, Molson Coors could escalate its equity stake in the JV from 42 per cent to 50 per cent.

And that was where preparation came in. Eric had learned to be ready for any eventuality ever since Tom and Hartland failed to reserve the right to buy back the Canadiens from their cousins. In the case of MillerCoors, that safeguard came in the form of a change of control clause. "When Sam Walker, our chief legal officer, and his team pulled together the MillerCoors JV for us, they did a brilliant job," says Eric. "They made sure we were equipped. So when AB InBev made a play for SABMiller, we had an option to raise our stake in the MillerCoors business to 50 per cent at a good price. And that's what we did."

But there was more. By making a bid to take over its closest rival, AB InBev anticipated the inevitable antitrust issues. So in countries where the combined market share of the merged company seemed excessive, it opted to take preventative measures. In the United States, for example, it decided to sell its entire 58 per cent stake in the MillerCoors JV to Molson Coors – not just the 8 per cent required by the change of control clause. (Even after this sale, it would still have 45 per cent of the US market.)

The pre-emptive move worked. On 20 July 2016, AB InBev got the okay from US antitrust authorities to finalize the buyout of SABMiller. That cleared the way for Molson Coors. On 11 October 2016, Molson Coors purchased its joint venture partner for US$12 billion. It got full ownership of the US MillerCoors beer business, gained worldwide control of the Miller brand name, and doubled its size. The Street heralded the move. The stock, which had hovered around US$40/share four years before, soared to over US$100/share.

Molson Coors was now the third-largest brewer in the world.

"Getting to number three is a game-changer for us," says Eric. "It makes us stronger for the future. We could never figure out how to get a good foothold in the States. We tried a bunch of things, the Hamm deal, exporting to the US, setting up a separate US business ... but we could never get it right. Then we diversified. But when we got back to beer, we still needed the States. So, first we partnered with Coors. Then we did the JV with SABMiller. And look where we are now: we own Miller and we're number three in the world!"

Sandy Riley admires Eric's fortitude. "I think what's happened with the Miller deal must be a nice feeling of vindication for Eric. Because Eric believed that there was a role for the family in a global beer company. In order to do that, he had to tough it out. He had to get the transaction with Coors done in the face of all that Ian was doing. He had to make some concessions with respect to where the main head office was to be located. And he had to make compromises with respect to his family's right to collect the same economic rewards that other shareholders were getting in terms of the special dividend. All because he believed that, at the end of the day, the family would continue to be a significant player in a global beer company that could stand on its own two feet for decades to come.

"For the longest time, you could question whether it was going to work. But by hanging in there and staying in the game, keeping going, and doing the MillerCoors JV and buying StarBev in Central Europe and kind of being there, it's like watching the clouds pass. All of a sudden the clouds cleared, and a path appeared that has taken the company to a position where it's a top-three world brewing company. And throughout that process, the Molson family has continued to maintain its position as one of the controlling shareholders."

Leo Kiely agrees. He sees Eric's vision to build a sustainable, global brewery as having played out. "This is the closing chapter of an era in the beer world. When Anheuser-Busch got bought by InBev, that was huge, right? But then, AB InBev consolidating SABMiller and becoming the juggernaut they are – that's going to another level. And Molson Coors getting control of a large share of the US business as a result? I think that's full circle to a sustainable business … From the beginning, Eric wanted to remain in the brewing business for the long term, right? With all that's happened, I think Molson Coors is now set up to do that. I think that's really cool."

When he learns of Kiely's comments, Eric smiles. "It *is* cool." After all he went through, this was his payoff.

Throughout his journey, Eric was guided by his unwavering vision of Molson as a global player. He used persuasion and influence as his tools and only pulled out the heavy artillery of control ("the hydrogen bomb," as Luc Beauregard once called it) when it was critical to the survival of the company.

"I never wanted to give up control," says Eric. "I almost lost it back in the 1990s with Mickey Cohen and then again later with Ian. Then I realized that not only do we need control – even if it's shared control, like what we have with Coors – but we need to exercise our position of control in line with our Family Principles. That way everyone benefits, employees, shareholders, and all other stakeholders, and our long-term future is secured."

Yet he remains realistic. He knows that with the continuing consolidation, it's not certain that the family will be able to keep its position of control in a brewing giant. He maintains, however, that there is one thing the family can (and must) continue to control and to enhance: the Molson name. "That's why I created the 'Molson Brothers' concept," he says, "which we now use to make investments and to make charitable donations … The Molson name is more than a good glass of beer. It's a name with a strong image. It's a Canadian name, one that represents solid citizens who contribute to their communities. We need to keep building on that."

❦

The Order of Canada is the nation's highest civilian distinction and serves to recognize those who have "demonstrated outstanding achievement, dedication to the community and service to the nation." The honour was bestowed upon Eric on 26 October 2007 for both his business career as the leader of the oldest brewery in North America and his multiple philanthropic undertakings – especially regarding the Montreal General Hospital and Concordia University.

Eric chuckles as he remembers a conversation about Concordia with Stephen years ago after he returned from a lunch with its president, Dr Fred Lowy.

"How was it?" Stephen asked.

"Very nice." Eric hung up his overcoat. "We went to that Newtown place on Crescent Street. I like spending time with Fred." Eric first met Lowy in 1995 when he recruited him to become president and vice-chancellor of Concordia. Over the years, the two men worked together and grew close.

"Did you talk about the business school?" Stephen asked.

"Well, it seems they need more money." After a pause he added, "I may have agreed to extend our foundation's gift for a few extra years. I think I mentioned five extra years to him."

"You what?" cut in Stephen. "Eric, that's an extra $5 million!"

Eric looks at me and smiles sheepishly. "Stephen hasn't stopped bugging me on that one. I coughed up an extra five million bucks by having a nice lunch with Fred Lowy! I mean, the Molson Foundation was already supporting Concordia. It was our target university for a long time. But when I told Fred, 'Yes, let's go for it, we'll extend our contribution longer into the future,' I didn't have any kind of official approval. Stephen, as the head of the foundation, obviously had something to say about that!" Eric laughs. "I mean, I like to do things properly, but I just forgot about asking for approval for that one. The Creep keeps bugging me about it. I just figured the foundation would want to do it. For years we had been working on making Concordia better. In the end it worked out well."

Fred Lowy remembers his initial appeal to Eric. "I sat with Eric to talk to him about the project. Back then the business school was good, but it was scattered all over the place in all kinds of different rented properties. I told Eric it would become an even better business school if they had their own building. Eric completely agreed. He took the ball and ran with it. He worked hard to help us get the funds we needed.

"The total contribution from the Molson family was $25 million," says Lowy. "At the time, it was a very substantial gift. These days, the way money is being thrown around at universities, it may not seem as significant, but at the time, it really moved the university forward."

There was also the question of how to name Concordia's business school. "There were a lot of ideas floating around," Lowy says. "One of them was to name it after Eric. It could have been the Eric Molson

School of Business. After all, he took a leadership role in getting this done. But of course Eric wanted no part of that. Instead, he and Stephen came up with the idea of naming it after John Molson – you know, to honour the entrepreneur and founder of the Molson dynasty. We all agreed."

On 8 September 2009, the John Molson School of Business opened its doors to faculty, staff, and 8,500 students in a new, innovative, seventeen-storey tower downtown.

Over the years, Eric's devotion to his community has extended far beyond Concordia. In addition to giving financial support to multiple causes, personally and through the Molson Foundation, he has worked many hours as a volunteer board member for other institutions, in education (Princeton University, McGill University, Bishop's University, Bishop's College School, Selwyn House School, and the Toronto French School), health (the Montreal General Hospital Foundation and the Montreal Neurological Institute), and the arts (Les Grands Ballets Canadiens de Montréal and *Vie des Arts* magazine). Quoting John Molson, he reminds us, "We're all members of a larger community which depends on everyone playing a part."

Eric's involvement has served as a model not only to those closest to him, like his sons, but to many others who have seen him at work. Pierre Boivin, for example, says Eric was an inspiration. "Eric is a model for us. Look at what he's done in terms of our medical and academic institutions, like the Montreal General Hospital and Concordia University. Hats off! He's been instrumental to their evolution. It's not just the capital the family has put into the Molson Foundation and the money they give out, but it's also their personal implication that's impressive. I personally was not all that involved in community work before starting at Molson. And when I look back at my career, I see that my first real influence in terms of community involvement was the Molson family."

❦

Luc Beauregard, long-time Molson board member and founder of National Public Relations, was also inspired by Eric. (Sadly, Luc died of cancer on 26 July 2013, one week shy of his seventy-second birthday.) He said he admired Eric's moral compass, his community involvement, and his long-term mindedness. The respect went both ways. Luc was always there for Eric when it mattered. And as Eric neared the end of his career and contemplated how to transfer his patrimony to the seventh generation, Luc indirectly played a role.

The hand-over to one's successors takes years to orchestrate. Eric says it begins in early childhood. "You set the right example. You give them a good education. And the whole time, you watch them like a hawk. But you've also got to give them room … enough room to make their own choices and their own mistakes, but not so much that they fall flat and they can't get up again. It's a delicate balance."

When the Molson Coors merger closed in 2005, Eric was sixty-seven. He had been observing and guiding his sons for years. It was time to make a move. "I wanted to help my sons by investing in their businesses while I was still alive. You don't want to wait for someone to read a will to transfer stuff. I thought it was better to pass on responsibility while I was still there. That way you can see what happens. You can observe how they handle themselves and how they work together."

It was around this time that Andrew approached his father with an opportunity: what if they made an offer to buy National? The public relations firm started by Beauregard in 1976 had grown to become Canada's largest. By 2004, Andrew had worked there for seven years and loved the place.

"I approached Luc to see if he would be interested in selling the business to me," Andrew says. "At first he was hesitant. Over the years, we had worked closely together, but this was different. I wanted to buy him out. He eventually warmed to the idea … But before doing anything, I spoke to Dad. It was going to be an important investment for our family, and it was the first time we would be branching outside Molson. I needed to make sure Dad was as convinced as I was."

Eric knew his son was committed to National. "Andrew came to see me and asked, 'Can we do it?' I thought it was a good idea. Andrew was passionate about the PR business. He worked hard at it. Also, Luc wanted him to take over. So it made sense."

Eric contemplated how to configure the investment amongst his sons. Fairness was key. "I insist that all three brothers be joint investors in the businesses they get into," he says. "We share everything. To a certain extent, I wanted to make sure that if one of the boys made a fortune doing something, the other guys got in on the gravy. That's the way we structured it. We did it that way with hockey as well: everyone's in on the gravy. If somebody is doing more work, then that person gets a salary for it. But the investment in the business amongst the brothers is the same."

Luc Beauregard eventually agreed to sell National to Andrew, partly because of his unobtrusive style. "Andrew is a bit like his dad," he told journalists in 2005, "in the sense that he's very intense, but very discreet – not a flashy person." But mostly it was because Beauregard knew Andrew shared Eric's principles. "Andrew is a professional shareholder. He's committed to the sustainability of his businesses … When I sold to him, I knew he wouldn't turn around and flip the firm after two years. It's not a family trait."

Andrew's discretion and humility facilitated the transition with Beauregard. Instead of stepping into the shoes of his old boss and aggressively taking over as soon as he became the majority owner, Andrew showed the restraint he learned from his father. He became chairman only when Beauregard indicated he was ready to step aside and assume the honorary title of "founding president." That was on 1 January 2012, seven years after the transfer of ownership to the Molsons.

In the meantime, Eric observed how his sons acted as business partners. "This deal to buy National with Luc and Andrew was a good test case for me. I got to see how the boys worked together. Did they argue? No. Did they only think of their own interests? No. After that, I knew things were going to turn out all right."

The National deal played another role. It paved the way for a much more public and emotional transaction – the buy-back of the Montreal Canadiens. "Andrew led the way by doing the deal with Luc," continues Eric. "He bought National and paved the way for the Canadiens' deal. It showed us how we could structure it to make it work."

🍁

Rumours started circulating in early 2009. Cash-strapped George Gillett Jr would either sell his stake in the Montreal Canadiens or face bankruptcy. After buying 80.1 per cent of the club and its Bell Centre (then called Molson Centre) arena from Molson in January 2001, Gillett had gone on a buying spree. He had picked up 50 per cent of England's Liverpool soccer club, a NASCAR team, ski resorts, golf courses, car dealerships, and more. Having spread himself thin, he faced a dire situation in 2008 when the global economic crisis hit.

On 23 March 2009, the Canadiens' organization confirmed the club was for sale: "The Gillett family has retained the services of BMO Capital Markets and the process is under way." Habs CEO Pierre Boivin conceded, "We're not hiding it. We're going through a very difficult economic period ... Banks are reluctant to finance even very good projects."

Right away, speculations began. Would the team be bought by Guy Laliberté, founder of the Cirque du Soleil? What about Stephen Bronfman of Claridge Investments Inc.? Was the Desmarais family of Power Corp. interested? How about Joey Saputo, son of cheese magnate Lino Saputo? Could it be a celebrity like Céline Dion and husband-manager René Angelil? What about Jim Balsillie of BlackBerry fame? Of course, there was also Québecor's Pierre Karl Péladeau ... Hypotheses filled pages of local and national papers for days.

Once the due diligence started, a shroud of secrecy cloaked the process. Potential bidders signed thick confidentiality agreements to look at the hockey franchise's books. Their deadline to submit a formal offer was set for Thursday, 9 April 2009, at 5:00 p.m.

Despite the covertness of the operation, Geoff Molson followed it intently. As the designated representative of Molson Coors on the Canadiens' board of directors (the brewery owned 19.9 per cent of the club), Eric's youngest son had a distinct vantage point. It was a delicate position to be in. His family had such a long history with the team that everyone felt it was not implausible for them to join in the bidding process. To mitigate the potential conflict of interest, Geoff took a step back. He didn't sit on the board committee overseeing the sale, and he was excluded from all discussions around it. He could neither see who was bidding nor what they were offering.

Yet he couldn't stop thinking about it.

The week before the sale was announced, Gillett had approached him after a board meeting. "Listen, Geoff," he said, "I respect your family. I think you guys are the best. So I want to give you a chance to buy the team from me before I go public."

Although he remained visibly impassive, Geoff now admits, "My first thought was, 'Wow! Wouldn't that be great?'" Imagine being part of something with such a glorious record, something that fuels such palpable passion, something that's part of the identity of so many, regardless of race, gender, age, politics, or religion. Geoff was almost lightheaded.

The Molson family's involvement with the team dated back to 1924 when Geoff's great-grandfather and four other relatives were among the first investors in the Canadian Arena Company (the entity that held the Habs and the Forum). Then Tom and Hartland bought the team in 1957 and owned it for fourteen years. Later, the family stayed indirectly involved when the brewery bought the team from the Bronfmans in 1978. Even when Gillett became the principal owner in 2001, Molson kept a 19.9 per cent interest in it. But the family's ties to the Habs were more than financial: they were emotional. Just like many other Montrealers and Québécois, the Molsons were diehard fans.

The day after Gillett's overture, Geoff had a breakfast meeting with Eric and Andrew. As soon as they ordered, Geoff began. "George has approached me. He's selling the team and he wants to know if we're interested."

Eric saw the ardour in his son's eyes and was careful not to inflame it. "You must be crazy, Geoff," he said. "Forget it. You don't want to invest in something that has up and down cycles like that." Eric made a roller-coaster motion with his hand. "You win a Stanley Cup, you make more money. You don't make the playoffs, you're down in the dumps. You don't want that in your investments."

After a long discussion, the three agreed that Geoff would decline Gillett's offer. "So I called George back and said no … but I still wanted to do it," Geoff says. "Then I saw all these people building partnerships to buy the team, and I thought, 'Our family won't buy the team alone, but what if we found partners and did it with other people?'" If he found a way to spread the risk, Eric might be more open to the idea.

Geoff called for a second breakfast meeting with his father and brother. This time, they met at Eggspectation on the corner of de la Montagne Street and de Maisonneuve Boulevard. "I think we can do this," he told Andrew and Eric. "But I can't do it without your permission, Dad, and I can't do it without it becoming public."

He drew a pie chart on a napkin. "As a family we could get 20 per cent. Molson would keep its 20 per cent. And for the remaining 60 per cent, we could talk to these people." He wrote down several names.

Andrew backed his brother. "With the right partners, we can make this work."

Eric watched Geoff and Andrew become enlivened as they debated who to include as partners in the Molson deal team. His boys were different: Geoff was outspoken and unshrinking in front of the cameras, while Andrew was more a behind-the-scenes networker. Both, however, were intelligent, resolute, and hard-working. What mattered most to Eric was that they worked well together. They were partners who had each others' backs.

"What about Justin?" asked Eric.

"He'll go along with it," replied Geoff. "He loves the Habs."

"Well, he's got to be part of it. This will be a Molson Brothers project."

Geoff and Andrew agreed.

"We'll need to manage all potential conflicts of interest," added Andrew. "You know, put up Chinese walls and all that."

Geoff agreed. "I'll talk to Sam Walker" – Molson Coors' chief legal officer. "We'll see what he thinks we should do." Given his positions as both an employee and board member of Molson Coors, as well as his director position on the board of the Canadiens, Geoff knew he was walking a fine line by spearheading the bid to buy the team.

The next day, he met with Pierre Boivin and announced that his family wanted to participate in the bidding process. The Habs' CEO was surprised. "I mean, George Gillett and I were sure that the Molson family would be the best buyer for the team," he says, "but they had initially said no to George's offer. And when the Molson Brothers said

Andrew and Geoff Molson, on their way to deliver the Molson Brothers bid for the Montreal Canadiens on 10 June 2009. Photo by Martin Roy.

they wanted to be in the race, it was very late in the process. We were already in the second round. We were down to three or four finalists who were fighting to get it. But, because it was the Molson family, we allowed them to come in. I mean, they already owned 20 per cent through the company, Geoff was on the board, they had a long history with the organization … We decided it made sense to let them in."

The Molson Brothers submitted their bid for the Habs on 10 June 2009. Albeit late to join, they were now part of the race and soon leading the pack.

The next day, Serge Savard dropped his bid and stepped out of the sales process. He said, "On a monté un dossier pour l'achat du Canadien et on est prêt, mais la venue des Molson a changé la donne. J'ai toujours été intimement lié à la famille et je n'ai pas le goût de me battre contre eux. Je suis donc sur les lignes de côté" ("We've put together a bid to buy the Canadiens and we're ready, but the arrival of the Molsons has changed the game. I've always been very close to the family and I don't feel like fighting against them. I will therefore stand on the sidelines"). After announcing that he was not going to fight the Molson family, he said that the three Molson brothers "are there for the right reasons; they're there for the love of hockey." They should be the front-runners.

The Molsons were grateful for the hockey legend's endorsement. "Serge Savard has a lot of credibility in the public as a hockey man," says Andrew. "The fact that he openly came out and said he was disengaging from the bidding process because it was almost natural for the Molson Brothers to get it was very helpful. It was especially helpful when you have the *Journal de Montréal* insinuating that we shouldn't get the team because the Molsons are not real Québécois. The fact that Serge Savard came out and basically said the reverse was very meaningful."

On Saturday, 20 June 2009, Geoff Molson and George Gillett shook hands. They had reached an agreement. Although there were still details to be resolved, the Molson Brothers' offer had topped the bidding war.

Reactions from both the media and the public were enthusiastic. The headline of one local paper read, "Welcome Back Molsons: The

Sale of the Canadiens Ended with the Best of All Possible Results." Jean Béliveau, one of the greatest captains in the team's history, was unequivocal: "It's excellent news for everyone. The Molson Brothers are continuing the tradition of their forefathers … As I know them, the Molsons will take all means necessary to make the Canadiens a winning team once again." Even NHL commissioner Gary Bettman called the sale to the Molsons "a real plus for the franchise and the fans of Montreal. We're always looking for owners who are passionate about hockey." The team going back to the family under whose tutelage it won fourteen of its twenty-four Stanley Cups seemed like a restoration of the natural order of things.

In the midst of all this positive feedback, however, there was still work to be done. The financing had to be finalized and the partners in the venture confirmed. Inevitably, there were surprises. The most important one came from the least expected place – Molson Coors. Based on the feedback he'd received, Geoff assumed that the brewery would keep its 19.9 per cent investment in the team intact. Yet the board still had not given its approval.

"The hardest part of the whole deal for me was that I couldn't convince Molson Coors to stay in as an investor," says Geoff. "It got to the point where the board felt uncomfortable with my attempts to persuade the company to keep its investment in the Habs." Sensing the rising tension amongst his fellow directors, Geoff backed off. Ultimately, the board chose to sell the brewery's stake in the team.

Looking back on the experience, Eric acknowledges that "the whole situation with Molson Coors and the purchase of the team could have been better handled. Geoff was new to the board back then, and he was poorly advised on how to approach them with it. He assumed the CEO and the directors would want to continue with the Habs. His advisors on the inside said it was going to be all right … What we should have done is softened up the board beforehand. But we didn't, and when the time came to do the deal, we ended up having to buy out the brewery … The good thing that came of it was that Andrew and Geoff worked well together through that situation. They were allies and partners, and that's important to me."

On 1 December 2009, three days before the Montreal Canadiens celebrated the hundredth anniversary of their first game, the NHL board of governors announced the approval of the sale to Molson Brothers and its partners. Geoff would become the organization's next CEO. Luc Bertrand would be chairman of the board of the new CH Group and Andrew one of its directors.

So far, the family's investment is proving to be a good one. According to *Forbes* magazine, the team in 2009 was worth about US$334 million. In their 2016 ranking, it had risen to the second-highest valued team in the NHL, at US$1.2 billion. The only thing that's left to win is that elusive twenty-fifth Stanley Cup.

"I'm proud of what Geoff and his gang have done," says Eric. "It's like I told Morgan McCammon back in 1978, 'You didn't just buy a hockey team. You bought an entertainment business and the hockey team is one of your acts.' As a businessman you have to have a bigger vision. And Geoff has that. Their entertainment business is booming, and they're also developing a real estate business.

"It's the same with Andrew and his business. The public relations group he's building with his partners has an excellent reputation. But, just like the hockey business, you can go through fluctuations because you can lose your talent. They can walk out the door on you. So you have to be bigger, spread yourself out more, and that's what Andrew has done. Now they're growing internationally and they have offices in New York, San Francisco, London, Copenhagen ... Amazing!"

Eric pauses and asks rhetorically, "Who would have thought we would be on top of the number-three brewery in the world? That we would own the Canadiens once again? And that we'd have a firm like National that's so intimately involved with the public affair issues of the country? ... It's going to be all right, because of the boys. Andrew and Geoff are now both on the board of Molson Coors, and they don't fight, they're smart, they stick to our principles, and they work hard. Thanks to them, we are strong influencers at the board level. And they're in there together, real partners. They're also lucky because they have Justin. Justin is like Stephen: he's the solid, quiet partner behind the scenes. He doesn't really care about money, but he has the right values, and if there's ever a problem, he'll be there. There's a real satisfaction in knowing that it's going to be all right."

❧

Looking back, Sandy Riley summarizes Eric's time as chairman. "At heart, Eric is a brewer. He's a guy who loves beer: loves making it, has a passion for the product, and harbours a strong sense of the family connection. But what he got involved in was some pretty nasty corporate infighting and some pretty big transactions in order to get the family business to a place where it could become what it's becoming. It wasn't easy, but he did it. He got the company to where he wanted it … And now Molson Coors is a major player in the global beer market."

In 2010, Eric retired. "After fifty years, it's time for me to hang up my skates," he announced. And although he may have started as a reluctant chairman, once he uncovered his passion and made it his mission, he was hard to stop.

Along the way, many people underestimated him. His non-confrontational manner and propensity to give others the limelight allowed for some more ego-driven people to take centre stage. "Eric gives everybody a lot of space," says Leo Kiely. "You could argue *too much* space … I think there were some people who took advantage of him. That would be my impression – and I'm talking back to the conglomerate days, and so forth. With that style of chairmanship, people can start thinking it's their company. But make no mistake, it's Eric's company."

In his influential book *Good to Great*, American business author Jim Collins discusses what constitutes a "Level 5 leader." At the peak of the five-tier hierarchy of leadership that Collins delineates is not the individual known for flash and charisma (i.e., a big ego) but rather someone who embodies a "paradoxical mix of personal humility and professional will." That could be Eric that Collins is describing.

Eric shouldered the roles of chairman, controlling shareholder, and family patriarch without complaint, even though he might have had different aspirations when he was younger. "If I hadn't had the Molson business to carry forward, I might have ended up in the lab, doing research or teaching," Eric muses. "It would have been fun, but in the end it wouldn't have been nearly as interesting or satisfying as what I ended up doing."

He made it interesting by making it his own. He accepted the responsibility that came with his family legacy but didn't just blindly execute what was started before him. "When I became chairman, it took me a while to figure out what was best for the corporation and allow myself to bring it back to what I cared most about. Beer was what I understood and what I was passionate about. So we did it, and it worked. That's why, in terms of educating my boys, I let them choose. They have to find what they love, pursue it, and work hard at building it up. If you do that, it doesn't even feel like work."

"There's a grit to it," says Kiely. "Guys like Pete or Eric don't need this for their personal wealth or for their family's wealth. There's a grit that comes with legacy ... When it came down to it, Eric didn't care what anybody thought about his decisions regarding the beer business. He didn't care what anybody thought about his sons buying the Canadiens. He felt that was his DNA, right? And I think there's real grit to that. That might take a whole lifetime to learn how to apply and make happen. And it's pretty damned cool."

Still, Eric passes on the credit. "I may have had grit, but I couldn't have done it without Jane. When I think of all that she's had to put up with over the years – all the beer talk, the hockey, and all that bathroom humour ... Poor Jane!"

He gets a little emotional. "It's been a blessing to me: the love, the understanding, and the support I've had from her through it all ... I couldn't have done it without her. She's raised our three boys to be good, solid citizens, contributing to their communities, respecting all cultures, and upholding the values we have as a family."

Values define and differentiate Eric. Some have called him "naive" and "idealistic" (giving up the $51 million special dividend, for example), but his principles are what make him unique and a leader in his own quiet way. His choices show that one does not have to be an underhanded, selfish manipulator to win at the game of business. You can play by the rules, set the right example, and still come out on top.

"It is true, that to be good at what you do, you have to know your stuff," Eric told an auditorium-full of Concordia graduates in 2006.

"But if you want to be a leader, if you dream of making the world a better place, then it is your strong values that will be your beacon. These values will keep you focused on achieving your goals, and will guide you when you are making a tough decision, especially when that decision might affect others. Values help you understand what integrity means and what it means to have respect for others. Imagine a world where no one played his or her part. Every man and woman for themselves. A world of greed and thoughtlessness. We would soon see the results."

It seems there are many more examples of greed and its nefarious consequences in business than there are of benevolence and concern for others. Eric is different. Like the yeast that makes beer, he worked quietly in the background, followed his principles, and took the brewery to a new level. Without him, Molson wouldn't be what it is today.

🍁

In early fall each year, the Montreal Canadiens launch their hockey season with an opening ceremony on home ice. A burning torch is passed from former Habs legends to a current team member, and it travels from player to player until finally the team's captain is left standing in the middle of the rink holding up the flame to thunderous applause.

The ceremony is a re-enactment of John McCrae's "To you from failing hands we throw the torch; be yours to hold it high." This passage had been on the wall of the Canadiens' dressing room since 1952, when general manager Frank J. Selke put it up.

Explains Ken Dryden, Hockey Hall of Fame Canadiens goaltender, "The notion of throwing or passing the torch is not only an aspirational concept – it's true. We all pass the torch to anybody who comes next. We do it as parents, as our parents did for us. We do it with co-workers … Those who set a certain standard and generated a certain expectation – of course, that's what this is. The Montreal Canadiens decided to do it in not just a conceptual way but in a visible, ceremonial way."

The tradition resonates with Eric. "You want to pass on something that's better than what you got. Which is what we're doing. I got a conglomerate of businesses from my father. We then went back to beer.

And now we're the number-three brewer in the world, with Andrew and Geoff on the board."

Eric passed the torch to the seventh generation despite multiple obstacles. All along, he conducted himself "with the kind of responsibility and sense of stewardship you would hope to see in someone in his position," according to Sandy Riley. "It's a privilege nowadays to be the controlling shareholder of a public company with a multiple vote share structure. People have to keep that privilege in mind, and they have to manage their involvement in the business on that basis. And to their credit, first Eric, and now Andrew and Geoff, have lived up to that obligation."

"The boys are doing a good job of making the Molson name better," Eric says. "There will be something 'Molson' in the future. The institution will survive. I consider Molson – the name, the family, the past, the heritage – as an institution. It's associated with breweries, hockey, public relations, the foundation ... and our job is to protect, preserve, and enhance it. It's laced with integrity, which is easy to lose and impossible to buy. Integrity is what's helped us over the centuries.

"So you can buy and sell businesses – and we have – but all along you try to keep the institution in good shape. And to do that, you've got to watch out for family dynamics. We now have the eighth generation coming up. What are they going to be like? Will they go around thinking they're something special just because of their last name? I don't think so, but who knows? Will they work hard? Will they work well together? Will they care about and contribute to their communities and to Canada? Will they work to enhance the reputation of Molson? Are they going to make the image better? I don't know. That's why I keep a close eye on them."

In the background, I hear the screech of children playing. Eric pauses for a minute to look out at his grandchildren roughhousing on the lawn. My gaze follows, and I see my daughters and their cousins making big piles of the maple leaves on the ground. Their cheeks are flushed by the activity and cool air. The eighth generation ... I wonder what the future holds for them.

"Is that it?" he asks, turning towards me. "Do you have all you need?"

"I think so." I switch off my tape recorder.

Is this really it? Is it over? It is Saturday, 8 October 2016. My first interview with Eric was on Tuesday, 27 August 2013. Not wanting to completely close the door on our conversations, I add, "But can we sit down again for another session if I realize I'm missing something?"

"Sure, no problem." He picks up his cup of coffee. "You better get your questions in fast, though. My memory is not what it used to be." He smiles.

Eric Molson on the roof of the Molson Brewery on Notre Dame Street looking out over Montreal. Cover of the September 1993 issue of *Concordia University Magazine*. Photo by Nicholas Amberg.

ACKNOWLEDGMENTS

While I was working on *Back to Beer*, I often got the same kind of re-action from friends who heard about the project. "A biography of your father-in-law? How interesting ... But isn't it a little risky?"

Anxiety would then surface: What if they were right? What if it was too risky? What if my in-laws hated it? Would I become that relative everyone tries to avoid at dinner parties? Or worse, would I be "fired" from the family? My safeguard was my husband, Andrew. He'd look at me and say, "Trust yourself, Helen. Dad does." I banked on that and kept going.

One thing is certain: had it not been for Eric's transparency and his largesse in terms of time and information, I could never have written this book. Imagine what it took for someone like him – an introvert who never wants to be the centre of attention – to spend hours talk-ing and revealing his thoughts and emotions. Imagine what it was like for him to be grilled on past decisions and events, some painful and well tucked away, for the sake of what others could learn from them. Imagine his doing all this and then declining my offer to let him read the manuscript before publication because he did not want to interfere with my writer's prerogative to tell the story as I saw it. If you can pic-ture all that, you realize the depth of gratitude I feel towards Eric.

My mother-in-law, Jane, was equally open to this venture. She trusted me not to make a hash of it, and her unwavering support gave me confidence. Geoff and Justin were also well disposed to my doing this work about their father. They were encouraging and there for me when I needed them. The same is true of my sisters-in-law, Kate and Julia.

In fact, the entire "Tom Molson gang" was incredibly generous with me. Without hesitation, Stephen, Nancy, Deirdre, and Cynthia agreed to be interviewed and willingly shared their memories and insights. I am also very grateful to Eric and David Stevenson and Brian, Colin, and James Baxter.

Although my side of the family didn't play an active role in this project, my mother, Garyfallia Bouchelou, my brother, John Antoniou, and his spouse, Johanna Choremis, have always supported me in my endeavours. They are a wellspring of comfort and strength for me.

Loyal friends are my other source of fortitude. The Greek philosopher Epicurus once said, "It is not so much our friends' help that helps us as the confidence of their help." Michel de la Chenelière gave me this kind of self-assurance right from the start. When I told him I was thinking of writing a book on Eric, he immediately volunteered to be my literary agent. I grabbed that lifeline he proffered and relied on his wisdom since then. Michel has been by my side throughout this endeavour and I am very grateful to him.

Nathalie Bissonnette guided me in a different way. A talented film executive who produced a documentary about her own family, she inspired me to find the delicate balance of giving an objective account while being an insider. Nathalie also introduced me to Joseph Campbell's *The Hero with a Thousand Faces*. Together, we delved into the journey of Campbell's hero, which ultimately helped me gain a deeper insight into Eric's personal odyssey.

When my friend Anne Fortier learnt of my project, she too spontaneously offered her help. This *New York Times*–bestselling author became my writing partner and unofficial editor. Whenever I was blocked or had a question or a crazy idea, I would send Anne an email. She was always ready to brainstorm and give her opinion. Moreover, her replies were filled with such humour and wit that I'd often be laughing long after I closed my inbox.

I am equally grateful for the counsel of other close friends who reviewed the manuscript in progress: Gregory Charles, Nicole Collet,

Adriana Embiricos, Christiane Germain, Vicki Light, Tom Pollack, Lynn Schoener, Howard Steiger, and Lorne Steinberg. Thank you to all.

Of course, *Back to Beer* could not have become what it is without the superb professionals at McGill-Queen's University Press. Philip Cercone, MQUP's executive director, enthusiastically embraced the project. Maureen Garvie, an amazing editor, was indefatigable in her review and suggestions. Her sensitivity and nuanced approach made this biography far better than it would otherwise have been. Rachel Martinez, an award-winning translator, was not only able to express my words in French but also managed to capture my voice. She was supported in her work by an exceptional French-language editor, Sophie Sainte-Marie. David Drummond used his artistry to create a captivating cover design. Other members of the MQUP team were equally wonderful: Natalie Blachere, Ryan Van Huijstee, Jacqueline Michelle Davis, Susan McIntosh, and Elena Goranescu – thank you.

From the Molson Foundation, Simonne Bienvenue was vital in unearthing some of the archives and photographs for the book. Eric's assistant, Patricia Dell'Elce, was also very supportive. From Molson Coors, Lori Ball and Emily Bone helped me with pictures and questions of copyright. From the Club de hockey Canadien, I thank Florence Labelle, who helped me find some great shots of the Habs, and France Margaret Belanger for her advice. And from National Public Relations, Nicole Delorme's expertise in strategic communications was invaluable to me.

The team at Concordia University Library, Guylaine Beaudry, Dee Winn, Danielle Dennie, and Satya Miller, was amazing. Until this book, I never realized the hoops one had to go through to get copyright clearance for photos. Satya, who carried the brunt of the load, worked diligently to get the appropriate permissions. Thank you, Alan Shepard, president of Concordia University, for introducing me to these wonderful people.

To all of the above and the many others who are not mentioned by name but contributed so much to this project, I borrow Sebastian's words from Shakespeare's *Twelfth Night* (act III, scene 3) and say, "I can no other answer make but thanks, and thanks, and ever thanks."

There is one person, however, to whom I owe much more than thanks, and that's my husband, Andrew. Without him I would never have found the confidence to embark on this venture. He not only encouraged me to do it but helped me stay the course and smoothed the way. He set up interviews, gave me feedback on multiple versions of the text, and tirelessly shared his perspective on everything from Quebec politics to corporate governance. He never complained, not even during the fourteen-month stint when my alarm clock rang at 4:45 every morning so I could write for a couple of hours before the baby woke up. But more than that, Andrew made me laugh and enjoy this learning journey. He is the reason I smile every day and, along with our daughters, he is my inspiration and the love of my life.

INDEX

Baxter, née Molson, Cynthia, 14, 20,
22, 160, 216, 237, 246, 247, 248,
265, 327, 329, 345, 346, 359, 384–5,
387, 401, 404; childhood, 7, 9–11,
33; school, 16, 25, 28; and Tom
Molson's passing, 119–20, 383
Baxter, James, 329, 383–4
B B Bargoons, 168, 177. *See also*
Molson Companies Ltd
Beauregard, Luc, 202–4, 312, 334,
403, 407, 414; as advisor, 208,
251, 258, 291, 326, 333; as board
director, 232, 241, 286, 292, 333,
338, 339, 341, 342, 343, 344, 373,
414; National Public Relations,
416–18. *See also* Molson, Eric
Beaver Lumber Company Ltd, 154,
168, 190–2, 201, 245. *See also*
Molson Companies Ltd
beer: brewing process, vii, 29, 47,
69, 107–8, 238; consolidation
and globalization, 169, 176,
205, 257, 283, 314–15, 321, 325,
328, 334, 368, 383, 390, 394, 396;
exemption from Canada-US Free
Trade Agreement, 143–5, 169;
industry evolution, 89, 127, 136;
interprovincial trade barriers,
143–4; yeast, viii–ix, 29–30. *See
also* Molson, Eric
Béliveau, Jean, 125, 147, 148, 185,
239–41, 248, 424
Bell Centre, 201, 305, 419
Bellini, Francesco, 232, 241, 286, 290,
291, 324, 338–9, 342, 343, 344, 358,
373, 394–5
Bemberg family, 206, 283
Bensimon Byrne, 266
Berry, Bob, 142
Bertrand, Luc, 425

Bettman, Gary, 219, 424
Beutel Goodman, 392
BHP Company, 242
Black, Conrad, 232, 342, 353, 355
Black, James (Jim), 75, 112, 129–30,
162, 181, 185; buying Diversey,
115–17; as CEO, 99–101, 137, 142,
153, 154; as chairman, 154, 155, 221;
as Eric's "godfather," 100, 111, 155;
replaced by Eric, 154–6, 161. *See
also* Molson Companies Ltd
Blake, Hector (Toe), 93, 147, 148, 201
Blank, Arthur, 190
Boivin, Pierre, 268, 416; as president
of the Montreal Canadiens, 263–
4, 269–70, 419, 421, 423;
recruitment of, 262–3. *See also*
O'Neill, Dan
Boston Bruins, 46, 125, 136
Bouchard, Lucien, 219, 220
Bourassa, Robert, 112–13, 146
Bourne, Gordon, 105
Bourque, Pierre, 219
Brace, Hollis, 103, 129–31
Brador beer, 89–91
Braehead, 246
Brahma Brewery, 282
Brito, Carlos, 411
Bronfman, Edward and Peter, 94,
126, 127, 133, 215, 420. *See also*
Montreal Canadiens
Buckley, Peter, 312–13, 335, 361. *See
also* Caledonia Investments plc
Budweiser beer, 136, 143, 408
Buffett, Warren, 394, 411
Burden, Brian, 403
Burgundy Asset Management, 389,
395

Cadbury, Adrian, 307–9

McNiven, Bruce, 356

Mendeleev, Dmitri, 3, 20

Miller Brewing Company, 106, 180, 182–3, 195, 196–8, 199, 200, 204, 230, 234, 235, 236, 241, 242–3, 245, 253, 274, 275, 319. *See also* Molson Companies Ltd; Molson Coors Brewing Company; SABMiller

MillerCoors, 318, 410, 411–12, 413. *See also* Molson Coors Brewing Company; SABMiller

Mitchell, Antonia (Tonia), 57

Mitchell, Margaret, 59, 61, 62

Mitchell, William, 63–4

Molson, Andrew T., 3, 4, 37–8, 45, 55, 69, 84, 85, 86, 87, 88, 102, 113, 117, 124–5, 201, 205, 212–4, 239, 279, 298, 311, 315, 329, 346, 349, 376, 380, 400–2; board director, 290, 291, 309, 317–20, 373, 375, 398, 407–8, 429; on corporate governance, 206, 294–5, 308, 373–4, 406–7; education, 131, 132–5; Montreal Canadiens purchase, 420–1, 422, 423, 424, 425; National Public Relations, 361, 417–18, 425; professional development, 205–6, 290, 373

Molson, née Stewart, Beatrice (Auntie Bea), 52, 117, 119

Molson, Betty, 16

Molson, Bill (brother of Ian), 344–5, 355–7, 357–8, 359

Molson, David, 73, 91–3, 94–6, 126, 127, 215. *See also* Montreal Canadiens

Molson, Dorothy, 16

Molson, née Lyall, Elizabeth, 214

Molson, née Pentland, Elizabeth (Bessie), 23

Molson, Eric H.: on advisors, 122, 175, 217, 251, 308, 346, 374; on Arnett, 225, 230–2 (hiring), 236, 250, 254, 267–9 (firing), 368; as assistant to Hartland Molson, 53–4; back to beer, 176–8, 180, 181, 182, 186, 202–4, 205, 208, 220, 222–3, 225, 226, 228, 232, 234, 239, 244, 245, 251, 252, 309, 345, 368, 413, 427, 428; on Beauregard, 208, 232, 251; becoming board director, 109–10; on beer, 68–70, 175–6, 204; and Brador, 89–91; chairman of the board, 154–7, 161–2, 341–2; on being a sidewalk man, 54, 139, 141, 187, 262, 269; at Bishop's College School, 16–20; on Brazil investment, 286–7, 288, 299, 301, 303, 306; as brewmaster, 48, 77–8; buying Formosa brewery, 106–8; buying SABMiller's US business, 412–13; chancellor of Concordia University, 185–6, 187–9, 201; on Cohen, 157–61 (hiring), 174, 175, 183, 187, 189, 192–3, 199–200, 202, 205, 207–9 (firing), 368; on contingency plans, 96, 243, 412; on contractual dispute with Coors, 198–200, 226–7; on control, 41, 82–3, 122, 138, 238, 275, 388, 391, 405, 414; on corporate governance, 98, 142, 172, 232, 258–9, 277, 286, 289, 291–3, 294–5, 300, 307–11, 331, 342, 344, 354, 379, 380–1; as deputy chairman, 142, 221; on Diversey, 115–16, 176, 194–6, 202; on diversification, 70–1, 76–7, 82, 111, 137, 176, 193, 205–6, 209–11; on education, 102, 131–4, 186; early years, 7–11,

MOLSON CEO-CHAIR TIMELINE

MOLSON IPO

DIVERSIFICATION

JO[...]

ERIC MOL[...]

JIM BLACK – PRES & CEO

BUD WILLMOT – CHAIRMAN

BUD WILLMOT – DEPUTY CHAIRMAN

BUD WILLMOT – PRES & CEO

DAVE CHENOWETH – PRES

P.T. MOLSON – PRES

HARTLAND MOLSON – CHAIRMAN

HARTLAND MOLSON – PRES

TOM MOLSON – CHAIRMAN

BERT MOLSON – CEO

1945   1950   1955   1960   1965   1970   1975